AF798491

Cognitive Technologies

Editor-in-Chief

Daniel Sonntag, German Research Center for AI, DFKI, Saarbrücken, Germany

Titles in this series now included in the Thomson Reuters Book Citation Index and Scopus!

The Cognitive Technologies (CT) series is committed to the timely publishing of high-quality manuscripts that promote the development of cognitive technologies and systems on the basis of artificial intelligence, image processing and understanding, natural language processing, machine learning and human-computer interaction.

It brings together the latest developments in all areas of this multidisciplinary topic, ranging from theories and algorithms to various important applications. The intended readership includes research students and researchers in computer science, computer engineering, cognitive science, electrical engineering, data science and related fields seeking a convenient way to track the latest findings on the foundations, methodologies and key applications of cognitive technologies.

The series provides a publishing and communication platform for all cognitive technologies topics, including but not limited to these most recent examples:

- Interactive machine learning, interactive deep learning, machine teaching
- Explainability (XAI), transparency, robustness of AI and trustworthy AI
- Knowledge representation, automated reasoning, multiagent systems
- Common sense modelling, context-based interpretation, hybrid cognitive technologies
- Human-centered design, socio-technical systems, human-robot interaction, cognitive robotics
- Learning with small datasets, never-ending learning, metacognition and introspection
- Intelligent decision support systems, prediction systems and warning systems
- Special transfer topics such as CT for computational sustainability, CT in business applications and CT in mobile robotic systems

The series includes monographs, introductory and advanced textbooks, state-of-the-art collections, and handbooks. In addition, it supports publishing in Open Access mode.

Md Zia Uddin

Trustworthy Multimodal Intelligent Systems for Independent Living

Springer

Md Zia Uddin
Department of Sustainable Communication
Technologies
Sintef Digital
Oslo, Norway

ISSN 1611-2482 ISSN 2197-6635 (electronic)
Cognitive Technologies
ISBN 978-3-031-97358-1 ISBN 978-3-031-97359-8 (eBook)
https://doi.org/10.1007/978-3-031-97359-8

© The Editor(s) (if applicable) and The Author(s), under exclusive license to Springer Nature Switzerland AG 2025

This work is subject to copyright. All rights are solely and exclusively licensed by the Publisher, whether the whole or part of the material is concerned, specifically the rights of translation, reprinting, reuse of illustrations, recitation, broadcasting, reproduction on microfilms or in any other physical way, and transmission or information storage and retrieval, electronic adaptation, computer software, or by similar or dissimilar methodology now known or hereafter developed.
The use of general descriptive names, registered names, trademarks, service marks, etc. in this publication does not imply, even in the absence of a specific statement, that such names are exempt from the relevant protective laws and regulations and therefore free for general use.
The publisher, the authors and the editors are safe to assume that the advice and information in this book are believed to be true and accurate at the date of publication. Neither the publisher nor the authors or the editors give a warranty, expressed or implied, with respect to the material contained herein or for any errors or omissions that may have been made. The publisher remains neutral with regard to jurisdictional claims in published maps and institutional affiliations.

This Springer imprint is published by the registered company Springer Nature Switzerland AG
The registered company address is: Gewerbestrasse 11, 6330 Cham, Switzerland

If disposing of this product, please recycle the paper.

Preface

In an increasingly interconnected and technologically advanced world, the quest for enhancing independent living has emerged as a crucial frontier in artificial intelligence (AI) and assistive technologies. Individuals with diverse needs, ranging from the elderly population to those with disabilities or chronic health conditions, often encounter challenges that impede their ability to live autonomously and maintain a high quality of life. Addressing these challenges requires innovative solutions leveraging intelligent systems' power to provide personalized support and assistance tailored to individual needs. This book explores the concept of trustworthy multimodal intelligent systems and their transformative potential in enabling independent living. At the heart of this exploration lies the fusion of data, synthetic data generation techniques, and explainable AI (XAI) principles, all driven by sophisticated deep learning algorithms. Integrating these components seamlessly aims to develop advanced assistive technologies and ensure their reliability, transparency, and user acceptance. To embark on this journey, it is imperative first to understand the landscape of independent living and the challenges faced by individuals who require assistance in various aspects of their daily lives. Aging populations are growing worldwide, accompanied by an increased prevalence of age-related health conditions and disabilities. As individuals age, they often encounter difficulties performing routine tasks, managing their health, and maintaining social connections. Similarly, individuals with disabilities face unique obstacles that can hinder their mobility, communication, and overall independence. In response to these challenges, the concept of independent living has gained prominence, advocating for the empowerment of individuals to live as autonomously as possible, regardless of age or ability. Central to the concept is enabling individuals to make informed choices, access essential services, and participate fully in society. However, achieving independence requires more than physical accessibility; it demands holistic support systems that address diverse needs and preferences. This is where intelligent systems play a pivotal role. By harnessing the capabilities of AI, sensor technology, and data-driven insights, we can create assistive solutions that adapt to individual needs, preferences, and contexts. Multimodal data, encompassing information from various sources such as wearable devices, environmental sensors, and digital health records, offers a rich source of information for understanding user behavior, health status, and environmental factors. At the core of these intelligent systems lie deep learning algorithms, which have demonstrated remarkable success in various AI tasks, from image recognition to natural language understanding. Fueled by vast amounts of data and computational power, deep learning models can learn complex patterns and relationships, making them well-suited for analyzing multimodal data and extracting actionable insights. However, adopting AI in critical domains such as healthcare and assisted living necessitates a deeper understanding of model behavior and decision-making processes. Black-box models, which lack transparency and interpretability, pose significant challenges regarding trust, accountability, and ethical implications. To address these concerns, explainable AI (XAI) has emerged, focusing on developing techniques that elucidate the inner workings of AI systems and provide meaningful explanations for their decisions. In this book, we explore trustworthy multimodal intelligent systems guided by the principles of data-driven innovation, synthetic data generation, deep learning, and explainable AI. We dive into the intricacies of sensor technology, synthetic data generation techniques, deep learning architectures, and XAI principles, culminating in practical applications using the Python programming language. Through theoretical insights, practical examples, and hands-on tutorials, we aim to equip readers with the knowledge and tools to design, develop, and deploy intelligent systems supporting independent living. By fostering a deeper understanding of the interplay between data, algorithms, and user needs, we strive to empower individuals to lead more autonomous, fulfilling lives, fostering a more inclusive and equitable society.

Oslo, Norway Md Zia Uddin

Acknowledgements I would like to dedicate this book to my family, especially my elder brothers (Mohammed Monir Uddin, Shaifuddin Khalad, and Md Rayhan Uddin).

The book is partly supported (i.e., Chap. 3: Synthetic Data) by Invest4Health (Mobilising novel finance models for health promotion and disease prevention) project by European Union's Horizon Europe, under Grant Agreement No. 101095522.

Competing Interests The author has no competing interests to declare that are relevant to the content of this manuscript.

Contents

Chapter 1
AI for Independent Living

Abstract Trustworthy multimodal intelligent systems hold immense promise for enabling independent living among older adults, individuals with disabilities, and those managing chronic conditions. By integrating diverse data streams—such as motion sensors, audio inputs, environmental measurements, and wearable devices—these systems provide a comprehensive view of daily activities. Unlike single-sensor setups, multimodal approaches can capture more nuanced patterns, ensuring reliable event detection and personalized interventions without overburdening users or disrupting their usual routines. Establishing trust in such complex environments requires robust strategies to address privacy, transparency, and fairness. Because these systems operate in highly personal spaces, residents and caregivers need reassurance that their sensitive information will not be misused. One way to achieve this is by processing large portions of data locally, within edge-computing devices, which helps keep personal details off external servers. Additionally, synthetic data generation techniques support model development by simulating real-life patterns. This artificial data allows researchers to train algorithms on varied scenarios—like detecting falls or monitoring medication schedules—without exposing genuine, identifying information. Combined with strong encryption and access controls, these methods help preserve resident privacy while still providing accurate, data-driven insights. Multimodal inputs give rise to potent machine learning models capable of detailed behavior analysis, anomaly detection, and predictive analytics. For example, a system may integrate motion patterns from room sensors, heart-rate data from wearables, and acoustic signals from smart speakers. By synthesizing these signals, the system can more reliably detect events such as a fall, a sudden shift in routine, or signs of emotional distress. Furthermore, predictive analytics can forecast elevated health risks, giving residents and caregivers the opportunity to intervene proactively. Such anticipatory support offers real benefits, including early medical checks or personalized reminders that can prevent hospitalizations and maintain quality of life. Yet even the most accurate models will falter if they are perceived as opaque or prone to bias. Explainable AI (XAI) techniques can alleviate these concerns by revealing the factors behind an algorithm's suggestions or alerts. Residents and family members who understand how the system interprets sensor data are more likely to accept its recommendations and respond correctly. This transparency also shines a light on

© The Author(s), under exclusive license to Springer Nature Switzerland AG 2025
M. Z. Uddin, *Trustworthy Multimodal Intelligent Systems for Independent Living*, Cognitive Technologies, https://doi.org/10.1007/978-3-031-97359-8_1

possible biases, helping developers refine algorithms so they work equitably across varying health profiles, mobility levels, and cultural backgrounds. As part of a broader ethical approach, designers must also consider user autonomy, allowing residents to adjust the frequency or types of notifications and to override automated decisions when appropriate.

1.1 Introduction

Independent living has always been important for people of different ages and abilities. Whether we are talking about older adults who wish to stay in the comfort of their own home instead of moving to a nursing facility, or younger adults with disabilities who want to maintain their personal autonomy, the common goal is the same: to live in a place where they feel safe, comfortable, and in control of their own choices. In recent years, technology has created new opportunities to help more people achieve this goal. One of the most promising ideas is the concept of smart assisted homes [1–3]. These are living spaces that use a combination of advanced sensors, communication devices, and software tools to make everyday life easier and safer. This introduction explores how technology, particularly artificial intelligence (AI), machine learning (ML), and the Internet of Things (IoT), is reshaping the way we think about independent living. We will also discuss how synthetic data and explainable AI (XAI) fit into this picture.

To begin, it is important to recognize why independent living matters so much. For older adults, there is a strong desire to remain at home for as long as they can. This is often called aging in place. Many older adults feel more at ease in a familiar environment, close to friends, neighbors, and family members. They might have lived in the same community or house for many years, and leaving it can be emotionally challenging. Research suggests that people who can stay in their own homes or remain in a community setting tend to have higher levels of happiness and satisfaction with life. They often feel a stronger sense of identity and control, which in turn can support their emotional well-being. For adults with disabilities, whether these disabilities are physical, sensory, or cognitive, independent living is equally important. It allows them to participate in everyday activities on their own terms, using their own methods. Independence contributes to feelings of empowerment and self-efficacy.

But remaining independent can be difficult for some people. An older adult may feel unsteady on their feet, worried about falling while climbing stairs or bending down to pick something up. Someone with a visual impairment might find it difficult to manage the stove or see visitors coming to the front door. A person with a chronic health condition may need regular checks of vital signs, such as blood pressure or blood sugar, which can be time-consuming or demanding without help. These challenges can interfere with daily life, making tasks like cooking, bathing, or cleaning more complicated. In many cases, family members or professional caregivers step in to help, but 24-h assistance can be expensive or impractical. Some people also feel uneasy about giving up their privacy or sense of control, no matter how well-intentioned their helpers might be. Smart assisted homes present a possible solution to many of these challenges. The phrase smart assisted home can mean many things, but usually it refers to a house or apartment that includes multiple sensors and connected devices that keep track of a person's environment and health, often through non-intrusive methods. Instead of having cameras placed in every room, a smart assisted home might rely on motion sensors, pressure sensors, or temperature sensors that can detect when someone gets out of bed, when a door opens, or when a person might have fallen down [3]. These devices are typically linked to a central system that can analyze the incoming signals and figure out if something is wrong. For example, if a sensor in the kitchen notices that the stove has been left on for an unusual amount of time, the system might send an alert to the resident's phone or their caregiver's phone, prompting them to switch off the stove for safety. Alternatively, the system might do it automatically if certain triggers are reached. Moreover, wearable sensors are becoming very popular. These could be smartwatches that track heart rate, step count, and sleep patterns. They could also be small devices that one wears on a belt or around the neck to detect falls. If the wearable senses a sudden impact combined with a period of no movement, it might notify emergency services or a family member [4]. These wearables can also have features like GPS tracking, which is useful if someone wanders off or gets lost, a concern for people living with certain types of dementia. This constant flow of information from sensors in the home and on the person can help create a complete picture of daily life without needing someone to be monitored in person.

AI and machine learning have become major topics of interest when we talk about smart assisted homes. AI can be defined simply as the ability of a computer program or machine to think and learn, usually inspired by how human brains operate. Machine learning is a field within AI that focuses on algorithms that can learn patterns from data. In a smart assisted home, there is a continuous flow of data from various sensors—motion sensors, temperature sensors, blood pressure monitors, etc. This data is not only large in volume but also changes over time. Machine learning algorithms can examine the data to spot trends, predict future events, and make suggestions about how to improve the resident's well-being. For example, an AI might notice that a resident's average daily step count has been dropping over the last two weeks, which could indicate deteriorating mobility or the onset of health issues. It could then remind the person to do some gentle exercises, notify a caregiver, or offer tips on improving balance. The combination of AI with IoT sensors can also enable a concept known as ambient intelligence. Ambient intelligence is when the environment itself seems to be aware of the user's presence and can respond to their needs proactively. For instance, the lights in a hallway can brighten if the system detects that the user has gotten up in the middle of the night, helping them see and avoid bumping into furniture. If the AI predicts the person might have low blood sugar soon (perhaps due to consistent patterns in meal times, medication schedules, or wearable glucose monitor readings), the system might display a reminder or suggest a snack. These kinds of smart actions reduce the chance of accidents or emergencies while helping the user maintain control over their daily routine.

However, to build sophisticated AI models, developers need a great deal of training data. Ideally, this data would come from real people in real-life situations. But there are serious concerns about privacy. Storing or sharing large amounts of a person's daily activity and health data could lead to data breaches or unauthorized surveillance, which many find unacceptable. This is where synthetic data becomes very useful. Synthetic data is artificially generated data that mirrors the statistical patterns of real data but does not contain any actual personal information. In other words, it simulates possible scenarios without revealing anyone's identity or private details. For example, if a research team wants to train a fall-detection algorithm, they could create virtual models of people falling. They could use computer simulations that emulate an older adult's movements at home, generating sensor outputs for thousands of hypothetical fall events. Then the algorithm can learn to detect the patterns associated with falls without real people having to fall again and again, which is obviously dangerous. Synthetic data can also help ensure algorithms are robust by exposing them to diverse conditions that might be hard to capture in small real-life datasets. While AI can learn to make accurate predictions and quick decisions, it often acts as a black box, meaning that it is not always obvious to human users how or why the AI made a certain choice. This can create issues of trust. If a system decides to send an alert to paramedics, the person might want to know: This is particularly sensitive for older adults or people with disabilities who might worry that the system is making assumptions about them. Explainable AI (XAI) comes into play here. The purpose of XAI is to make AI-driven decisions easier to understand. Instead of just providing an outcome, an explainable AI system can say: "I detected a sudden downward acceleration from the wearable device, followed by a lack of motion for 30 s. Therefore, I flagged a potential fall." By offering these insights, XAI builds trust among residents, caregivers, and family members. It ensures that if errors happen, it is easier to figure out what went wrong and improve the system. This level of transparency is crucial in healthcare settings, including smart assisted homes, because lives can literally be on the line.

Trust also depends on how ethical and responsible the AI is. Data collection within the home must be done lawfully and with the resident's clear consent [5]. The system should give users control over what information is stored, who can see it, and when. Another ethical concern is bias. If an AI system is trained mostly on data from people of a certain demographic group, it might make poor or incorrect decisions for other groups. For example, older adults from different cultural backgrounds may have very different daily schedules and routines. If the AI is not aware of these differences, it might mistakenly flag normal cultural practices as signs of abnormal behavior. To be equitable, algorithms should be trained on data that covers a broad range of users. While synthetic data can help diversify training sets, real-world validation is still important [6].

In the years ahead, we can expect these technologies to keep improving. Advances in ambient computing will allow the entire home environment to be more seamlessly responsive, almost like having an invisible butler who quietly pays attention to the resident's habits. AI models will likely become more predictive, anticipating potential hazards or health changes before they happen. This might involve analyzing changes in walking speed, voice patterns, or even how a person normally interacts with household objects. If something shifts significantly, the AI can suggest a checkup with a doctor or remind the user to do mobility exercises. Robotics could also merge with smart home systems, enabling tasks like picking up dropped items, assisting with laundry, or guiding someone through physical therapy exercises. Despite the bright prospects, making sure this technology is both effective and respectful of individual rights remains a big challenge. Collaborations between healthcare experts, computer scientists, ethicists, and community organizations are key. Policymakers, too, have to set clear guidelines on privacy and accountability. If these issues are addressed, the technology can move forward in a way that helps everyone who wants to live independently.

1.2 Smart Assisted Homes for Independent Living

Smart assisted homes have emerged as an important area of innovation for supporting independent living, especially among older adults, people with disabilities, and individuals managing chronic health conditions. Although the idea of a smart home once seemed futuristic, the growth of sensors, connected devices, and artificial intelligence (AI) has turned this idea into reality. The primary goal behind these developments is to allow residents to remain as independent as possible in their own living spaces, while still having access to features that enhance safety, convenience, and overall well-being.

At the heart of smart assisted homes are sensor networks and connected devices that gather and share information about what is happening in the house. These can include motion sensors that detect a person's movement in hallways or rooms, pressure sensors under mats to see if someone has gotten out of bed, and environmental sensors that measure temperature, humidity, or lighting. Some systems also use cameras, though they often raise privacy concerns, so many researchers and developers turn to non-visual or low-resolution sensors to reduce the feeling of surveillance. Regardless of the specific type, the sensors typically connect to a central controller or a cloud-based platform that monitors all data in real time. When AI algorithms receive this data, they can identify patterns and detect unusual events. For example, if a resident usually wakes up around 7 a.m. but has remained in bed until noon, the system might alert a caregiver to check on them. If the data indicates that someone fell in the bathroom, an automatic call could go out to emergency services. These capabilities significantly reduce the risk that a person in need of urgent help will remain unattended for too long.

Smart assisted homes are not just about detecting dangers or accidents. They also strive to increase overall comfort. For instance, a person with mobility issues may want to control lights, doors, and appliances through voice commands or smartphone apps [7, 8]. AI-enabled thermostats can learn the temperature preferences of residents and automatically adjust the heat or air conditioning at certain times of the day. Such conveniences, while seemingly small, can provide a meaningful boost to autonomy,

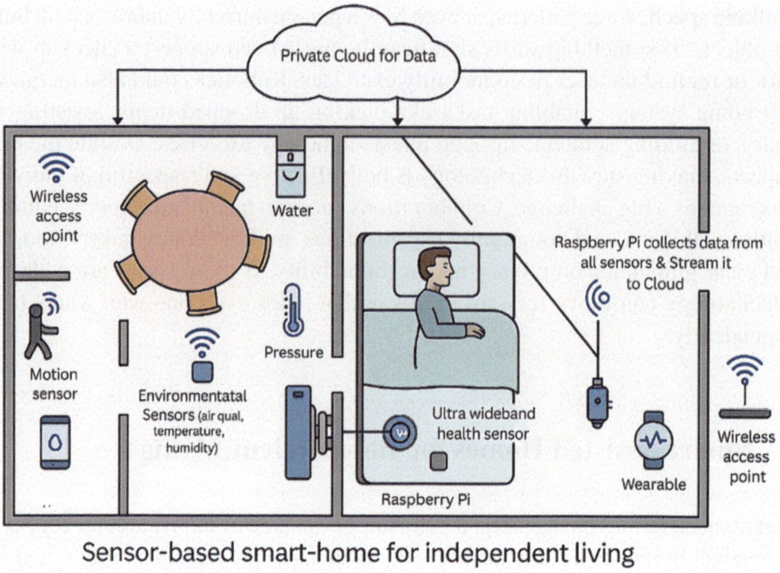

Fig. 1.1 An example of a smart apartment for independent assisted living

because the resident does not have to rely on outside help for simple tasks. Figure 1.1 shows an example of a smart apartment for independent assisted living.

In many current implementations, these systems integrate seamlessly with existing supportive services, such as telehealth. If a resident has a chronic condition like diabetes or hypertension, they can use wearable health monitors or in-home medical devices that collect physiological data—such as blood sugar or blood pressure readings—and share it with healthcare professionals in real time. This constant flow of information helps doctors and nurses intervene earlier if they notice any worrisome trends. It also means the resident may not have to travel as often for routine check-ups, which can be convenient for those with mobility restrictions or transportation issues. However, building these systems and making them effective requires a lot of data. AI models need plenty of examples to learn how to differentiate between normal and abnormal behavior. They also need to generalize well, meaning they should work correctly for many different users, even those with unique habits or living arrangements. Collecting large datasets from real homes can be difficult and raises concerns about privacy. For this reason, many researchers have turned to synthetic data, which is generated artificially by computers and can be used to train AI algorithms without relying on real personal details. Furthermore, once the models are trained, a mechanism to explain their decisions is essential. This is where explainable AI (XAI) fits in. XAI ensures that caregivers, residents, and family members understand how and why an algorithm made a certain judgment—like triggering a fall alert or suggesting that the resident should check their blood pressure again.

1.2.1 Data and Synthetic Data in Smart Assisted Homes

As mentioned, real-world data is critical for training the AI and machine learning models that control a smart assisted home. Yet collecting and sharing this kind of personal data has risks. Imagine placing dozens of sensors in a private residence and continuously storing data about a person's movements, sleep habits, and even vital signs on cloud servers. Even with strong security measures, there remains the possibility of data breaches or misuse. It's understandable that many people, especially older adults who are unfamiliar with data-sharing technologies, might feel uncomfortable at the thought of their personal routines being recorded and processed by others.

Synthetic data offers a creative solution. In simple terms, synthetic data is computer-generated information that closely resembles real data but does not come from any one individual's actual life. It mirrors the statistical patterns or distributions found in genuine datasets, enabling machine learning models to learn the same kinds of patterns they would see in real data—yet there is no direct one-to-one mapping to a real person. For smart assisted homes, this could mean simulating different daily activities, health conditions, or emergency scenarios. Researchers may use simulated environments to emulate the layout of a typical house, the walking speeds of an older adult, or the time intervals in which they might use the restroom. They can script a wide range of normal and abnormal events—such as cooking, sleeping, reading, falling, or leaving the house unexpectedly—to create synthetic sensor readings.

By using these generated datasets, researchers can train AI models to recognize events like falls, medication-taking routines, or even changes in gait that could signal upcoming mobility issues. When the models are finally deployed in a real home, they are better prepared to handle unusual but important scenarios—like a fall in the kitchen at 3 a.m.—even if they did not have real data on such an event. This approach is particularly helpful for capturing rare incidents. Falls may not happen often (which is good in real life), so it can be challenging to gather enough examples to train an accurate detection algorithm. Synthetic data can fill in these gaps.

Another benefit is that synthetic data can help avoid certain biases. Suppose a research group only has access to data from a small number of older adults living in a specific geographic region. That data might not generalize well to other cultures, climates, or housing designs. By generating synthetic data that spans many potential living conditions, the AI becomes more flexible. Developers can even adjust parameters to represent different styles of furniture, different schedules, or multiple occupant types. This diversity in the training process helps produce AI tools that work for a wider range of individuals. Of course, synthetic data has its limitations. If the artificial scenarios do not accurately reflect how people truly behave, the AI might learn patterns that are too simplistic or unrealistic. A system trained heavily on synthetic data might struggle when faced with the unpredictable variety of real-world life. That is why many researchers follow a hybrid method: they create synthetic data but also gather some real data from volunteers to check if the models are performing well [5]. Despite these challenges, synthetic data remains a powerful resource for addressing privacy issues and ensuring that developers can refine their algorithms without risking personal data leakage.

1.2.2 Explainable AI for a Trustworthy System

Even the most sophisticated AI systems will fail to gain acceptance if they are not perceived as trustworthy, fair, and transparent. This is where Explainable AI (XAI) becomes vital. XAI refers to methods that make it easier for human beings to understand the logic behind AI decisions. In a smart assisted home, explanations can take different forms. For instance, if an AI system flags a possible emergency, residents or caregivers may want to see a statement such as: Alert generated because the user's wearable registered sudden impact followed by inactivity for over 60 s. By revealing this reasoning, the system clarifies that it did not randomly raise the alarm, but rather acted upon specific indicators that could be a sign of a fall.

Why is this transparency so important? One obvious reason is trust. Many people, especially older adults, may feel uneasy about surrendering control to technology they do not fully understand. If the AI does something unexpected—like turning off the lights or adjusting the thermostat—they might worry it is malfunctioning or even that it is attempting to spy on them. Knowing exactly why the system took a certain action can ease those fears. When a person can see that the system is simply reacting to energy-saving preferences or typical user schedules, they are more likely to feel comfortable.

Moreover, trust in healthcare and monitoring contexts is essential because errors can have serious consequences. If a system consistently sends false alarms, emergency responders and family members may begin ignoring these notifications. Yet if the system cannot offer an explanation for why it believed there was an emergency, it is harder to correct the underlying logic. With XAI techniques, developers can pinpoint what sensor reading or data pattern triggered a false alarm, fix any misinterpretation, and improve the algorithm. This feedback loop becomes crucial for maintaining a high standard of care. Explainable AI also helps reduce the risk of bias or unfair treatment. As AI systems take on more responsibilities in deciding whether someone needs help, or in predicting a person's future health risks, it becomes possible that inaccuracies or prejudices in the training data will appear in the system's decisions [8]. For instance, imagine an AI that learned mostly from data about men and did not account for certain physical differences in women, or an AI that was trained on a younger subset of individuals but has trouble adjusting to the slower movements of older adults. If the AI is opaque, it might be very difficult to find these biases. If the AI is explainable, however, we can see what features it looked at to make decisions and correct it if those features are not relevant or if they lead to skewed outcomes. This kind of scrutiny is particularly needed in smart assisted homes, where the aim is to serve all residents equally well.

There are a number of technical approaches to achieving explainable AI. Some rely on visualizations such as heat maps or feature-importance plots, showing which parts of the data most influenced a decision. Others produce textual explanations in plain language, or rely on simpler rules-based systems for critical decisions. In many smart home experiments, developers have integrated small dashboards or mobile apps that offer real-time alerts and the reasoning behind them. Another approach is to design the core AI models in a more interpretable manner from the outset, although that can make them less flexible than complex, black box models like deep neural networks. The key is to balance accuracy with transparency in a way that makes sense for the user population. XAI is not just a technical detail; it reflects an ethical stance on how these systems should be designed and deployed in environments where people live. Transparent decision-making is vital to respecting the residents' autonomy, dignity, and comfort. It ensures that while the technology may be sophisticated, it remains approachable and accountable. As smart assisted homes continue to evolve, XAI will remain a cornerstone for building systems that people can rely on with confidence.

1.3 Independent Living with AI-Driven Personalization

One of the key strengths of modern technology is its capacity to learn from individual preferences and habits. In the context of smart assisted homes, AI-driven personalization means the system gradually becomes more aware of its residents' unique routines, likes, dislikes, and health conditions. Instead of offering generic, one-size-fits-all solutions, a well-designed system can tailor its services to the specific needs of each occupant [9, 10]. This approach not only improves comfort but can also play a crucial role in preventing emergencies and maintaining well-being over the long term.

Consider an older adult with arthritis who prefers a warmer room temperature, especially in the mornings when joint pain can be more pronounced. A personalized smart home system might learn this preference from daily interactions with thermostats and motion sensors, then automatically raise the heat a bit before the person wakes up. Another individual could have a schedule that varies significantly from day to day—perhaps they work part-time, volunteer in the community, or have grandchildren visiting unexpectedly. The smart home can adapt by learning that certain lights, appliances, or security settings need to be adjusted at irregular intervals. These may seem like small gestures, but over weeks and months, such personalization can greatly enhance the resident's quality of life [11, 12].

There is also a deeper dimension to personalization: predictive analytics. By analyzing ongoing data from the environment and any wearable devices, machine learning algorithms can begin to predict what might happen next. For example, if a resident's mobility data, heart rate, or sleep quality starts trending downward, the system could proactively recommend more frequent rest breaks, prompt them to do gentle exercise, or even schedule a doctor's visit [13]. This kind of prediction extends beyond comfort and into the realm of preventive healthcare, which can be transformative for aging adults or individuals with chronic conditions [14].

1.3.1 Behavioral Analysis for Personalized Assistance

To offer truly personalized assistance, a smart home must first understand how its residents live on a regular basis. This is where behavioral analysis comes into the picture. Instead of making decisions purely on rules established by programmers, AI algorithms can observe patterns emerging from sensor data [15]. Over time, they can develop an internal model of each resident's daily activities, preferences, and typical habits.

Monitoring Daily Routines

A foundational aspect of behavioral analysis is identifying daily routines such as mealtimes, bathing schedules, sleeping patterns, and time spent outside the home. Suppose an older adult typically has breakfast around 8 a.m., leaves for a morning walk at 9 a.m., returns by 10 a.m., and naps in the afternoon. Motion sensors, combined with door sensors, can provide enough evidence to map out these habits. A wearable device might capture step counts, heart rate, and overall physical activity during the walk, while a bed sensor or a contact-free radar sensor monitors sleep quality at night. Over several weeks, the AI system develops a behavioral profile for that individual. This profile becomes the backbone of personalization. If, on a particular day, the system detects that the resident skipped their morning walk or did not open the fridge when they usually have breakfast, it might send a subtle reminder: Would you like to prepare breakfast, or should I order groceries? If the user often forgets to lock the door after returning from a walk, the system could remind them or automatically lock the door. It is essential to note that the AI should offer these interventions gently, without overriding the resident's autonomy, in order to strike a balance between helpfulness and respect for personal freedom.

Tracking Cognitive and Emotional Well-Being

Beyond physical routines, behavioral analysis can also consider cognitive and emotional states, although this aspect is more complex. For instance, the frequency of certain types of interactions—like phone calls, social gatherings, or video chats—can give the AI system insight into how socially active the resident is. If someone who is usually very sociable suddenly withdraws or isolates themselves, the system might notice a shift. It could suggest that they call a friend, ask a caregiver to check in, or propose an engaging indoor activity. Early detection of changes in social behavior can be a key indicator of depressive symptoms in older adults. Even changes in speech patterns or daily step counts might offer hints about a decline in mental sharpness or the onset of mild depression. Through careful, privacy-conscious data gathering, the AI might detect these shifts and recommend supportive measures, such as scheduling a virtual consultation with a mental health professional or gently encouraging more social interaction. While such capabilities must be handled delicately and with the user's consent, they highlight the potential of behavioral analysis to go beyond mere convenience into the realm of holistic well-being.

Personalized Health Management

People who live with chronic conditions—diabetes, heart disease, or respiratory issues—often have unique daily routines that revolve around medication schedules, dietary restrictions, or exercise programs. By analyzing the resident's ongoing behavior, the AI can deliver reminders aligned with each individual's needs. For example, if a person with diabetes is supposed to check their blood sugar levels three times a day, the system can compare actual check times with the recommended schedule. If it notices missed tests, the system can send a friendly nudge via a phone notification or a voice assistant. Furthermore, the AI can draw connections between different data streams. If an individual's blood sugar readings appear high in the afternoon on days when they skip a walk, the system might suggest a short stroll or a light indoor exercise session. Over time, the resident receives tailored guidance that responds to real-life patterns rather than generic advice. This approach can not only improve health outcomes but also reduce frustration by avoiding one-size-fits-all solutions that might not be suitable for everyone. At the same time, respect for privacy remains crucial. Residents must have options to limit data collection or override certain recommendations. Some might wish to keep their medication schedule completely private, while others may welcome as many helpful prompts as possible. The system must be designed to handle these differing preferences gracefully, providing robust data security and clear consent mechanisms.

Safety and Emergency Alerts

Behavioral analysis can also enhance safety in subtle ways. Anomalies in routine, such as a lack of motion during daytime hours or unusual restlessness at night, can trigger early alerts. If a resident often visits the kitchen for water multiple times each night but suddenly stops getting up, the system could interpret this as potential dehydration or an indication of reduced mobility. It might issue a non-intrusive reminder or prompt a caregiver to check in. In emergency scenarios, personalized knowledge makes alerts more accurate. A typical fall-detection mechanism might trigger a call for help when it senses a sudden drop in height, but if it also knows that the resident frequently practices seated yoga exercises, it might interpret certain movements differently to avoid false alarms. Likewise, an individual who occasionally takes naps on the floor (perhaps for back pain relief) would have a different baseline from someone who never lies down outside of a bed or sofa. Customizing these thresholds can significantly reduce erroneous alerts and build trust in the system's reliability.

1.3.2 Adaptive Assistance with Predictive Models

Behavioral analysis primarily deals with what is happening in the present. Predictive models, on the other hand, look toward the future. They tap into historical and current data to forecast possible outcomes, allowing the system to offer assistance before problems escalate. Predictive models vary widely in complexity, from basic statistical approaches (like linear regression) to advanced machine learning techniques (like neural networks or reinforcement learning) [13]. In a smart assisted home, these models empower the system to act proactively rather than merely reacting to events.

Anticipating Health Risks

One of the most transformative uses of predictive modeling is anticipating health issues. Consider a resident who has a history of high blood pressure. Over time, the smart home records patterns in their blood pressure readings, exercise routines, meal times, and sleep quality. The AI might notice correlations—perhaps on days when they do not sleep well, their blood pressure is higher the next morning. By combining these insights with a broader medical risk model, the system can forecast when the resident is at a higher risk of a blood pressure spike. It might then take preventative measures like dimming lights at bedtime to promote relaxation, reminding them to drink enough water, or even scheduling a virtual consultation with a healthcare provider. For older adults who have an elevated risk of falling, predictive modeling can look at changes in gait speed detected by motion sensors or wearable accelerometers. If the AI sees a steady decline in gait speed, it might predict a higher risk of falls in the coming weeks. Early interventions might include recommending balance exercises, adjusting furniture placement for easier movement, or having a physical therapist do a home visit. By taking these steps before an actual fall occurs, the system helps preserve independence and avoid injuries that could otherwise lead to a hospital stay.

Medication and Appointment Management

Complex medication schedules often lead to confusion, especially for individuals who take multiple prescriptions at varying times. Predictive models can analyze which medications have been missed in the past and predict the times or conditions under which a resident might be most likely to forget them. For instance, a model might reveal that missed doses tend to occur on weekends or when the resident has visitors. Armed with that knowledge, the smart system can send extra reminders during those times or even lock down certain medication dispensers until the correct medication is taken (with user consent). These predictive capabilities can extend to appointments, too. If the resident has a history of forgetting their telehealth check-ins, the system can predict which future appointments are at the highest risk of being overlooked. It might then send repeated notifications via a smartphone or a voice assistant leading up to the appointment time. Similarly, if the system is integrated with a transportation service, it could ensure a ride is arranged well in advance. This approach is especially useful for those with memory impairments who want to maintain some level of self-reliance.

Energy and Resource Optimization

Predictive models do not just help with health and safety—they can also make daily life more efficient. By analyzing data about how often lights, heating, or cooling systems are used at various times, the AI can anticipate the best ways to save energy without causing discomfort. If the resident typically uses the living room in the evenings, the system can keep that area at a comfortable temperature, while reducing air conditioning or heating in rooms that are rarely used after a certain hour. Over time, these small adjustments can lower utility bills, which is especially helpful for people on fixed incomes. More importantly, it can do so in a way that respects the resident's preferences, ensuring that it does not, for example, turn off the heat in a room where the resident might spontaneously decide to read.

Proactive Social Engagement

Another fascinating application of predictive modeling is related to social engagement. Isolation and loneliness can be major concerns for older adults or people with limited mobility, and these factors can seriously affect physical and mental health [15]. The system might learn that a resident tends to become more withdrawn on days after poor sleep or stressful events. It could predict future days when these conditions might repeat and recommend enjoyable activities, such as watching a favorite show, playing a digital game, or phoning a relative. In more advanced configurations, if the resident has given permission, the system might even contact a family member or friend to prompt a quick conversation or plan an outing. Essentially, the AI can anticipate moments of isolation and intervene early with supportive suggestions.

1.4 Challenges and Ethical Considerations

Smart assisted homes offer a range of benefits for people who want to continue living independently, yet developing and deploying these systems also brings up several significant challenges and ethical questions [16]. As sensors collect continuous streams of personal data, serious concerns arise about how that information is stored, shared, and used. Residents may worry about outsiders accessing their data, possibly misusing it, or even committing fraud. At the same time, the deployment of artificial intelligence (AI) in such sensitive contexts introduces issues of fairness, transparency, and accountability. AI models, after all, can be influenced by biases in the data they learn from, and their decision-making processes are not always easy for people to understand. In a home environment—where decisions might affect a resident's safety and well-being—ensuring trust in the system becomes even more critical.

People who move into or adopt a smart assisted home frequently have vulnerabilities. They could be older adults who rely on health monitoring, individuals with disabilities that affect their mobility or sensory perception, or individuals with chronic illnesses that require constant attention. For these populations, any misstep in the technology's design or functionality can have serious repercussions. Therefore, topics like data privacy, system security, ethical AI practices, and user control must remain at the forefront of design considerations. This section explores both the technical and social aspects of these challenges, illustrating why they are so important and suggesting some strategies for mitigating potential harms.

1.4.1 Data Privacy and Security

Privacy is a core human right. That principle becomes especially delicate in a smart assisted home, where an array of sensors is constantly collecting details about a resident's daily life. These details might include their sleeping schedule, mobility patterns, medication routines, and health indicators like blood pressure or heart rate. Such data, if compromised, could expose very personal information about an individual's health or habits. In the worst cases, it might be used for discrimination (e.g., insurance companies setting higher premiums) or criminal activities like identity theft. Older adults and individuals with disabilities can be particularly vulnerable to scams, so safeguarding data in these systems is paramount [6]. One strategy for ensuring privacy is to keep data collection to the minimum needed for the system to function effectively. Rather than constantly uploading all raw data to a remote server, developers can use edge computing. With edge computing, much of the data processing and analysis happens on a local device inside the home—like a dedicated hub or even a powerful home computer. For example, an AI fall detection algorithm might operate directly on sensor inputs without sharing them with a cloud service. Only when a fall is detected would a short notification get sent to caregivers or emergency responders. This design limits data exposure, as raw sensor streams are not continuously transmitted over the internet.

Where data must be transmitted, robust encryption protocols are essential. Systems should use secure channels (e.g., HTTPS, SSL/TLS) to move data from home-based sensors to the cloud or other external services. The data at rest—whether on local devices or on cloud servers—should also be encrypted, making it difficult for attackers to read the contents even if they gain access to the physical storage or intercept the data flow. Access controls, such as requiring strong authentication and regularly rotating keys or passwords, provide further layers of defense. Some researchers and companies experiment with blockchain-based authentication or identity management, where each sensor or device has a unique digital signature that confirms its authenticity. Such approaches can prevent malicious actors from inserting fake data into the system or impersonating legitimate devices. While blockchain solutions can be more resource-intensive, they may become more widespread if they prove able to deliver stronger, decentralized security without overly complicating the user's experience.

To develop AI models, large amounts of real-world data are typically necessary. Yet fully relying on real data can create privacy risks, as individuals' sensitive information might be exposed to researchers or developers [17]. As discussed earlier, synthetic data has become an appealing solution. By generating data that mirrors real usage patterns without tying them to actual residents, developers can train and validate AI algorithms while preserving privacy. Even so, organizations should supplement synthetic data with small-scale, carefully anonymized real-world datasets to ensure the models capture genuine edge cases and remain accurate in real environments. Anonymization, however, is not foolproof. If an attacker obtains multiple pieces of anonymized data about the same person from different sources, they might still piece together identifying details. Therefore, data minimization, encryption, and strict access policies remain critical. Residents must also be informed about how their data—even if anonymized—could be employed for research or product development, giving them a say in whether they want to participate.

Smart assisted homes need to comply with relevant data protection laws and regulations. Depending on the region, these could include frameworks like the General Data Protection Regulation (GDPR) in the European Union or the Health Insurance Portability and Accountability Act (HIPAA) in the United States for healthcare-related data. Compliance not only protects residents but can also guide developers toward best practices [15]. For instance, GDPR promotes data minimization and transparency, requiring developers to justify each type of data they collect. These rules can encourage more ethical designs that inherently protect user privacy, rather than making privacy an afterthought. Despite best efforts, security threats will continue to evolve. Hackers might target a smart assisted home's cameras, microphones, or motion sensors, either to gain private information or even to harass the occupant. Denial-of-service attacks could disrupt essential services, like emergency alerts. Such events highlight the need for rigorous software updates, vulnerability testing, and secure hardware. Device manufacturers and service providers must cooperate to issue patches when vulnerabilities are discovered. Automated update systems can help ensure that devices remain secure without the user needing to manually install updates, which some older adults may find difficult.

Ethical Concerns in AI Decision-Making

An ethical smart assisted home system must function fairly for everyone. However, AI models can inadvertently absorb biases from the data used to train them. For instance, if most training data comes from physically active older men, the system might fail to interpret the signals or patterns relevant to older women with different lifestyles. This could result in missed alerts or unnecessary notifications for certain groups. Similarly, if the system was never tested with individuals who use wheelchairs, it might misunderstand wheelchair movements as irregular or interpret normal wheelchair maneuvers as falls. Such mistakes can undermine trust in the system and lead to inequitable service. Developers and healthcare stakeholders must therefore ensure diverse data collection during the design phase. It is also crucial to test AI models with a wide array of user groups and living situations. If biases are discovered, the system should be retrained or adjusted to correct them. This is where explainable AI (XAI) is particularly useful [18]. By revealing how decisions are made, developers and testers can spot skewed reasoning—like over-reliance on certain features that are not relevant for all users—and then refine the algorithm accordingly.

Respecting Autonomy and Informed Consent

Smart assisted homes are meant to preserve autonomy, yet certain technologies can inadvertently limit it. Automated decision-making—like automatically calling an ambulance if a fall is detected—might strip residents of the choice to decide for themselves whether they actually need emergency care. Some individuals might prefer waiting, perhaps due to cost concerns or personal reasons. To address this, systems should be designed with adjustable settings and override options. For instance, if the user is fully conscious after a detected fall, they can dismiss the alert instead of letting it escalate. Ethical deployment also demands informed consent. Residents must understand which data is collected, how AI algorithms analyze it, and under what conditions alerts are sent to outside parties. They need to know the limits of the system—no AI can be correct 100% of the time—and the potential risks if a malfunction happens. This transparency allows people to make choices about whether to use certain features. In some cases, family members or caregivers who help oversee the system may need legal or ethical frameworks that clarify decision-making rights, especially for users with cognitive impairments.

Transparency and Accountability

The use of AI in critical decisions—like determining whether a resident is in danger—calls for high levels of transparency and accountability. If an AI system errs, the developers should be able to trace the error back to a specific model component or data input [19]. They should then make improvements or at least explain to the resident (and possibly regulators) how the mistake happened. This level of accountability is difficult if the AI model is opaque, a situation frequently described as a black box. Although deep learning architectures are powerful, they can be complex and hard to interpret. Tools such as local interpretable model-agnostic explanations (LIME) and SHAP (Shapley Additive Explanations) can help illuminate which features most influence a prediction. This transparency is especially crucial in healthcare-oriented scenarios, where a single incorrect judgment can greatly affect a user's well-being. At the organizational level, accountability might take the form of clear policies on how to handle user complaints, systematic reviews of AI decisions, and ongoing audits to spot anomalies or biased patterns [20]. For instance, a smart home provider might keep logs of all alerts triggered by the system, ensuring they can investigate any claim that the system failed to alert someone about a genuine emergency or triggered a false alarm. Some experts also recommend setting up independent ethics boards or committees to oversee AI deployment in settings like assisted living, ensuring that community and user perspectives are considered.

Balancing Human Care with Automation

Even the most advanced smart home systems cannot replace human empathy and judgment. A concern among some critics is that care providers might rely too heavily on AI, leading to a reduction in in-person visits and genuine human interaction. For residents who already feel isolated, a fully automated approach might exacerbate loneliness. On the flip side, others argue that because smart homes can handle many routine monitoring tasks, caregivers can dedicate more time to meaningful human engagement. Finding the right balance is an ethical challenge. Designers, policymakers, and care institutions have to figure out where to draw the line between AI-driven interventions and human-based care. For example, an AI might handle preliminary health checks and remind users about medications, but a live nurse or family member can still do a more thorough wellness check or emotional support call once a week. The system could also be set up to invite more frequent human check-ins if it detects signs of social withdrawal or emotional distress. This human-technology hybrid approach aims to maintain efficiency without losing the personal touch that many people want and need.

Inclusive Design and Accessibility

Another ethical dimension is designing smart assisted homes that cater to people with diverse abilities. For a user who is visually impaired, voice interfaces or tactile feedback may be crucial. For a user with hearing loss, visual alerts or haptic notifications might be more appropriate. If a resident has mobility limitations, the system should be navigable from a wheelchair or through accessible touchscreens. AI speech recognition must be tested with multiple accents, speaking styles, and potentially slurred or slow speech, a scenario often faced by older adults or those with certain medical conditions. An inclusive design philosophy can go a long way toward preventing marginalization. By involving user groups in the development process—through focus groups, usability testing, and pilot programs—developers can refine the system to meet actual needs rather than assumptions. This approach not only improves the user experience, but also addresses broader ethical responsibilities like equity and social justice.

1.5 Discussion

The promise of smart assisted homes for independent living is both exciting and multifaceted. As we have explored throughout this chapter, such homes leverage a network of sensors—often ambient and wearable—that provide continuous monitoring of a resident's daily activities. Building upon that foundation, artificial intelligence (AI) and machine learning (ML) algorithms can identify patterns, detect risks, and deliver timely assistance, all aimed at helping individuals maintain autonomy in their own residences. The scope of beneficiaries is broad: older adults seeking to age in place, individuals living with disabilities, and those managing chronic conditions who prefer the familiarity and comfort of home.

However, harnessing these technological tools requires attention to critical aspects such as privacy, security, ethical considerations, and trust. Synthetic data generation has emerged as a creative way to train machine learning models without compromising real user data, while explainable AI (XAI) offers transparency by illuminating how automated decisions come about [21]. Taken together, these elements form a cohesive ecosystem that balances the technical demands for robust data with the ethical imperative to respect personal boundaries.

1.6 Conclusion

The transition to widespread smart independent living technology is part of a broader cultural shift in how we approach caregiving, aging, and independent living with disabilities. Advanced sensors, AI algorithms, and integrated IoT systems are reshaping the relationship between residents, their homes, and the caregiving ecosystem. On the most practical level, these technologies promise early emergency detection, simplified daily routines, and improved health outcomes. But they also symbolize a redefinition of autonomy: individuals can take control of their environment in ways that were not feasible before. We must remember, though, that technology is not a silver bullet. It should not be seen as a universal fix for the social, emotional, and psychological aspects of aging or living with disabilities. Many individuals desire social interaction, meaningful activity, and respect for their personal choices, beyond the scope of a purely sensor-driven system. A well-designed smart home recognizes this fact—it enhances the user's abilities without diminishing their personal agency.

References

1. A. Vrančić, H. Zadravec, and T. Orehovački, "The role of smart homes in providing care for older adults: A systematic literature review from 2010 to 2023," Smart Cities, vol. 7, Art. no. 62, 2024.
2. S. Wilhelm and F. Wahl, "Emergency detection in smart homes using inactivity score for handling uncertain sensor data," Sensors, vol. 24, Art. no. 6583, 2024.
3. C. Lázaro and C. Angulo, "Using UMAP for partially synthetic healthcare tabular data generation and validation," Sensors, vol. 24, Art. no. 7843, 2024.
4. M. Alqulaity and P. Yang, "Enhanced conditional GAN for high-quality synthetic tabular data generation in mobile-based cardiovascular healthcare," Sensors, vol. 24, Art. no. 7673, 2024.
5. J. Lange, N. Wenzlitschke, and E. Rahm, "Generating synthetic health-sensor data for privacy-preserving wearable stress detection," Sensors, vol. 24, Art. no. 3052, 2024.
6. C. Lázaro and C. Angulo, "Iterative application of UMAP-based algorithms for fully synthetic healthcare tabular data generation," Algorithms, vol. 17, Art. no. 591, 2024.
7. C. Metta, A. Beretta, R. Pellungrini, S. Rinzivillo, and F. Giannotti, "Towards transparent healthcare: Advancing local explanation methods in explainable artificial intelligence," Bioengineering, vol. 11, Art. no. 369, 2024.
8. G. Vardakis, G. Hatzivasilis, E. Koutsaki, and N. Papadakis, "Review of smart-home security using the Internet of Things," Electronics, vol. 13, Art. no. 3343, 2024.
9. M. J. C. S. Reis and C. Serôdio, "Edge AI for real-time anomaly detection in smart homes," Future Internet, vol. 17, Art. no. 179, 2025.
10. Y. Li, L. Zhou, M. Wang et al., "Research on designing context-aware interactive experiences for sustainable aging-friendly smart homes," Electronics, vol. 13, Art. no. 3507, 2024.
11. G. P. Pinto, P. K. Donta, S. Dustdar, and C. Prazeres, "A systematic review on privacy-aware IoT personal data stores," Sensors, vol. 24, Art. no. 2197, 2024.
12. M. Moure-Garrido, C. Garcia-Rubio, and C. Campo, "Reducing DNS traffic to enhance home-IoT device privacy," Sensors, vol. 24, Art. no. 2690, 2024.
13. O. Alshamsi, K. Shaalan, and U. Butt, "Towards securing smart homes: A systematic literature review of malware-detection techniques and recommended prevention approach," Information, vol. 15, Art. no. 631, 2024.

14. M. Shalan, M. R. Hasan, Y. Bai, and J. Li, "Enhancing smart-home security: Blockchain-enabled federated learning with knowledge distillation for intrusion detection," Smart Cities, vol. 8, Art. no. 35, 2025.
15. Z. Sadeghi, R. Alizadehsani, M. A. Çifçi, and R. Kausar, "A review of explainable artificial intelligence in healthcare," Computers & Electrical Engineering, vol. 118, Art. no. 109370, 2024.
16. Q. Sun, A. Akman, and B. W. Schuller, "Explainable artificial intelligence for medical applications: A review," arXiv:2412.01829, 2024.
17. M. Fiori, G. Civitarese, P. Bettini et al., "Leveraging large language models for explainable activity recognition in smart homes: A critical evaluation," arXiv:2503.16622, 2025.
18. M. Fiori, G. Civitarese, C. Bettini, "GNN-XAR: A graph neural network for explainable activity recognition in smart homes," arXiv:2502.17999, 2025.
19. J. Daun, S. Zugal, and M. Tiefenau, "Explainable activity recognition for smart-home systems," ACM Trans. Interactive Intell. Syst., early-access, 2023.
20. C. I. Nwakanma, G. O. Anyanwu, and D.-S. Kim, "A review of thermal-array-sensor-based activity detection in smart spaces using AI," ICT Express, vol. 10, pp. 1–12, 2024.
21. A. Luz, T. Ferreira, V. Souza et al., "Enhancing smart environments with context-aware chatbots powered by large language models," arXiv:2502.14469, 2025.

Chapter 2
Multimodal Systems for Independent Living

Abstract The advancement of multimodal sensing technologies has significantly enhanced independent living, particularly for older adults and individuals with disabilities. This chapter explores diverse sensor modalities used in smart home environments to monitor daily activities, detect anomalies, and ensure safety. Key categories include wearable devices, ambient sensors, camera systems, acoustic methods, pressure and floor sensors, radar and RF-based approaches, and smart objects. Wearable sensors, such as accelerometers, gyroscopes, and physiological monitors, offer real-time data for tracking movement, posture, heart rate, and respiration, supporting applications like fall detection and health monitoring, though they face challenges like limited battery life, data reliability, and user adherence. Ambient sensors—motion detectors, door/cabinet sensors, and smart appliances—enable passive monitoring of activity patterns and risks such as inactivity or unusual usage. Camera-based systems leverage computer vision, depth imaging, and techniques like skeleton tracking and convolutional neural networks (CNNs) for activity recognition, though privacy concerns demand solutions such as edge processing and anonymized data extraction. Acoustic sensing employs audio features such as Mel-Frequency Cepstral Coefficients (MFCCs), spectrograms, and beamforming to detect distress signals and anomalies. Pressure sensors embedded in furniture and floors analyze weight distribution, occupancy, and gait stability, complementing other sensing approaches. Radar and RF-based solutions, including Wi-Fi Channel State Information (CSI), provide contactless monitoring of motion and vital signs, making them suitable for privacy-sensitive environments, although signal interference and environmental factors can affect performance. Sensor-augmented objects like smart canes and pill dispensers enable tracking of mobility, medication adherence, and daily habits without relying on wearables. The integration of heterogeneous data sources remains a key challenge, with methods such as hierarchical fusion, temporal alignment, and contextual correlation improving detection accuracy and reducing false positives. Longitudinal data analysis facilitates early identification of health trends such as mobility decline or cognitive impairment. Ethical considerations—including data privacy, transparent decision-making, and adaptability to user lifestyles—are critical for acceptance and success. By combining advanced sensing with machine learning-based analysis,

© The Author(s), under exclusive license to Springer Nature Switzerland AG 2025
M. Z. Uddin, *Trustworthy Multimodal Intelligent Systems for Independent Living*, Cognitive Technologies, https://doi.org/10.1007/978-3-031-97359-8_2

these systems offer scalable, adaptive, and privacy-conscious solutions to support independent living and improve the quality of life for vulnerable populations.

2.1 Introduction

The aging population across the globe is growing at a rapid pace, and with it comes an urgent need to devise, adopt, and refine technologies that support independent living. In response, researchers and industry professionals have focused increasingly on the idea of multimodal systems, which combine various types of sensors, devices, and analytical methods into unified frameworks that help older adults or individuals with special needs to remain in their homes longer, live safer lives, and maintain a higher quality of day-to-day existence [1–3]. Although many of these systems are also suitable for younger people with disabilities or those requiring rehabilitative support, the greatest emphasis has historically been on older adults, partly due to the larger share of healthcare costs that arise in old age and partly because many seniors express a clear desire to remain in familiar environments.

This chapter presents a comprehensive, descriptive overview of multimodal systems for independent living. We will explore the evolution of these systems from early prototypes that monitored only a single parameter (for instance, a simple motion sensor to detect presence in a hallway) to the sophisticated, networked solutions of today that combine wearable sensors, ambient intelligence, robotic assistance, artificial intelligence (AI), big data analytics, and Internet of Things (IoT) infrastructures. Though such systems can appear complex, they share a unifying mission: to create a supportive environment that can detect threats or anomalies (e.g., a fall, changes in gait, deviations in routine, or unusual physiological readings), intervene proactively (e.g., sending an alert to a caregiver, activating an emergency service, or adjusting environmental parameters like temperature), and thereby uphold the independence of the user [4]. Figure 2.1 shows a generic flowchart of training and testing of data and event-based approaches via machine learning. In conceptualizing these multimodal systems, we see that the term multimodal implies the integration of multiple streams of data. This can include:

- Physiological signals (e.g., heart rate, breathing rate, temperature), frequently captured by wearable or non-contact devices.
- Environmental measurements (e.g., motion, humidity, temperature, indoor air quality, presence and occupancy data, door or cabinet usage).
- Vision-based information (e.g., images or depth maps from cameras, or optical sensors tracking the silhouette and skeleton joint movements of a user).
- Acoustic data (e.g., audio signals to detect falls, calls for help, or relevant sound patterns).
- Radar and radio-frequency analyses (e.g., changes in radar signal reflection patterns or Wi-Fi channel variations, used to detect movement or even vital signs).

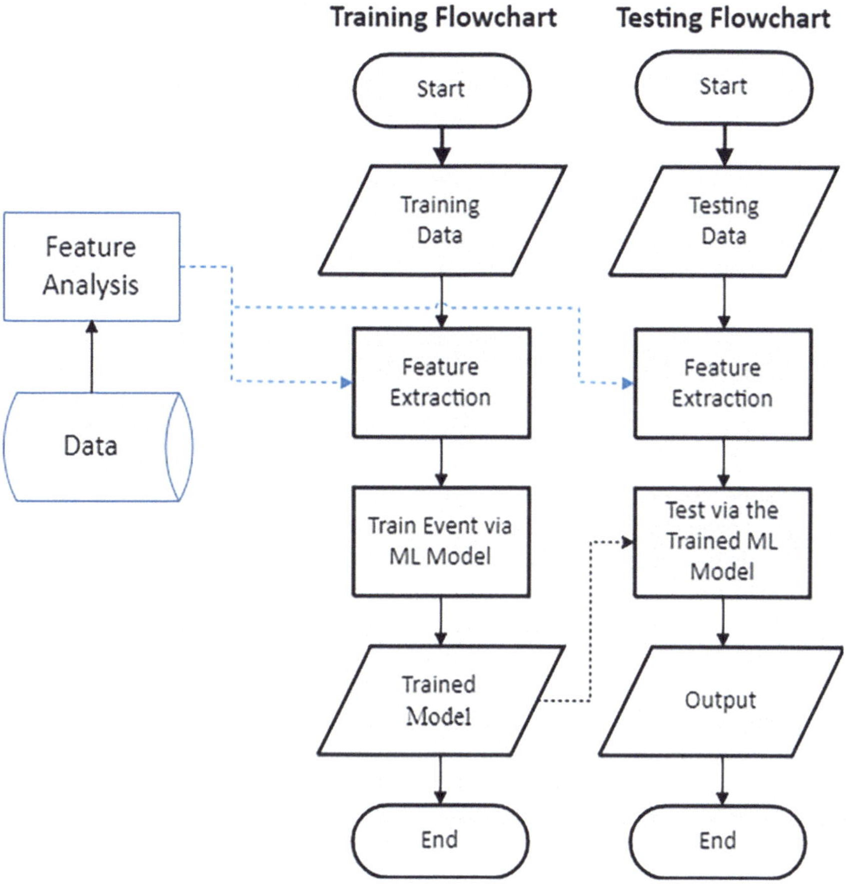

Fig. 2.1 A generic flowchart of training and testing of data and event-based approaches via machine learning

- Smart objects and furniture (e.g., sensor-equipped refrigerators, bedding, cushions, or pill boxes that record user interactions to infer daily activities or adherence to medication schedules).
- Robotic and assistive devices (e.g., robotic systems with integrated sensors that can help with mobility, carry items, or facilitate telepresence).

2.1.1 Independent Living Technologies

Global demographics have shifted dramatically in recent decades. As life expectancy increases, there is a higher proportion of older adults in many populations, especially in developed nations. Healthcare systems must respond to the needs and preferences of these seniors, the majority of whom prefer to remain in their own homes rather than move into assisted-living facilities or nursing homes. This preference for aging in place has led to the exploration of practical, cost-effective solutions that promote autonomy and reduce the burden on healthcare resources [5]. Early telecare systems emerged as phone-based mechanisms through which a user could call for help by pressing a button. This is still widely used, yet far from sufficient for more holistic care. Individuals who fall or become disoriented might not be able to press a button, leading to potential delays in emergency response. Technological developments such as cheaper microelectronics, improved battery life, the ubiquity of wireless Internet, and ever-smaller sensors have made advanced monitoring more feasible. In parallel, growth in machine learning, cloud computing, and edge devices has delivered more powerful ways to analyze and react to sensor data in near real-time. Twenty years ago, it was unusual to see a health-monitoring system that could automatically detect and classify activities of daily living (ADLs). Nowadays, there are prototypes and commercial products that can identify whether a person is cooking, bathing, or resting, using data from motion sensors, cameras, and wearables.

Early attempts at remote monitoring for older adults often relied on a single data source, such as an infrared motion sensor in key points of the house, or a wearable panic button. Such isolated methods provided minimal context. A motion sensor, for instance, might detect that someone is in the living room, but not how they are moving, whether they have fallen, or how long they have remained inactive. Recognizing the limitations, researchers began to consider combining multiple sensing modalities. This approach has proven far richer and more robust; data from different sensors can be cross-referenced to confirm anomalies, reduce false alarms, and provide a comprehensive assessment of a user's daily patterns.

2.1.2 Multimodal System for Independent Living

A multimodal system for independent living aims to track and interpret a variety of signals that capture both the person's state (physiological, behavioral, emotional) and the environment's state (location, temperature, air quality, presence of potential hazards, and so forth).

Sensors attached to the user can capture physiological parameters, such as heartbeat, electrocardiogram (ECG) signals, oxygen saturation, and respiration rate. They can also detect motion signatures—allowing for identification of gait speed or postural transitions (standing, walking, sitting, etc.). Modern devices like smartwatches, wristbands, and specialized chest straps or patch sensors can collect this data continuously and transmit it to a local hub or the cloud for analysis.

Environmental sensors, typically installed around the home, capture data like temperature, humidity, carbon dioxide levels, presence or location, sound or acoustic patterns, and household device usage. For instance, a stove sensor can detect if the stove remains on for too long, or a water-flow sensor can detect potential flooding or identify usage patterns that deviate from routine (e.g., lack of water use may indicate that the person has not performed certain daily tasks). Cameras, depth sensors, or thermal imaging devices provide valuable insights into posture, location, and sometimes emotional expression. They can capture subtle changes in gait or sudden falls. However, concerns about privacy have led researchers to investigate alternative approaches such as radar-based, infrared-based, or radio frequency-based solutions that do not record identifiable video footage.

Certain daily objects can be integrated with sensors or connectivity modules. Examples include smart pill dispensers that track medication intake, sensor-equipped beds that measure sleep patterns or restlessness, and service robots that help carry objects, remind users about medication times, or monitor overall home safety. In advanced scenarios, social robots can also engage in conversation and help users with mental stimulation, providing cues for daily tasks or even companionship. The data streams from these devices need to be combined in a well-orchestrated fashion. This typically involves a local processing system (e.g., a small computer, a home server, or an embedded controller) and possibly remote servers (cloud-based). The system uses data fusion algorithms to make sense of multiple inputs—for example, combining motion sensor data with a wearable accelerometer can confirm if a user has truly fallen or merely sat down abruptly. This fusion significantly reduces false alarms.

Higher-level analytics interpret the fused data, looking for patterns such as changes in daily routines, signs of cognitive decline, or risk factors like repeated near-falls. This analytics layer might also incorporate machine learning models, rules-based engines, or statistical methods. Outputs can include alerts (text messages or calls to caregivers), local automated adjustments (such as turning off the stove if it was left on by mistake), or logs for professional healthcare staff to review. Information should be presented in an accessible, non-intrusive manner, whether it is for the older adult, who might receive gentle reminders or notifications on a tablet, or for remote family members and caregivers, who require timely alerts in the event of a health issue or security risk. The overall design must strike a balance between offering thorough monitoring and respecting the user's privacy and autonomy.

2.1.3 The Socio-technical Context

While the technical details of multimodal systems are fascinating, they cannot be divorced from the broader socio-technical context in which these systems operate. Adoption depends heavily on acceptance by the elderly themselves, their families, and professional caregivers. Several social and ethical dimensions warrant careful consideration. One of the most frequently cited barriers to widespread deployment of cameras or advanced sensing systems in a home is the fear of constant surveillance. Many older adults worry about losing their dignity and autonomy if they are monitored too extensively. Therefore, designers often look to non-visual or privacy-preserving technologies, or ensure that any camera-based monitoring uses sophisticated encryption and local processing that does not store raw images.

For a system to be genuinely helpful, users must feel comfortable with wearing sensors or having them embedded in their environment. Devices that appear too clinical or medical may be perceived as stigmatizing, reminding individuals of frailty rather than promoting independence. Carefully designed, discreet systems that blend seamlessly into daily life have a higher likelihood of adoption. With massive amounts of personal, sensitive data being collected, questions of data ownership, sharing, and ethical usage arise. Different stakeholders—technology providers, healthcare agencies, insurance companies, or families—may have divergent motivations or claims on the data. Legal frameworks differ by country, and many remain ambiguous in how they handle the emerging complexities of continuous health data. Even the most advanced technology cannot make a meaningful impact unless it is affordable or covered by healthcare insurance. Large-scale adoption often requires collaboration between government agencies, insurance providers, and local healthcare authorities. The cost of sensors, internet connectivity, system maintenance, and potential home modifications can pose financial obstacles. Nonetheless, when weighed against the cost of institutionalization or repeated hospital stays, a well-designed system may prove cost-effective in the long run.

Independent living solutions must account for the cultural, linguistic, and personal preferences of users. Activities of daily living vary widely by culture; for example, meal patterns or religious rituals might influence how a monitoring system interprets normal or abnormal behaviors. The system must also accommodate different living arrangements. Some older adults live entirely alone, others with family members, and still others in shared housing. Each scenario creates unique data profiles and potential sensors' placements.

2.1.4 Key Motivations for Multimodal Approaches

A single sensor, no matter how well-designed, inevitably fails to capture the complexity of daily life. Motion sensors alone might trigger frequent false positives, while relying solely on wearable technology can produce data gaps if the user forgets or refuses to wear the device. By combining data sources—e.g., motion sensors, pressure mats, and wearable accelerometers—it is possible to cross-verify events, drastically reducing false alarms and missed detections. Beyond detecting something like a fall event, a multimodal system can interpret context. Is the user alone in the living room, or is another household member present? Did the user just walk in from outside, or have they been cooking? Is the house temperature unusually high, raising the risk of dehydration? By layering multiple channels of information, the system can provide deeper, contextually informed interventions.

Over time, the system learns each individual's unique lifestyle and preferences. If someone always takes a nap at a certain time or routinely walks slowly, the system can adapt its thresholds accordingly. In other words, the baseline patterns come from the user's own data. Multimodal inputs accelerate and improve this personalization process, since the system can cross-reference signals and calibrate more precisely. One of the primary aims of an independent living solution is to identify subtle changes that indicate a problem in its early stages—cognitive decline, frailty, depression, or undiagnosed medical conditions. Gait analysis, for example, reveals tiny variations in walking speed or stride length that might precede an actual fall. A system that looks only at raw motion sensor data might miss these changes, but a multimodal approach that includes wearables, video-based pose detection, and radar-based signals can pick up micro-level deviations early.

When systems provide varied types of feedback—reminders, suggestions for physical exercises, or occasional alerts about household conditions—they can also foster better engagement. For instance, a system may gently recommend more frequent hydration if it detects high humidity and limited fluid intake. Multimodal data enables the system to issue recommendations that are more precise and user-centric.

2.1.5 Challenges and Opportunities Moving Forward

With multiple sensors collecting continuous streams of data, the system must handle massive volumes of information. Efficient data management strategies, including edge computing (processing data locally to reduce bandwidth and latency) and robust algorithms for filtering noise, remain crucial. While many projects succeed in tightly controlled laboratory or pilot settings, scaling up to hundreds or thousands of homes introduces complexities in installation, support, and maintenance. Homes differ in layout and materials, and older adults themselves vary in health conditions and technology literacy. Various hardware and software platforms must work together seamlessly. The absence of standardization can slow the implementation of new features or hamper the ability to integrate an additional sensor type. Even the most accurate system is of limited value if it fails to align with the user's lifestyle. Acceptance requires trust, ease-of-use, and minimal intrusion. The system must adapt to the person, rather than forcing the person to adapt to it.

Funding the deployment of these systems remains a concern, especially in regions where healthcare support is heavily regulated or reliant on public insurance. Demonstrating cost savings (for instance, by reducing hospitalization rates) can encourage healthcare providers to subsidize the systems. By identifying risk factors early, these systems encourage proactive interventions—preventing small issues from becoming severe. This has the potential to transform the way eldercare is delivered. Machine learning models can become hyper-personalized, capturing an individual's unique trajectory of movement, heart rate trends, or medication adherence patterns. Over time, the system grows more accurate for that specific user. With telemedicine becoming increasingly mainstream, data from a multimodal system can be shared seamlessly with healthcare professionals, enabling remote consultations that are more evidence-based and timely. Beyond mitigating dangers, these systems can contribute to overall well-being. For example, automated lighting and temperature controls that respond to daily habits can create an environment that is comfortable and supportive, reducing loneliness by facilitating social interactions through integrated communication platforms. Large deployments of multimodal systems could create unprecedented datasets on aging populations, revealing correlations and patterns that advance our understanding of health trajectories and inform policy decisions.

2.2 Sensor Modalities

In designing a robust multimodal system for independent living, one of the first and most critical steps is to select the right collection of sensors. These sensors must gather data on the person's well-being, detect the environment's state, and discern relevant daily activities that could provide early clues about health changes [6, 7]. Just as a comprehensive medical check-up relies on multiple tests and measurements to understand a patient's overall condition, a multimodal system integrates different sensory pathways to create a broad and nuanced overview of daily life. It is helpful to remember that each sensor type has its own strengths, limitations, costs, and privacy implications. In real-world applications, the art lies in combining sensors in a way that aligns with the user's lifestyle, the architectural constraints of a home, and the practicalities of system maintenance. Figure 2.2 shows the connection of sensors and devices that can be used for smart independent assisted living.

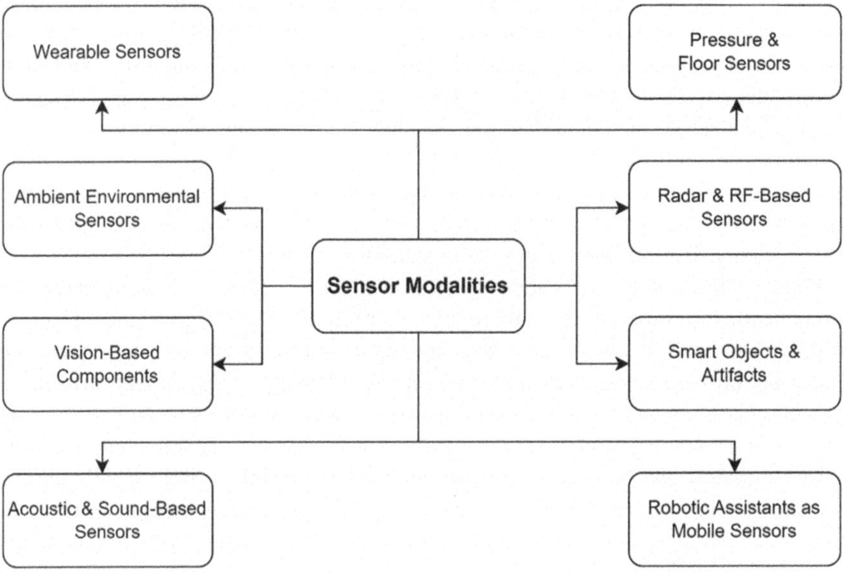

Fig. 2.2 Sensors and devices that can be used for smart independent assisted living

2.2.1 Wearable Sensors

Wearable sensors hold a special place in the modern ecosystem of independent living technologies because they collect firsthand data about the user. They are often attached to the wrist, chest, or foot, or sometimes embedded within common personal items like eyeglasses or belts. Wearable devices can measure a wide range of parameters—acceleration, gyroscopic movements, heart rate, skin temperature, and even electrodermal activity, which can hint at stress levels. They can also act as mobile computing platforms, especially in the case of smartwatches or smartphones that the user already owns [5]. This capability means some data processing can be done locally before transmitting relevant findings to the central system.

The earliest examples of wearable technology in eldercare involved simple accelerometers that sent an alert if a sudden impact was detected, signifying a possible fall. Modern incarnations have evolved dramatically. Current commercial smartwatches can track walking speed, analyze gait irregularities, and even measure electrocardiograms. Additionally, continuous monitoring is possible, though this depends on device battery life, user compliance in charging or wearing the sensor, and robust connectivity. Wearables often face the challenge that some older adults are reluctant to wear them consistently or find charging them tedious. This reluctance is sometimes due to appearance-related concerns (some are bulky or look clinical) or personal discomfort at having a device strapped on. Designers must address these concerns through ergonomic shapes and subtle aesthetics. From a technical standpoint, many wearable sensors rely on short-range wireless connections—commonly Bluetooth or Bluetooth Low Energy—to communicate with either a smartphone or a home gateway. This pathway ensures a low power profile. In terms of data, the device can often store raw signals temporarily before performing local feature extraction and sending only higher-level indicators, such as step count, heart rate, or sudden acceleration. Though these summarized metrics are essential for daily monitoring, more specialized research systems might store and analyze the full raw signal for in-depth analysis. For example, a system in a research setting might want to study whether an older adult's micro-step variability correlates with early cognitive decline, and that level of detail requires deeper signal processing.

Wearable sensors are a powerful tool for collecting close-to-the-body data. They capture subtle bodily changes—ranging from increased resting heart rate to slight modifications in gait—and transform these metrics into insights that can be seamlessly integrated into a broader home monitoring platform. However, system designers must be mindful of user acceptance, battery life, and potential data gaps when the individual removes the device or forgets to charge it.

2.2.2 Ambient Environmental Sensors

Ambient sensors differ from wearables in that they reside not on the body but in the living space. They passively gather data about presence, movement, temperature, lighting, and various other attributes of the home environment [8–11]. Because they are integrated into walls, ceilings, floors, and everyday objects, they often intrude less on the user's sense of personal space or body than wearables do. Moreover, because ambient sensors do not rely on the user to remember to wear or charge anything, they can deliver more consistent data over time.

One of the most common categories of ambient sensors consists of motion detectors, such as passive infrared (PIR) sensors. PIR sensors detect changes in infrared radiation associated with the movement of warm objects, typically humans, within their field of view. While PIR sensors alone cannot confirm the exact nature of the activity (for example, cooking versus resting in a chair), they can provide essential cues about the person's location and general motion. If carefully positioned, they can detect repeated movement patterns, track transitions from one room to another, and signal long periods of inactivity that might indicate a fall or some other immobilizing event. Many modern systems also integrate door or cabinet sensors, which detect whether a refrigerator or medicine cabinet has been opened and for how long. These data points shed light on daily routines, such as mealtimes, medication adherence, or overall activity. Additional sensors might track water usage at sinks or in the shower, electricity usage of appliances, and even subtle changes in air quality. By correlating these signals, the system can form an approximate picture of how the older adult goes about daily tasks—whether they have cooked a meal, bathed, or opened the door to greet a visitor.

Temperature and humidity sensors are similarly valuable. Deviations in a home's usual temperature-humidity profile may indicate that the user forgot to turn off the stove or an air conditioner, or that they have opened a window at an unusual time. Such changes become relevant if they point to a behavior shift or a potential hazard, like extremely high heat or poor indoor air quality. In cold climates, these sensors can also help ensure that the heating system is working correctly and that the user is not at risk of hypothermia. A notable advantage of ambient sensors is that many of them operate at low power and can function for years on a single battery or from a wired power supply, minimizing maintenance overhead [10, 11]. They also typically generate relatively small amounts of data (binary on–off events or periodic measurements like temperature every few minutes), meaning that communication bandwidth is rarely a bottleneck. The trade-off is that ambient sensors alone often cannot confirm the exact nature of an activity. For instance, a motion sensor might detect a person moving around the living room at midday, but it provides no definitive information about whether they are exercising or pacing due to restlessness. Such nuances often require more advanced sensing, like vision or radar, or context from other sensing streams such as wearables.

2.2.3 *Vision-Based Components*

Vision-based sensors, typically in the form of conventional video cameras or depth cameras, can detect a wide range of user activities with relatively high accuracy. From gait analysis to posture classification, cameras can capture and interpret subtle actions that simpler sensors miss. For instance, a camera-based system can differentiate between someone lying on the floor deliberately for a stretching exercise and someone who has collapsed due to a fall [12]. By examining frames over time, a vision-based system can also identify major changes in daily movement patterns or the onset of tremors and other neurological symptoms. However, cameras introduce significant concerns around privacy. Many older adults, especially those who live alone, do not want to feel that someone is watching them all the time. This factor often limits widespread deployment of conventional RGB video in bedrooms, bathrooms, or other personal spaces. As a consequence, many researchers and product designers have turned toward technologies like depth cameras, which capture a three-dimensional silhouette rather than a detailed color image, or thermal cameras, which produce heatmaps of the environment. Both approaches can deliver valuable insights into body posture and motion without depicting facial or room details.

Advanced methods that go beyond simple background subtraction and detect skeleton joints or track contours allow for real-time activity recognition. Some systems incorporate machine learning models that analyze sequences of frames to detect transitions from walking to sitting, lying down, or falling. Others use more complex architectures, such as deep neural networks, to label ongoing activities (e.g., cooking, cleaning, picking up an object) or detect anomalies indicative of health risks. Depth cameras and optical sensors can also be combined with other data streams to minimize false positives. For instance, if a motion sensor indicates the user is in the living room while a wearable accelerometer shows rapid acceleration and a vision system sees a collapse, the system becomes much more certain that a fall has occurred. Despite these advantages, vision-based approaches demand higher computational resources. Processing video or depth data can be both CPU- and GPU-intensive, often requiring local edge computing solutions or robust cloud infrastructure, depending on how large the environment is and how many sensors are in use. Network constraints and the high data bandwidth of raw video must be carefully managed. As a result, some systems perform on-camera or on-sensor processing, sending only high-level events (like fall detected) to the system's central hub rather than raw images. This method not only saves bandwidth but also helps address privacy concerns, since images are not stored or transmitted.

In an ideal multimodal system, the camera's strengths—granular event detection and posture analysis—counterbalance the limitations of simpler sensors. Meanwhile, the presence of other sensor streams ensures that if the camera feed is obscured (by darkness, obstruction, or power failure), the system still has partial functionality to detect some relevant activities.

2.2.4 Acoustic and Sound-Based Sensors

Sound-based monitoring relies on microphones or arrays of microphones placed around the home. The system can analyze patterns in captured audio signals, looking for distinct acoustic signatures such as a cry for help, the sound of a fall, or the clang of dishes. This approach can be more subtle than a visual feed, in the sense that privacy is less visibly compromised (though audio collection raises concerns about eavesdropping). Nonetheless, older adults or family caregivers may feel uneasy about continuous audio recording within the home. As with camera data, some solutions address this by processing audio signals locally and transmitting only recognized events, rather than streaming raw audio. Detecting falls via sound involves training an algorithm to recognize the characteristic thump or crash that accompanies a person hitting the floor. However, objects can also fall and produce very similar acoustic patterns. Therefore, acoustic detection systems often must differentiate between the sound of a book dropping, for example, and the more distressing pattern of a body's impact. This is where advanced classification approaches can help, examining features such as frequency distribution and temporal progression. The system might also look for a subsequent cry or moan that often follows a genuine fall event, further clarifying context.

Microphone arrays can offer directionality, locating the source of a sound in space. That capability helps a system pinpoint which room or area a concerning noise came from, potentially speeding up emergency response. Some research projects have also developed solutions that analyze the pitch and cadence of speech, detecting signs of confusion or distress, though these are more experimental and raise additional privacy implications. Acoustic sensors can play a particularly valuable role in certain specific scenarios. For instance, if a person in a wheelchair drops a pot in the kitchen, the system can capture the sound of the impact, notice that the person is still present (from PIR sensors), and possibly prompt them visually or audibly: Is everything okay? Press a button if you need assistance. By cross-referencing data streams, it can distinguish a harmless event from a more serious scenario. The flexibility and non-intrusiveness of audio make it attractive, but high false-positive rates remain a risk unless carefully mitigated through data fusion or well-tuned detection algorithms.

2.2.5 Pressure and Floor Sensors

Pressure sensors are commonly associated with beds, chairs, and floors. They gather information about the distribution and magnitude of weight in a specific area, sometimes resolving it into an approximate body outline if multiple sensing points are used. When embedded in mattresses or cushions, these sensors can estimate heart and respiration rates by picking up micro-movements of the body, as well as track restlessness, changes in posture, or the amount of time spent in bed. Some sophisticated bed sensor systems incorporate ballistocardiography techniques, detecting the subtle mechanical vibrations that correspond to each heartbeat. Floor sensors, including pressure-sensitive mats or tiles, can do more than simply register presence. They can track footsteps as a person moves through a corridor, sometimes inferring gait speed and stride length by monitoring the progression of pressure patterns. Detecting a sudden heavy impact might point to a fall. Similarly, analyzing repeated sequences might reveal that the person is pacing—potentially a sign of agitation, confusion, or pain.

Because pressure sensors are typically hidden inside or beneath existing surfaces, they rarely generate the user acceptance challenges that cameras or wearables do. They function invisibly, requiring minimal effort from the user. That said, installation can be tricky if the home has carpeting, complex floor structures, or limited space. Additionally, these sensors must be robust to normal household usage: daily vacuuming, pets walking over them, or visitors wearing high heels should not produce a flurry of false alerts. As with other types of sensors, pressure data alone has limited interpretive power. A reading that indicates a person has been lying in bed for many hours could be a sign of normal sleep, illness, or simply a day of quiet rest. Data from motion sensors, wearables, or sound detection can bring context to the situation and help the system decide whether an alert or notification is warranted. Nonetheless, the ability of pressure sensors to unobtrusively collect data about positioning and movements makes them a vital piece of a multimodal system.

2.2.6 Radar and Radio-Frequency-Based Sensors

In response to the privacy challenges of cameras, researchers have explored radio-frequency (RF) solutions, including radar and Doppler sensing. These methods work by sending out radio waves and measuring the reflections as they bounce off objects—most importantly, the human body. Doppler radars can detect small motions like breathing and heartbeat fluctuations, while more general-purpose radars can track a person's location and movements. A distinct advantage is that these methods generally do not produce an image of the person, thus substantially reducing privacy concerns. Wi-Fi-based sensing has also garnered interest in the research community. In this approach, common Wi-Fi signals are analyzed to see how a person's presence or movement alters the channel state information. The subtle fluctuations in signal strength across different frequencies can reveal gait speed, posture changes, or the presence of multiple individuals. The key strength here is that many homes already have a Wi-Fi infrastructure, so no specialized hardware is required aside from minor firmware or driver modifications in some cases. However, the method requires complex signal processing and can be affected by interference from other Wi-Fi devices or multi-path reflections in cluttered homes.

Radar-based solutions can achieve precise detection of micro-movements—for example, distinguishing between someone who is standing still, breathing, or engaged in fine hand gestures. These systems can also identify falls by the velocity profile of the body as it abruptly changes. In earlier implementations, radar devices were expensive or power-hungry, but with the miniaturization of technology, small, power-efficient modules have become viable for home use. The main consideration for RF sensors is that they can be sensitive to obstacles, changes in furniture layout, or the presence of visitors. The signals may be absorbed, reflected, or scattered in ways that complicate interpretation. A well-calibrated system includes adaptive algorithms that understand the baseline environment and can adapt to slight changes. When integrated into a broader multimodal setup, radar data can be cross-validated with, for instance, motion sensors or wearable accelerometers for more accurate event detection.

2.2.7 Smart Objects and Everyday Artifacts

Beyond discrete sensors mounted on walls or placed in corners, a growing trend involves embedding sensors into everyday objects such as refrigerators, pill dispensers, canes, and utensils. This idea capitalizes on the fact that older adults are already accustomed to using these items daily, so no additional routine must be learned. A smart refrigerator, for example, can track how often it is opened, detect if items are removed, and estimate consumption patterns. A sensor-augmented cane might record the user's walking patterns or the frequency of cane usage. One particularly useful application is the smart pill dispenser, which lights up or emits a sound at specific times, then logs whether the compartment was opened. This helps track medication adherence and prevents overdosing or forgetting doses. Some dispensers automatically alert a caregiver if a dose is missed or if the user is about to take the wrong medication. Similarly, a smart cooking pot can monitor temperature and fluid levels, ensuring safety and providing data on nutritional habits. These smart objects can become nodes in a larger sensor network, offering real-time data on how the older adult interacts with their home environment. Because these objects directly reflect daily routines, they provide context that might be more precise than environmental sensors alone. However, each smart object must be carefully designed to balance technological complexity with user-friendliness. If the object becomes too cumbersome or visually distracting, the user might reject it altogether. Additionally, maintenance and battery replacement can become issues if too many smart objects are deployed without a clear plan.

2.2.8 Robotic Assistants as Mobile Sensor Platforms

Although robots in the context of eldercare are often envisioned primarily as service providers—carrying items, opening doors, or facilitating communication—they can also function as mobile sensor platforms. Equipped with cameras, depth sensors, radar modules, or even arms that can lightly touch a user's wrist to measure heart rate, a single robot might gather as much data as numerous static sensors around the home. By moving to areas of interest, the robot can gain vantage points that static sensors cannot. If an anomaly is detected in one part of the house—say, the motion sensors have not recorded any movement in the kitchen for an unusually long period—the robot can navigate there and investigate. Furthermore, the robot can engage in direct interaction with the older adult, asking if they feel dizzy or need assistance. If a user collapses, a robot with appropriate mobility can move closer, use its camera or radar to assess the situation more thoroughly, and even communicate with emergency services or a remote caregiver. Advanced models include integrated speech recognition and natural language processing, allowing the user to converse with the robot. This verbal interface can provide valuable clues regarding the user's cognitive and emotional state.

From a design perspective, robots must be carefully tested for reliability, especially if they are expected to perform physically assistive tasks. They also demand significantly more resources in terms of battery, computing, and maintenance compared to static sensors. The cost factor is non-trivial, and for some households, installing a range of simpler sensors might be more feasible and less expensive than introducing a sophisticated robotic system. Nonetheless, for those who do employ a robot, it can become a versatile and dynamic component of the multimodal infrastructure.

2.2.9 Synergistic Integration of Multiple Sensing Modalities

While each sensor type described has intrinsic value, the real power of a multimodal system emerges from how these various streams work in tandem. The interactions can be conceptualized in several ways. Different sensors can confirm or refute one another's signals, decreasing the likelihood of false alarms. A loud crash might be detected acoustically, but the floor sensor might reveal that no significant weight impacted the floor. This contradiction suggests an object fell, not a person. If, however, the floor sensor also shows a sudden pressure spike, the system can be more confident that it was truly a fall event. Each sensor offers a distinct perspective. A wearable accelerometer can detect subtle changes in gait dynamics, while a camera might provide evidence of the user's posture [14, 15]. Combined, they paint a fuller picture of mobility and balance. This richer insight allows for advanced analytics that can detect early markers of frailty or gait instability.

Ambient sensors might indicate that the user has entered the kitchen and turned on the stove, while a wearable sensor logs prolonged standing and minimal foot movement. Simultaneously, a vision-based system might interpret gestures that imply the person is chopping vegetables. Together, these data streams confirm that the user is cooking. If this cooking session extends far longer than usual, or if the stove remains on after the user's motion data shows they have returned to the living room, the system can alert them to avoid a fire risk. Over time, the system learns baseline behaviors. Perhaps a specific user frequently takes short naps in the afternoon, so motion sensors record minimal activity for an hour. In a single-sensor system, this might be flagged as a potential emergency. But by noticing that wearable data still indicates normal heart rate, and acoustic sensors register occasional coughs or sighs, the system realizes the user is merely resting. As a result, it can adapt thresholds and reduce nuisance alarms.

A user might wear an intelligent watch that detects elevated heart rate, while an ambient sensor records abnormally high indoor temperature. By linking these data points, the system can suggest the user hydrate or turn on a fan. If a robotic assistant is present, it can bring a glass of water or open a window. The synergy is not just about data correlation but proactive, context-aware action.

Practical Considerations in Sensor Selection and Deployment

When planning a multimodal setup, it is not enough simply to list desired sensors. Designers and caregivers must address practical constraints, such as cost, installation complexity, maintenance, user acceptance, and integration with existing home infrastructure [16]. They must also respect the diverse living arrangements of older adults. Some older adults reside in single-story homes, while others occupy multilevel houses or small apartments. Some live alone; others share space with spouses or adult children, creating multiple moving persons that the system must differentiate [17, 18].

During installation, sensor placement is crucial. Motion sensors must not be obstructed by furniture. Cameras need unobstructed views. Pressure sensors in floors or beds demand careful calibration. Wearables depend on consistent usage patterns and user compliance. Some sensors may require stable network connectivity—whether Wi-Fi or a dedicated radio protocol—so coverage must be tested in the far reaches of the home. Additionally, homes vary widely in building materials, and thick walls or metal structures can impede wireless signals. Software integration is another significant challenge. Each sensor typically has its own data format, update rate, and operational quirks. A unified data fusion layer or middleware must abstract these details, presenting consistent interfaces to the higher-level algorithms that interpret events. This layer must also handle time synchronization, which can be complicated if devices report data asynchronously. In some systems, an event-driven architecture triggers analysis as soon as data arrive. In others, data are aggregated in short intervals and then processed in batches.

Power supply is equally important. While some devices can be plugged into wall outlets, others might rely on batteries for portability or to facilitate flexible placement. Regular battery checks or self-reporting features that warn of low battery are vital to prevent sensor failures going unnoticed. If the user or caregiver must replace batteries frequently, it could reduce the system's overall effectiveness. Finally, user training or orientation should not be overlooked. Even if sensors are designed to be unobtrusive, the older adult or their family members need at least a basic understanding of what is being monitored and why. Clear communication helps them appreciate the benefits and fosters trust. For instance, if they are aware that cameras are depth-based or anonymized, it can alleviate privacy concerns.

2.3 Architecture and Data Fusion in Multimodal Systems

A set of sensors, no matter how carefully chosen or installed, represents just the initial piece of a larger puzzle in independent living technologies. For these sensors to provide meaningful insights, they must be integrated within a coherent system architecture—one that securely and reliably transports, processes, and interprets the data in real time (or near real time). In other words, the raw signals from sensors must be channeled through a layered infrastructure that includes communication, data storage, intelligent analysis, and user-facing interfaces [19, 20]. The bedrock of the solution often lies in advanced data fusion techniques, which synthesize multiple sources of information into a single representation of what is happening at any given moment.

2.3.1 Common Architectural Layers

Multimodal systems are typically structured using a layered architecture that promotes modular design and ease of maintenance [21]. At the base is the Sensing and Actuation Layer, which comprises environmental sensors and devices such as robotic arms or alarms that can respond based on system logic. These components connect via various communication technologies like Wi-Fi, ZigBee, or Bluetooth, and the diversity of manufacturers results in a wide range of hardware protocols and data types. Above this is the Communication Layer, responsible for transferring sensor data to processing hubs, either locally or in the cloud, using different networking standards, including IP-based and publish-subscribe models. This layer also incorporates essential security features, such as encryption, to safeguard personal and health-related information. The Data Management and Processing Layer follows, where incoming data are stored, time-stamped, validated, and standardized—ensuring consistency and enabling synchronization across multiple sources. The system's core functionality resides in the Intelligence Layer, which leverages signal processing, machine learning, and rule-based systems to interpret data, detect critical events, and monitor behavioral trends over time. It also performs data fusion, combining inputs from different sensors into unified insights. The Application and Interaction Layer presents these insights through user interfaces such as mobile apps or dashboards, and may also automate actions like sending alerts or controlling devices. Closely linked is the User Interface Layer, which governs how individuals—such as older adults, caregivers, or clinicians—interact with the system through tools like notifications, voice assistants, or social robots, with a focus on usability, personalization, accessibility, and privacy preferences.

2.3.2 *Centralized Versus Distributed Architectures*

In broad terms, system designers may opt for either a centralized or a distributed approach. Each has advantages and challenges, influencing factors like latency, reliability, and data privacy. In a centralized model, all (or most) sensor data are sent to a single computing node—often a local gateway or a cloud server—for storage and processing. On the one hand, this simplifies architecture: sensors only need to know how to transmit data to that central location, and there is a single place to implement and update analytics algorithms. On the other hand, a strong dependence on one node can create a single point of failure. If that node goes offline or the Internet connection fails, the entire system may be compromised [22]. Additionally, continuous data streaming to the cloud can raise bandwidth and privacy concerns, particularly with video or audio data.

A distributed or edge-heavy architecture places more intelligence at the edges of the network—potentially inside each sensor module or a series of local microcontrollers that do preliminary processing before sharing only summarized events or relevant features. This arrangement can improve resilience. Even if one sensor fails or loses its connection to the home gateway, other parts of the system can still function. Distributed approaches also help with privacy: raw data (especially images or audio) may never leave the home network, as only event-level information is transmitted outward. However, distributing intelligence comes with added complexity in design, firmware updates, and synchronization across multiple nodes. Many real-world deployments combine elements of both models. They might analyze high-frequency signals locally (e.g., using on-device AI for fall detection from a camera) and only send higher-level summaries (like Fall detected at 14:15 in the living room) to the cloud for logging and caregiver notifications.

2.3.3 *Data Fusion: The Heart of Multimodal Integration*

When we talk about multimodal or multi-sensor systems, we imply that various streams of data are not just collected but combined intelligently to provide deeper insights. This merging is known as **data fusion**. In practice, data fusion can occur at different points within the architecture:

For low-level fusion (signal-level fusion), raw signals from multiple sensors are combined to form a new signal. For instance, if we have two microphones that record audio at slightly different frequencies, or two radars scanning overlapping areas of the environment, we might merge their streams to reduce noise or to create a more precise measurement of a phenomenon (e.g., location or velocity).

For intermediate-level fusion (feature-level fusion), sensors each produce features—like average speed from an accelerometer, presence/absence from a PIR sensor, or spectral components from an audio signal. These features are then merged into a single feature vector for subsequent classification or interpretation. An example might be combining the variance of accelerometer data (indicating restlessness or rapid movement) with the PIR count of room entries/exits to identify an agitation pattern.

For high-level fusion (decision-level fusion), each sensor or sensor group arrives at an independent decision or label, and these decisions are fused. For example, a wearable might classify the user's activity as walking, while a camera-based system identifies the same activity, and a PIR sensor confirms motion in the hallway. If all are in agreement, the fused decision is strong. If they conflict, the system may perform additional checks or adopt a confidence-based method to decide whose output is more trustworthy in that scenario.

2.3.4 Machine Learning for Inferences

Increasingly, data fusion in multimodal independent living systems is driven by machine learning (ML) or artificial intelligence (AI). These methods can capture subtle correlations between sensor signals that traditional rule-based approaches might overlook. Often the simplest approach, a rule-based system uses if–then statements crafted by domain experts. For instance, If accelerometer indicates a severe change in velocity, and the floor sensor indicates a sudden impact, then label as fall. Fuzzy logic can soften these rules so they accommodate uncertainty. This method is straightforward, transparent, and easy to debug, but it struggles with the complexity of continuous streams and overlapping behaviors. Hidden Markov Models (HMMs) or Gaussian Mixture Models (GMMs) can model time-series data and classify events like falls, wandering, or transitions (e.g., standing to sitting). Support Vector Machines (SVMs) are popular for feature-based classification, helping the system decide among discrete activity labels (walking, cooking, lying down, etc.). These methods require carefully engineered features and can yield strong results if those features capture the essence of the user's motion or environment changes. Convolutional Neural Networks (CNNs) or Recurrent Neural Networks (RNNs) can directly learn from raw signals (such as images, depth maps, or acceleration waveforms). CNNs, for instance, might be used for posture recognition from video or skeletal data, while RNNs (including LSTM or GRU variants) are well-suited for sequential data like accelerometer or acoustic signals. Figure 2.3 shows a basic CNN, LSTM, and GRU architecture of machine learning. CNN uses convolutional and pooling layers to extract spatial features from input data before classification through fully connected layers, LSTM processes sequential data using specialized gates—forget, input, and output—and a cell state to retain long-term dependencies. GRU (Gated Recurrent Unit) is a simplified recurrent neural network that models sequential data using update and reset gates to control the flow of information without an explicit cell state.

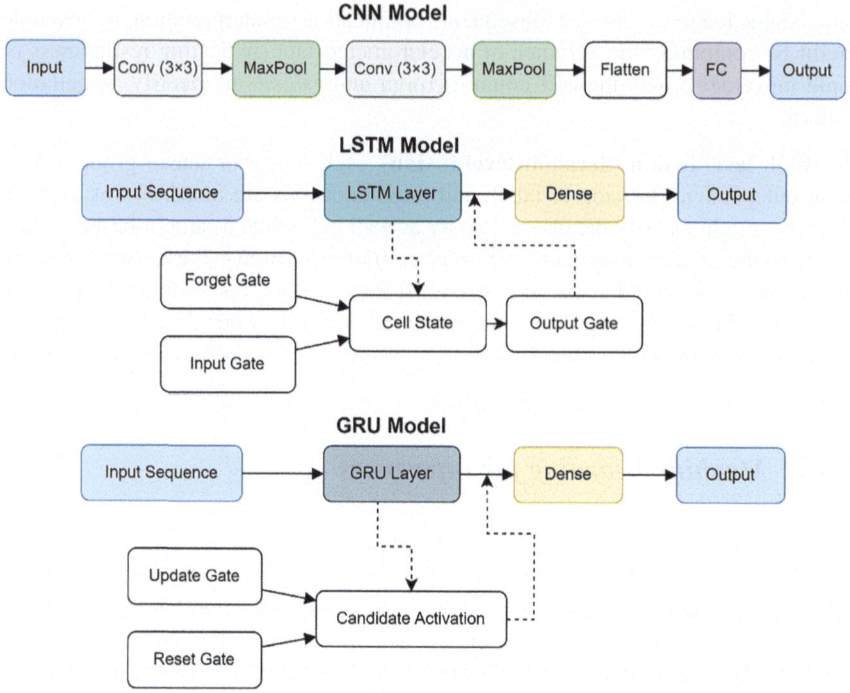

Fig. 2.3 A basic CNN, LSTM, and GRU architecture of machine learning

In a multimodal scenario, a late fusion approach might train separate neural networks for each sensor type, then concatenate the final feature vectors before a classification layer. Alternatively, early fusion might merge sensor signals at an early stage. Deep learning models typically require large labeled datasets, which can be challenging in older adults' homes, but they often outperform simpler methods when enough training data are available. Some systems combine rule-based logic for critical safety events (like immediate fall detection) with deeper ML models for more nuanced monitoring (like gradual changes in gait or cognitive patterns). The rule-based logic ensures rapid response to emergencies, while the ML subsystem identifies trends over time that do not demand instant alerts. Many older adults have unique patterns of movement or cognitive function, and these can change over time (due to illness, medication changes, or recovery from injury). Adaptive or online learning algorithms can update themselves continually, personalizing the detection thresholds or classifier boundaries for the specific user. For instance, an older adult might have a baseline gait speed that is slower than average, so an unpersonalized system might erroneously flag them as at risk, whereas an adaptive system becomes familiar with the individual's normal parameters.

2.3.5 *Managing Time, Synchronization, and Data Quality*

A crucial but sometimes underestimated aspect of data fusion is the accurate synchronization of data streams. Because different sensors operate at different sampling rates or update intervals, the system must align them on a common timeline or at least interpolate approximate values. For instance, a camera might run at 10 frames per second, whereas a wearable accelerometer might produce data at 50 samples per second, and a PIR sensor might only send data when motion changes occur [23]. Aligning these signals can be complicated by network delays, sensor clocks drifting over time, or temporary disconnections.

Systems also must cope with data quality issues. Sensor noise, temporary occlusions (for cameras), or out-of-range measurements (for wireless signals) all degrade reliability. Data fusion logic often includes confidence estimates and filters (like Kalman filters or particle filters) that smooth raw data and help the system gracefully handle missing or unreliable signals. Where possible, sensor calibration routines—run periodically or at installation—establish baseline conditions to reduce drift and false positives.

2.3.6 *Real-Time Versus Batch Processing*

The term real-time can be somewhat ambiguous, but in eldercare scenarios, the system typically needs to detect and respond to critical events (e.g., falls) with minimal delay. This means some portion of the analytics pipeline must run in real time or near real time to trigger immediate alarms. In the same system, there may be modules for more leisurely batch analysis—processing large accumulations of data at night or during idle times to identify patterns of change over weeks or months.

Online pipeline focuses on short-term event detection and rapid response. Figure 2.4 represents a continuous learning and testing of a user interaction-based AI approaches. Usually a combination of direct sensor input, quick data fusion, and thresholds or classifiers that can act promptly. **Offline or batch pipeline h**andles historical data, applying more compute-intensive analyses like deep learning-based anomaly detection or trend analysis. Results feed back into the real-time pipeline in the form of updated thresholds or newly learned models. Balancing these two modes ensures that the user remains safe (immediate alerts) while the system continually refines its understanding of the user's long-term health trajectory (batch analysis).

2.3.7 *Example Data Flow: From a Fall Event to an Alert*

It may be helpful to visualize a concrete scenario that ties together the elements discussed so far. Imagine an older adult, living alone, who unexpectedly trips over a

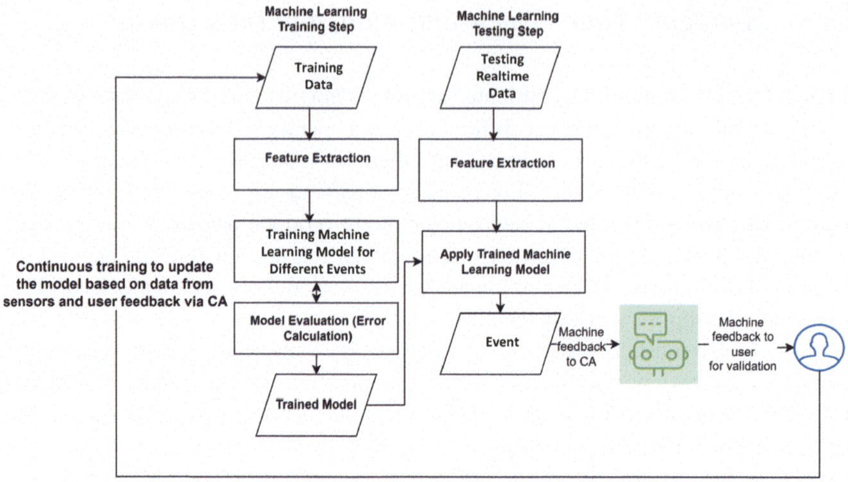

Fig. 2.4 Continuous learning and testing of a user interaction-based AI approaches

small stool in the kitchen. Figure 2.5 shows an example data flow of a fall event to alert. The data flow in a fused, layered system might proceed as follows:

A wearable accelerometer detects a sharp deceleration as the person crashes to the floor. Simultaneously, a pressure sensor beneath the kitchen floor notes a sudden impact. An overhead depth camera registers that the user's silhouette has changed from vertical to horizontal. The accelerometer's microcontroller classifies the movement as potentially indicative of a fall and immediately raises a local alarm. The camera's edge-based analytics quickly identifies a fall posture, tagging the event with

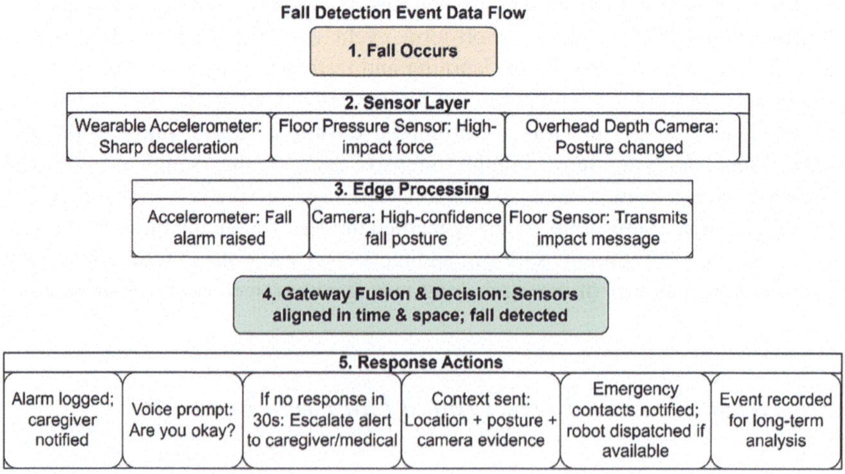

Fig. 2.5 Example data flow of a fall event to alert

high confidence. The floor sensor transmits a short message that a high-impact force was detected. At the local gateway, incoming data from the wearable, camera, and floor sensor are time-aligned. The system notices that three distinct triggers coincide in time and location. It concludes with near certainty that a fall has occurred.

A Fall Detected alarm is immediately logged and communicated to a caregiver application. The system attempts to make contact with the user's wearable device or a nearby smart speaker: It appears you have fallen. Are you able to respond? If the user does not respond within, say, 30 s, the system escalates the alert to a designated caregiver or medical service, including contextual data (e.g., location: kitchen, camera-based evidence of the user's posture). A service robot, if available, navigates to the kitchen to assess the situation or provide immediate help (e.g., bringing a phone, water, or first aid kit). The user's emergency contacts receive a smartphone notification. In parallel, the event is also recorded for long-term analysis, so the system can track whether falls are becoming more frequent and potentially alert medical professionals to an underlying deterioration.

2.4 Implementation and Real-World Deployment Challenges

Having addressed the broad landscape of sensors, system architecture, and data fusion strategies, we now turn to the realities of bringing these multimodal solutions into people's homes and communities. Real-world deployment is rarely a straightforward process, even for well-designed prototypes. In actual living spaces, technology encounters all the unpredictability of daily life—unanticipated user behaviors, varying environmental conditions, diverse home layouts, and cultural and social factors that may not have been fully captured in a laboratory setting [24]. As a result, developers and stakeholders often discover that the transition from concept to reality demands ongoing adaptation, continuous user feedback, and a willingness to rethink system assumptions.

2.4.1 The Human Factor: User Acceptance and Adoption

Multimodal systems, no matter how advanced, only succeed if the people they serve are comfortable using them and trust them. In eldercare, there is a natural tension between the need for comprehensive, real-time monitoring and the desire to protect privacy and personal dignity. Many older adults have lived decades without constant digital observation and may be wary of cameras, microphones, or wearable devices that feel too clinical or intrusive. Several strategies can help mitigate these concerns. First, transparent communication about the system's purpose, capabilities, and data practices is essential. By explaining that certain sensors (like depth cameras) do not produce identifiable images, or that local processing eliminates the need to store raw video in the cloud, developers can reassure users that the main intent is safety, not surveillance. Additionally, a phased introduction can be beneficial. Rather than installing the full suite of sensors immediately, some deployments begin with a minimal, less intrusive setup—perhaps a few ambient sensors combined with a simple wearable device—so that the user can become accustomed to mild monitoring before additional technologies are added. If individuals see tangible benefits early on (for instance, timely alerts when they need assistance or helpful daily reminders), they may be more inclined to accept additional features.

2.4.2 Infrastructure and Installation Complexities

In laboratory settings, system designers often have full control over sensor placement, lighting conditions, network quality, and power supply, allowing them to fine-tune sensor configurations until performance is optimal. By contrast, in real homes, each installation must adapt to existing floor plans, furniture arrangements, and occupant preferences. No two houses are identical: some have thick walls that degrade wireless signals, others have multiple stories that require separate sensor clusters, and many older homes have electrical wiring that complicates the power supply for certain devices. One of the first considerations is whether a home has reliable internet. If connectivity is poor or nonexistent, a purely cloud-dependent system would not function consistently. In these cases, an edge-first approach that performs most processing locally is more practical. Battery-powered devices often require periodic recharging or replacement, and older users may not have the dexterity or inclination to handle frequent battery swaps. This reality pushes many system implementers toward sensors powered from wall outlets or integrated wiring, if feasible, though that might mean more intrusive installation work.

2.4.3 System Reliability and Redundancy

A single sensor malfunction should not cripple an entire monitoring system. Because older adults rely on these solutions for safety and assistance, continuous availability is paramount. This is a major reason why a multimodal approach is favored in the first place: multiple sensors can confirm an event, limiting the risk of false positives or missed detections if one sensor fails. Yet ensuring robust redundancy goes beyond installing multiple sensors. It requires designing the system architecture to handle errors gracefully. For instance, if the main hub loses connectivity, local sensors might still store data or issue alarms via alternative channels, such as a cellular connection. Emergency backups and offline functionality help maintain service during power outages. Some advanced homes have battery backups for key sensors and routers. Others incorporate a low-power mode in which essential functions (like detecting large motions that could indicate a fall) remain active. Additionally, field reports often reveal that electronics placed in kitchens or bathrooms can suffer from humidity or heat damage. This highlights the need for ruggedized devices or protective casings—choices that might not be obvious in the early design phase.

2.4.4 Ethical, Legal, and Policy Considerations in Deployment

When shifting from controlled experiments to everyday living environments, ethical and regulatory demands come to the fore. Health-related data, such as daily patterns or physiological signals, typically falls under strict privacy regulations in many countries. In the European Union, for example, the General Data Protection Regulation (GDPR) imposes obligations on data controllers to obtain clear consent, minimize data collection, and offer data access or deletion upon request. Similar frameworks exist in other parts of the world, though they differ in scope and enforcement. Implementers must ensure that older adults (and any involved family members) genuinely understand their rights regarding data. This means presenting consent forms and privacy agreements in accessible language—avoiding legalistic jargon. Local laws may require that cameras never capture areas considered highly private, such as bathrooms, unless a strong medical rationale exists. Even then, some form of user-initiated activation might be necessary to avoid continuous recording. Meanwhile, audio-based systems can risk wiretapping concerns if they inadvertently capture private conversations, so developers must weigh the benefits of acoustic monitoring against the potential intrusion.

2.4.5 Family and Caregiver Engagement

Multimodal systems do not only support the individual user; they often benefit extended networks of family, friends, and professional caregivers. In many cases, family members live far from older relatives and depend on periodic phone calls or infrequent visits to check on their welfare. A sensor-driven system that provides timely updates—like notifications if the user failed to get out of bed at their usual time—can be deeply reassuring to loved ones [25]. Similarly, professional caregivers can monitor multiple clients remotely, allocating in-person visits to those who show the greatest signs of risk. That said, families and caregivers also bring their own perspectives and concerns. Some worry about receiving too many alerts, fearing information overload. Others may be uncomfortable with video or microphone data, or conversely, they might feel the system is insufficient if it does not include visual or audio checks. In certain communities, having adult children or friends watch over an older adult through technology might be culturally sensitive. Families can sometimes perceive remote monitoring as a replacement for personal interaction, an interpretation that can generate guilt or tension. Encouraging a supportive mindset—where technology complements rather than replaces human care—helps alleviate such fears.

2.4.6 Balancing Autonomy and Safety

A fundamental tension inherent in assisted living technologies is the balance between promoting the user's autonomy—allowing them maximum freedom to live as they wish—and ensuring their safety through monitoring. Overly aggressive monitoring can feel infantilizing or oppressive, potentially leading the user to reject the system altogether. Conversely, a too-lenient system might miss critical events or patterns of decline. One approach is to allow the older adult to configure privacy zones or quiet times. For instance, they might prefer not to have camera coverage in certain rooms, or they might want sensors deactivated during bathing. The system can still maintain emergency capabilities (e.g., a waterproof wearable in the shower for fall detection), but it avoids continuous camera streaming. Similarly, quiet times can be scheduled so that the system is not collecting or transmitting data during the user's usual period of restful solitude unless there is a major event. Such flexibility may require advanced planning in the data fusion logic to account for incomplete data. If the user is in a privacy zone, the system relies on other sensors or uses predictive logic to track the user's general status. The user's chosen autonomy thus shapes the performance envelope of the system. To mitigate risks, some solutions allow break glass overrides for emergencies, meaning that if a critical sensor (like a wearable) suddenly detects a severe incident, the privacy preference might be temporarily lifted to permit an essential visual or acoustic check. The system architecture must carefully incorporate these exceptions, ensuring they are truly reserved for dire situations, or else trust may be eroded.

2.4.7 Maintenance, Updates, and Long-Term Support

Many technology projects falter not during initial deployment but in the months or years after. Sensors need software updates, new firmware, or recalibrations. Cloud-based analytics platforms can change or be superseded by newer AI models. If the supporting organization (such as a startup) closes or merges with another company, will the older adult's system still be maintained? These questions underline the importance of designing for long-term support. To address this, some institutions partner with established technology vendors or academic consortia that can offer continuity of service. Clear maintenance protocols—like monthly self-checks or remote diagnostics—prevent small issues from becoming major failures. Centralized dashboards can indicate if any sensor battery is low, or if data streams have dropped out. Without such oversight, a user might live for weeks with a broken camera or disconnected wearable, mistakenly believing they are still protected. Careful versioning of software and machine learning models also matters. Even if a sensor is physically stable, an abrupt software update might alter how data is interpreted, leading to unexpected behaviors. Rolling out updates gradually, with a mechanism to revert to a previous version, can minimize disruption. Some older adults are adept at using modern technology; others might feel overwhelmed if asked to navigate complex update procedures. Hence, remote, automatic updates or visits from a trained technician can relieve this burden.

2.5 Conclusions

Multimodal systems for independent living stand at a crossroad of urgent societal demand (driven by aging populations), rapid technological innovation, and profound ethical considerations. Their promise is clear: a future in which older adults can remain in familiar environments longer, savor greater autonomy, and enjoy reassurance that help is always nearby. Their complexity is also clear: these systems must navigate user acceptance, data security, cultural differences, and the very real possibility that technology might unintentionally replace social interactions or introduce new kinds of risk. Yet, the spirit of innovation remains strong. Researchers are constantly experimenting with next-generation sensors that vanish into everyday objects, with AI that understands the ebb and flow of life's routines, and with robots that offer a friendly hand or a voice of companionship. Policymakers and healthcare providers, too, are gradually recognizing that investing in these technologies can stave off more expensive interventions down the road. In parallel, older adults themselves—often mischaracterized as technophobic—are discovering that these systems can provide a sense of empowerment and peace of mind, as long as they retain control and choice. The success of multimodal systems for independent living hinges on the recognition that technology must serve people, not the other way around. By staying rooted in empathy, carefully balancing autonomy with safety, and fostering an ecosystem of interdisciplinary collaboration, we can craft solutions that uplift the lives of countless individuals in their golden years. In doing so, we also lay the groundwork for a broader societal shift—a move toward more preventive, personalized, and humane healthcare that sees the home as a vital space of care, connection, and well-being.

References

1. Md. Zia Uddin, Weria Khaksar and Jim Torresen, "Ambient Sensors for Elderly Care and Independent Living: A Survey," Sensors, vol. 18, no. 7, art. 2027, pp. 1–31, Jul. 2018.
2. George Demiris and B. Kay Hensel, "Technologies for an Aging Society: A Systematic Review of 'Smart Home' Applications," Yearbook of Medical Informatics, vol. 17, pp. 33–40, 2008.

3. Eva Oswald, Frank Wahl and Oliver Schilling, "Relationships Between Housing and Healthy Ageing in Very Old Age," The Gerontologist, vol. 47, no. 1, pp. 96–107, Feb. 2007.
4. Parisa Rashidi and Diane J. Cook, "Activity Knowledge Transfer in Smart Environments," Pervasive and Mobile Computing, vol. 7, no. 3, pp. 331–343, Jun. 2011.
5. Mara Rantz, Marilyn Skubic, Brad Miller and Mihail Popescu, "Automated In-Home Fall Risk Assessment and Detection Sensor System for Elders," The Gerontologist, vol. 55, suppl. 1, pp. S78–S87, Jun. 2015.
6. Saisakul Chernbumroong, Seng Cang and Huiru Yu, "Genetic Algorithm-Based Classifiers Fusion for Multisensor Activity Recognition of Elderly People," IEEE Journal of Biomedical and Health Informatics, vol. 19, no. 1, pp. 282–289, Jan. 2015.
7. Y. Chen, H. Lee and J. Kim, "Smart Floor Mats for a Health Monitoring System Based on Textile Sensors," Sensors, vol. 23, no. 15, art. 6512, 2023.
8. Jane Chung, George Demiris and Hilaire J. Thompson, "Ethical Considerations Regarding the Use of Smart Home Technologies for Older Adults: An Integrative Review," Annual Review of Nursing Research, vol. 34, pp. 155–181, 2016.
9. Xiangbo Shu, Jiawen Yang, Rui Yan and Yan Song, "Expansion-Squeeze-Excitation Fusion Network for Elderly Activity Recognition," arXiv preprint arXiv:2112.10992, pp. 1–10, Dec. 2021.
10. M. Ahmed, T. Alzahrani and J. Singh, "An Edge AI-Enabled IoT Healthcare Monitoring System for Smart Cities," Computers & Electrical Engineering, vol. 96, art. 107524, Aug. 2021.
11. Sonia Cañete, Carlos Gómez and Daniel Rodríguez, "Edge AI-Enabled Real-Time Healthcare Monitoring System for Smart Cities," Computers & Electrical Engineering, vol. 96, art. 107534, Aug. 2021.
12. Amina Frik, Yasemin Acar and Serge Egelman, "Privacy and Security Threat Models and Mitigation Strategies of Older Adults for Smart Home Healthcare," in Proc. 15th USENIX Symposium on Usable Privacy and Security (SOUPS), pp. 429–448, Aug. 2019.
13. Alexandru Rancea, Ionuţ Anghel and Tudor Cioara, "Edge Computing in Healthcare: Innovations, Opportunities and Challenges," Future Internet, vol. 16, no. 9, art. 329, pp. 1–28, Sep. 2024.
14. X. Gao, P. He, Y. Zhou and X. Qin, "A Smart Healthcare System for Remote Areas Based on the Edge–Cloud Continuum," Electronics, vol. 13, no. 21, art. 4152, 2024.
15. Sara Kang, Haesun Park and Crystal Lee, "Data Privacy and Smart Home Technology Adoption: Older Adults' Attitudes and Beliefs," in Proc. 9th Int. Conf. on Human Aspects of IT for the Aged Population (ITAP), LNCS 14018, pp. 101–115, Jul. 2023.
16. Jessica Percy Campbell et al., "User Perception of Smart Home Surveillance Among Adults Aged 50 Years and Older: Scoping Review," JMIR mHealth and uHealth, vol. 12, e48526, pp. 1–18, Jan. 2024.
17. Elif Tural, Danni Lu and D. Austin Cole, "Safely and Actively Aging in Place: Older Adults' Attitudes and Intentions Toward Smart Home Technologies," Gerontology and Geriatric Medicine, vol. 7, pp. 1–12, May 2021.
18. Christina Aggar, Golam Sorwar, Carolyn Seton and Anastasia Ward, "Smart Home Technology to Support Older People's Quality of Life: A Longitudinal Pilot Study," International Journal of Older People Nursing, vol. 18, no. 1, e12489, 2023.
19. Wei Wang, Alex X. Liu and Muhammad Shahzad, "Gait Recognition Using WiFi Signals," in Proc. ACM UbiComp 2026 (Intl. Joint Conf. Pervasive & Ubiquitous Computing), pp. 363–373, Sep. 2016. ACM Digital Library.
20. Ahmad Almadhor et al., "Wrist-Based Electrodermal Activity Monitoring for Stress Detection Using Federated Learning," Sensors, vol. 23, no. 8, art. 3984, Apr. 2023.
21. Shunsuke Hirayama and Daigo Misaki, "Development of a Smart Pillbox with Passive RFID to Support Prospective Memory and Medication Adherence," in Proc. AHFE 2023, paper 1004374, Jul. 2023.
22. Rui Chang Yang, Kofi Boakye Eddiano and Lu Lu, "Deep Learning-Based Sound Classification for Home Care Monitoring," Applied Sciences, vol. 11, no. 9, art. 3991, May 2021.

23. Patrick E. Ralston, Danielle Y. Gray, Daniel E. Larsen and Marisol W. Gonzales, "Energy Disaggregation as a Sensor for Eldercare," Sensors, vol. 23, no. 4, art. 2070, Feb. 2023.
24. Jingyi Li, Zhen Wang and Ling Chen, "FedHome: Cloud-Edge-Based Personalized Federated Learning for Smart Homes," arXiv preprint arXiv:2012.07450, 2020.
25. Han Liu, Ying Zhang, Rui Wang and Xiaoyan Zhao, "Real-Time Acoustic Scene Recognition for Elderly Daily Routines Using Edge Computing," Sensors, vol. 25, no. 6, art. 1746, Mar. 2025.

Chapter 3
Synthetic Data

Abstract This chapter takes a closer look at what synthetic data is, why it matters, and how it fits into data science and artificial intelligence. Since collecting real-world data often comes with privacy risks and biases, synthetic data provides a safe alternative by mimicking the patterns of real data without exposing sensitive details. One of the key focus areas of this chapter is how synthetic data is making a difference in assisted living. In healthcare, for example, researchers can use synthetic patient data to train AI models for detecting diseases, monitoring patients, and predicting health outcomes—without compromising anyone's private information. Beyond healthcare, synthetic data is also driving progress in the automotive industry, security systems, and natural language processing. We also explore different ways to create synthetic data, from traditional statistical methods to modern machine learning techniques like Generative Adversarial Networks (GANs). Various types of GAN models, including CTGAN, CycleGAN, MedGAN, and WGAN, are discussed to show how they generate realistic and diverse datasets. This is especially useful in assisted living, where high-quality synthetic data can improve AI-powered tools like fall detection systems, behavioral analysis, and personalized care solutions. Another important topic is fairness in synthetic data. AI models trained on biased data can lead to unfair outcomes, which is a serious issue in healthcare and assisted living. This chapter explains how to create fair synthetic data and reduce bias so that AI models work equally well for everyone. Techniques such as balancing class distributions and adversarial debiasing are introduced to ensure synthetic datasets are both accurate and ethical. To help readers put theory into practice, we include step-by-step guidance on generating synthetic data using Python. Examples cover applications in regression, classification, and clustering, as well as generating tabular synthetic data using GANs. By applying these methods, professionals working in healthcare, security, and AI development can overcome data limitations and improve their models in meaningful ways. Synthetic data is proving to be a powerful tool for AI, especially in fields where privacy, fairness, and data quality are essential. This chapter aims to give readers a well-rounded understanding of what synthetic data is, how it works, and how it can be used to solve real-world challenges.

© The Author(s), under exclusive license to Springer Nature Switzerland AG 2025
M. Z. Uddin, *Trustworthy Multimodal Intelligent Systems for Independent Living*, Cognitive Technologies, https://doi.org/10.1007/978-3-031-97359-8_3

3.1 Introduction

Synthetic data is a rapidly growing field within data science and artificial intelligence, offering a myriad of benefits and applications. At its core, synthetic data refers to data that is artificially generated rather than collected from real-world events or observations. This data is created using sophisticated algorithms and simulations designed to replicate the statistical properties and patterns of real data. The creation of synthetic data involves generating data points that are statistically similar to real data, ensuring that the synthetic data can be used in place of real data for various purposes. One of the primary reasons synthetic data has garnered significant attention is its ability to address privacy concerns. In an era where data privacy regulations like GDPR and CCPA are becoming increasingly stringent, synthetic data offers a way to use data without compromising individual privacy. Since synthetic data does not contain any real personal information, it can be used freely without the risk of exposing sensitive data. This makes it particularly valuable in fields such as healthcare and finance, where data privacy is paramount.

Moreover, synthetic data is cost-effective. Collecting real data can be an expensive and time-consuming process, often requiring extensive resources and infrastructure. In contrast, synthetic data can be generated quickly and at a fraction of the cost, making it an attractive alternative for many organizations [1]. This is especially useful in scenarios where data collection is challenging or impractical, such as in rare event modeling or when dealing with highly sensitive information. Synthetic data has become an increasingly important tool in modern data science and artificial intelligence (AI). As the demand for large-scale datasets grows, traditional methods of data collection often prove inadequate due to concerns related to privacy, cost, and accessibility. This chapter explores the concept of synthetic data, its significance, and its applications in AI and data science [2]. By understanding synthetic data, data practitioners can leverage its advantages to enhance model training, improve robustness, and tackle real-world challenges that arise from limited or sensitive datasets. In the context of independent living, it plays a key role in remote health monitoring, activity recognition, fall detection, cognitive assistance, and personalized support systems. This review looks at how synthetic data contributes to independent living, its benefits, challenges, and where research might go in the future.

Independent living is about people, especially older adults and those with disabilities, being able to manage on their own with little to no outside help. As the global population ages and more people require home-based care, technology is stepping in to provide support. AI-driven systems can make independent living easier, but they need large, high-quality datasets to function well [3]. Collecting real-world data isn't easy due to privacy laws, ethical concerns, and practical limitations. Synthetic data offers a way around these challenges by creating realistic, privacy-friendly datasets that allow AI models to be trained effectively. There are several ways to generate synthetic data, including generative adversarial networks (GANs), variational autoencoders (VAEs), agent-based simulations, and rule-based modeling [1]. GANs can create synthetic images, sensor data, and human activity patterns, which are useful for machine learning applications in healthcare and smart homes. VAEs generate diverse synthetic data by learning from real-world variations. Agent-based simulations mimic real-life interactions between people and their environments, helping researchers develop more realistic datasets. Rule-based modeling allows for datasets tailored to specific situations, such as home environments or healthcare scenarios. One major area where synthetic data is making a difference is in human activity recognition (HAR). HAR is crucial for monitoring daily routines, identifying unusual behaviors, and triggering interventions when necessary. Traditional datasets used for HAR often have limitations, including small sample sizes, lack of diversity, and privacy restrictions. Synthetic data helps fill these gaps by providing a wide range of activity scenarios for different ages, mobility levels, and home environments. Machine learning models trained on these diverse datasets perform better and work well across different populations. Fall detection is another area where synthetic data is proving useful. Falls are a serious risk for older adults, leading to injuries and loss of independence. AI-based fall detection systems rely on large datasets of both falls and regular activities to train accurate models. However, real-world fall datasets are imbalanced since falls are relatively rare. Synthetic data helps solve this problem by generating realistic fall scenarios, including variations in posture, movement speed, and environmental conditions. When synthetic data is added to training datasets, AI models become more reliable, reducing false alarms and missed detections.

Remote health monitoring also benefits greatly from synthetic data, especially when it comes to wearable devices that track things like heart rate, blood pressure, and movement. While these devices collect valuable health information, obtaining large, diverse datasets is difficult due to privacy regulations and recruitment challenges. By generating synthetic physiological data using GANs and VAEs, researchers can train AI systems to detect early signs of health issues such as cardiovascular diseases, diabetes, and neurodegenerative conditions. Synthetic data also helps clinical research by providing a wider variety of patient profiles, making health monitoring systems more effective. Synthetic data is also useful in cognitive assistance for individuals with dementia, autism, and other cognitive impairments. Smart assistants and conversational AI systems rely on large datasets to understand user behaviors and provide relevant support [4]. Synthetic data can simulate different speech patterns, interaction styles, and contextual situations, making AI-powered cognitive assistance systems more adaptable. Additionally, facial recognition and emotion detection systems benefit from synthetic datasets that model different facial expressions and behaviors, improving their ability to detect mood changes and cognitive decline. Despite its advantages, synthetic data comes with some challenges. The quality and realism of synthetic data are critical because poor-quality data can introduce biases and inaccuracies into AI models. To ensure synthetic data is useful, it needs to be carefully validated using methods like adversarial testing, domain adaptation, and comparison with real-world datasets. Another issue is the ethical and legal side of using synthetic data. While it helps protect privacy, there are still questions about data ownership, consent, and bias. Regulations like GDPR and HIPAA must be followed when synthetic data is used in healthcare and independent living technologies.

Another challenge is that AI models trained on synthetic data can be hard to interpret. Many deep learning models work like black boxes, meaning it's not always clear how they make decisions. This lack of transparency can make it difficult for caregivers and healthcare professionals to trust AI predictions. Efforts are being made to improve explainability using techniques from explainable AI (XAI), which help users understand how AI systems make their decisions. Looking ahead, synthetic data is expected to play an even bigger role in independent living technologies. As generative models improve, synthetic data will become more realistic and useful. Combining synthetic data with real-world datasets through semi-supervised learning could further enhance AI model accuracy. Federated learning, which allows AI models to be trained on decentralized devices without sharing data, could work well alongside synthetic data to improve privacy and security [5]. These advancements will help create scalable and effective independent living solutions. Another promising area is the personalization of independent living technologies using synthetic data. AI-driven systems that adapt to an individual's needs, preferences, and environment will make independent living easier and more comfortable. Future research should focus on developing adaptive synthetic data generation methods that respond to real-time user interactions. The combination of synthetic data with edge computing, IoT, and 5G networks could also improve smart home technologies, enabling real-time decision-making and seamless human–computer interaction. Synthetic data is changing the way AI-driven independent living technologies are developed by solving data limitations, protecting privacy, and improving AI performance. Its applications in activity recognition, fall detection, remote health monitoring, and cognitive assistance show how it can enhance autonomy and well-being.

Challenges related to data quality, ethics, and AI interpretability must be addressed to ensure its effectiveness. As research progresses, synthetic data, combined with new AI technologies, will continue to support independent living, making life easier and safer for people who want to maintain their independence.

3.2 Synthetic Data

Synthetic data refers to artificially generated data that mimics the characteristics and statistical properties of real-world data. Unlike real data, which is collected from direct observations or measurements, synthetic data is created using various computational techniques, including generative models, simulations, and statistical methods [1]. The primary goal of synthetic data is to provide a dataset that serves as a viable substitute for actual data while preserving the essential structure and patterns found in the original data. The process of generating synthetic data involves different approaches depending on the specific needs of a given application. Rule-based generation relies on predefined conditions to create datasets, ensuring consistency and control over the data attributes. Statistical methods involve drawing samples from probability distributions that match the characteristics of real data, making it useful in modeling and simulation tasks. More advanced methods use machine learning models, such as generative adversarial networks (GANs) and variational autoencoders (VAEs), to create high-quality synthetic datasets that can replicate complex structures found in real-world data. Another approach is simulation-based generation, where environments are modeled computationally to produce realistic scenarios for training AI models, such as those used in robotics or autonomous systems.

Synthetic data exists in multiple forms and is applicable across a range of domains. Structured synthetic data, commonly used in finance and healthcare, maintains well-defined attributes similar to real-world tabular datasets [6]. Unstructured synthetic data, such as images, text, and audio, is widely employed in applications like computer vision, natural language processing, and speech recognition. Time-series synthetic data is used for forecasting and anomaly detection in industries such as finance, cybersecurity, and industrial operations.

Figure 3.1 presents a comparison between real and synthetic heart rate data in an assisted living setting. The green line represents real heart rate data collected from a simulated patient, exhibiting natural fluctuations around a baseline of 70 beats per minute (BPM). These variations are small, within a ± 3 BPM range, reflecting realistic physiological changes due to factors such as movement, stress, or normal cardiovascular function.

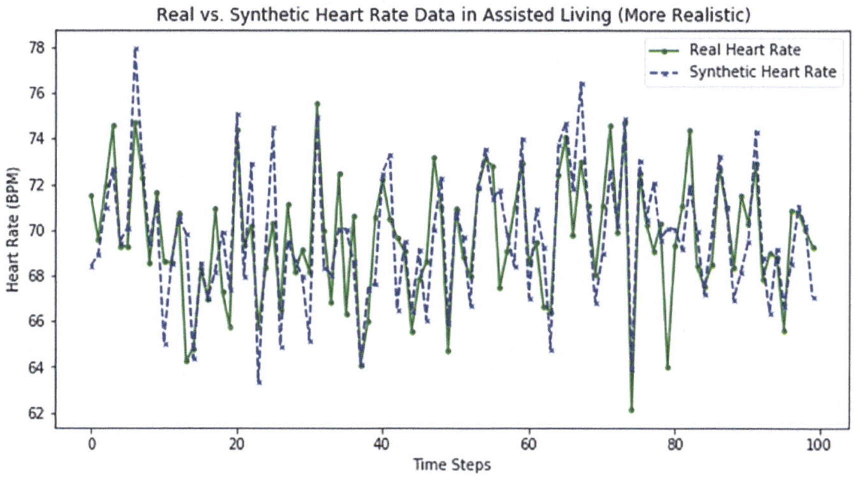

Fig. 3.1 Example of time-series synthetic and real data

The blue dashed line represents synthetic heart rate data, which is generated to closely follow the real data while introducing slight differences. Instead of randomly generating synthetic values, the approach maintains 90% of the real data characteristics, incorporating minor controlled noise and a 10% lagged real data component. This method ensures that the synthetic heart rate values retain realistic trends while introducing subtle variations, making them useful for research and model training. Unlike traditional synthetic data generation methods that might introduce unnatural variations, this approach maintains a realistic range of 60–90 BPM, preventing extreme fluctuations. This is particularly important in assisted living environments, where accurate heart rate tracking is crucial for detecting anomalies such as arrhythmias or sudden heart rate drops. The figure also tries to demonstrate how synthetic data can mimic real physiological patterns while preserving patient privacy. Such data is valuable for machine learning model training, anomaly detection, and healthcare research when access to real patient data is limited. This approach allows researchers to develop robust health-monitoring systems while ensuring realistic yet privacy-friendly datasets for experimentation.

```
import numpy as np
import pandas as pd
import matplotlib.pyplot as plt

# Generate realistic assisted living heart rate dataset
np.random.seed(42)
time_steps = np.arange(0, 100, 1)

# Simulate real heart rate data with small random variations around a baseline
(e.g., 70 BPM)
real_heart_rate = 70 + np.random.normal(0, 3, 100) # Baseline with small
fluctuations

# Generate synthetic heart rate data that closely follows real data with realistic
variations
```

```
synthetic_heart_rate = real_heart_rate * 0.9 + np.random.normal(0, 2, 100) + 0.1 * np.roll(real_heart_rate, shift=1)

# Ensure synthetic data remains within a plausible range by slightly smoothing abrupt changes
synthetic_heart_rate = np.clip(synthetic_heart_rate, 60, 90)  # Keeping values within a reasonable BPM range

# Create DataFrame for visualization
df_assisted_living = pd.DataFrame({"Time": time_steps, "Real Heart Rate": real_heart_rate, "Synthetic Heart Rate": synthetic_heart_rate})

# Plot the real and synthetic time series data without grid lines
plt.figure(figsize=(10, 5))
plt.plot(df_assisted_living["Time"], df_assisted_living["Real Heart Rate"], label="Real Heart Rate", linestyle="-", marker="o", markersize=3, color="green")
plt.plot(df_assisted_living["Time"], df_assisted_living["Synthetic Heart Rate"], label="Synthetic Heart Rate", linestyle="--", marker="x", markersize=3, color="blue", alpha=0.8)
plt.xlabel("Time Steps")
plt.ylabel("Heart Rate (BPM)")
plt.title("Real vs. Synthetic Heart Rate Data in Assisted Living (More Realistic)")
plt.legend()
plt.show()
```

3.3 Importance of Synthetic Data

The significance of synthetic data arises from its ability to overcome many of the challenges associated with real-world data collection and usage. One of its primary benefits is addressing privacy concerns. With regulations such as GDPR and HIPAA imposing strict restrictions on handling sensitive information, organizations struggle to obtain sufficient data for analysis and AI training. Synthetic data offers a way to generate realistic datasets without exposing personally identifiable information, making it an essential tool for privacy-preserving data science [7]. Beyond privacy, synthetic data is also cost-effective and efficient. Collecting large-scale datasets manually requires extensive resources, including time, personnel, and infrastructure. The process can be cumbersome, particularly in industries like healthcare and autonomous systems, where real-world data acquisition is either expensive or logistically challenging. Synthetic data reduces these constraints by providing an alternative that can be generated rapidly and at scale, without the need for physical data collection.

Another crucial advantage of synthetic data is its ability to mitigate data imbalance, a common problem in real-world datasets where certain categories or events are underrepresented. In applications such as fraud detection, rare diseases, and cybersecurity, the lack of sufficient instances of critical events makes model training difficult. Synthetic data generation helps address this by artificially increasing the number of samples in minority classes, allowing machine learning models to learn more effectively from balanced datasets. Moreover, synthetic data enables improved AI model training and validation. AI and machine learning algorithms require diverse and comprehensive datasets to generalize effectively. When real data is scarce, synthetic data provides an alternative that allows models to be trained on a variety of scenarios. This is particularly useful in areas such as self-driving cars, where synthetic environments simulate different road conditions and driving behaviors, allowing AI models to learn and adapt before being deployed in real-world situations. Similarly, in medical imaging, synthetic patient data enables the training of diagnostic models without violating privacy regulations.

Synthetic data also enhances model robustness and generalization. AI models trained on limited datasets are prone to overfitting, meaning they perform well on training data but fail when exposed to new examples. By incorporating synthetic data into training pipelines, AI systems can be exposed to a broader range of variations, reducing biases and improving their ability to generalize. This is particularly relevant in fields such as computer vision, where synthetic images can augment real-world datasets by introducing controlled variations in lighting, angles, and backgrounds. Additionally, synthetic data facilitates experimentation and prototyping without risks. In industries such as finance, healthcare, and security, working directly with real-world data carries legal and ethical implications. Organizations often struggle with regulatory compliance and must find ways to develop and test their models without exposing sensitive data. Synthetic datasets offer a safe alternative by allowing researchers and developers to test algorithms, evaluate methodologies, and refine AI models in controlled environments before transitioning to real-world deployment.

3.4 Synthetic Data for Artificial Intelligence

The integration of synthetic data into data science and AI has transformed how models are developed, tested, and deployed. In machine learning, the ability to generate synthetic datasets enables researchers and engineers to experiment with different training approaches, optimize hyperparameters, and evaluate models without being constrained by the limitations of real-world data availability [7–9]. For example, in supervised learning tasks, synthetic labels can be generated to supplement training data, improving model accuracy and performance.

In computer vision, synthetic data has played a crucial role in advancing object detection, segmentation, and recognition models. GANs and 3D simulation tools allow researchers to create photorealistic images that train AI models to recognize objects under varying conditions. These synthetic datasets help address challenges such as data scarcity and annotation costs, making it feasible to develop AI applications for industries like healthcare, security, and retail. Similarly, in natural language processing, synthetic text is used to train models for chatbots, machine translation, and text summarization. By generating artificial conversations, researchers can fine-tune AI models to understand context, sentiment, and intent without relying entirely on real-world text corpora. Speech processing and audio analysis also benefit from synthetic data, particularly in applications like automatic speech recognition and voice synthesis. Generating synthetic audio datasets enables AI models to be trained on a diverse set of voices, accents, and languages, improving their robustness. This is particularly valuable in applications like virtual assistants and accessibility technologies, where AI systems must handle diverse speech patterns effectively.

Synthetic data plays a pivotal role in bias mitigation and fairness in AI. Many real-world datasets contain biases, leading to AI models that reinforce societal inequalities. By generating synthetic data with balanced demographic distributions, researchers can mitigate biases and ensure fairer decision-making in AI-driven applications. For example, synthetic resumes and job applications can be created to test hiring algorithms for potential biases and improve fairness in recruitment processes.

Another critical area where synthetic data is making a significant impact is in training autonomous systems and robotics. Simulated environments provide a safe and scalable platform for developing AI models used in self-driving cars, industrial automation, and drone navigation. These synthetic environments allow AI systems to learn from a diverse set of scenarios, including rare and hazardous conditions that would be challenging to encounter in real-world training. Healthcare and medical research also benefit from synthetic data, particularly in areas where real patient data is difficult to obtain due to privacy concerns [10]. Synthetic medical records and imaging datasets allow researchers to develop diagnostic AI models without exposing sensitive patient information. For instance, AI models for disease detection can be trained on synthetic X-rays and MRIs, enabling progress in medical AI without breaching confidentiality regulations. In cybersecurity, synthetic data is used to generate attack simulations and threat detection scenarios. By modeling cyber threats and fraudulent transactions, AI-driven security systems can be trained to recognize malicious activities without relying on sensitive real-world data. This approach is especially valuable for developing robust security solutions that can detect and respond to evolving cyber threats in real time. The use of synthetic data extends to digital twins and simulations, where virtual models of real-world systems are created for predictive analysis and optimization. These applications are particularly beneficial in manufacturing, logistics, and urban planning, where AI-driven simulations enable organizations to make data-informed decisions without disrupting real-world operations.

Synthetic data continues to drive innovation across multiple domains, offering solutions to data scarcity, privacy concerns, and model bias. As advancements in generative AI and data synthesis techniques progress, synthetic data will play an increasingly vital role in shaping the future of AI and data science.

3.5 The Lifecycle of Data

Understanding the lifecycle of data is essential for ensuring data quality, security, and compliance in synthetic data generation. The lifecycle consists of multiple stages, beginning with data creation or acquisition, followed by data storage, processing, usage, sharing, and eventual archiving or deletion. Each stage presents unique challenges and considerations. Figure 3.2 represents a life cycle of synthetic data. During the data creation phase, data can be generated from sensors, user inputs, simulations, or synthetic generation models. Storage involves structuring and maintaining data in secure repositories, ensuring accessibility while mitigating risks such as unauthorized access. Data processing includes cleaning, transformation, and augmentation to make it suitable for analysis. When using data in AI applications, it is critical to balance usability and privacy concerns. Sharing data, whether internally or externally, requires careful governance to prevent privacy violations or data breaches. Lastly, data archiving or deletion follows regulatory requirements and policies that dictate how long data should be retained before disposal.

Synthetic data follows a similar lifecycle, with added considerations for validation and monitoring to ensure it aligns with real-world distributions. By simulating real-world patterns, synthetic data maintains its relevance and usability while preserving privacy.

3.6 Data Collection Versus Privacy

Data collection is a fundamental part of AI and machine learning, but it raises significant concerns regarding privacy. The growing volume of personal and sensitive data being collected for various applications has led to increasing scrutiny over how data is obtained, stored, and used. Regulatory frameworks such as GDPR and CCPA emphasize the need for responsible data collection and require organizations to implement strict measures for data protection [11–13]. Balancing data collection with privacy is challenging because data-driven systems thrive on large and diverse datasets. Traditional methods of anonymization and encryption help protect sensitive information, but they often reduce data utility. Differential privacy techniques add noise to datasets to obscure individual identities while preserving statistical insights. However, these methods are not always sufficient in high-dimensional data scenarios.

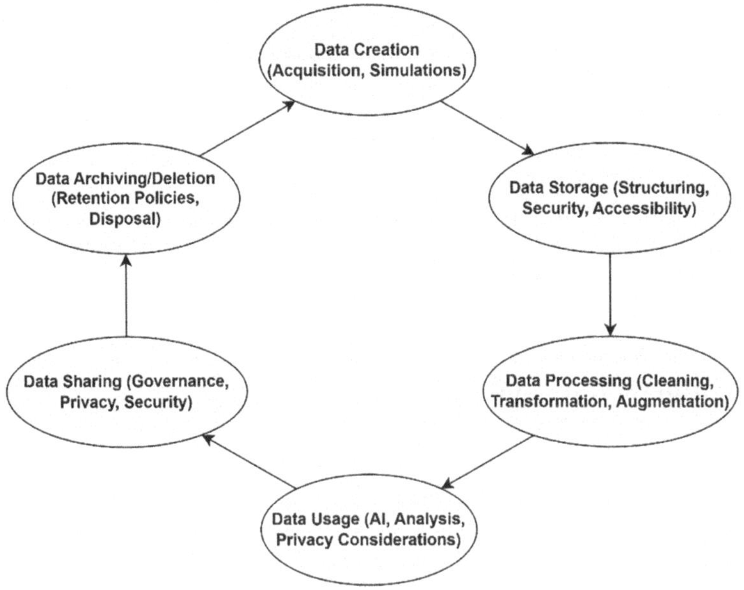

Fig. 3.2 Life cycle of synthetic data

Synthetic data presents a compelling solution to this dilemma. By generating artificial datasets that retain statistical properties without including real personal information, organizations can bypass privacy restrictions while maintaining data usability. This allows companies to innovate and develop AI models without exposing individuals to privacy risks. As AI continues to advance, synthetic data will play a key role in enabling privacy-preserving data collection practices.

3.7 Data Privacy and Synthetic Data

Privacy concerns have become a major barrier to data access and sharing, especially in industries dealing with sensitive information such as healthcare, finance, and cybersecurity. Traditional anonymization techniques, while useful, do not fully eliminate the risk of re-identification when combined with other datasets [14, 15]. As a result, synthetic data has emerged as a robust alternative for maintaining privacy while supporting AI development. Synthetic data helps organizations navigate regulatory landscapes by allowing them to create datasets that are free from personally identifiable information. This is particularly beneficial for sectors where data sharing is heavily restricted. For instance, in healthcare, synthetic patient records can be used to train AI models for disease diagnosis without exposing real patient details. Similarly, financial institutions can generate synthetic transaction data for fraud detection models without compromising customer information.

Another advantage of synthetic data in privacy protection is its ability to create diverse and unbiased datasets. Bias in AI models often stems from real-world data limitations and imbalances. By carefully curating synthetic data, organizations can ensure fair representation across different demographic groups, leading to more ethical AI applications. Despite its benefits, synthetic data privacy measures must be continually evaluated to ensure they do not inadvertently reproduce patterns that could lead to re-identification. Techniques such as adversarial testing and statistical validation help assess the privacy strength of synthetic datasets and ensure compliance with data protection regulations.

3.8 Synthetic Data and Data Quality

High-quality data is crucial for the success of AI and machine learning models. Poor data quality can lead to biased models, inaccurate predictions, and unreliable outcomes. The challenge with synthetic data is ensuring that it accurately represents real-world patterns while maintaining its unique advantages. Data quality in synthetic datasets depends on several factors, including fidelity, completeness, consistency, and representativeness [16]. Fidelity refers to how well synthetic data preserves statistical relationships found in real data. Completeness ensures that synthetic data captures all relevant aspects of real-world scenarios, preventing gaps that could impact model performance. Consistency refers to maintaining logical relationships between data points, ensuring that synthetic records do not contain unrealistic or conflicting information. Representativeness ensures that synthetic data generalizes well to unseen real-world cases.

The process of generating high-quality synthetic data involves using advanced generative models such as GANs, VAEs, and transformer-based approaches [17]. These models learn the distribution of real data and create synthetic versions that closely match original characteristics. However, synthetic data should always undergo rigorous validation to confirm its accuracy and utility. Another key factor in data quality is diversity. Many real-world datasets suffer from imbalances that impact AI model performance. Synthetic data can be designed to fill these gaps, ensuring that underrepresented groups or rare events are adequately covered. This enhances AI model generalization and reduces biases in decision-making. While synthetic data offers significant advantages, it is not a one-size-fits-all solution. Its effectiveness depends on the domain, application, and the underlying data generation techniques [18]. Organizations must carefully evaluate synthetic data quality through benchmarking against real data, measuring statistical properties, and assessing model performance to ensure its reliability. By maintaining high data quality, synthetic data becomes a powerful tool for AI innovation, enabling safe, ethical, and effective machine learning applications.

3.9 Applications of Synthetic Data

Synthetic data is widely used across various industries to address challenges related to data scarcity, privacy, and model training [18]. It enables organizations to develop and deploy AI models while mitigating risks associated with real-world data collection. Several sectors have embraced synthetic data to improve efficiency, enhance security, and ensure compliance with data protection regulations.

Healthcare is one of the most significant beneficiaries of synthetic data. Medical records, imaging data, and patient histories are highly sensitive, making it difficult for researchers and AI developers to access real-world datasets [19]. Synthetic data helps bridge this gap by providing realistic yet anonymized patient data that preserves essential statistical properties without exposing individual identities. AI-driven diagnostics, drug discovery, and treatment recommendation systems benefit immensely from synthetic medical data. For example, synthetic X-ray or MRI images are used to train deep learning models for disease detection without relying on actual patient scans [20]. This approach allows medical institutions to enhance diagnostic accuracy while maintaining compliance with privacy regulations such as HIPAA and GDPR.

The automotive industry, particularly in autonomous vehicle development, relies heavily on synthetic data. Self-driving car models require extensive datasets to train and validate perception algorithms under diverse conditions. Since capturing real-world driving scenarios can be costly and time-consuming, synthetic environments are used to simulate complex road situations, including adverse weather conditions, pedestrian interactions, and unexpected obstacles. Simulation-based synthetic data provides the flexibility to test autonomous vehicles in rare and dangerous scenarios that may not be frequently encountered in real-world datasets. By using synthetic data, car manufacturers and AI developers can accelerate the testing and deployment of autonomous systems while improving vehicle safety and reliability. Cybersecurity and fraud detection systems require large amounts of data to identify malicious activities and prevent cyber threats. However, real-world security data is often classified or unavailable due to confidentiality concerns. Synthetic data addresses this issue by generating artificial datasets that mimic real cyberattack patterns, allowing security analysts to train and test intrusion detection systems without exposing sensitive information. In fraud detection, synthetic transaction data helps financial institutions train AI models to recognize fraudulent behaviors while avoiding the risk of violating customer privacy. Banks and financial organizations use synthetic data to refine fraud detection algorithms, ensuring that they can identify suspicious activities without compromising legitimate customer transactions.

Natural Language Processing (NLP) applications benefit from synthetic text generation to train chatbots, translation models, and sentiment analysis tools. Collecting and labeling large-scale text datasets can be expensive and biased, making it difficult to develop fair and effective NLP models. Synthetic data helps overcome these challenges by generating diverse text samples that represent different linguistic patterns, dialects, and cultural contexts. AI-driven content moderation and speech recognition systems use synthetic data to enhance their accuracy, ensuring they can handle various real-world scenarios. Additionally, in AI-driven customer support, synthetic conversations allow chatbots to be trained on realistic yet artificially generated dialogues, improving user interactions without exposing personal conversations.

3.10 Synthetic Data for Independent Living

Synthetic data has a wide range of applications in assisted living, transforming how caregivers and healthcare professionals provide care to elderly residents. One key area is fall detection and prevention. AI models trained on synthetic motion and activity data can identify fall risks in real-time, alerting caregivers to potential hazards before an incident occurs [21]. By simulating various mobility patterns, synthetic data ensures that detection models are comprehensive and adaptive to different resident behaviors.

Another important application is personalized care planning. Assisted living facilities rely on detailed health and behavioral records to create customized care plans. However, privacy concerns limit access to real-world data. Synthetic data offers a privacy-preserving alternative, allowing AI-driven systems to analyze trends in resident health conditions, predict deterioration, and recommend proactive interventions [22]. This leads to more personalized, data-driven decision-making that enhances quality of care. Cognitive health monitoring is another area where synthetic data plays a crucial role. AI models trained on synthetic speech and behavioral data can assist in detecting early signs of dementia and cognitive decline. By generating realistic but artificial speech and interaction patterns, these models can improve diagnostic accuracy and provide caregivers with early warnings about cognitive impairment.

Synthetic data also enhances smart home automation for assisted living. AI-powered systems that control lighting, temperature, and security can be trained using synthetic datasets that simulate real-world resident interactions. This ensures that automation systems are better suited to elderly individuals' needs, creating a safer and more comfortable living environment. Furthermore, synthetic data supports medication adherence monitoring. By generating synthetic logs of medication intake and patient responses, AI-driven adherence monitoring systems can detect irregularities in medication usage, helping caregivers intervene when necessary. This reduces the risk of missed medications and ensures that residents follow their prescribed treatment plans. The Integration of synthetic data. In assisted living enables safer, more efficient, and privacy-preserving AI applications. From fall prevention to cognitive health monitoring and personalized care, synthetic data-driven models are transforming elderly care, improving quality of life, and reducing risks in assisted living environments.

3.11 How to Generate Fair Synthetic Data

Fairness in AI is a growing concern, as biased datasets can lead to discriminatory decision-making and unintended ethical consequences. Ensuring that synthetic data is fair and unbiased requires careful planning, diverse data generation, and rigorous validation techniques.

One of the most effective ways to generate fair synthetic data is by ensuring that the underlying data sources are diverse and representative of different demographic groups. Training generative models on biased real-world data may result in synthetic data that replicates and amplifies these biases. To prevent this, data engineers must incorporate fairness-aware techniques such as reweighting, debiasing algorithms, and adversarial testing.

Another approach involves using fairness constraints during the data generation process. By setting predefined conditions, AI developers can ensure that synthetic datasets reflect equal representation across race, gender, socioeconomic status, and other critical attributes. This method helps create unbiased training data for AI applications in hiring, credit scoring, and law enforcement, where fairness is paramount. Evaluation metrics such as disparate impact analysis, demographic parity, and equalized odds testing should be applied to synthetic datasets to assess their fairness. These techniques help detect and mitigate biases before deploying AI models in real-world applications.

Transparency and explainability in synthetic data generation also play a crucial role in ensuring fairness. Organizations should document the methods used to generate synthetic data, providing clear insights into how biases were addressed and what measures were taken to improve data equity. Open-source frameworks and collaborative efforts within the AI community can further enhance the development of fair synthetic data practices. By integrating fairness-aware synthetic data generation techniques, AI developers can reduce biases in machine learning models, enhance trust in AI systems, and promote ethical decision-making across various industries. Synthetic data offers a pathway to building responsible AI solutions that are both privacy-preserving and equitable, ensuring that technological advancements benefit all users regardless of their background.

3.12 GANs

Generative Adversarial Networks (GANs) have revolutionized the field of synthetic data generation by enabling the creation of highly realistic artificial data. GANs consist of two neural networks, a generator and a discriminator, that work against each other in a competitive framework. The generator aims to create realistic data samples, while the discriminator tries to distinguish between real and synthetic data. Over time, the generator improves, producing increasingly convincing data that can be used for various applications, including image synthesis, text generation, and tabular data augmentation.

GANs have had profound impacts on artificial intelligence, particularly in the domains of computer vision, speech processing, and biomedical research. By using adversarial learning, GANs refine their ability to generate data that closely mirrors real-world distributions. Researchers have used GANs to develop synthetic video datasets that assist in training machine learning models for action recognition, significantly reducing the need for expensive data collection. Additionally, in the entertainment industry, GANs have been employed to generate realistic digital characters, de-aging effects in movies, and even enhancing low-resolution images for video restoration. The training process of GANs Is Inherently unstable, as both the generator and discriminator are constantly evolving in response to each other. This dynamic nature can lead to challenges such as mode collapse, where the generator repeatedly produces limited variations of data rather than diverse examples. To mitigate these issues, advanced variations of GANs have been developed, each addressing specific limitations and enhancing the quality of generated data.

3.13 Different GANs

GANs have demonstrated their capability in producing realistic images, videos, and structured data. For example, GANs have been used to generate synthetic human faces that are indistinguishable from real photographs, as seen in projects like This Person Does Not Exist. In financial modeling, GANs generate realistic stock market simulations, allowing AI systems to develop trading strategies without using real market data [23, 24]. Beyond finance, GANs have found applications in creating synthetic speech datasets, improving automatic speech recognition systems, and helping in dialect and accent adaptation for virtual assistants.

Conditional Tabular GAN (CTGAN) is specifically designed for generating tabular data. Unlike traditional GANs, which struggle with categorical and imbalanced data, CTGAN uses conditional sampling and mode-specific normalization to create high-quality synthetic tables. For example, CTGAN has been used to generate synthetic health insurance claims data, preserving statistical characteristics while ensuring privacy compliance. The technique has also been applied in fraud detection models by generating realistic but synthetic financial transactions, enabling robust anomaly detection without risking exposure of real customer information.

CTGAN can be used to generate synthetic resident health data, helping researchers develop predictive models for chronic illness monitoring. Figure 3.3 shows the output of the following code example of CTGAN.

Fig. 3.3 Output of code CTGAN displaying synthetic data of age, blood pressure, and fall risk of different people

	Age	Blood_Pressure	Fall_Risk
0	80	145	1
1	85	138	1
2	79	138	0
3	80	140	1
4	84	150	0

```
From sdv.tabular import CTGAN
import pandas as pd

# Load assisted living dataset
real_data = pd.DataFrame({
    'Age': [70, 75, 80, 85, 90],
    'Blood_Pressure': [130, 140, 135, 145, 150],
    'Fall_Risk': [1, 0, 1, 0, 1]
})

# Train CTGAN model
ctgan = CTGAN()
ctgan.fit(real_data)

# Generate synthetic data
synthetic_data = ctgan.sample(5)
print(synthetic_data)
```

SurfelGAN is a specialized GAN model used for rendering and reconstructing 3D surfaces. It is applied in computer graphics and virtual simulations, particularly in generating synthetic 3D scenes for training autonomous systems. For instance, autonomous vehicle manufacturers use SurfelGAN to simulate urban environments, helping AI-driven vehicles learn to navigate complex traffic conditions. Additionally, in the field of archaeology and cultural heritage preservation, SurfelGAN has been utilized to reconstruct 3D models of ancient artifacts and historical sites from incomplete data. CycleGAN enables the transformation of images from one domain to another without requiring paired training data. One of its famous applications is converting images of horses into zebras and vice versa. In medical imaging, CycleGAN has been used to transform CT scans into MRI scans, allowing doctors to utilize additional diagnostic information without collecting new data. Another novel application includes converting satellite images taken in different seasons to create seamless environmental monitoring tools for tracking climate changes and deforestation trends.

MedGAN is designed for generating high-fidelity medical data, including electronic health records (EHRs) and diagnostic images. It has been successfully used to generate synthetic patient records that help train AI models for disease prediction without violating patient privacy laws. MedGAN has been instrumental in developing AI-based early detection systems for diseases such as cancer and Alzheimer's, where access to diverse and extensive medical data is often restricted due to regulatory policies. MedGAN can generate synthetic medical records of assisted living residents while preserving privacy. Figure 3.4 shows the output of following code of MedGAN.

```
from sdv.timeseries import PAR

# Load sample medical dataset
ehr_data = pd.DataFrame({
    'Resident_ID': [1, 2, 3],
    'Heart_Rate': [72, 85, 78],
    'Blood_Pressure': [120, 135, 140]
})

# Train MedGAN model
medgan = PAR()
medgan.fit(ehr_data)

# Generate synthetic medical records
synthetic_ehr = medgan.sample(5)
print(synthetic_ehr)
```

Deep Convolutional GAN (DCGAN) is a popular variant of GANs that incorporates convolutional layers to enhance the quality of generated images. DCGAN has been widely used to generate art, such as anime character portraits, and improve

Fig. 3.4 Output of code MedGAN

	Resident_ID	Heart_Rate	Blood_Pressure
0	1	73	124
1	2	84	135
2	3	78	139
3	2	74	118
4	2	83	135
5	3	78	139
6	1	71	122
7	2	85	135
8	3	78	140
9	1	72	121
10	2	85	135
11	3	78	140
12	1	71	123
13	2	85	135
14	3	78	140

Heart Rate	Motion	Step Count	Respiration	Fall Risk	Temperature	Sleep Quality	Pain Level
0.76	-0.11	0.18	-0.13	-0.41	0.08	0.24	0.30
0.39	0.10	-0.14	-0.20	-0.50	-0.17	0.53	0.20
0.20	-0.07	0.00	-0.14	-0.23	-0.19	0.50	-0.05
0.17	-0.23	0.33	-0.05	-0.32	-0.18	0.46	0.13
0.00	-0.04	-0.13	-0.11	0.09	0.00	0.21	0.08

Fig. 3.5 Output of code WGAN

image super-resolution techniques in photography. Furthermore, DCGAN has been leveraged in biomedical research to generate synthetic cell images for drug discovery and enhance microscopy images for better disease diagnosis. DCGAN can generate synthetic images of assisted living environments for training AI models in facility management. Wasserstein GAN (WGAN) improves upon traditional GANs by stabilizing training and addressing mode collapse issues. One application of WGAN is in generating high-quality synthetic speech for voice assistants like Alexa and Google Assistant, allowing them to sound more natural. WGAN has also been used to create hyper-realistic digital fashion models for the virtual clothing industry, enabling companies to showcase apparel without needing physical runway shows. Wasserstein GAN (WGAN) improves stability in training GANs for synthetic patient data and activity monitoring in assisted living. Figure 3.5 shows the output of the following code for WGAN.

```
import torch
import torch.nn as nn
import torch.optim as optim


# Set device for computation (use GPU if available)
device = torch.device("cuda" if torch.cuda.is_available() else "cpu")


# Define the WGAN Generator
class WGANGenerator(nn.Module):
    def __init__(self, noise_dim=10, output_dim=10):
        super(WGANGenerator, self).__init__()
        self.model = nn.Sequential(
            nn.Linear(noise_dim, 64),
```

```
                nn.ReLU(),
                nn.Linear(64, output_dim)
            )

        def forward(self, z):
            return self.model(z)

# Define the WGAN Critic (used instead of a discriminator in WGAN)
class WGANCritic(nn.Module):
    def __init__(self, input_dim=10):
        super(WGANCritic, self).__init__()
        self.model = nn.Sequential(
            nn.Linear(input_dim, 64),
            nn.ReLU(),
            nn.Linear(64, 1)
        )

    def forward(self, x):
        return self.model(x)

# Initialize the WGAN Generator and Critic
generator = WGANGenerator().to(device)
critic = WGANCritic().to(device)

# Optimizers (WGAN uses RMSprop or Adam, here we use RMSprop)
lr = 1e-4
g_optimizer = optim.RMSprop(generator.parameters(), lr=lr)
c_optimizer = optim.RMSprop(critic.parameters(), lr=lr)

# Simulated real patient activity data (100 samples, each with 10 features)
real_data = torch.randn(100, 10).to(device)

# WGAN Training Loop Parameters
```

```
batch_size = 32
epochs = 1                # One epoch for demonstration
critic_steps = 5          # Number of critic updates per generator update

# --- WGAN Training Loop ---
for epoch in range(epochs):
    for i in range(0, real_data.size(0), batch_size):
        real_batch = real_data[i:i+batch_size]

        # --- Train the WGAN Critic ---
        for _ in range(critic_steps):
            z = torch.randn(real_batch.size(0), 10).to(device)
            fake_data = generator(z).detach()

            critic_real = critic(real_batch).mean()
            critic_fake = critic(fake_data).mean()
            loss_critic = -(critic_real - critic_fake)   # WGAN loss

            c_optimizer.zero_grad()
            loss_critic.backward()
            c_optimizer.step()

            # WGAN weight clipping (simple constraint on Lipschitz continuity)
            for p in critic.parameters():
                p.data.clamp_(-0.01, 0.01)

        # --- Train the WGAN Generator ---
        z = torch.randn(real_batch.size(0), 10).to(device)
        fake_data = generator(z)
        loss_generator = -critic(fake_data).mean()   # WGAN generator loss

        g_optimizer.zero_grad()
        loss_generator.backward()
```

```
        g_optimizer.step()

    print(f"Epoch [{epoch+1}/{epochs}] - WGAN Critic Loss: {loss_critic.item():.4f} | Generator Loss: {loss_generator.item():.4f}")

# --- Generate Synthetic Patient Activity Data Using WGAN Generator ---
with torch.no_grad():
    z = torch.randn(5, 10).to(device)
    synthetic_data = generator(z)

# Print final output
print(synthetic_data.cpu())
# Define human-readable feature names
feature_names = [
    "Heart Rate ",
    "Motion ",
    "Step Count",
    "Respiration ",
    "Fall Risk ",
    "Temperature (°C)",
    "Sleep Quality",
    "Pain Level "
]

# Convert tensor to DataFrame
df = pd.DataFrame(synthetic_data.numpy(), columns=feature_names)
print("\n🧪 Synthetic Patient Activity Monitoring Data (Generated by WGAN):\n")
```

SeqGAN extends the capabilities of GANs to sequential data, making it suitable for generating text and time-series data. SeqGAN has been applied in chatbot training, where it generates realistic conversational dialogues to enhance the performance of AI-driven virtual assistants. In addition, SeqGAN has been used in financial markets to generate synthetic but realistic stock price sequences for training predictive models.

SeqGAN is useful for generating sequential data such as patient medication logs and daily activity patterns.

```
import torch
import torch.nn as nn

# Define a simple SeqGAN generator
class SeqGAN(nn.Module):
    def __init__(self):
        super(SeqGAN, self).__init__()
        self.model = nn.Sequential(
            nn.Linear(5, 32),
            nn.ReLU(),
            nn.Linear(32, 32),
            nn.ReLU(),
            nn.Linear(32, 5)
        )

    def forward(self, x):
        return self.model(x)

# Generate synthetic daily routine data
generator = SeqGAN()
z = torch.randn((10, 5))
synthetic_sequences = generator(z)
print(synthetic_sequences)
```

Conditional GAN (cGAN) introduces additional control variables to steer the data generation process. For example, cGAN can be used to generate images of handwritten digits from the MNIST dataset, conditioned on specific numbers, enabling fine-tuned data augmentation for handwritten recognition systems. It has also been used to generate synthetic medical images with controlled attributes, helping in the development of AI-assisted radiology tools.

Conditional GAN (cGAN) allows synthetic data generation conditioned on resident health status, useful for predicting future care needs. Figure 3.6 represents the output using following code for cGAN.

```
Sample 1 :  [0.148102268576622, -0.018659986555576324, 0.15971159934997559]
Sample 2 :  [0.13335107266902924, 0.0034852996468544006, 0.1537148356437683]
Sample 3 :  [0.16320505738258362, 0.00460737943649292, 0.16138580441474915]
Sample 4 :  [0.14277933537960052, -0.11140552163124084, 0.1811046004295349]
Sample 5 :  [0.22561725974082947, 0.07654038071632385, 0.189470574259758]
```

Fig. 3.6 Output of code cGAN

```
import torch
import torch.nn as nn


class CGAN(nn.Module):
    def __init__(self, condition_dim, noise_dim, output_dim):
        super().__init__()
        self.model = nn.Sequential(
            nn.Linear(condition_dim + noise_dim, 64),
            nn.ReLU(),
            nn.Linear(64, 64),
            nn.ReLU(),
            nn.Linear(64, output_dim)
        )
    def forward(self, noise, cond):
        return self.model(torch.cat((noise, cond), 1))


torch.manual_seed(42)                    # reproducible demo
gen = CGAN(condition_dim=2, noise_dim=5, output_dim=3)


cond = torch.tensor([[1., 0.]])       # e.g. fall-risk = 1, med-cond = 0


for i in range(5):
    z = torch.randn(1, 5)                  # fresh noise each time
    print(f"Sample {i+1} : ", gen(z, cond).squeeze().tolist())
```

Synthetic Data Vault (SDV) is an ecosystem of generative models designed for creating synthetic tabular data. It includes various GAN-based methods such as CTGAN and TVAE (Tabular Variational Autoencoder). SDV has been used in the banking sector to generate synthetic customer transaction records for fraud detection model training.

Fig. 3.7 Output of code CTGAN highlighting the relationship between age, blood pressure, and fall risk

	Age	Blood_Pressure	Fall_Risk
0	80	132	1
1	75	138	1
2	78	141	1
3	80	150	1
4	70	130	1

GANs and their various extensions continue to play a crucial role in synthetic data generation, providing innovative solutions across multiple domains. By leveraging these advanced generative models, organizations can unlock new possibilities for AI training, data augmentation, and privacy-preserving data sharing. The Synthetic Data Vault (SDV) provides tools for generating realistic tabular data for resident health records and facility management. Figure 3.7 shows the output of the following code using CTGAN.

```
from sdv.tabular import CTGAN
import pandas as pd

# Load assisted living facility dataset
real_data = pd.DataFrame({
    'Age': [70, 75, 80, 85, 90],
    'Blood_Pressure': [130, 140, 135, 145, 150],
    'Fall_Risk': [1, 0, 1, 0, 1]
})

# Train SDV model
ctgan = CTGAN()
ctgan.fit(real_data)

# Generate synthetic facility data
synthetic_data = ctgan.sample(5)
print(synthetic_data)
```

GAN-based synthetic data generation enhances assisted living solutions by creating artificial but realistic data that preserves privacy while improving predictive analytics for health monitoring, mobility tracking, and fall detection. By utilizing these techniques, researchers and caregivers can develop AI-powered tools that enhance the quality of life for elderly residents.

3.14 Generating Synthetic Images

Generating synthetic images involves using artificial intelligence models to create visual content that mimics real-world images. These models, such as GANs and diffusion models like Stable Diffusion, learn from large datasets and can generate images from text prompts, existing images, or random noise. The process enables the creation of realistic, high-resolution visuals for various applications, including art, marketing, virtual environments, and data augmentation. Synthetic image generation offers a cost-effective and scalable solution for producing visuals without relying on traditional photography or manual design. It also opens creative possibilities by allowing fine control over style, content, and composition through simple input prompts. Stable Diffusion is a type of deep learning model designed to create synthetic images based on text descriptions, rough sketches, or existing pictures [25, 26]. It belongs to a group of generative models called diffusion models, which work by transforming random noise into a coherent image through a step-by-step denoising process. Unlike earlier models like GANs (Generative Adversarial Networks), diffusion models tend to be more stable during training and offer greater control during image generation, making them well-suited for creative applications. The core advantage of Stable Diffusion lies in its ability to produce visually rich and detailed images that closely follow the instructions given in natural language prompts. The model generally uses a U-Net architecture along with a text encoder—often based on models like CLIP—to understand and respond to prompts. It generates images in a compressed representation known as latent space, which helps reduce memory and processing demands. Different versions of Stable Diffusion have been developed over time, each offering improvements in image quality, realism, and flexibility. Versions like v1.4 and v1.5 were widely used for their high-quality outputs. Later releases, such as v2.0 and v2.1, introduced better support for depth, resolution, and diverse visual styles. There are also specialized tools such as image-to-image and inpainting pipelines that let users alter images or create new ones based on a reference.

Frameworks like Hugging Face's 'diffusers' library make it easy to use these models by providing ready-to-use pipelines. Stable Diffusion is now commonly used in art, design, content creation, and more, enabling users to generate visuals without traditional design skills. Figure 3.8 shows the output of the following code using Stable Diffusion.

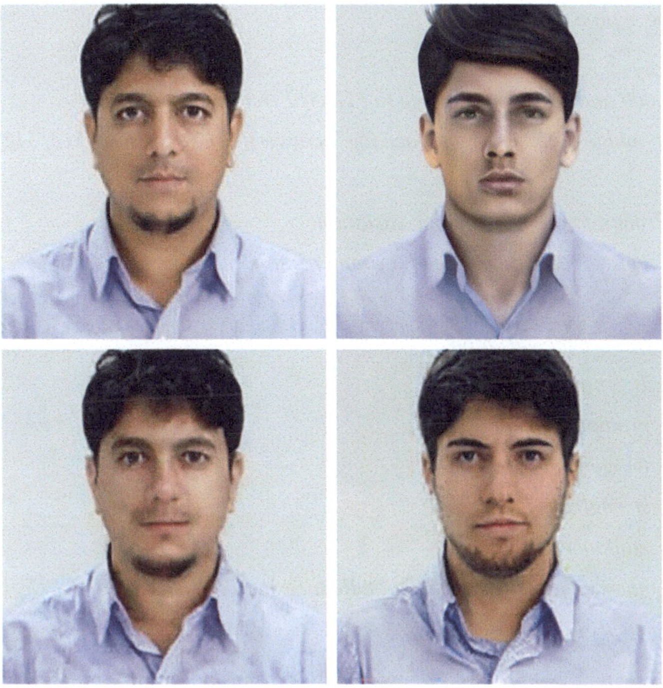

Fig. 3.8 Output of code stable diffusion

```
from diffusers import StableDiffusionImg2ImgPipeline
from PIL import Image
import torch

# Load the model on CPU
pipe = StableDiffusionImg2ImgPipeline.from_pretrained(
    "runwayml/stable-diffusion-v1-5",
    torch_dtype=torch.float32   # Use float32 for CPU
)
```

```
pipe = pipe.to("cpu")

# Load and resize your image to 512x512 (required input size)
init_image = Image.open("face.jpg").convert("RGB").resize((512, 512))

# Prompt to guide the image variation
prompt = "realistic image of a young person"

# Generate the variation
result = pipe(
    prompt=prompt,
    image=init_image,
    strength=0.5,
    guidance_scale=7.0,
    num_inference_steps=30    # Reduce steps to speed up on CPU
).images[0]

# Save result
result.save("face_variation.jpg")
print("Variation saved as face_variation.jpg")
```

3.15 Generating Synthetic Text Data

Synthetic text data means creating text using computer programs instead of collecting it from real people. This is useful when you don't have enough real data or when you want to protect people's privacy. It also helps when you want to teach a program how to understand language but don't have examples of every situation [27]. For example, if you are training a chatbot and you want it to answer questions it has never seen before, you can create fake (but realistic) questions and answers to practice on.

One common way to make synthetic text is by using a language model. A language model is a computer program that has learned how words usually go together. You give it a starting sentence or topic, and it writes something that sounds natural. These models have been trained on a lot of books, websites, and conversations, so they can write about many topics. Synthetic text can be used for many things, like training chatbots, making fake customer reviews for testing, writing practice questions for students, or creating examples of conversations. It helps save time and effort because you don't need people to write everything manually. There are many tools and models for generating text. One of the popular ones is called GPT (Generative Pre-trained Transformer), which can create full sentences and paragraphs based on a short prompt [28]. With just a few lines of code, you can make a program that writes its own text. Here is a simple example using Python and the Hugging Face Transformers library GPT-2: Fig. 3.9 shows the output of the following code using GPT-2.

```
from transformers import pipeline, set_seed

# Load a text generation pipeline using GPT-2
generator = pipeline("text-generation", model="gpt2")
set_seed(42)  # Set seed for consistent output

# Give a prompt
prompt = "relation between data and synthetic data is"

# Generate synthetic text
results = generator(prompt, max_length=50, num_return_sequences=1)

# Print the generated text
print("Generated Text:\n", results[0]['generated_text'])
```

```
=== Generated Text (1) ===
relation between data and synthetic data is often characterized by fidelity and utility. Synthetic data is generated to mimic the statistical properties of real data without exposing sensitive information, allowing models to be trained in a privacy-preserving manner. It can fill in gaps,...

=== Generated Text (2) ===
relation between data and synthetic data is unlike traditional data sources because it's created through computational models rather than real-world observation. While raw data carries inherent biases from collection processes, synthetic data can be crafted to correct imbalances, augment small...

=== Generated Text (3) ===
relation between data and synthetic data is fundamentally about approximation—synthetic data strives to reproduce key patterns and distributions found in original datasets. This approximation enables testing and development when access to real data is limited, yet it also introduces challenges…
```

Fig. 3.9 Output of code GPT-2

Here is also another Python program that uses the Faker library to generate a small dataset of synthetic text data including names, emails, addresses, phone numbers, jobs, and short bios. This example creates 5 fake user profiles and prints them (Fig. 3.10).

```
User 1
Name:       David Davis
Email:      williamcunningham@example.net
Phone:      001-981-568-2964x52628
Address:    4673 Bailey Grove, West Jenniferfort, WI 39180
Job Title:  Sports therapist
Bio:        Peace majority finish article.
--------------------------------------------------
User 2
Name:       Kevin Goodwin
Email:      kathleen90@example.org
Phone:      001-880-731-0927x5784
Address:    59652 Johnson Isle, Ryanview, NE 78939
Job Title:  Heritage manager
Bio:        Car economy pass report certain light involve. School try lose tree live big picture.
--------------------------------------------------
User 3
Name:       Valerie Barrera
Email:      hunter08@example.com
Phone:      (689)020-5839x955
Address:    66245 Hannah Gardens, Cindychester, MO 35442
Job Title:  Geophysical data processor
Bio:        Many term song old create young pretty. Eat a the money consumer.
--------------------------------------------------
User 4
Name:       Nicole Johnson
Email:      warrenlaura@example.com
Phone:      +1-621-971-4480x428
Address:    79561 Christopher Pike Suite 164, North Marissahaven, MS 64586
Job Title:  Presenter, broadcasting
Bio:        Rich either product pick my film little.
--------------------------------------------------
User 5
Name:       Vanessa Wang
Email:      johncombs@example.org
Phone:      963-670-1942x30520
Address:    98892 Christopher Dam Suite 931, Port Tarafort, OR 43572
Job Title:  Music tutor
Bio:        Word degree physical kind cell all behind simple.
```

Fig. 3.10 Output of code faker

```
from faker import Faker

# Create a Faker instance
fake = Faker()

# Generate 5 fake user profiles
for i in range(5):
    print(f"User {i+1}")
    print("Name:        ", fake.name())
    print("Email:       ", fake.email())
    print("Phone:       ", fake.phone_number())
    print("Address:     ", fake.address().replace('\n', ', '))
    print("Job Title: ", fake.job())
    print("Bio:         ", fake.paragraph(nb_sentences=2))
    print("-" * 50)
```

3.16 Synthetic Data Generation for Regression, Classification, and Clustering

Python has become the dominant programming language for synthetic data generation, thanks to its rich ecosystem of libraries and frameworks. Various Python packages, such as NumPy, Pandas, Scikit-learn, PyTorch, and TensorFlow, provide powerful tools for creating synthetic data in different domains, including structured tabular data, images, and text. The flexibility of Python allows researchers and developers to create high-fidelity synthetic datasets for machine learning applications while preserving privacy and data utility [29].

The process of synthetic data generation in Python can be accomplished using statistical methods, rule-based simulations, or deep learning models such as Generative Adversarial Networks (GANs) and Variational Autoencoders (VAEs). Each approach has its strengths, depending on the use case. For example, simple statistical techniques may suffice for generating random yet structured tabular data, whereas deep learning-based generative models are more effective for creating highly complex data, such as human-like images or realistic financial transactions.

Several open-source libraries specialize in synthetic data generation. For structured tabular data, the Synthetic Data Vault (SDV) provides models such as CTGAN and TVAE that generate privacy-preserving synthetic records. For computer vision applications, PyTorch and TensorFlow offer GAN implementations to synthesize realistic images. Meanwhile, text generation can be achieved using Natural Language

Processing (NLP) models like GPT-based transformers. Understanding how to generate synthetic data in different contexts allows data scientists to augment datasets, balance class distributions, and comply with privacy regulations while maintaining the statistical integrity of the data [30].

3.16.1 Synthetic Data Generation in Regression Problem

Assisted living environments rely on predictive models to monitor and improve the well-being of elderly individuals. Regression models play a crucial role in predicting continuous health-related variables, such as blood pressure, mobility scores, or cognitive function decline, based on sensor data and medical history. However, real-world datasets often suffer from missing values, limited sample sizes, or privacy concerns. Synthetic data generation helps mitigate these issues by providing additional training samples that maintain the statistical properties of real-world healthcare data.

Python offers various techniques to generate synthetic data for regression problems in assisted living scenarios. One straightforward approach is to use NumPy and Scikit-learn to create structured datasets that mimic patient health trends. By defining mathematical relationships or probabilistic distributions, researchers can generate synthetic datasets that simulate real-world conditions.

For instance, we can generate synthetic data representing the relationship between daily step count (X) and blood pressure (y) in elderly individuals (Fig. 3.11).

```
import numpy as np
import matplotlib.pyplot as plt

# Generate synthetic regression data for assisted living
np.random.seed(42)
X = np.linspace(1000, 10000, 100)  # Daily step count
y = 120 - 0.005 * X + np.random.normal(0, 2, size=X.shape)  # Blood pressure
trend

# Visualizing the synthetic data
plt.scatter(X, y, label='Synthetic Health Data')
plt.xlabel('Daily Step Count')
plt.ylabel('Blood Pressure (mmHg)')
plt.title('Synthetic Regression Data for Assisted Living')
plt.legend()
plt.show()
```

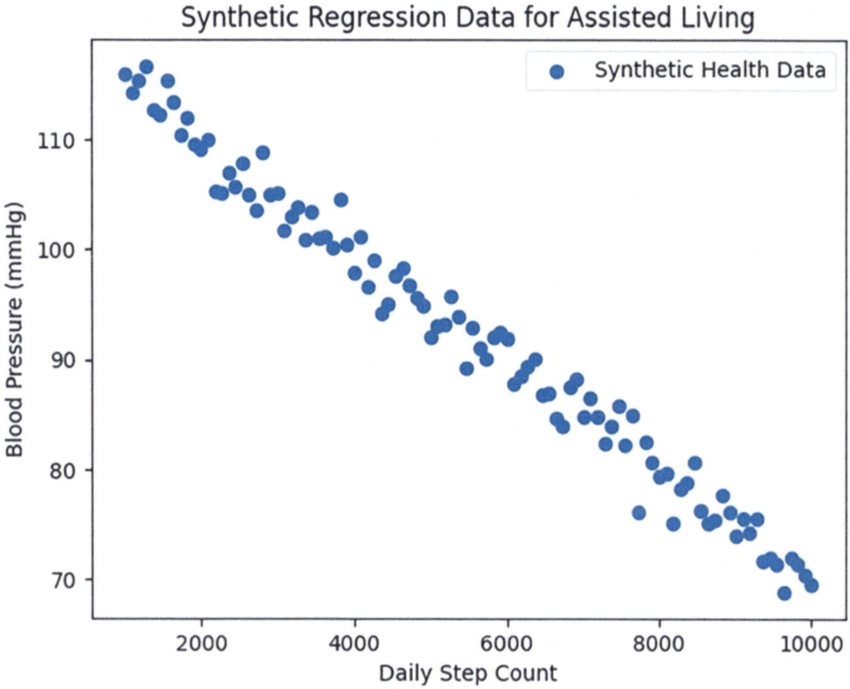

Fig. 3.11 Regression example

This approach enables researchers to simulate different healthcare scenarios, such as the effects of physical activity on blood pressure trends, by modifying the function governing the target variable. Scikit-learn also provides functions like make_regression to generate synthetic regression datasets, which can be tailored for healthcare applications. Here's an example of generating synthetic patient health data with multiple features (Fig. 3.12).

	Heart Rate	Daily Steps	Sleep Hours	Blood Pressure
0	-0.189120	-1.330314	0.921650	20.115212
1	-0.653329	-0.474945	1.765454	61.205711
2	-0.224856	0.076852	-0.650003	89.551861
3	0.570599	-0.662624	-0.763259	104.676878
4	0.327880	-0.125454	0.085893	137.961125

Fig. 3.12 Example synthetic data for regression

```
from sklearn.datasets import make_regression
import pandas as pd

# Generate synthetic patient health data
X, y = make_regression(n_samples=1000, n_features=3, noise=5.0,
random_state=42)
# Convert to DataFrame
synthetic_df = pd.DataFrame(X, columns=["Heart Rate", "Daily Steps", "Sleep
Hours"])
synthetic_df["Blood Pressure"] = y + 120  # Adjusting baseline

print(synthetic_df.head())
```

This method is particularly useful for generating high-dimensional healthcare datasets, where multiple biometric features influence patient outcomes. Researchers can fine-tune parameters such as noise levels and feature importance to create realistic data reflecting different patient conditions.

Deep learning models like GANs and VAEs further improve synthetic data generation by learning latent representations of patient health trends. PyTorch provides tools to train deep learning models that generate high-quality synthetic datasets. Below is an example using a simple neural network-based generator to create synthetic patient health data (Fig. 3.13).

```
import torch
import torch.nn as nn
import torch.optim as optim
import pandas as pd

# Define the synthetic data generator
```

Heart Rate	Temperature	Step Count	Predicted Wellness Score
0.882	0.915	0.383	0.133
0.959	0.390	0.601	0.182
0.257	0.794	0.941	0.266
0.133	0.935	0.594	0.220
0.869	0.568	0.741	0.200

Fig. 3.13 Prediction of wellness score from the synthetic data

```
class HealthDataGenerator(nn.Module):
    def __init__(self, input_dim, output_dim):
        super(HealthDataGenerator, self).__init__()
        self.model = nn.Sequential(
            nn.Linear(input_dim, 64),
            nn.ReLU(),
            nn.Linear(64, 64),
            nn.ReLU(),
            nn.Linear(64, output_dim)
        )

    def forward(self, x):
        return self.model(x)

# Set random seed for reproducibility
torch.manual_seed(42)

# Simulate input features (e.g., heart rate, temperature, step count)
X_synthetic = torch.rand((100, 3))

# Generate synthetic target values (e.g., wellness score)
generator = HealthDataGenerator(input_dim=3, output_dim=1)
y_synthetic = generator(X_synthetic).detach().numpy()

# Create a DataFrame with meaningful column names
df = pd.DataFrame(X_synthetic.numpy(), columns=["Heart Rate",
"Temperature", "Step Count"])
df["Predicted Wellness Score"] = y_synthetic

# Display the first 5 rows in a readable format
print(" Generated Synthetic Patient Health Data (first 5 samples):\n")
print(df.head().to_string(index=False, float_format="%.3f"))
```

By generating realistic synthetic healthcare data, researchers and developers can create robust predictive models for assisted living applications while ensuring privacy and mitigating data scarcity. These synthetic datasets support the development of AI-driven health monitoring systems, fall detection algorithms, and personalized intervention strategies for elderly individuals in assisted living environments. This deep learning-based approach is particularly useful when real regression data is scarce or when there is a need for synthetic data augmentation to improve model performance. By training a GAN or VAE on existing regression datasets, researchers can generate new, realistic data points that maintain the statistical integrity of the original dataset.

Synthetic data generation for regression problems is crucial in various domains, including finance, healthcare, and engineering. In finance, synthetic stock market data can be generated to test risk models without exposing proprietary trading data. In healthcare, synthetic patient biomarker data can be used to develop predictive models for disease progression without violating patient confidentiality. In engineering, synthetic sensor data can simulate machine performance under different operating conditions, enabling predictive maintenance models. By leveraging Python-based synthetic data generation techniques, data scientists can create high-quality regression datasets that enhance model training, reduce bias, and facilitate data-driven decision-making in various industries.

3.16.2 Synthetic Data Generation for Classification

Classification problems involve categorizing data into discrete labels or classes based on input features. Machine learning models rely on large, well-balanced, and diverse datasets for training to achieve optimal performance. However, real-world classification datasets often suffer from class imbalance, limited sample sizes, or privacy restrictions. Synthetic data generation provides an effective solution by augmenting datasets with realistic but artificial samples, thereby improving model generalization and fairness.

Python offers various methods for generating synthetic classification data, ranging from simple statistical techniques to advanced deep learning-based methods. One commonly used approach is Scikit-learn's make_classification function, which enables users to create synthetic classification datasets with adjustable parameters such as the number of classes, features, informative features, and class imbalance. Following is an example of generating a synthetic classification dataset for independent living using Scikit-learn (Fig. 3.14).

```
from sklearn.datasets import make_classification
import pandas as pd

# Generate synthetic dataset (e.g., for predicting patient health risk)
X, y = make_classification(
    n_samples=1000,
    n_features=5,
    n_classes=3,
    n_informative=3,
    weights=[0.6, 0.3, 0.1],
    random_state=42
)

# Convert to DataFrame with meaningful feature names
synthetic_df = pd.DataFrame(X, columns=[
    "Heart Rate",
    "Daily Steps",
    "Sleep Quality",
    "Cognitive Score",


        "Activity Level"
    ])

    # Map numeric classes to risk categories
    risk_labels = {0: "Low", 1: "Medium", 2: "High"}
    synthetic_df["Risk Level"] = [risk_labels[r] for r in y]

    # Round values for better readability
    synthetic_df = synthetic_df.round(2)

    # Display the first 5 rows
    print("🧪 Sample Synthetic Patient Risk Prediction Data:\n")
    print(synthetic_df.head().to_string(index=False))
```

This method is particularly useful for generating health-related classification datasets, such as predicting risk levels for falls, cardiovascular disease, or cognitive

Heart Rate	Daily Steps	Sleep Quality	Cognitive Score	Activity Level	Risk Level
1.56	0.63	-0.57	-2.55	-1.58	High
-1.76	-0.42	0.35	2.38	0.17	Low
-0.33	-0.46	-1.18	1.44	-1.23	Low
-1.80	0.08	1.62	1.22	1.05	Low
0.54	-0.60	-1.20	0.87	0.19	Low

Fig. 3.14 Prediction of risk level classification from the synthetic data

impairment. Researchers can modify parameters to simulate different health risk distributions in assisted living populations. Following is an example of generating synthetic health classification data using a GAN (Fig. 3.15).

```
import torch
import torch.nn as nn
import numpy as np
import pandas as pd

# Define a simple generator to simulate health risk classification
class HealthClassificationGenerator(nn.Module):
    def __init__(self, input_dim, output_dim):
        super(HealthClassificationGenerator, self).__init__()
        self.model = nn.Sequential(
            nn.Linear(input_dim, 64),
            nn.ReLU(),
            nn.Linear(64, 64),
            nn.ReLU(),
            nn.Linear(64, output_dim),
            nn.Softmax(dim=1)  # Outputs probabilities across risk classes
        )
```

```
    def forward(self, x):
        return self.model(x)

# : Simulate input health metrics (e.g., heart rate, sleep, activity, etc.)
torch.manual_seed(42)
X_synthetic = torch.rand((100, 5))  # 100 synthetic patients × 5 health features

# : Generate predicted risk class probabilities
generator = HealthClassificationGenerator(input_dim=5, output_dim=3)
y_synthetic = generator(X_synthetic).detach().numpy()

# : Create a readable table
risk_df = pd.DataFrame(y_synthetic, columns=["Low Risk", "Medium Risk",
"High Risk"])
risk_df = risk_df.round(3)

# : Display first 5 synthetic patients
print(" Predicted Health Risk Probabilities for Synthetic Patients:\n")
print(risk_df.head().to_string(index=False))
```

Deep learning-based synthetic classification data generation is especially valuable in assisted living for handling imbalanced datasets, such as when there are fewer samples of high-risk patients. By generating additional samples for underrepresented health conditions, classification models can be trained more effectively, reducing bias and improving diagnostic accuracy in healthcare applications. This enhances AI-driven risk prediction, fall detection, and personalized intervention strategies, ultimately improving elderly care in assisted living facilities.

```
Predicted Health Risk Probabilities for Synthetic Patients:

Low Risk  Medium Risk  High Risk
   0.353        0.368      0.279
   0.358        0.361      0.282
   0.341        0.374      0.285
   0.338        0.374      0.288
   0.353        0.365      0.282
```

Fig. 3.15 Prediction of different health risk levels from the synthetic data

3.16.3 Synthetic Data Generation for Clustering

Clustering is an unsupervised learning technique that groups data points based on similarity. Unlike classification, clustering does not rely on predefined labels, making synthetic data generation more challenging. Synthetic clustering datasets help test and validate clustering algorithms by providing controlled environments where ground truth relationships are known. Python provides various methods for generating synthetic clustering data, including Scikit-learn's make_blobs and make_moons functions. These functions allow the creation of datasets with distinct clusters, noise levels, and customizable distributions, which are particularly useful for simulating health-related patient groups. Following is an example of generating a synthetic clustering dataset for assisted living using Scikit-learn (Fig. 3.16).

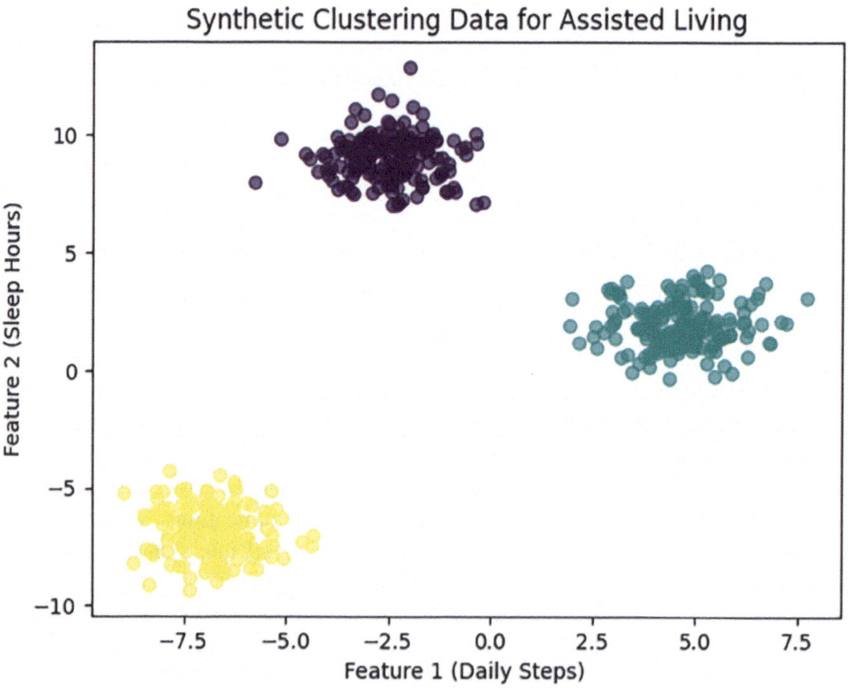

Fig. 3.16 A clustering example

```
from sklearn.datasets import make_blobs
import matplotlib.pyplot as plt

# Generate synthetic clustering data for patient activity patterns
X, y = make_blobs(n_samples=500, centers=3, cluster_std=1.0,
random_state=42)

# Visualizing the synthetic clusters
plt.scatter(X[:, 0], X[:, 1], c=y, cmap='viridis', alpha=0.6)
plt.xlabel("Feature 1 (Daily Steps)")
plt.ylabel("Feature 2 (Sleep Hours)")
plt.title("Synthetic Clustering Data for Assisted Living")
plt.show()
```

This method allows researchers to test clustering algorithms such as K-Means, DBSCAN, and hierarchical clustering on simulated patient groups, activity levels, and health conditions. By adjusting parameters, researchers can mimic various healthcare clustering scenarios, such as identifying groups with similar mobility patterns or monitoring cognitive decline. Following is another example.

```
import torch
import numpy as np
import torch.nn as nn
import matplotlib.pyplot as plt
from sklearn.cluster import KMeans

# Define a simple generator for clustering health data
class HealthClusteringGenerator(nn.Module):
    def __init__(self, input_dim, output_dim):
```

```
        super(HealthClusteringGenerator, self).__init__()
        self.model = nn.Sequential(
            nn.Linear(input_dim, 64),
            nn.ReLU(),
            nn.Linear(64, 64),
            nn.ReLU(),
            nn.Linear(64, output_dim)
        )

    def forward(self, x):
        return self.model(x)

# : Generate synthetic input features (e.g., activity + sleep)
torch.manual_seed(42)
X_synthetic = torch.rand((300, 2))

# : Generate synthetic outputs using the generator
generator = HealthClusteringGenerator(input_dim=2, output_dim=2)
```

```
y_synthetic = generator(X_synthetic).detach().numpy()

# --- Plot raw synthetic data ---
plt.figure(figsize=(7, 6))
plt.scatter(y_synthetic[:, 0], y_synthetic[:, 1], alpha=0.6)
plt.xlabel("Feature 1 (Mobility Index)")
plt.ylabel("Feature 2 (Cognitive Score)")
plt.title(" Synthetic Health Data (Unclustered)")
plt.grid(True)
plt.show()

# --- Apply KMeans clustering and plot clustered data ---
kmeans = KMeans(n_clusters=3, random_state=42)
cluster_labels = kmeans.fit_predict(y_synthetic)

plt.figure(figsize=(7, 6))
scatter = plt.scatter(
    y_synthetic[:, 0],
    y_synthetic[:, 1],
    c=cluster_labels,
    cmap='viridis',
    alpha=0.7
)
plt.xlabel("Feature 1 (Mobility Index)")
plt.ylabel("Feature 2 (Cognitive Score)")
plt.title("Clustered Synthetic Health Data (via KMeans)")
plt.colorbar(scatter, label="Cluster Group")
plt.grid(True)
plt.show()
```

For more complex clustering scenarios, Generative Adversarial Networks (GANs) can be employed to create high-fidelity synthetic clustering datasets. A specialized ClusterGAN approach combines supervised and unsupervised loss functions to learn meaningful latent representations, which can reflect natural patient clusters in healthcare. Synthetic clustering data is essential in healthcare applications such as

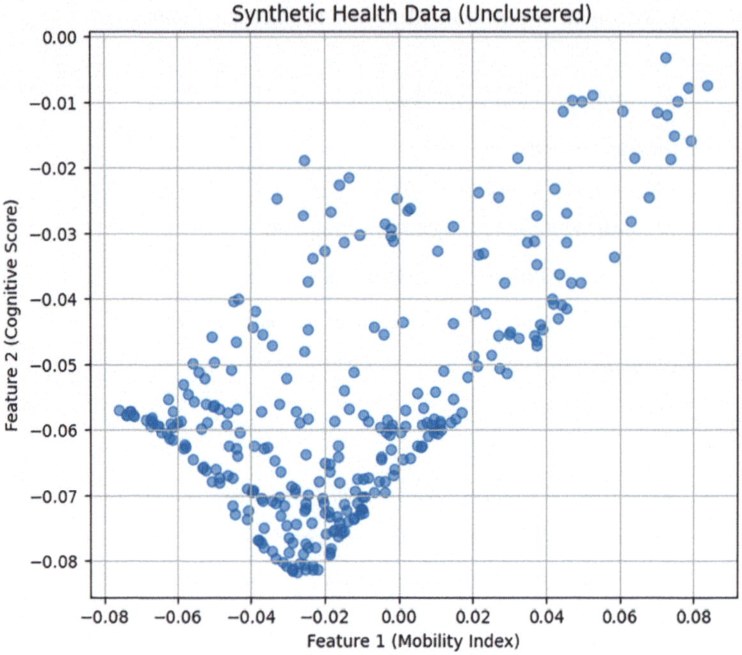

Fig. 3.17 Unclustered synthetic data

anomaly detection, patient segmentation, and personalized intervention planning. By generating diverse patient clusters, researchers and clinicians can improve clustering model performance and validate their robustness in various assisted living scenarios (Figs. 3.17 and 3.18).

Leveraging Python-based synthetic data generation tools, assisted living research can benefit from privacy-preserving, high-quality synthetic datasets that enable the development of more reliable AI-driven health monitoring and risk assessment models.

3.16.4 An Example of VAE for Regression, Classification, and Clustering Data

His codes snippet demonstrates how to apply a Variational Autoencoder (VAE) to synthetic data for multiple tasks: regression, classification, and clustering. First, it generates three separate datasets using scikit-learn's make_regression, make_classification, and make_blobs, providing different feature shapes and labels. Then, it defines a simple feed-forward VAE in PyTorch. The VAE includes an encoder that maps input features to latent variables, followed by a reparameterization step that samples from a normal distribution, and a decoder that reconstructs the original

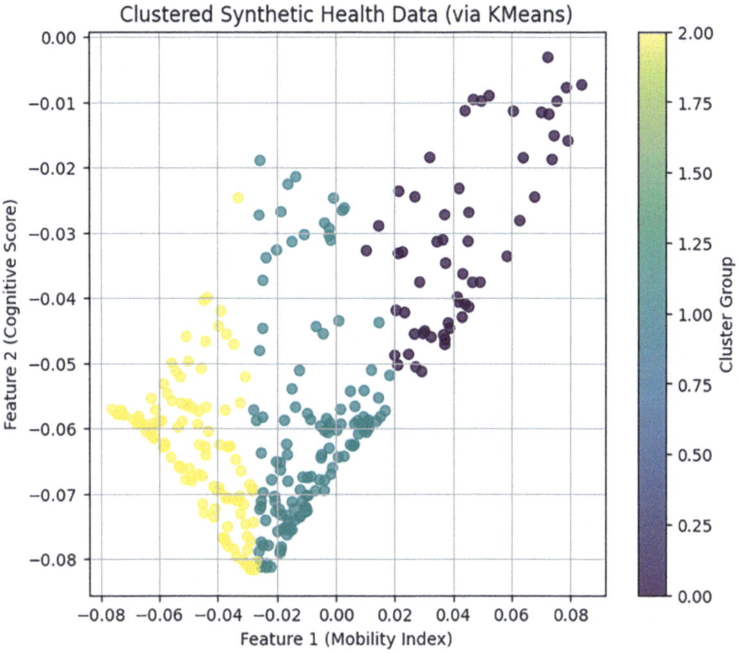

Fig. 3.18 Clustered synthetic data represented in different colors

inputs. The training loop uses a combination of mean squared error for reconstruction followed by regularizing the latent space. The code trains a VAE on each dataset without using labels, because a VAE is inherently unsupervised. Once trained, it extracts the latent representations for each data point. For regression, these representations become inputs to a linear model predicting numeric targets. For classification, they feed a logistic regression that distinguishes classes. Lastly, for clustering, it applies K-means to the latent embeddings to see how well they align with known clusters. By systematically training the model and extracting embeddings, the code demonstrates a flexible approach that can generalize to real-world scenarios. While not fully optimized for production, this example clarifies how one unsupervised model can generate embeddings useful for multiple downstream tasks.

```
import numpy as np
import torch
import torch.nn as nn
import torch.optim as optim
from torch.utils.data import DataLoader, TensorDataset
from sklearn.datasets import make_regression, make_classification,
make_blobs
from sklearn.model_selection import train_test_split
from sklearn.preprocessing import StandardScaler
from sklearn.cluster import KMeans
from sklearn.linear_model import LogisticRegression
from sklearn.metrics import accuracy_score, mean_squared_error

# ---------------------------------------------------------------------------
# 1) Generate Synthetic Data
# ---------------------------------------------------------------------------

# A. Regression dataset (X_reg: features, y_reg: numeric target)
X_reg, y_reg = make_regression(n_samples=500, n_features=4, noise=10.0,
random_state=42)

# B. Classification dataset (X_clf: features, y_clf: class labels)
X_clf, y_clf = make_classification(n_samples=500, n_features=4,
n_informative=2,
                                   n_redundant=0, n_classes=2,
random_state=42)

# C. Clustering dataset (X_clu: features, y_clu: cluster memberships)
X_clu, y_clu = make_blobs(n_samples=500, n_features=4, centers=3,
                          cluster_std=1.5, random_state=42)
```

```
# We'll ignore y_clf and y_reg when training the VAE (unless doing a
conditional VAE).
# We'll only use them AFTER the VAE is trained, to build a separate
classifier/regressor or evaluate embeddings.

# ---------------------------------------------------------------------------
# 2) Define a Simple MLP VAE
#    We'll create a small VAE that can handle a generic input_dim.
#    We won't do label conditioning here (purely unsupervised).
# ---------------------------------------------------------------------------

class VAE(nn.Module):
    def __init__(self, input_dim=4, latent_dim=2, hidden_dim=32):
        super(VAE, self).__init__()

        # Encoder
        self.encoder = nn.Sequential(
            nn.Linear(input_dim, hidden_dim),
            nn.ReLU()
        )
        self.fc_mu = nn.Linear(hidden_dim, latent_dim)
        self.fc_logvar = nn.Linear(hidden_dim, latent_dim)

        # Decoder
        self.decoder = nn.Sequential(
            nn.Linear(latent_dim, hidden_dim),
            nn.ReLU(),
            nn.Linear(hidden_dim, input_dim),
        )

    def encode(self, x):
        h = self.encoder(x)
```

```
        mu = self.fc_mu(h)
        logvar = self.fc_logvar(h)
        return mu, logvar

    def reparameterize(self, mu, logvar):
        std = torch.exp(0.5 * logvar)
        eps = torch.randn_like(std)
        return mu + eps * std

    def decode(self, z):
        return self.decoder(z)

    def forward(self, x):
        mu, logvar = self.encode(x)
        z = self.reparameterize(mu, logvar)
        recon = self.decode(z)
        return recon, mu, logvar

def vae_loss(recon_x, x, mu, logvar):
    # Mean Squared Error (reconstruction)
    recon_loss = nn.functional.mse_loss(recon_x, x, reduction='sum')
    # KL divergence
    kld = -0.5 * torch.sum(1 + logvar - mu.pow(2) - logvar.exp())
    return recon_loss + kld

# ---------------------------------------------------------------------------
# Helper: Train a VAE on a given dataset (X only)
# ---------------------------------------------------------------------------
def train_vae(X, input_dim=4, latent_dim=2, epochs=20, batch_size=64):
    # Normalize or scale data
    scaler = StandardScaler()
    X_scaled = scaler.fit_transform(X)
```

```
    # Convert to Torch
    dataset = TensorDataset(torch.from_numpy(X_scaled).float())
    loader = DataLoader(dataset, batch_size=batch_size, shuffle=True)

    # Instantiate model + optimizer
    model = VAE(input_dim=input_dim, latent_dim=latent_dim,
hidden_dim=32)
    optimizer = optim.Adam(model.parameters(), lr=1e-3)

    model.train()
    for epoch in range(1, epochs + 1):
        total_loss = 0
        for (batch_x,) in loader:
            optimizer.zero_grad()
            recon, mu, logvar = model(batch_x)
            loss = vae_loss(recon, batch_x, mu, logvar)
            loss.backward()
            optimizer.step()
            total_loss += loss.item()
        # Print average epoch loss
        avg_loss = total_loss / len(loader.dataset)
        if epoch % 5 == 0:
            print(f"Epoch [{epoch}/{epochs}], Loss: {avg_loss:.4f}")

    # Return the trained model and the scaler
    return model, scaler

# ------------------------------------------------------------------------------
# 3) Example A: Using VAE for Regression (as an Unsupervised Feature
Extractor)
# ------------------------------------------------------------------------------
print("\n=== VAE on Regression dataset ===")
model_reg, scaler_reg = train_vae(X_reg, input_dim=4, latent_dim=2)
```

```
    # We'll now show how to use the VAE's latent space to help a separate
regressor
    # A. Extract latent embeddings for each sample
    model_reg.eval()
    with torch.no_grad():
        X_reg_scaled = torch.from_numpy(scaler_reg.transform(X_reg)).float()
        mu, _ = model_reg.encode(X_reg_scaled)
        z_reg = mu.numpy()    # [n_samples, latent_dim]

    # B. Train a standard regressor (e.g., linear) on the latent space
    X_train_z, X_test_z, y_train_reg, y_test_reg = train_test_split(z_reg, y_reg,
test_size=0.2, random_state=42)

    regressor = torch.nn.Linear(2, 1)   # simple linear regression in torch, or use
sklearn's LinearRegression

    # (Here we'll just do a quick MSE check with a torch training loop or we can
do an sklearn approach.)
    # For brevity, let's do a simple sklearn approach for the regression on z_reg:
    from sklearn.linear_model import LinearRegression
    reg_sklearn = LinearRegression()
    reg_sklearn.fit(X_train_z, y_train_reg)
    y_pred_reg = reg_sklearn.predict(X_test_z)
    mse_reg = mean_squared_error(y_test_reg, y_pred_reg)
    print(f"Regression on VAE latent space MSE: {mse_reg:.2f}")

    # ------------------------------------------------------------------------
    # 4) Example B: Using VAE for Classification
    # ------------------------------------------------------------------------
    print("\n=== VAE on Classification dataset ===")
    model_clf, scaler_clf = train_vae(X_clf, input_dim=4, latent_dim=2)
```

```
# A. Extract latent embeddings
model_clf.eval()
with torch.no_grad():
    X_clf_scaled = torch.from_numpy(scaler_clf.transform(X_clf)).float()
    mu, _ = model_clf.encode(X_clf_scaled)
    z_clf = mu.numpy()

# B. Train a classifier on the latent space
X_train_zc, X_test_zc, y_train_clf, y_test_clf = train_test_split(z_clf, y_clf,
test_size=0.2, random_state=42)

clf_lr = LogisticRegression()
clf_lr.fit(X_train_zc, y_train_clf)
y_pred_clf = clf_lr.predict(X_test_zc)
acc_clf = accuracy_score(y_test_clf, y_pred_clf)
print(f"Classification on VAE latent space accuracy: {acc_clf:.2f}")

# ---------------------------------------------------------------------------
# 5) Example C: Using VAE for Clustering
# ---------------------------------------------------------------------------
print("\n=== VAE on Clustering dataset ===")
model_clu, scaler_clu = train_vae(X_clu, input_dim=4, latent_dim=2)

model_clu.eval()
with torch.no_grad():
    X_clu_scaled = torch.from_numpy(scaler_clu.transform(X_clu)).float()
    mu, _ = model_clu.encode(X_clu_scaled)
    z_clu = mu.numpy()

# If we know the ground-truth labels (y_clu), we can see how well a standard
# clusterer (like k-means) performs in the 2D latent space:
kmeans = KMeans(n_clusters=3, random_state=42)
pred_clusters = kmeans.fit_predict(z_clu)
```

```
# Evaluate how well the discovered clusters match the ground-truth y_clu
# We'll do a simple "completeness" or "homogeneity" or "accuracy" measure if the labels match exactly:
from sklearn.metrics import accuracy_score
# But cluster labels might not match exactly. For a quick hack, we can reorder the predicted labels if desired.
# Let's do a naive approach: if we know y_clu = {0,1,2}, we could attempt a best matching.
# For demonstration, let's see if we can find a direct accuracy or not.
# In practice, you'd do something like a Hungarian algorithm or count permutations.

# Quick example (not always accurate if permutations differ):
acc_clu = accuracy_score(y_clu, pred_clusters)
print(f"Clustering on VAE latent space (raw label matching) accuracy: {acc_clu:.2f}")
```

The output is as shown in Fig. 3.19.

3.17 Cross-Validation in Machine Learning

In machine learning, cross-validation is a method used to evaluate how well a model performs on data it hasn't seen before. Instead of using a single split of the data for training and testing, cross-validation divides the dataset into several equal-sized parts or folds. In a typical k-fold cross-validation, the model is trained on k − 1 folds and tested on the remaining one [31]. This process repeats k times, with each fold used once as the test set. The final performance is calculated as the average across all folds, giving a more balanced view of the model's accuracy and reducing the chance of overfitting. In contrast, non-cross-validation, often called the hold-out method, separates the dataset into two distinct sets—one for training and one for testing—usually in a fixed ratio like 80% training and 20% testing. This approach is straightforward and quick, which makes it suitable for large datasets or when computational resources are limited. However, it may produce unreliable results if the data is not well-distributed or if the dataset is small, as the performance depends heavily on the specific data split used. Choosing between these two approaches depends on the size of the dataset and the goal of the analysis. Cross-validation is more thorough and is preferred when accuracy and model robustness are critical. It is commonly used in tasks such as model comparison and hyperparameter tuning. On the other hand, the

```
=== VAE on Regression dataset ===
Epoch [5/20], Loss: 4.0755
Epoch [10/20], Loss: 3.9670
Epoch [15/20], Loss: 3.9684
Epoch [20/20], Loss: 3.8970
Regression on VAE latent space MSE: 611.51

=== VAE on Classification dataset ===
Epoch [5/20], Loss: 4.0256
Epoch [10/20], Loss: 3.9592
Epoch [15/20], Loss: 3.9018
Epoch [20/20], Loss: 3.8459
Classification on VAE latent space accuracy: 0.73

=== VAE on Clustering dataset ===
Epoch [5/20], Loss: 4.0399
Epoch [10/20], Loss: 3.9343
Epoch [15/20], Loss: 3.2466
Epoch [20/20], Loss: 2.7531
Clustering on VAE latent space (raw label matching) accuracy: 1.00
```

Fig. 3.19 A VAE example of regression, classification, and clustering

hold-out method may be adequate for simpler tasks or initial testing. Overall, cross-validation offers a more comprehensive evaluation of a model's ability to generalize, which is essential for building reliable and effective machine learning systems.

3.18 Akaike Information Criterion (AIC) and the Bayesian Information Criterion (BIC)

The Akaike Information Criterion (AIC) and the Bayesian Information Criterion (BIC) are widely used for selecting the most appropriate model from a set of candidates [32]. These criteria help evaluate how well a model fits the data while accounting for its complexity. They are particularly valuable in fields like regression analysis and time series forecasting, where multiple models may offer reasonable explanations for the observed data. AICis designed to measure the quality of a model by assessing its fit to the data and penalizing it for having too many parameters. The idea is to discourage models that are overly complex and risk fitting noise instead of actual patterns. A lower AIC score suggests a model that achieves a good balance between accuracy and simplicity, making it more likely to generalize well to unseen data. BIC performs a similar function but is more stringent when it comes to penalizing complexity. It incorporates the size of the dataset into its evaluation, leading it to favor simpler models as the number of data points increases. This makes BIC especially useful in scenarios where model interpretability and avoiding overfitting are priorities. Like AIC, a lower BIC value points to a more suitable model among the options. Although both AIC and BIC aim to identify the best model, they do so with slightly different priorities. AIC is often used when the goal is better predictive performance, as it tends to allow more complexity. In contrast, BIC is typically applied when a simpler, more generalizable model is desired. Considering both can offer a more nuanced perspective on model selection, especially when the best choice is not immediately clear.

The following code performs fivefold and tenfold cross-validation on various classical machine learning models using random synthetic data. Additionally, it calculates AIC and BIC values exclusively for likelihood-based models such as Logistic Regression, Gaussian Naive Bayes, and Linear Discriminant Analysis, providing both performance and model selection metrics. Figure 3.20 shows cross-fold validations on different ML models, AIC, and BIC. The lower the AIC and BIC the better the model is. Hence, logistic regression is better than Naïve Bayes in this example.

Model	5-Fold Accuracy	10-Fold Accuracy	AIC	BIC
Logistic Regression	0.73	0.745	244.17	280.45
LDA	0.73	0.75		
Gaussian NB	0.755	0.755	246.73	283.01
Gradient Boosting	0.79	0.79		
SVM	0.815	0.805		
Decision Tree	0.775	0.815		
Random Forest	0.825	0.825		
Extra Trees	0.845	0.835		
K-NN	0.84	0.85		

Fig. 3.20 Cross-fold validations on different ML models, AIC, and BIC

```
from sklearn.datasets import make_classification
from sklearn.model_selection import cross_val_score
from sklearn.linear_model import LogisticRegression
from sklearn.tree import DecisionTreeClassifier
from sklearn.ensemble import RandomForestClassifier,
GradientBoostingClassifier, ExtraTreesClassifier
from sklearn.naive_bayes import GaussianNB
from sklearn.neighbors import KNeighborsClassifier
from sklearn.svm import SVC
from sklearn.discriminant_analysis import LinearDiscriminantAnalysis
from sklearn.metrics import log_loss
import pandas as pd
import numpy as np

# Generate synthetic classification data
X, y = make_classification(n_samples=200, n_features=10, n_informative=5,
                           n_redundant=2, random_state=42)

# Define models to evaluate
models = {
    "Logistic Regression": LogisticRegression(max_iter=1000),

            "Decision Tree": DecisionTreeClassifier(),
            "Random Forest": RandomForestClassifier(),
            "Gradient Boosting": GradientBoostingClassifier(),
```

```
        "Extra Trees": ExtraTreesClassifier(),
        "Gaussian NB": GaussianNB(),
        "K-NN": KNeighborsClassifier(),
        "Support Vector Classifier": SVC(probability=True),
        "LDA": LinearDiscriminantAnalysis()
    }

# Function to calculate AIC and BIC (for applicable models only)
def calculate_aic_bic(model, X, y):
    model.fit(X, y)
    probs = model.predict_proba(X)
    log_likelihood = -log_loss(y, probs, normalize=False)
    num_params = X.shape[1] + 1   # number of features + intercept
    aic = 2 * num_params - 2 * log_likelihood
    bic = np.log(len(y)) * num_params - 2 * log_likelihood
    return aic, bic

#Run evaluation and store results
results = []

for name, model in models.items():
    scores_5 = cross_val_score(model, X, y, cv=5)
    scores_10 = cross_val_score(model, X, y, cv=10)

    if name in ["Logistic Regression", "Gaussian NB", "Linear Discriminant
Analysis"]:
        aic, bic = calculate_aic_bic(model, X, y)
    else:
        aic, bic = np.nan, np.nan   # Not applicable
```

```
    results.append({
        "Model": name,
        "5-Fold Accuracy": round(scores_5.mean(), 4),
        "10-Fold Accuracy": round(scores_10.mean(), 4),
        "AIC": round(aic, 2) if not np.isnan(aic) else None,
        "BIC": round(bic, 2) if not np.isnan(bic) else None
    })

# Convert to DataFrame and display
final_df = pd.DataFrame(results).sort_values(by="10-Fold Accuracy",
ascending=True)
print(final_df)
```

3.19 Conclusion

AI and machine learning rely on good data, but getting high-quality, unbiased, and privacy-safe datasets is often a challenge. That's where synthetic data steps in—it offers a way to train AI models while avoiding privacy risks, data shortages, and biases. This chapter has explored the key aspects of synthetic data and how it is shaping AI applications, particularly in assisted living. In assisted living settings, AI-powered systems need reliable data to improve patient care and daily life. However, real data is often difficult to collect and raises privacy concerns, especially in healthcare. Synthetic data allows AI models to be trained on realistic patient information without exposing sensitive details, making it an ethical and practical solution. This means AI can support personalized care, track health patterns, and improve safety without putting real individuals at risk. One of the biggest advantages of synthetic data is its ability to balance data accessibility with privacy protection. Unlike anonymized data, which still carries a risk of being traced back to real individuals, synthetic data ensures full confidentiality while keeping the statistical characteristics needed for AI training. In assisted living, this means AI can recognize patterns in patient behavior and health trends without ever handling real personal data. Another major focus of this chapter has been fairness in synthetic data. AI systems trained on biased data can lead to unfair predictions, particularly in healthcare, where biased models could lead to incorrect treatments or disparities in care. We have discussed various methods to reduce bias in synthetic data, including adversarial debiasing and fairness-aware data balancing, to ensure AI technologies serve diverse populations more equitably. Modern generative models like GANs have transformed how synthetic data is created. GAN-based methods, including CTGAN, MedGAN, and

WGAN, help generate high-quality synthetic datasets that improve AI models, especially in assisted living scenarios. By generating realistic yet privacy-preserving data, these models support the development of smarter, more adaptable AI solutions. On a practical level, this chapter also provided hands-on examples for generating synthetic data using Python. Whether for regression, classification, or clustering, synthetic data generation techniques can help AI professionals overcome data limitations. This is particularly valuable in assisted living, where gathering real-world data can be difficult, and ethical considerations are paramount. In summary, synthetic data is proving to be an essential tool in AI, allowing researchers and developers to build effective, unbiased, and privacy-conscious solutions. Whether in healthcare, security, or AI-driven applications, the ability to generate realistic and fair synthetic data is transforming how we develop and deploy AI. This chapter serves as a guide to understanding and applying synthetic data, equipping readers with the knowledge and tools to use it effectively in real-world scenarios.

References

1. N. Patki, R. Wedge, and K. Veeramachaneni, "The Synthetic Data Vault," in Proc. IEEE Int. Conf. on Data Science and Advanced Analytics (DSAA), 2016, pp. 399–410.
2. A. Torfi, E. A. Fox, and C. K. Reddy, "Differentially Private Synthetic Medical Data Generation Using Convolutional GANs," Information Sciences, vol. 563, pp. 323–340, 2021.
3. R. Torkzadehmahani, P. Kairouz, and B. Paten, "DP-CGAN: Differentially Private Synthetic Data and Label Generation," arXiv:2001.09700, 2020.
4. L. Rosenblatt, X. Liu, S. Pouyanfar, E. de Leon, A. Desai, and J. Allen, "Differentially Private Synthetic Data: Applied Evaluations and Enhancements," arXiv:2011.05537, 2020.
5. D. Pujol, A. Gilad, and A. Machanavajjhala, "PreFair: Privately Generating Justifiably Fair Synthetic Data," Proc. VLDB Endowment, vol. 16, no. 8, pp. 1573–1586, 2023.
6. B. Chaudhari, H. Chaudhary, A. Agarwal, K. Meena, and T. Bhowmik, "FairGen: Fair Synthetic Data Generation," arXiv:2210.13023, 2022.
7. I. J. Goodfellow, J. Pouget-Abadie, M. Mirza, B. Xu, D. Warde-Farley, S. Ozair, A. Courville, and Y. Bengio, "Generative Adversarial Nets," in Advances in Neural Information Processing Systems, vol. 27, 2014, pp. 2672–2680.
8. M. Arjovsky, S. Chintala, and L. Bottou, "Wasserstein GAN," in Proc. 34th Int. Conf. on Machine Learning (ICML), 2017, pp. 214–223.
9. T. B. Brown, B. Mann, N. Ryder, M. Subbiah, J. Kaplan, P. Dhariwal, A. Neelakantan, P. Shyam, G. Sastry, A. Askell, S. Agarwal, A. Herbert-Voss, G. Krueger, T. Henighan, R. Child, A. Ramesh, D. M. Ziegler, J. Wu, C. Winter, C. Hesse, M. Chen, E. Sigler, M. Litwin, S. Gray, B. Chess, J. Clark, C. Berner, S. McCandlish, A. Radford, I. Sutskever, and D. Amodei, "Language Models Are Few-Shot Learners," in Advances in Neural Information Processing Systems, vol. 33, 2020, pp. 1877–1901.
10. R. J. Chen, M. Y. Lu, T. Y. Chen, D. F. K. Williamson, and F. Mahmood, "Synthetic Data in Machine Learning for Medicine and Healthcare," Nature Biomedical Engineering, vol. 5, pp. 493–497, 2021.
11. A. Tucker, Z. Wang, Y. Rotalinti, and P. Myles, "Generating High-Fidelity Synthetic Patient Data for Assessing Machine-Learning Healthcare Software," npj Digital Medicine, vol. 3, Article 147, 2020.
12. L. Xu, M. Skoularidou, A. Cuesta-Infante, and K. Veeramachaneni, "Modeling Tabular Data Using Conditional GAN," in Advances in Neural Information Processing Systems, vol. 32, 2019, pp. 7333–7343.

13. L. Xie, K. Lin, S. Wang, F. Wang, and J. Zhou, "Differentially Private Generative Adversarial Network," arXiv:1802.06739, 2018.
14. M.-L. Fang, D. S. Dhami, and K. Kersting, "DP-CTGAN: Differentially Private Medical Data Generation Using Conditional GANs," arXiv:2202.00128, 2022.
15. J. Yoon, M. Mizrahi, N. Farhady Ghalaty, T. Jarvinen, A. S. Ravi, P. Brune, F. Kong, D. Anderson, G. Lee, A. Meir, F. Bandukwala, E. Kanal, S. Ö. Arık, and T. Pfister, "EHR-Safe: Generating High-Fidelity and Privacy-Preserving Synthetic Electronic Health Records," npj Digital Medicine, vol. 6, Article 141, 2023.
16. J. Yoon, D. Jarrett, and M. van der Schaar, "TimeGAN: Time-Series Generative Adversarial Networks," in Advances in Neural Information Processing Systems, vol. 32, 2019, pp. 10319–10330.
17. M. Abadi, A. Chu, I. Goodfellow, H. B. McMahan, I. Mironov, K. Talwar, and L. Zhang, "Deep Learning with Differential Privacy," in Proc. ACM SIGSAC Conf. on Computer and Communications Security (CCS), 2016, pp. 308–318.
18. X. Yue, H. A. Inan, X. Li, G. Kumar, J. McAnallen, H. Shajari, H. Sun, D. Levitan, and R. Sim, "Synthetic Text Generation with Differential Privacy: A Simple and Practical Recipe," in Proc. 61st Annual Meeting of the Association for Computational Linguistics, 2023, pp. 1321–1342.
19. A. Yale, S. Dash, R. Dutta, I. Guyon, A. Pavao, and K. P. Bennett, "Assessing Privacy and Quality of Synthetic Health Data," in Proc. Conf. on Artificial Intelligence for Data Discovery and Reuse (AIDR), 2019, pp. 1–4.
20. S. Gambs, F. Ladouceur, A. Laurent, and A. Roy-Gaumond, "Growing Synthetic Data Through Differentially-Private Vine Copulas," Proceedings on Privacy Enhancing Technologies, Issue 3, pp. 122–141, 2021.
21. S. Hinterstoisser, V. Lepetit, P. Wohlhart, and K. Konolige, "On Pre-Trained Image Features and Synthetic Images for Deep Learning," in Proc. European Conf. on Computer Vision Workshops (ECCV-W), 2018, pp. 682–699.
22. Y. Zhang, H. Ling, J. Gao, K. Yin, J.-F. Lafleche, A. Barriuso, A. Torralba, and S. Fidler, "DatasetGAN: Efficient Labeled Data Factory with Minimal Human Effort," in Proc. IEEE/CVF Conf. on Computer Vision and Pattern Recognition (CVPR), 2021, pp. 10197–10207.
23. M. Heusel, H. Ramsauer, T. Unterthiner, B. Nessler, and S. Hochreiter, "GANs Trained by a Two Time-Scale Update Rule Converge to a Local Nash Equilibrium," in Advances in Neural Information Processing Systems, vol. 30, 2017, pp. 6626–6637.
24. D. Li, H. Ling, S. W. Kim, K. Kreis, A. Barriuso, S. Fidler, and A. Torralba, "BigDatasetGAN: Synthesizing ImageNet with Pixel-Wise Annotations," arXiv:2201.04684, 2022.
25. C. Yan, Z. Zhang, S. Nyemba, and Z. Li, "Generating Synthetic Electronic Health Record Data Using Generative Adversarial Networks: Tutorial," JMIR AI, vol. 3, 2024, e52615.
26. J. Jordon, J. Yoon, and M. van der Schaar, "PATE-GAN: Generating Synthetic Data with Differential Privacy Guarantees," in Proc. Int. Conf. on Learning Representations (ICLR) Workshops, 2019.
27. J. Kim, C. Lee, and N. Park, "STaSy: Score-Based Tabular Data Synthesis," in Proc. Int. Conf. on Learning Representations (ICLR), 2023.
28. H. Zhang, J. Zhang, Z. Shen, B. Srinivasan, X. Qin, C. Faloutsos, H. Rangwala, and G. Karypis, "Mixed-Type Tabular Data Synthesis with Score-Based Diffusion in Latent Space," in Proc. Int. Conf. on Learning Representations, 2024.
29. Z. Lin, S. Gopi, J. Kulkarni, H. Nori, and S. Yekhanin, "Differentially Private Synthetic Data via Foundation Model APIs," in Proc. Int. Conf. on Learning Representations, 2024.
30. M. Guillaudeux, O. Rousseau, J. Petot, Z. Bennis, C.-A. Dein, T. Goronflot, N. Vince, S. Limou, M. Karakachoff, M. Wargny, and P.-A. Gourraud, "Patient-Centric Synthetic Data Generation: No Reason to Risk Re-Identification in Biomedical Data Analysis," npj Digital Medicine, vol. 6, Article 37, 2023.
31. T. Liu, J. Fan, G. Li, N. Tang, and X. Du, "Tabular Data Synthesis with Generative Adversarial Networks: Design Space and Optimizations," The VLDB Journal, vol. 33, pp. 255–280, 2024.
32. N. Park, M. Mohammadi, K. Gorde, S. Jajodia, H. Park, and Y. Kim, "Data Synthesis Based on Generative Adversarial Networks," Proc. VLDB Endowment, vol. 11, no. 10, pp. 1071–1083, 2018.

Chapter 4
Trustworthy AI and Explainability

Abstract Trustworthy multimodal intelligent systems hold immense promise for enabling independent living among older adults, individuals with disabilities, and those managing chronic conditions. By integrating diverse data streams—such as motion sensors, audio inputs, environmental measurements, and wearable devices—these systems provide a comprehensive view of daily activities. Unlike single-sensor setups, multimodal approaches can capture more nuanced patterns, ensuring reliable event detection and personalized interventions without overburdening users or disrupting their usual routines. Establishing trust in such complex environments requires robust strategies to address privacy, transparency, and fairness. Because these systems operate in highly personal spaces, residents and caregivers need reassurance that their sensitive information will not be misused. One way to achieve this is by processing large portions of data locally, within edge-computing devices, which helps keep personal details off external servers. Additionally, synthetic data generation techniques support model development by simulating real-life patterns. This artificial data allows researchers to train algorithms on varied scenarios—like detecting falls or monitoring medication schedules—without exposing genuine, identifying information. Combined with strong encryption and access controls, these methods help preserve resident privacy while still providing accurate, data-driven insights. Multimodal inputs give rise to potent machine learning models capable of detailed behavior analysis, anomaly detection, and predictive analytics. For example, a system may integrate motion patterns from room sensors, heart-rate data from wearables, and acoustic signals from smart speakers. By synthesizing these signals, the system can more reliably detect events such as a fall, a sudden shift in routine, or signs of emotional distress. Furthermore, predictive analytics can forecast elevated health risks, giving residents and caregivers the opportunity to intervene proactively. Such anticipatory support offers real benefits, including early medical checks or personalized reminders that can prevent hospitalizations and maintain quality of life. Yet even the most accurate models will falter if they are perceived as opaque or prone to bias. Explainable AI (XAI) techniques can alleviate these concerns by revealing the factors behind an algorithm's suggestions or alerts. Residents and family members who understand how the system interprets sensor data are more likely to accept its recommendations and respond correctly. This transparency also shines a light on

© The Author(s), under exclusive license to Springer Nature Switzerland AG 2025

M. Z. Uddin, *Trustworthy Multimodal Intelligent Systems for Independent Living*, Cognitive Technologies, https://doi.org/10.1007/978-3-031-97359-8_4

possible biases, helping developers refine algorithms so they work equitably across varying health profiles, mobility levels, and cultural backgrounds. As part of a broader ethical approach, designers must also consider user autonomy, allowing residents to adjust the frequency or types of notifications and to override automated decisions when.

4.1 Introduction

Artificial Intelligence (AI) has rapidly become an integral part of modern technological advancements. It influences numerous fields, including healthcare, finance, transportation, and security. The increasing reliance on AI-driven decision-making has raised concerns regarding transparency, interpretability, and trustworthiness [1]. AI models, particularly deep learning systems, function as complex black-box mechanisms, making it difficult to understand how they derive conclusions. This lack of transparency presents a challenge when AI systems are deployed in critical areas where human lives and ethical considerations are involved. Figure 4.1 shows different branches and relation with machine learning components including XAI.

Explainable Artificial Intelligence (XAI) has emerged as a field dedicated to enhancing AI transparency and interpretability. The goal of XAI is to develop models that not only perform well but also provide justifiable and understandable results. The need for explainability becomes even more significant when AI models make decisions that directly affect individuals, such as medical diagnoses, financial loan approvals, and judicial sentencing recommendations [2–4]. The discussion highlights how AI's complexity has evolved, transitioning from traditional expert systems to sophisticated deep learning architectures. The balance between performance and interpretability is explored, along with the ethical and practical implications of opaque decision-making models.

Artificial Intelligence has undergone multiple phases of development. Early AI systems were based on symbolic reasoning and rule-based logic, where human experts explicitly defined decision-making processes. These systems were transparent and interpretable, allowing users to trace how conclusions were reached. However, their ability to handle large-scale, unstructured data was limited. With the advent of machine learning (ML) and deep learning (DL), AI models have achieved unprecedented accuracy and efficiency in solving complex tasks. Deep Neural Networks (DNNs) and ensemble learning methods have enabled breakthroughs in areas such as natural language processing, image recognition, and autonomous systems. Despite these advancements, the inherent complexity of these models makes them difficult to interpret. Unlike traditional rule-based AI, deep learning models operate through intricate mathematical transformations that are challenging to decipher [5, 6].

The shift toward data-driven AI has introduced black-box decision-making—a scenario where even AI developers struggle to explain why a model produces a particular output. This opacity raises several issues, including ethical concerns

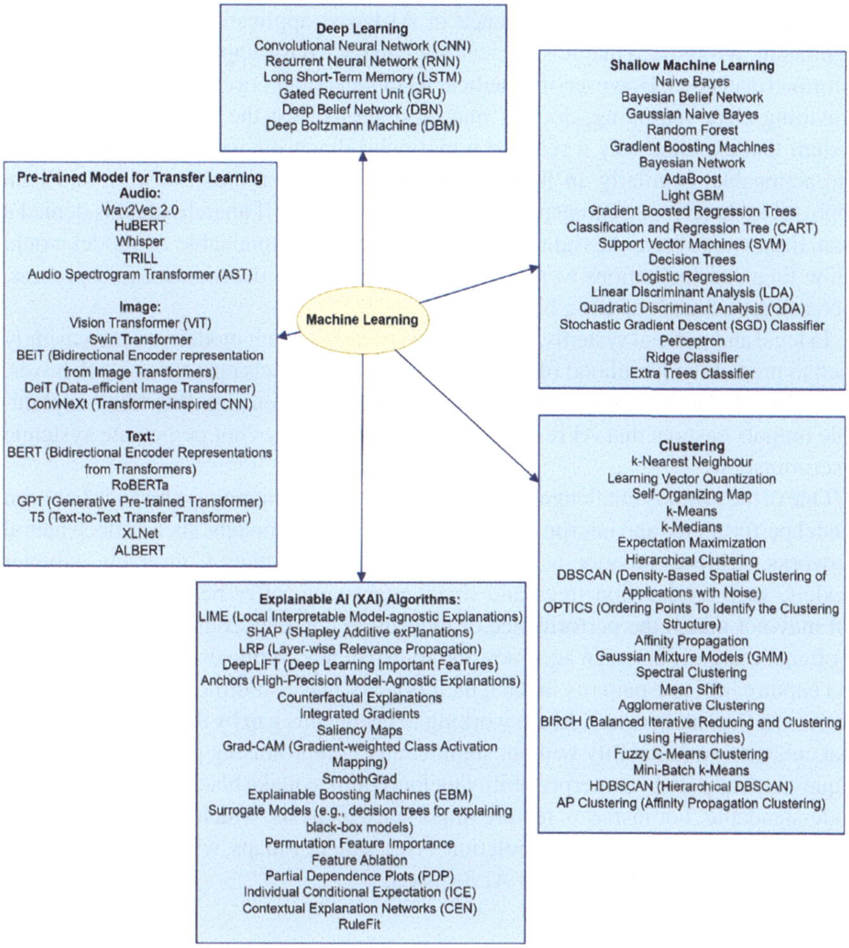

Fig. 4.1 Machine learning and XAI

regarding bias and fairness, regulatory challenges in ensuring AI compliance with laws and policies, trust deficits among users and stakeholders, and security risks related to adversarial attacks and data privacy.

4.1.1 The Importance of Explainability in AI

Explainability is a critical factor in ensuring AI's reliability, accountability, and fairness. When AI systems are applied in fields where human decisions have traditionally been the standard, it becomes essential to understand the reasoning behind their outputs. Lack of explainability can result in unjustified decisions, potential legal disputes, and loss of confidence in AI-based applications. For instance, in healthcare, AI-assisted diagnosis systems are expected to support doctors in making informed decisions. However, if a medical AI model predicts a certain disease without providing clear reasoning, doctors may hesitate to trust the result. A transparent system that explains why it reached a particular diagnosis would be more reliable and actionable. Similarly, in financial services, AI-driven credit scoring and loan approval systems require transparency to ensure fairness. If an individual is denied a loan, they should have the right to understand why. An explainable AI model would allow financial institutions to provide insights into their decision-making process, increasing trust and reducing biases.

In legal and judicial systems, AI-powered risk assessment models are increasingly used to predict the likelihood of reoffending. If these models operate as black boxes, they may reinforce existing biases, leading to unfair sentencing. Providing explainable outputs ensures that AI remains accountable and does not perpetuate systemic discrimination.

One of the primary challenges in AI development is maintaining a balance between model performance and interpretability. Highly complex models, such as deep neural networks, achieve superior accuracy but lack transparency. Conversely, simpler models, such as decision trees and linear regression, offer better interpretability but may not match the performance of their more complex counterparts [7]. There is often a trade-off between accuracy and transparency. While deep learning models can capture intricate patterns in data, their opacity makes it difficult to validate their decisions. Researchers in XAI are working to bridge this gap by developing methods that enhance explainability without significantly compromising performance. Techniques such as post-hoc interpretability methods aim to make black-box models more understandable. For instance, feature importance analysis, which identifies the most influential factors in a model's prediction. Also, saliency maps, which highlight areas of input data that contribute to an AI decision.

4.1.2 Ethical Considerations and Trust in AI

The ethical implications of AI decision-making have become a central concern in AI governance. Without transparency, AI systems risk propagating bias, discrimination, and social harm. The lack of interpretability can lead to algorithmic unfairness, where certain groups are disproportionately affected by AI-driven decisions.

For example, biased training data can result in discriminatory AI models. If an AI-based hiring system is trained on biased historical data, it may favor certain demographics while disadvantaging others. Transparency allows developers to detect and mitigate biases, ensuring fairer outcomes.

To promote responsible AI, organizations and regulatory bodies are advocating for explainability standards. The European Union's General Data Protection Regulation (GDPR) includes provisions for the right to explanation, requiring AI systems to provide justifiable reasoning for their decisions. Similar initiatives are being proposed in other countries to enforce accountability in AI systems [8]. Trust is a fundamental component of AI adoption. Users are more likely to embrace AI technologies when they understand and trust the decision-making process. In high-stakes applications such as autonomous driving, medical diagnosis, and cybersecurity, trust is paramount. If AI fails to justify its actions, users may reject its recommendations, even if they are statistically accurate.

Transparency and user-friendly explanations improve AI adoption. When users can question and verify AI decisions, they develop confidence in its reliability. This is especially important in business applications, where stakeholders need assurance that AI models align with organizational goals and ethical guidelines. The future of artificial intelligence (AI) hinges on enhancing explainability while maintaining efficiency and scalability. Key areas of focus include developing inherently interpretable models that offer transparency without compromising accuracy, standardizing evaluation metrics for explainability, and improving human-AI interaction through intuitive interfaces that allow users to understand and query AI decisions. Legal and policy frameworks must also evolve to ensure ethical compliance. As AI systems grow more complex, the need for transparency becomes increasingly critical. Explainability not only builds trust but also ensures fairness and alignment with human values. It is a foundational aspect of responsible and trustworthy AI. Addressing the challenges posed by opaque, black-box models is especially important in high-risk applications where interpretability is essential. Advancements in explainability research will shape the next generation of AI, and a collaborative effort among researchers, policymakers, and industry leaders is vital to embed transparency, fairness, and accountability into AI development. This section has introduced the significance of explainable AI (XAI) and set the stage for deeper exploration into its taxonomy, post-hoc techniques, and its role in responsible AI [9].

4.2 Taxonomy of Explainability in AI

Artificial Intelligence has transformed industries by providing advanced decision-making capabilities, but as AI models become more sophisticated, the ability to interpret their internal workings diminishes. This growing complexity raises significant concerns regarding transparency and accountability. Trustworthy AI must not only produce accurate predictions but also provide explanations that make its decisions understandable to humans [10]. Explainability, therefore, plays a crucial role in fostering trust, regulatory compliance, and ethical deployment of AI systems. A structured taxonomy of explainability is necessary to categorize different AI models and their varying levels of interpretability. By classifying AI models based on their transparency, it becomes easier to determine which systems can be directly understood and which require additional techniques to explain their behavior [7]. The need for a taxonomy arises from the diversity of AI models and their different levels of transparency. Some models, such as linear regression and decision trees, are inherently interpretable, meaning that their structure allows humans to trace the logic behind their predictions without requiring additional tools. Other models, such as deep neural networks and ensemble learning methods, function as black boxes, making it difficult to understand how they arrive at particular decisions. The distinction between these models is crucial, especially in applications where AI influences human lives, such as medical diagnosis, financial decision-making, and legal proceedings. Understanding how AI reaches its conclusions is essential for ensuring fairness and preventing biases from being embedded into automated systems. Figure 4.2 shows the taxonomy of XAI where different methods related to XAI is represented.

Explainability in AI can be categorized based on the level of transparency a model offers. Some models are designed with interpretability in mind, making it possible for users to understand their outputs without requiring post-hoc techniques. These models fall into the category of transparent AI systems, which provide clear and structured insights into their decision-making process. Transparent models can be further classified based on their interpretability, ranging from models that are simple enough for a human to simulate, to those that require some degree of decomposition to understand their internal components. The highest level of transparency is found in algorithmically transparent models, where every step in the decision-making process follows a mathematically well-defined structure that can be analyzed and verified.

Models that are easily simulated by humans are considered the most interpretable. These models allow users to manually follow their steps and replicate their decision-making process without external tools. For example, a small decision tree with a limited number of branches can be fully understood by simply following the conditions that lead to a particular outcome. However, as decision trees grow in size and complexity, they become harder to simulate manually, reducing their interpretability. In cases where a model is too complex to be simulated but can still be understood by analyzing its components, it is classified as decomposable. A decomposable model consists of input features, parameters, and calculations that can be independently examined, providing a structured way to understand its predictions. Linear regression models fall into this category because they explicitly define the relationship between input variables and outputs, allowing analysts to determine which features contribute most to the final prediction. Algorithmic transparency represents another category of explainability, where models follow clear mathematical principles that define how they operate. Bayesian networks and Generalized Additive Models belong to this group, as their decision-making processes are guided by well-established statistical relationships. While these models are transparent in terms of their underlying logic, they may still be challenging for non-experts to interpret without a technical understanding of probability theory and mathematical functions. Despite this challenge, algorithmically transparent models are valuable in applications where mathematical rigor is required to justify predictions.

While transparent models provide a foundation for explainable AI, they often lack the complexity needed to achieve high performance in real-world applications. This has led to the rise of black-box models, which prioritize predictive accuracy over interpretability. Deep neural networks, support vector machines, and ensemble learning models fall into this category, as their intricate architectures and large parameter spaces make them difficult to interpret. These models achieve exceptional results

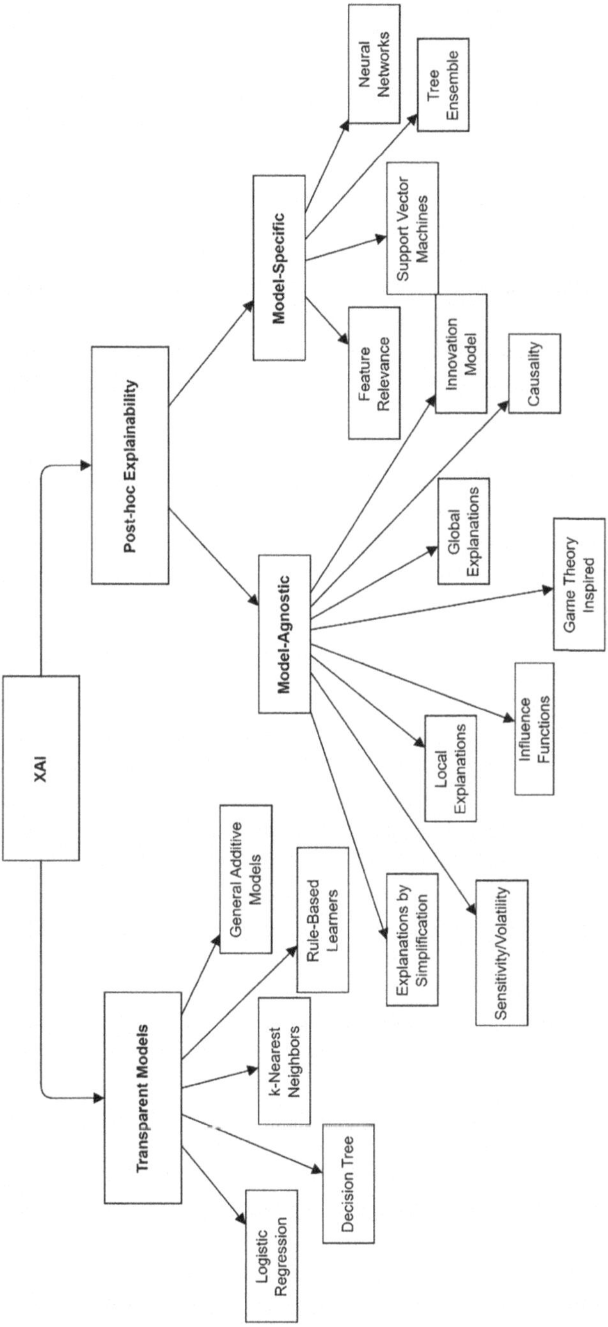

Fig. 4.2 Taxonomy of XAI

in tasks such as image recognition and natural language processing, but their decision-making processes remain opaque. In such cases, post-hoc explainability techniques become essential for extracting insights from these models. Post-hoc explainability methods aim to interpret the predictions of black-box models after they have been trained. These techniques help bridge the gap between high-performance AI and human interpretability by providing explanations for why a model made a particular decision. One common approach to post-hoc explainability involves simplifying a complex model by approximating it with a more interpretable one. Model simplification techniques create surrogate models that capture the general behavior of a black-box system while making it easier to understand. Local Interpretable Model-agnostic Explanations, commonly known as LIME, is one such technique that generates simplified models around individual predictions, allowing users to see which features influenced a particular decision. Decision tree approximation follows a similar approach by constructing an interpretable tree that mimics the behavior of a more complex AI model.

Another widely used post-hoc technique involves analyzing the importance of individual features in a model's decision-making process. Feature importance analysis identifies which input variables contribute most to a prediction, helping users understand the inner workings of an opaque AI system. The SHAP (Shapley Additive Explanations) method is a popular approach that assigns importance scores to features based on their contribution to a model's output. By quantifying how different features affect predictions, SHAP provides transparency into how an AI system weighs its inputs. Saliency maps are another method used in feature importance analysis, particularly in image classification tasks. These maps highlight the areas of an image that played a significant role in the model's decision, offering a visual representation of feature relevance. Local explanations provide another way to interpret black-box models by focusing on individual predictions rather than the entire system. Instead of attempting to explain an entire deep learning model, local explainability techniques generate insights for specific instances, making them particularly useful for complex models with non-linear decision boundaries. LIME is a prominent example of this approach, as it allows users to analyze the key factors influencing a single prediction without needing to understand the full model structure. Local explanations are valuable in applications where individual decisions need to be justified, such as loan approvals, medical diagnoses, or fraud detection.

Visual explanations enhance interpretability by presenting model outputs in a graphical format that highlights decision-making patterns. Some AI models, particularly in computer vision, can be interpreted through heatmaps and activation maps, which illustrate how different parts of an input influence the model's decision. Gradient-weighted Class Activation Mapping, or Grad-CAM, is a widely used technique that generates heatmaps to show which regions of an image were most important in making a classification. These visualizations provide intuitive explanations that make it easier to understand how neural networks process information. Explanation by examples is another approach to improving interpretability, where a model's decision is justified by referencing similar past cases. Case-based reasoning and K-Nearest Neighbors classification rely on example-based explanations, where predictions are made based on similarities to previously encountered instances. This approach is useful in domains such as medical diagnosis and legal decision-making, where human experts often rely on historical cases to support their reasoning.

While post-hoc explainability techniques provide valuable insights into black-box models, they do not fundamentally alter the opacity of the original system. As a result, researchers are exploring hybrid models that integrate transparency with high performance. These models aim to balance interpretability and accuracy by incorporating explainability mechanisms directly into their structure. Attention-based neural networks, for example, highlight important features during decision-making, allowing users to see which aspects of the input were most influential. Similarly, self-explaining models include built-in interpretability features that generate human-readable justifications for their predictions. The taxonomy of explainability in AI provides a structured approach to categorizing different levels of transparency and post-hoc techniques. Transparent models offer built-in interpretability but may lack the complexity required for high-performance applications. Opaque models achieve superior accuracy but require additional explainability methods to make their decisions understandable. The emergence of hybrid models represents a promising direction for AI development, as they seek to combine the strengths of both transparent and high-performance systems. By understanding this taxonomy, AI practitioners can make informed choices about which models to use in different contexts, ensuring that AI remains both effective and accountable in real-world applications.

4.3 Post-Hoc Explainability Techniques in AI

Artificial Intelligence has significantly advanced in recent years, with complex models such as deep learning architectures achieving remarkable accuracy in various tasks. However, as AI systems become more sophisticated, their decision-making processes grow more opaque, making it difficult for users to understand how predictions are made. This lack of transparency raises ethical, legal, and practical concerns, particularly in critical areas such as healthcare, finance, law enforcement, and autonomous systems. While inherently interpretable models provide some level of transparency, many high-performing AI systems, such as deep neural networks and ensemble models, require additional methods to make their inner workings understandable. Post-hoc explainability techniques address this challenge by providing insights into AI decision-making after the model has been trained and deployed [11–14].

Post-hoc explainability refers to the set of methods used to interpret and explain the predictions of black-box AI models. These techniques do not alter the underlying architecture of the model but instead provide external mechanisms to analyze and interpret how the model arrives at its conclusions. These methods help bridge the gap between accuracy and transparency, enabling users to gain trust in AI systems while maintaining their high performance. Post-hoc explainability techniques fall into several categories, including model simplification, feature importance analysis, local explanations, visual explanations, and explanation by example. Each of these approaches serves a specific purpose in improving AI transparency, allowing different stakeholders—such as researchers, developers, regulators, and end-users—to understand and trust AI-generated decisions. One of the most widely used post-hoc techniques is model simplification, which involves approximating a complex AI model with a more interpretable surrogate model. This approach provides a simplified representation of the black-box system while preserving its overall behavior. By creating a less complex model that mimics the original AI system's decision patterns, users can gain insights into how predictions are made. Local Interpretable Model-Agnostic Explanations (LIME) is a prominent model simplification technique that generates local approximations of an AI model. LIME creates a set of simplified models that explain how a black-box system makes predictions for specific instances. By perturbing input data and observing changes in predictions, LIME identifies the key features influencing a decision, allowing users to understand how the AI model behaves in different scenarios.

Another common approach to post-hoc explainability is feature importance analysis, which determines which input variables contribute most to a model's decisions. This method helps users identify the key factors that influence predictions, making it easier to interpret complex AI models. One of the most widely used feature importance techniques is SHapley Additive exPlanations (SHAP), which assigns importance scores to each feature based on its contribution to a model's output. SHAP is grounded in cooperative game theory and provides a mathematically sound way to quantify feature relevance. By analyzing feature importance scores, users can determine whether an AI model is making decisions based on meaningful and relevant information or if it is relying on spurious correlations in the data. This approach is particularly useful in applications such as medical diagnosis, credit scoring, and fraud detection, where understanding the factors influencing a decision is essential for ensuring fairness and accountability.

Local explanations provide another method for interpreting AI decisions by focusing on individual predictions rather than the entire model. Instead of attempting to explain how an AI system works as a whole, local explainability techniques generate insights for specific instances. LIME is an example of a local explanation method, as it provides instance-specific justifications for AI predictions. Another popular technique for local explanations is Counterfactual Explanations, which provides alternative scenarios where an AI model's decision would have changed. For example, in a loan approval system, a counterfactual explanation might indicate that if a person had a slightly higher income or better credit score, their loan application would have been accepted. These explanations help users understand what factors are influencing AI decisions and what changes could lead to different outcomes. Local explanations are particularly valuable in high-stakes applications where individual decisions need to be justified, such as hiring, legal rulings, and medical diagnoses. Visual explanations offer another way to interpret AI models by presenting explanations in a graphical format. This approach is especially useful for deep learning models used in image and text processing, where complex patterns and relationships are difficult to articulate in purely numerical or textual terms. Visualizations help users understand how AI models process data and highlight the key areas that influence their decisions. One of the most popular visual explanation techniques is Gradient-weighted Class Activation Mapping (Grad-CAM), which is used in convolutional neural networks (CNNs) for image classification tasks. Grad-CAM generates heatmaps that show which regions of an image were most influential in determining a classification. These visualizations provide intuitive insights into how deep learning models interpret images, making it easier to identify potential biases or errors in the model. Similarly, attention maps are used in natural language processing (NLP) models to highlight important words or phrases that contribute to AI-generated text classifications. These visual explanations help improve transparency in deep learning applications, making AI systems more interpretable for both experts and non-experts.

Another important post-hoc explainability technique is explanation by example, which provides insights into AI decisions by referencing similar past cases. This method is particularly useful in case-based reasoning systems, where predictions are made based on previously observed instances. K-Nearest Neighbors (KNN) is a classic example of an AI model that relies on example-based explanations, as it classifies new data points based on their similarity to existing cases. In medical diagnosis, explanation by example can be used to show similar patient cases that led to a particular diagnosis, allowing doctors to compare and validate AI-generated predictions. In legal applications, AI models that assist in case law analysis can provide similar past rulings to justify recommendations. Explanation by example is an intuitive way to enhance interpretability, as it aligns with human decision-making processes that often rely on analogies and past experiences. While post-hoc explainability techniques provide valuable insights into black-box models, they have certain limitations. These methods do not fundamentally alter the opacity of the original AI system; rather, they offer approximations and interpretations of its behavior. In some cases, post-hoc explanations may not fully capture the complexity of the AI model, leading to potential oversimplifications or misleading interpretations. Additionally, post-hoc techniques may not always be applicable across all types of AI models, requiring customized approaches for different architectures. Despite these challenges, post-hoc explainability remains an essential tool for improving AI transparency and trustworthiness.

As AI continues to advance, researchers are exploring new ways to enhance explainability while maintaining high performance. Hybrid models that integrate interpretability into AI architectures from the outset are gaining attention as a promising solution. These models combine the strengths of both transparent and high-performance systems, ensuring that AI remains both effective and accountable. Self-explaining AI models are being developed to provide built-in justifications for their predictions, reducing the need for external explainability techniques. Attention-based neural networks, for example, highlight the most important features during decision-making, allowing users to see which aspects of the input were most influential. These advancements represent a shift toward making AI systems more interpretable by design, reducing reliance on post-hoc methods.

The development of post-hoc explainability techniques has played a crucial role in making AI more transparent and understandable. These methods help bridge the gap between complex black-box models and human interpretability, ensuring that AI systems can be trusted in real-world applications. As the demand for explainability grows, ongoing research in this field will continue to refine and improve these techniques, making AI systems more accountable, fair, and ethically responsible. By combining post-hoc methods with advancements in inherently interpretable AI, the future of AI explainability is poised to evolve in a way that balances both performance and transparency, fostering greater trust and confidence in artificial intelligence.

4.4 Transparent Machine Learning Models

Artificial Intelligence is increasingly influencing key sectors such as healthcare, finance, and governance. As AI systems make decisions that impact human lives, the ability to understand and trust these decisions becomes paramount. While many advanced AI models function as black boxes, making it difficult to interpret their internal mechanisms, there exists another category of models known as transparent machine learning models, which are designed to be inherently interpretable. These models provide direct insights into their decision-making process, making them preferable in applications where accountability and transparency are critical. Transparent models allow users to trace and justify AI predictions without requiring additional post-hoc explanations. These models differ significantly from black-box models in that their structure and reasoning can be understood directly by examining their parameters, decision rules, and relationships between input features and outputs. Transparency ensures that users, regulators, and domain experts can verify predictions, detect biases, and validate AI-driven conclusions, making these models a cornerstone of trustworthy AI [7].

Unlike deep learning models, which consist of multiple layers of interconnected neurons that transform data through non-linear operations, transparent models rely on simpler mathematical structures that are more aligned with human reasoning. These models include linear regression, decision trees, rule-based systems, K-Nearest Neighbors (KNN), Bayesian models, and Generalized Additive Models (GAMs). Each of these models offers varying degrees of interpretability, and their applicability depends on the complexity of the task and the requirement for human understanding.

4.4.1 Linear and Logistic Regression

Linear regression is one of the simplest and most interpretable machine learning models, making it a preferred choice in applications where explainability is a priority. It establishes a direct relationship between input features and the predicted outcome by assigning weights to each feature. The coefficients of a linear regression model indicate how much a change in one variable affects the predicted result, making it easy to interpret the influence of different factors. This level of transparency allows researchers, policymakers, and practitioners to clearly understand the relationships between variables and make informed decisions.

Logistic regression extends this concept to classification tasks, where the outcome is categorical rather than continuous. Although the mathematical formulation of logistic regression involves a transformation function (sigmoid), the weights assigned to the features remain interpretable. A higher weight indicates a stronger influence of a particular variable on the probability of a certain class being predicted. This interpretability makes logistic regression widely used in fields such as medicine, where AI models are expected to provide understandable predictions. For example, a logistic regression model used to predict the likelihood of heart disease can indicate whether factors like cholesterol levels, age, and blood pressure significantly contribute to the risk assessment.

However, while linear and logistic regression models offer transparency, they have limitations. Their simplicity means they struggle with capturing complex, non-linear relationships between variables. This trade-off between interpretability and predictive power is one reason why more sophisticated AI models have become dominant in machine learning. Nonetheless, in many real-world applications where understanding the rationale behind predictions is more important than achieving the highest possible accuracy, regression models remain a crucial tool.

4.4.2 Decision Trees: Hierarchical Transparency

Decision trees are another class of inherently interpretable models that offer a structured, hierarchical approach to decision-making. A decision tree consists of nodes that represent decisions based on input features, leading to different possible outcomes. The tree structure enables a step-by-step explanation of how a prediction is made, allowing users to follow the path taken from input to output. The appeal of decision trees lies in their intuitive representation of AI logic. Unlike neural networks, which transform input data through multiple hidden layers, decision trees make explicit, human-readable choices at each step. For instance, a decision tree used in a loan approval system may have branches representing conditions such as credit score, annual income, and debt-to-income ratio. Each applicant's profile follows a clear path, leading to an approval or rejection decision. This level of interpretability makes decision trees an essential tool in applications where transparency and regulatory compliance are key concerns. Despite their strengths, decision trees have limitations. They can become overly complex when dealing with large datasets, leading to what is known as overfitting—a situation where the model captures noise rather than meaningful patterns. When a decision tree grows too deep, it loses its interpretability, making it difficult for users to understand all the decision rules involved. To mitigate this, techniques such as pruning are used to reduce tree complexity while retaining its interpretability. While single decision trees are transparent, combining multiple trees in ensemble methods—such as Random Forests or Gradient Boosting—reduces interpretability. Ensemble methods increase accuracy but make the model less explainable, as decisions are based on the aggregated outputs of numerous trees. Therefore, while decision trees remain an excellent choice for transparent AI, they must be used carefully to balance interpretability and performance.

4.4.3 Rule-Based Learning: Explicit Decision Logic in AI

Rule-based models represent another category of interpretable AI systems, where decisions are made based on explicitly defined rules. These models operate by applying if–then conditions to input data, generating an easily understandable reasoning process. Rule-based learning is commonly used in expert systems and domains where human-like decision-making is needed. Fuzzy rule-based systems extend this approach by allowing partial truth values rather than rigid yes/no conditions. This flexibility improves interpretability while maintaining a structured decision-making process. For example, a medical diagnosis system using rule-based AI may operate under conditions like "If blood pressure is high and cholesterol level is above a certain threshold, then the risk of cardiovascular disease is high." These kinds of models align closely with human reasoning, making them valuable in applications where transparency is non-negotiable. However, rule-based models face limitations when handling large datasets with numerous variables. As the number of rules increases, interpretability decreases, making it harder to understand the entire system. This is particularly problematic in complex AI applications where multiple factors interact in non-trivial ways. Nonetheless, in scenarios where AI-driven decisions require explicit justification, rule-based models remain a strong choice.

4.4.4 K-Nearest Neighbors (KNN): Instance-Based Interpretability

K-Nearest Neighbors (KNN) is a simple and interpretable model that classifies new data points based on their similarity to existing instances. Unlike models that learn patterns through complex transformations, KNN stores all training examples and makes predictions by comparing new inputs to their nearest neighbors in the dataset. The interpretability of KNN stems from its intuitive decision-making process. If a new input is classified as belonging to a particular category, users can examine its nearest neighbors to understand why the decision was made. For example, in a medical AI system, if a patient is diagnosed with a particular disease, doctors can look at past cases with similar symptoms and test results to justify the diagnosis. Despite its transparency, KNN has weaknesses. Its performance depends heavily on the choice of distance metric and the number of neighbors considered. Additionally, as the dataset size increases, KNN becomes computationally expensive, limiting its scalability. Nevertheless, its reliance on similarity-based reasoning makes it a valuable tool in fields where example-based explanations are required.

4.4.5 *Bayesian Models and Generalized Additive Models (GAMs): Statistical Transparency*

Bayesian models use probability distributions to represent uncertainty in decision-making. They provide explicit insights into how confident the model is about its predictions, making them useful in scenarios where uncertainty quantification is crucial. For example, in medical decision support systems, Bayesian models can estimate the probability that a patient has a particular disease based on prior knowledge and new test results. Generalized Additive Models (GAMs) offer another interpretable AI approach by combining multiple predictive features in an additive manner. Unlike standard linear regression, GAMs allow each feature to contribute non-linearly to the final prediction while maintaining a structure that remains easy to interpret. These models are widely used in finance, environmental science, and risk assessment, where decision-makers need clear justifications for AI-driven insights.

4.5 Challenges in Explainable AI

As artificial intelligence (AI) continues to shape decision-making in critical sectors, the demand for transparency and interpretability has grown significantly. From healthcare and finance to criminal justice and autonomous systems, the impact of AI-driven decisions underscores the importance of understanding how these systems function. Despite advancements in explainability techniques, key obstacles remain in making AI systems not only interpretable but also reliable, fair, and consistent with human values. These difficulties often arise from the complexity of machine learning models, the tension between model accuracy and clarity, the absence of standardized evaluation frameworks, and broader ethical concerns related to AI's role in society. Additionally, achieving explainability is complicated by the need to address other important factors such as user privacy, data security, and system transparency. Overcoming these issues is essential for building AI systems that are trustworthy, responsible, and aligned with societal interests [15].

One of the core tensions in explainable AI lies in the trade-off between performance and interpretability. Advanced models, particularly deep neural networks, have achieved remarkable results in fields like image classification, language modeling, and medical diagnostics. However, these models often function as "black boxes"—their internal decision processes are not easily accessible or understandable to users. Conversely, models designed for interpretability—such as decision trees, linear models, or rule-based approaches—offer clear reasoning but may fall short in predictive performance. This ongoing dilemma raises the question: should AI systems prioritize interpretability or accuracy? To address this, researchers have proposed hybrid strategies that aim to introduce interpretability into high-performance models. These include techniques like simplifying neural architectures, applying attention mechanisms, using feature attribution methods, and developing visualization tools that clarify how decisions are made. Still, a fully interpretable and highly accurate AI model remains an open challenge in the field.

Another major issue in the explainability landscape is the lack of a universally accepted definition of what it means for an AI system to be explainable. Different stakeholders bring different expectations: for instance, a physician may need a detailed rationale behind an AI-generated diagnosis, whereas a developer may focus on the mathematical significance of features or weight distributions [16]. This diversity in needs complicates efforts to create consistent evaluation standards. Some explanations might be technically correct but too complex for end-users to grasp, while others might be overly simplified, omitting critical reasoning steps. Without a shared framework or set of criteria for evaluating explainability, ensuring that AI systems are genuinely transparent and accountable across contexts remains a difficult task.

4.5.1 *Bias and Fairness in AI Decision-Making*

Bias in AI models remains a significant challenge, even in explainable AI systems. Many machine learning models are trained on historical data that may contain unintended biases. If these biases are not identified and corrected, AI systems can reinforce existing inequalities and make unfair decisions. For example, in the financial sector, AI-based credit scoring models might discriminate against certain demographics if the training data reflects historical biases in loan approvals. Similarly, in hiring processes, AI-powered recruitment tools may favor certain groups over others, reflecting past discriminatory hiring practices.

4.5.2 *Human-Centered Explainability: Making AI Understandable for All Users*

Another challenge in explainable AI is ensuring that explanations are accessible and understandable to different types of users. AI systems serve diverse audiences, including technical experts, domain professionals, regulators, and general users, each of whom requires a different level of explanation. For example, a doctor using AI-assisted medical diagnosis software may need an explanation that aligns with their clinical expertise, while a patient receiving an AI-generated diagnosis may require a simplified, easy-to-understand rationale. Similarly, a financial analyst may need detailed feature importance scores when evaluating AI-driven investment decisions, while a customer applying for a loan may want a clear, non-technical explanation of why they were approved or denied. Many current explainability methods focus on technical justifications rather than human-centered explanations. Achieving human-centered AI explainability requires designing customized explanations based on the knowledge level of the user, ensuring that AI explanations are intuitive and aligned with human reasoning, and allowing users to interact with AI explanations—such as by adjusting input parameters and observing changes in predictions [17]. Developing AI systems that provide clear, relevant, and actionable explanations for different audiences remains a major challenge. Future advancements in explainable AI must prioritize user-centered design principles to make AI explanations more meaningful.

4.5.3 Privacy and Security Concerns in Explainable AI

While transparency is essential for trustworthy AI, it must be balanced with privacy and security considerations. Some explainability techniques, such as feature attribution and model inversion methods, can unintentionally expose sensitive information about the underlying dataset. This raises concerns about data privacy, confidentiality, and adversarial attacks. For example, if an AI model used in healthcare provides overly detailed explanations about individual patient data, it could lead to privacy violations under regulations such as the General Data Protection Regulation (GDPR). Similarly, in financial applications, revealing too much information about an AI model's decision-making process could allow malicious actors to manipulate predictions for fraudulent activities. Explainability methods must be designed to provide sufficient transparency without compromising privacy or security. Some approaches to addressing this challenge include differential privacy, which ensures that explanations do not reveal specific details about individual data points; federated learning, which allows AI models to be trained without exposing raw data; and secure model-sharing techniques, which prevent adversaries from exploiting AI explanations to manipulate predictions. Balancing explainability, privacy, and security remains an ongoing challenge in the development of AI systems.

4.5.4 Regulatory and Legal Challenges in Explainable AI

Governments and regulatory bodies are increasingly emphasizing the need for explainable AI, particularly in high-risk applications where decisions can have significant consequences for individuals and society. Regulations such as the European Union's General Data Protection Regulation (GDPR) and the proposed Artificial Intelligence Act explicitly require AI systems to provide clear, understandable justifications for automated decisions [18]. Similar legal frameworks are also emerging in other regions around the world, setting expectations for fair, accountable, and transparent AI technologies. These developments reflect a growing recognition that the benefits of AI must be balanced with safeguards that protect human rights and uphold ethical standards.

However, enforcing these regulations presents substantial challenges due to the absence of universally accepted guidelines on how explainability should be operationalized in practice. Many organizations, especially those working at the cutting edge of AI innovation, struggle to comply with transparency requirements while preserving the efficiency, accuracy, and competitiveness of their AI systems. Additionally, the legal landscape for AI governance remains fragmented, with variations in regulatory approaches between countries and regions making it difficult to establish a coherent global standard for explainable AI. To effectively navigate this complex regulatory environment, organizations must take proactive steps, including the development of internal AI governance policies that explicitly prioritize explainability and accountability. They should adopt best practices for transparent AI development, such as thorough documentation, algorithmic audits, and user-centric design. Furthermore, meaningful collaboration with regulators, academic researchers, and industry leaders is essential to help shape evolving AI policies that strike the right balance between fostering innovation and ensuring public trust and safety. Despite significant progress in the field of explainable AI, numerous technical, legal, and ethical challenges remain in making AI systems genuinely transparent, fair, and accountable. Key obstacles include the ongoing tension between model accuracy and interpretability, the complexity of defining and measuring explainability, the persistence of algorithmic bias, and the critical need for explanations that are understandable and useful to human users. Moreover, the difficulty of balancing transparency with data privacy and security, while also managing the intricacies of emerging legal frameworks, adds further layers of complexity.

4.6 Responsible AI—Ethical and Practical Considerations

Artificial Intelligence (AI) has become deeply integrated into modern technologies, driving advancements across sectors such as healthcare, finance, education, and autonomous systems. As AI increasingly takes on roles that influence human well-being, there is growing concern over whether these systems operate in ways that align with ethical norms and societal expectations. In response, the concept of Responsible AI has gained prominence as a framework aimed at ensuring that AI technologies are created, implemented, and managed with a strong emphasis on ethical conduct, fairness, and accountability. This approach goes beyond optimizing for performance and accuracy—it also promotes core values like transparency, privacy, security, inclusivity, and social impact. The overarching goal is to develop AI systems that benefit society while avoiding the perpetuation of biases, unfair treatment, or unintended harm. Despite its importance, realizing Responsible AI in practice is complex. It involves addressing tensions between competing goals—for example, maximizing model accuracy without compromising fairness, complying with evolving regulatory landscapes, and embedding human values into algorithmic decision-making. This section delves into both the ethical imperatives and the practical challenges of Responsible AI, offering insights into how developers, institutions, and policymakers can work together to foster AI systems that are trustworthy, equitable, and aligned with the public good.

4.6.1 The Principles of Responsible AI

Developing Responsible AI requires adhering to a set of ethical guidelines that define how AI systems should operate. These principles guide AI development to ensure that models remain aligned with human rights, societal expectations, and regulatory standards. One of the core principles of Responsible AI is fairness, which ensures that AI models do not discriminate against individuals or groups based on factors such as race, gender, socioeconomic status, or disability. AI systems trained on biased data can unintentionally reinforce historical inequalities, leading to unfair outcomes in applications such as hiring, loan approvals, and law enforcement. Ensuring fairness in AI requires rigorous data auditing, bias mitigation techniques, and fairness-aware algorithms that detect and correct discriminatory patterns [19].

Another key principle is transparency, which ensures that AI decision-making is understandable and explainable. Transparency allows users to trust AI predictions, verify their validity, and challenge them when necessary. Explainable AI techniques play a crucial role in enhancing transparency by providing insights into how models arrive at their decisions. Organizations must design AI systems that provide clear explanations to stakeholders, including end-users, regulators, and industry professionals, ensuring that AI-driven decisions can be scrutinized and justified.

Accountability is another essential component of Responsible AI. When AI systems make errors or cause unintended harm, determining who is responsible can be challenging. Unlike traditional decision-making processes where humans are accountable, AI-driven decisions often involve complex algorithms and multiple stakeholders. Establishing clear accountability frameworks ensures that organizations take responsibility for their AI systems' outcomes. This includes setting up audit mechanisms, monitoring AI behavior over time, and establishing ethical AI governance committees to oversee AI implementations.

Finally, robustness and safety are critical for ensuring that AI systems function reliably in different environments. AI models can be vulnerable to adversarial attacks, where malicious actors manipulate inputs to deceive the system. Ensuring AI robustness involves rigorous testing, adversarial defense strategies, and continuous monitoring to detect and prevent vulnerabilities.

4.6.2 Fairness and Bias Mitigation in AI Systems

Fairness is one of the most challenging aspects of Responsible AI, as AI models learn patterns from historical data, which may contain societal biases and inequalities. If AI systems are trained on biased datasets, they can replicate and amplify existing prejudices, leading to unfair treatment of certain individuals or groups [20]. For example, hiring algorithms trained on past recruitment data may favor candidates from privileged backgrounds, reinforcing discrimination against marginalized communities.

Addressing bias in AI requires a multi-step approach that begins with ensuring that training data is diverse and representative of the population it serves. This involves conducting data audits to identify potential biases, removing discriminatory patterns, and balancing datasets to prevent certain groups from being underrepresented. Researchers have developed fairness-aware machine learning techniques that modify AI models to produce equitable predictions, ensuring that outcomes do not disproportionately favor or disadvantage specific groups. In addition to technical solutions, fairness in AI also involves ethical decision-making. Organizations must establish AI ethics guidelines and review processes to evaluate whether their AI systems align with fairness principles. This includes engaging ethicists, policymakers, and community representatives in AI design discussions to incorporate diverse perspectives. A responsible approach to AI fairness also involves transparency in AI audits, where organizations disclose potential biases and outline their strategies for addressing them.

Despite advancements in bias detection and fairness-aware algorithms, achieving perfectly fair AI remains an ongoing challenge. Fairness is often context-dependent, and different definitions of fairness may apply in different scenarios. For example, in credit scoring, should AI ensure equal outcomes for all applicants, or should it provide equal opportunities while allowing differences in creditworthiness? These ethical dilemmas highlight the complexity of fairness in AI and the need for continuous refinement of fairness frameworks.

4.6.3 Transparency and Explainability in Responsible AI

Transparency is a fundamental principle of Responsible AI, as it enables users to understand, trust, and verify AI decisions. A lack of transparency can lead to skepticism, particularly when AI is used in high-stakes applications such as healthcare, finance, and criminal justice. Ensuring that AI systems provide clear and comprehensible explanations is essential for gaining public trust and regulatory approval [21]. One of the key strategies for improving transparency is the adoption of XAI techniques that allow users to interpret model predictions. Different AI models offer varying levels of transparency. Decision trees, rule-based models, and linear regression provide built-in interpretability, while deep neural networks and ensemble learning methods require post-hoc explainability techniques, such as feature importance analysis, counterfactual explanations, and visualization methods.

Beyond technical transparency, organizations must also prioritize communication transparency, where AI decisions are explained in a way that is understandable to different stakeholders. AI explanations should be tailored to the needs of the audience, whether they are technical experts, business leaders, or general users. A doctor using an AI-powered diagnostic tool may require a detailed breakdown of which medical factors influenced a diagnosis, while a patient receiving the same diagnosis may need a simplified explanation that reassures them about the decision-making process. Transparency also plays a crucial role in regulatory compliance, as governments and legal institutions increasingly demand AI systems to provide explanations for automated decisions. Laws such as the General Data Protection Regulation (GDPR) in the European Union include provisions for the "right to explanation," requiring organizations to provide justifications for AI-driven decisions that affect individuals. AI developers must ensure that their models comply with these legal standards while maintaining ethical AI practices.

4.6.4 Accountability in AI Development and Deployment

AI accountability refers to the responsibility of organizations and developers in ensuring that AI systems function correctly and ethically. When AI models make incorrect predictions, cause harm, or exhibit biased behavior, determining responsibility becomes complex. Unlike traditional decision-making, where human accountability is clear, AI-driven decisions involve multiple stakeholders, including AI developers, data scientists, business leaders, and policymakers.

To ensure accountability, organizations must establish AI governance structures that oversee AI design, deployment, and monitoring. AI ethics committees, regulatory bodies, and industry standards can help enforce responsible AI practices and ensure that AI systems remain aligned with ethical principles. Algorithmic auditing is another essential aspect of accountability, where independent reviewers assess AI models for fairness, bias, and transparency. Organizations should also implement AI monitoring mechanisms to continuously track model performance. AI models evolve over time as they encounter new data, which means they can develop biases or unintended consequences. Regular audits and performance assessments help detect potential risks and adjust models accordingly.

Responsible AI is essential for ensuring that artificial intelligence is used ethically, fairly, and transparently. By prioritizing principles such as fairness, accountability, transparency, privacy, and robustness, organizations can develop AI systems that align with human values and societal expectations. While challenges remain in balancing accuracy with interpretability, mitigating bias, and maintaining regulatory compliance, continuous efforts in ethical AI research, fairness-aware algorithms, and AI governance frameworks will help shape AI technologies that are both powerful and responsible. Moving forward, collaboration between researchers, policymakers, industry leaders, and the public will be crucial in ensuring that AI remains a force for good in society.

4.7 The Focus in Explainable and Trustworthy AI

Artificial intelligence has made remarkable advancements, transforming industries and influencing decision-making in areas such as healthcare, finance, law enforcement, and autonomous systems. As AI becomes more integrated into society, ensuring that these systems are both explainable and trustworthy remains one of the most significant challenges in the field. Despite ongoing research and improvements, current methods for explainability still face limitations in scalability, accuracy, and usability. Additionally, ethical concerns surrounding fairness, accountability, and transparency continue to pose challenges for AI adoption.

Looking ahead, the future of Explainable AI (XAI) and Trustworthy AI will require continued research, technological innovation, and regulatory development. Advances in human-centered explainability, hybrid interpretability models, standardization of explainability metrics, and AI governance will shape the next generation of responsible AI systems. This section explores emerging trends, potential solutions, and key areas of focus in the future of XAI, with the goal of ensuring that AI remains transparent, ethical, and aligned with human values.

4.7.1 Advancing Human-Centered Explainability

One of the most promising directions in AI research is the development of human-centered explainability, which aims to make AI systems more understandable and useful for different audiences. Current explainability methods often focus on technical interpretations that may be meaningful to data scientists but not to end-users, decision-makers, or the general public. The challenge lies in bridging the gap between complex AI models and human reasoning, ensuring that explanations are accessible to diverse stakeholders. Future advancements in XAI will focus on customized and adaptive explanations, where AI systems provide different levels of interpretability depending on the user's expertise and needs. For example, a medical AI tool could offer detailed mathematical justifications for a data scientist while presenting simplified, intuitive explanations for a doctor making a clinical decision [22]. Similarly, an AI-powered financial system might provide a feature importance breakdown for analysts, while offering a plain-language summary for customers applying for loans.

Another key area of research is interactive AI explainability, where users can engage with explanations in a more dynamic way. Instead of receiving a static explanation, future AI systems could allow users to ask questions, explore different scenarios, and receive counterfactual explanations. For instance, an AI-driven hiring tool could explain why a particular candidate was not selected and offer insights into what changes would have resulted in a different outcome. This interactive approach to explainability will enhance trust and give users greater control over AI-assisted decision-making. Furthermore, multimodal explanations are gaining attention as a way to present AI explanations in more engaging and accessible formats. Instead of relying solely on text-based outputs, AI systems could leverage visualizations, audio narratives, and real-time feedback mechanisms to improve clarity. For example, AI-generated heatmaps, graphs, and voice-assisted explanations could provide users with a richer, more understandable overview of AI decision-making.

4.7.2 Hybrid Models: Integrating Transparency with Performance

As AI researchers strive to balance model interpretability and predictive accuracy, hybrid AI models are emerging as a potential solution. Traditional AI models often force a trade-off: simple models are more explainable but less accurate, while complex models are more accurate but difficult to interpret. Future advancements will focus on integrating explainability directly into deep learning architectures, reducing the need for post-hoc explanation methods. One promising approach involves self-explaining AI models, which embed interpretability into the AI system itself rather than relying on external tools to provide explanations. These models are designed to generate explanations alongside their predictions, ensuring that decision-making remains transparent throughout the process. Examples include attention-based neural networks, inherently interpretable deep learning architectures, and structured decision frameworks that provide built-in justifications.

Another area of innovation is the development of neurosymbolic AI, which combines deep learning with symbolic reasoning. Traditional deep learning models excel at pattern recognition but struggle with logical reasoning, while symbolic AI offers explicit rule-based decision-making but lacks adaptability. By merging these two approaches, AI systems can achieve both high accuracy and explainability, allowing them to reason like humans while remaining accountable. Additionally, causal AI models are being explored as a way to move beyond traditional statistical correlations. Instead of simply identifying patterns in data, future AI systems will be designed to understand cause-and-effect relationships, making their decisions more logical and interpretable. For example, in healthcare, a causal AI system could explain not only which symptoms correlate with a disease but also why certain risk factors lead to the development of that condition.

4.7.3 Standardizing Explainability Metrics and Evaluation Frameworks

A major challenge in the field of XAI is the lack of standardized metrics and evaluation frameworks for assessing explainability. Different AI models use different explainability techniques, making it difficult to compare their transparency levels objectively. Some explanations focus on feature importance, while others provide rule-based insights or counterfactual reasoning. Without a unified evaluation standard, determining which explainability method is the most effective remains challenging. AI researchers and regulatory bodies should work toward developing standardized benchmarks for explainability, ensuring that AI models are assessed based on clear, measurable criteria [23]. These standards may include: Quantitative explainability scores that evaluate the clarity, completeness, and coherence of AI explanations; User-centered metrics that measure how well end-users understand AI-generated explanations; Trustworthiness indices that assess the ethical and social implications of AI transparency.

4.7.4 Regulatory Developments and AI Governance

As AI adoption expands, government regulations and ethical guidelines will play an increasingly important role in shaping the future of XAI. Many policymakers are already developing legal frameworks that mandate AI transparency, fairness, and accountability, particularly in sensitive applications such as law enforcement, hiring, credit scoring, and healthcare [24]. The European Union's Artificial Intelligence Act, for example, categorizes AI systems into different risk levels and imposes strict explainability requirements on high-risk AI applications. Similarly, the General Data Protection Regulation (GDPR) enforces the "right to explanation," ensuring that individuals have access to justifications for AI-driven decisions that affect them. Other regions, including the United States, Canada, and China, are also developing AI policies that emphasize transparency and ethical considerations. In the coming years, AI governance frameworks will become more structured, requiring organizations to conduct regular AI audits, document their explainability processes, and comply with ethical AI standards. Regulatory agencies will likely establish AI oversight bodies, similar to existing financial regulatory authorities, to monitor AI systems and enforce responsible practices.

4.7.5 The Role of AI and Human Collaboration

As AI continues to evolve, its role in decision-making will shift toward collaborative intelligence, where AI and humans work together rather than AI replacing human decision-making entirely. Instead of operating as autonomous black-box systems, future AI models will function as assistive tools, providing insights and recommendations while allowing humans to retain control and oversight [25]. The future of AI explainability will focus on designing AI systems that enhance human judgment rather than replacing it. Human-in-the-loop AI models will become more common, where AI assists professionals—such as doctors, financial analysts, and legal experts—by offering explanations that complement human expertise. AI systems will provide recommendations, while humans make the final decisions based on a combination of data-driven insights and ethical considerations. Additionally, education and training programs will be essential in teaching professionals how to interpret AI explanations effectively. As AI becomes more prevalent in various industries, professionals must develop AI literacy skills, enabling them to critically assess AI-driven insights and ensure ethical decision-making.

4.8 Conclusion

Artificial intelligence has become a driving force in various industries, offering solutions that improve efficiency, accuracy, and decision-making. However, as AI continues to evolve, ensuring that it remains transparent, explainable, and responsible has become a critical challenge. AI models, particularly deep learning systems, often operate as black boxes, making it difficult to understand their decision-making processes. This lack of interpretability raises concerns about trust, fairness, accountability, and ethical implications in AI-driven decisions. Explainable AI (XAI) has emerged as a solution to this challenge, aiming to make AI systems more understandable and trustworthy. By providing insights into how AI models arrive at their conclusions, XAI enhances user confidence and regulatory compliance. The taxonomy of explainability categorizes AI models based on their level of transparency, distinguishing between inherently interpretable models (such as decision trees and linear regression) and black-box models that require post-hoc explainability techniques. Transparent models allow users to directly understand how decisions are made, while more complex models require explanations through feature importance analysis, local explanations, visualizations, and rule-based simplifications. Despite advancements in explainability methods, several challenges remain. The trade-off between accuracy and interpretability continues to be a major issue, as more interpretable models may lack the predictive power of black-box models. Developing fairness-aware AI requires bias detection, data auditing, and fairness-aware algorithms to ensure equitable outcomes. Another major challenge is balancing explainability with privacy and security. Some explainability methods may unintentionally expose sensitive information, raising concerns about data protection. Ensuring that AI systems remain transparent without compromising security requires careful implementation of privacy-preserving techniques, such as differential privacy and federated learning.

References

1. A. Adadi and M. Berrada, "Peeking inside the black-box: A survey on explainable artificial intelligence (XAI)," IEEE Access, vol. 6, 2018, pp. 52138–52160.
2. J. M. Barredo Arrieta, A. Díaz-Rodríguez, J. Del Ser, A. Bennetot, S. Tabik, A. Barbado, S. García, S. Gil-López, D. Molina, R. Benjamins, R. Chatila, and F. Herrera, "Explainable artificial intelligence (XAI): Concepts, taxonomies, opportunities and challenges toward responsible AI," Information Fusion, vol. 58, 2020, pp. 82–115.
3. O. Biran and C. V. Cotton, "Explanation and justification in machine learning: A survey," in Proc. IJCAI Workshop on Explainable AI, 2017, pp. 8–13.
4. N. Burkart and M. F. Huber, "A survey on the explainability of supervised machine learning," J. Artif. Intell. Res., vol. 70, 2021, pp. 245–317.
5. C. Chen, O. Li, C. Tao, A. J. Barnett, J. K. Su, and C. Rudin, "This looks like that: Deep learning for interpretable image recognition," in Adv. Neural Inf. Process. Syst. (NeurIPS), vol. 32, 2019, pp. 8928–8939.
6. U. Ehsan, P. Tambwekar, L. Chan, B. Harrison, and M. O. Riedl, "Automated rationale generation: Explainable AI for reinforcement learning," in Proc. AAAI Conf. Artif. Intell., vol. 33, 2019, pp. 9785–9793.
7. D. Gunning and D. W. Aha, "DARPA's explainable artificial intelligence (XAI) program," AI Mag., vol. 40, no. 2, 2019, pp. 44–58.
8. R. Guidotti, A. Monreale, S. Ruggieri, F. Turini, F. Giannotti, and D. Pedreschi, "A survey of methods for explaining black-box models," ACM Comput. Surv., vol. 51, no. 5, 2018, Art. no. 93.
9. A. Holzinger, C. Biemann, C. S. Pattichis, and D. B. Kell, "What do we need to build explainable AI systems for the medical domain?" arXiv:1712.09923, 2017.
10. S. M. Lundberg and S.-I. Lee, "A unified approach to interpreting model predictions," in Adv. Neural Inf. Process. Syst. (NeurIPS), vol. 30, 2017, pp. 4765–4774.
11. T. Miller, "Explanation in artificial intelligence: Insights from the social sciences," Artif. Intell., vol. 267, 2019, pp. 1–38.
12. G. Montavon, W. Samek, and K.-R. Müller, "Methods for interpreting and understanding deep neural networks," Digit. Signal Process., vol. 73, 2018, pp. 1–15.
13. M. T. Ribeiro, S. Singh, and C. Guestrin, "'Why should I trust you?' Explaining the predictions of any classifier," in Proc. ACM SIGKDD Int. Conf. Knowl. Discov. Data Min., 2016, pp. 1135–1144.
14. W. Samek, T. Wiegand, and K.-R. Müller, "Explainable artificial intelligence: Understanding, visualizing, and interpreting deep learning models," IT Inf. Technol., vol. 59, no. 6, 2017, pp. 385–394.
15. D. Shin, "The effects of explainability and causability on perception, trust, and acceptance: Implications for explainable AI," Int. J. Hum.-Comput. Stud., vol. 146, 2021, Art. no. 102551.
16. D. Alvarez-Melis and T. S. Jaakkola, "Towards robust interpretability with self-explaining neural networks," in Adv. Neural Inf. Process. Syst. (NeurIPS), vol. 31, 2018, pp. 7786–7795.
17. L. H. Gilpin, D. Bau, B. Z. Yuan, A. Bajwa, M. Specter, and L. Kagal, "Explaining explanations: An overview of interpretability of machine learning," in Proc. IEEE Int. Conf. Mach. Learn. Appl. (ICMLA), vol. 1, 2018, pp. 419–425.
18. M. Narayanan, J. Chen, J. He, B. Kim, S. Gershman, and F. Doshi-Velez, "How do humans understand explanations from machine learning systems? An evaluation of the interpretability of LIME and SHAP," arXiv:1802.07638, 2018.
19. S. Wachter, B. Mittelstadt, and C. Russell, "Counterfactual explanations without opening the black box: Automated decisions and the GDPR," Harvard J. Law Technol., vol. 31, no. 2, 2018, pp. 841–887.
20. A. Preece, D. Harborne, D. Braines, R. Tomsett, and S. Chakraborty, "Stakeholders in explainable AI," in AAAI Fall Symp. Artif. Intell. Gov. Public Sectors (FSS-18), 2018. arXiv:1810.00184.

21. S. Bach, A. Binder, G. Montavon, F. Klauschen, K.-R. Müller, and W. Samek, "On pixel-wise explanations for non-linear classifier decisions by layer-wise relevance propagation," PLoS ONE, vol. 10, no. 7, 2015, Art. no. e0130140.
22. P.-J. Kindermans, K.-T. Schütt, M. Alber, K.-R. Müller, D. Erhan, B. Kim, and S. Dähne, "Learning how to explain neural networks: PatternNet and PatternAttribution," arXiv:1705. 05598, 2017.
23. F. K. Dovsilovic, M. Katusic, D. Baranasic, and N. Hlupic, "Explainable artificial intelligence: A survey," in Proc. 41st Int. Conv. Inf. Commun. Technol., Electron. Microelectron. (MIPRO), 2018, pp. 0210–0215.
24. S. Chakraborty, R. Tomsett, R. Raghavendra, D. Harborne, M. Alzantot, F. Cerutti, M. B. Srivastava, A. D. Preece, S. Julier, R. M. Rao, T. D. Kelley, D. Braines, M. Sensoy, C. J. Willis, and P. Gurram, "Interpretability of deep learning models: A survey of results," in Proc. IEEE SmartWorld/SCALCOM/UIC/ATC/CBDCom/IOP/SCI, 2017, pp. 1–6.
25. F. Doshi-Velez and B. Kim, "Towards a rigorous science of interpretable machine learning," arXiv:1702.08608, 2017.

Chapter 5
Case Studies: Daily Activity Monitoring

Abstract This chapter focuses on practical, Python-based guidelines for analyzing human behavior and health data using wearable and ambient sensors, illustrating how deep learning and explainable artificial intelligence can support independent living and healthcare monitoring. The core motivation behind these methods lies in the limitations associated with wearable sensors—specifically, discomfort during prolonged use and potential rejection by elderly individuals who may find them cumbersome. Conversely, ambient or external sensors typically achieve higher acceptance in real-world settings, provided they reliably capture accurate data from a distance. The chapter brings attention to these trade-offs, introducing multiple strategies to handle challenges such as user compliance, data variability, and complex sensor installation procedures. Several publicly available datasets are explored, alongside actual real-time examples, to demonstrate the feasibility of implementing deep learning algorithms for behavior recognition. These datasets further validate the adaptability of Python-centric approaches, emphasizing how simple or advanced models (e.g., decision trees, random forests, support vector machines, and neural networks) can be implemented, optimized, and evaluated for real-time predictions. Code snippets and graphical outputs illustrate step-by-step methodology, ensuring readers can replicate or extend the experiments with minimal setup. The chapter also spotlights the Opportunity dataset, a richly labeled resource from a smart home environment that integrates signals from both body-worn sensors and ambient devices, reinforcing the importance of context in activity detection. Throughout, the narrative underscores the significance of explainable AI in transparent decision-making. Techniques like Local Interpretable Model-Agnostic Explanations (LIME) are showcased to interpret classifier outputs and uncover which features drive specific predictions. This transparency becomes vital for user trust, especially in healthcare scenarios where model recommendations may inform critical interventions or lifestyle adjustments. Ultimately, the chapter offers a comprehensive overview of sensor-based data collection, pre-processing pipelines, and modeling solutions under the umbrella of machine learning and explainable methods.

© The Author(s), under exclusive license to Springer Nature Switzerland AG 2025
M. Z. Uddin, *Trustworthy Multimodal Intelligent Systems for Independent Living*, Cognitive Technologies, https://doi.org/10.1007/978-3-031-97359-8_5

5.1 PAMAP2 Physical Activity Monitoring Dataset

One well-known resource in the field of wearable sensor data and human activity recognition is the PAMAP2 Physical Activity Monitoring dataset. Often referred to simply as "PAMAP2," it is available through the UCI Machine Learning Repository and is used extensively by researchers and practitioners aiming to develop and test methods for identifying physical activities based on sensor output. By collecting measurements from various body-worn devices, PAMAP2 offers a comprehensive view of how the human body moves and responds during different types of tasks, such as everyday activities, exercise, and household chores.

Researchers created this dataset by having several volunteers wear multiple sensors positioned on different parts of their bodies. In general, three inertial measurement units (IMUs) were attached: one on the wrist, another on the chest, and a third on the ankle. Alongside these devices, participants also wore a heart rate monitor to record their beats per minute (BPM). The inertial sensors gathered data like acceleration, angular velocity, and magnetic orientation at 100 samples per second (100 Hz), while the heart rate monitor typically recorded at around 9 Hz. This combination of detailed motion data and physiological signals yields a robust framework for investigating how people perform daily and athletic activities, making PAMAP2 a go-to choice for modeling human motion [1, 2]. A major strength of the PAMAP2 dataset is the wide array of activities it includes. Participants performed actions ranging from walking and running to Nordic walking, cycling, ascending and descending stairs, and more sedentary behaviors like sitting, standing, and lying down. It also includes certain household tasks such as ironing clothes and vacuum cleaning, giving the dataset a wide scope of real-life activities. This variety is invaluable for training and evaluating machine learning algorithms that aim to recognize and categorize different tasks based on body movements and heart rate patterns. Each recorded time segment has a corresponding activity label, typically denoted by numeric codes (for example, 1 for lying, 2 for sitting, etc.). This labeling strategy allows researchers to use PAMAP2 in supervised learning experiments, where the goal is to train a model that can automatically predict which activity someone is engaged in by analyzing the sensor outputs.

Because PAMAP2 provides raw data from each sensor, it requires some degree of preprocessing. Each data file is arranged in a table-like format, where each row corresponds to a time point and each column represents a sensor channel, such as acceleration in the x-direction, or heart rate. Data wrangling steps often include handling missing values, synchronizing sensor streams, and possibly resampling the data. Not all participants completed every activity, and the duration of each activity can vary among subjects, so researchers must account for these differences before building any classification models. Splitting the signals into small time segments (e.g., several seconds of data at a time) is a common approach. Each segment is then summarized by statistical features (like mean, variance, or signal magnitude) or frequency-domain characteristics (like power spectral density). These extracted features can serve as inputs for various machine learning algorithms. Beyond classic machine learning, the PAMAP2 dataset has attracted attention from those experimenting with deep learning, including convolutional neural networks (CNNs) and recurrent neural networks (RNNs). A notable advantage of deep learning is the potential to learn relevant representations straight from raw data, reducing the need for extensive feature engineering. However, neural networks typically demand a substantial amount of training data to avoid overfitting, and while PAMAP2 is sizable by wearable sensor standards, it may still be relatively small for some deep architectures. To tackle this, researchers might employ data augmentation strategies, regularization methods, or rely on transfer learning to improve model generalization.

One distinctive feature of PAMAP2 is the inclusion of heart rate data, which can substantially boost classification accuracy. When comparing similar types of movement—like walking slowly versus walking quickly—the heart rate can provide additional context that might not be as evident from acceleration or angular velocity alone. Moreover, by studying heart rate patterns, researchers can glean insights into energy expenditure and exertion levels, which in turn might help in health monitoring or rehabilitation contexts. Combining physiological signals with motion data enables a richer understanding of how people carry out activities and how those activities affect the body.

Figure 5.1 presents some initial rows of the PAMAP2 dataset, highlighting sensor readings and corresponding activity labels. Figure 5.2 illustrates the number of recorded samples per user, providing insight into data distribution across participants. The average heart rate for each subject is depicted in Fig. 5.3, offering a comparative view of physiological activity. Figure 5.4 visualizes the top five most important features identified by different shallow classifiers, helping to interpret their decision-making processes. Figure 5.5 provides the architectural summary of the LSTM model used for sequential activity recognition. The model's training and validation performance, in terms of accuracy and loss, is displayed in Fig. 5.6. Figure 5.7 reports the LSTM model's confusion matrix, revealing its prediction performance across various activities, while Fig. 5.8 employs LIME to explain the influential features in one of its predictions. The architecture of a simple RNN model is outlined in Fig. 5.9, and its training dynamics are captured in Fig. 5.10. Figure 5.11 presents the confusion matrix for the RNN model, and Fig. 5.12 complements it with a LIME-based explanation of a specific prediction. Figure 5.13 details the GRU model architecture, and Fig. 5.14 shows its training and validation curves. The GRU model's classification performance is summarized in Fig. 5.15 through a confusion matrix, followed by Fig. 5.16, which offers a LIME interpretation of a sample GRU prediction. The code is as follows:

	time_stamp	activity_id	heart_rate	hand_temperature	hand_3D_acceleration_16_x	hand_3D_acceleration_16_y
count	1.942872e+06	1.942872e+06	1.942872e+06	1.942872e+06	1.942872e+06	1.942872e+06
mean	1.705202e+03	8.081830e+00	1.074879e+02	3.275126e+01	-4.952973e+00	3.585079e+00
std	1.093463e+03	6.174789e+00	2.699215e+01	1.794162e+00	6.239663e+00	6.893705e+00
min	3.120000e+01	1.000000e+00	5.700000e+01	2.487500e+01	-1.453670e+02	-1.043010e+02
25%	7.445400e+02	3.000000e+00	8.600000e+01	3.168750e+01	-8.969760e+00	1.058210e+00
50%	1.480330e+03	6.000000e+00	1.040000e+02	3.312500e+01	-5.450280e+00	3.526550e+00
75%	2.663610e+03	1.300000e+01	1.240000e+02	3.406250e+01	-9.577087e-01	6.453505e+00
max	4.245680e+03	2.400000e+01	2.020000e+02	3.550000e+01	6.285960e+01	1.556990e+02

Fig. 5.1 Some initial rows of the PAMAP2 dataset

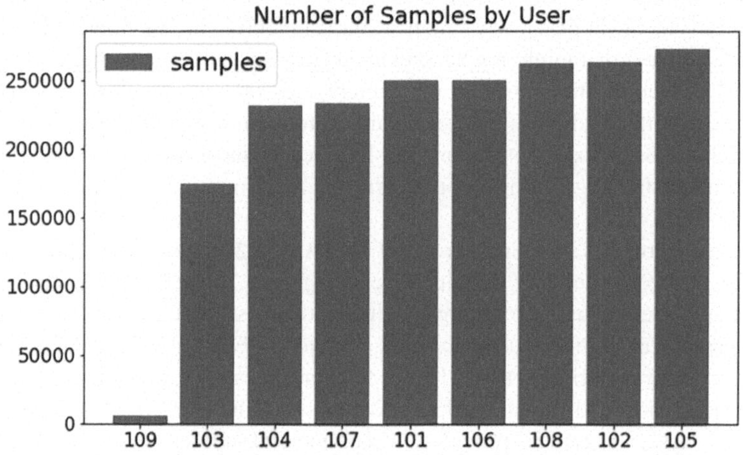

Fig. 5.2 Samples per user in the PAMAP2 dataset

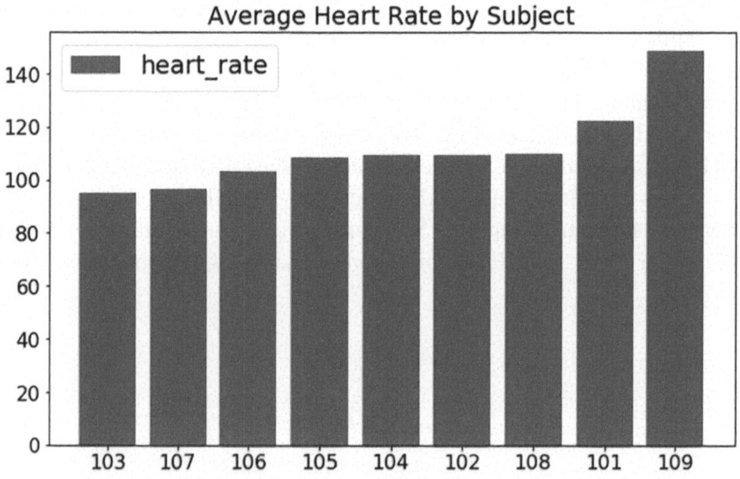

Fig. 5.3 Average heart rate per user in the PAMAP2 dataset

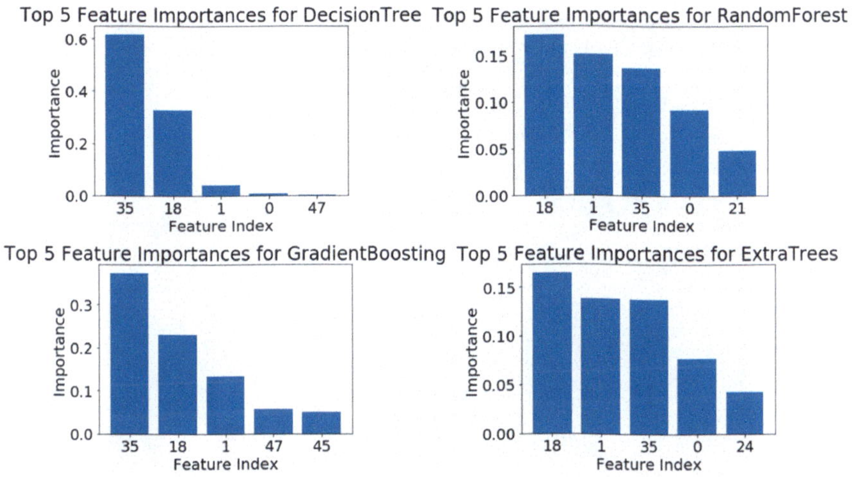

Fig. 5.4 Feature importance of different classifiers on the PAMAP2 dataset experiments

```
Model: "sequential"
_________________________________________________________________
Layer (type)                 Output Shape              Param #
=================================================================
lstm (LSTM)                  (None, 12)                3120
_________________________________________________________________
dense (Dense)                (None, 10)                130
_________________________________________________________________
dense_1 (Dense)              (None, 12)                132
=================================================================
Total params: 3,382
Trainable params: 3,382
Non-trainable params: 0
```

Fig. 5.5 Model summary of the LSTM on the PAMAP2 dataset

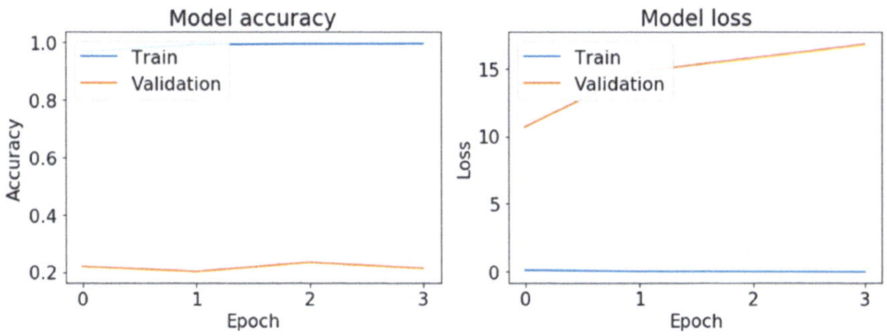

Fig. 5.6 LSTM model accuracy and loss on the PAMAP2 dataset

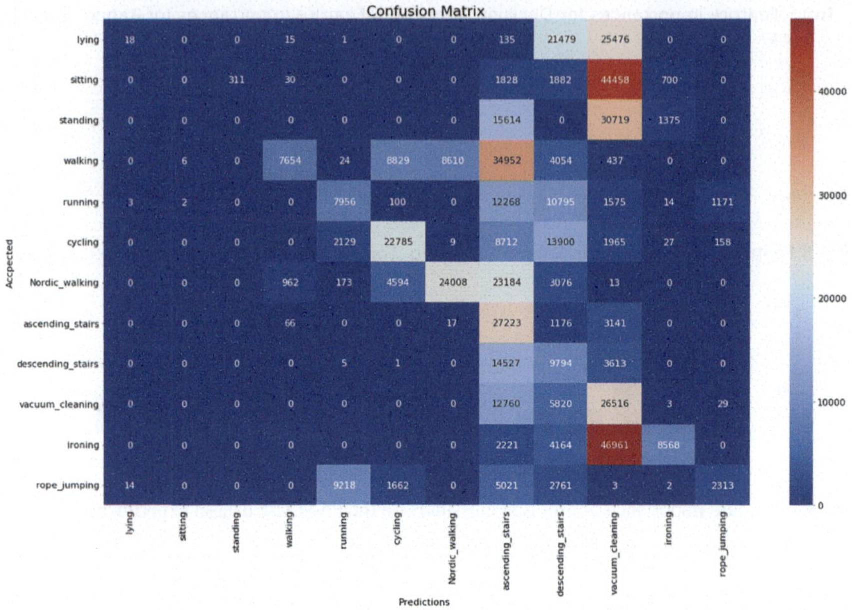

Fig. 5.7 Confusion matrix of LSTM on the PAMAP2 dataset

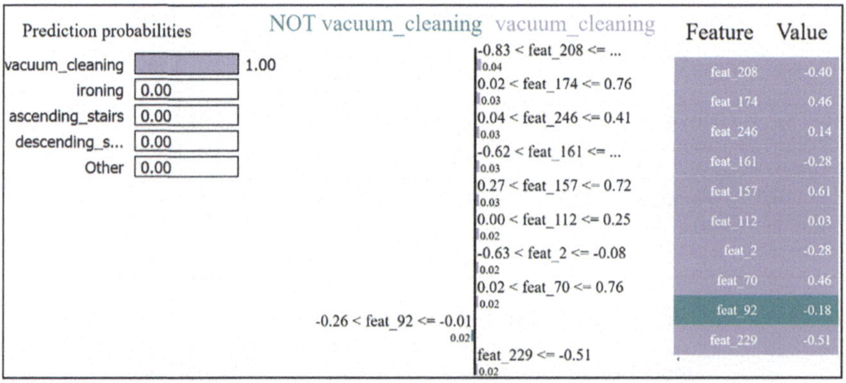

Fig. 5.8 LIME on LSTM on the PAMAP2 dataset

```
_________________________________________________________________
Layer (type)                 Output Shape              Param #
=================================================================
simple_rnn (SimpleRNN)       (None, 32)                2720
_________________________________________________________________
dense_2 (Dense)              (None, 16)                528
_________________________________________________________________
dense_3 (Dense)              (None, 12)                204
=================================================================
Total params: 3,452
Trainable params: 3,452
Non-trainable params: 0
_________________________________________________________________
```

Fig. 5.9 Model summary of the simple RNN on the PAMAP2 dataset

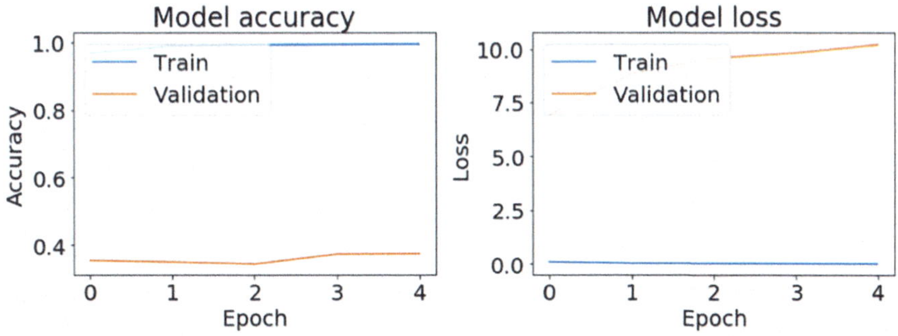

Fig. 5.10 Simple RNN model accuracy and loss on the PAMAP2 dataset

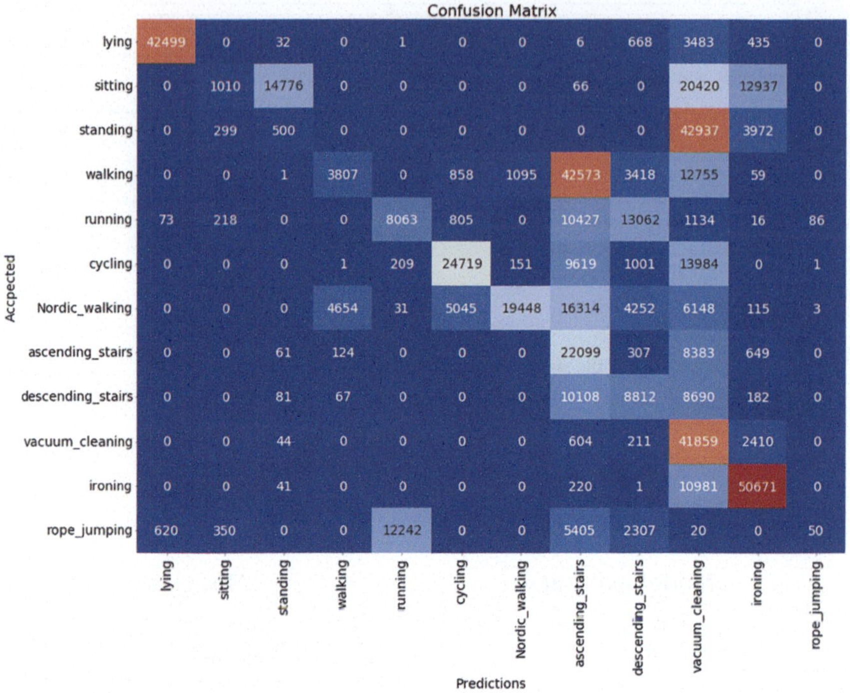

Fig. 5.11 Confusion matrix of simple RNN on the PAMAP2 dataset

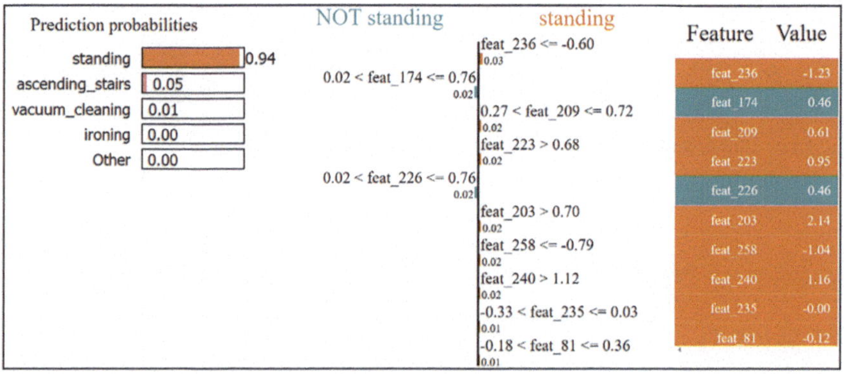

Fig. 5.12 LIME on simple RNN on the PAMAP2 dataset

```
Layer (type)                 Output Shape              Param #
=================================================================
gru (GRU)                    (None, 32)                8256

dense_4 (Dense)              (None, 16)                528

dense_5 (Dense)              (None, 12)                204
=================================================================
Total params: 8,988
Trainable params: 8,988
Non-trainable params: 0
```

Fig. 5.13 GRU model summary applied on the PAMAP2 dataset

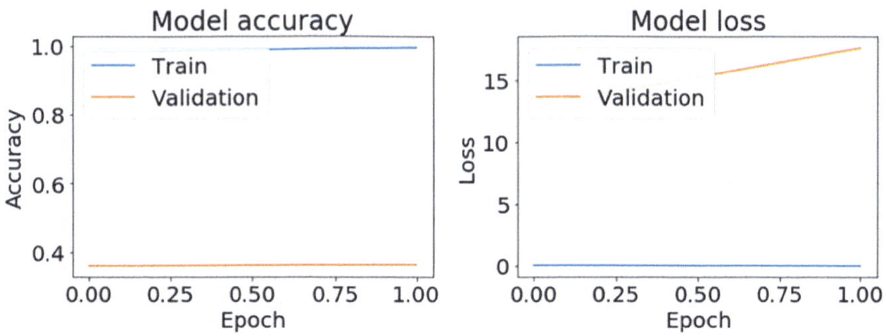

Fig. 5.14 GRU model accuracy and loss on the PAMAP2 dataset

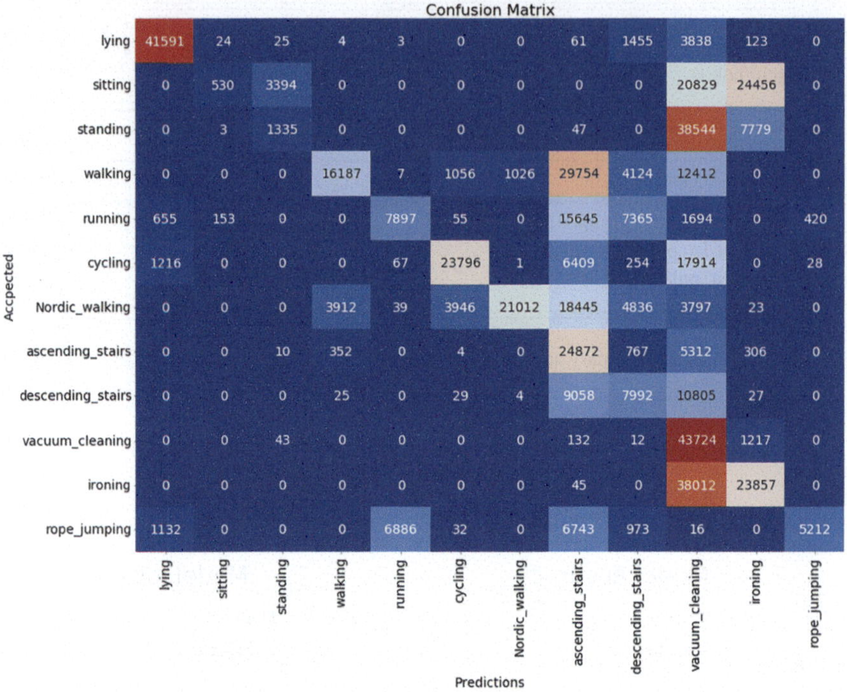

Fig. 5.15 Confusion matrix of GRU on the PAMAP2 dataset

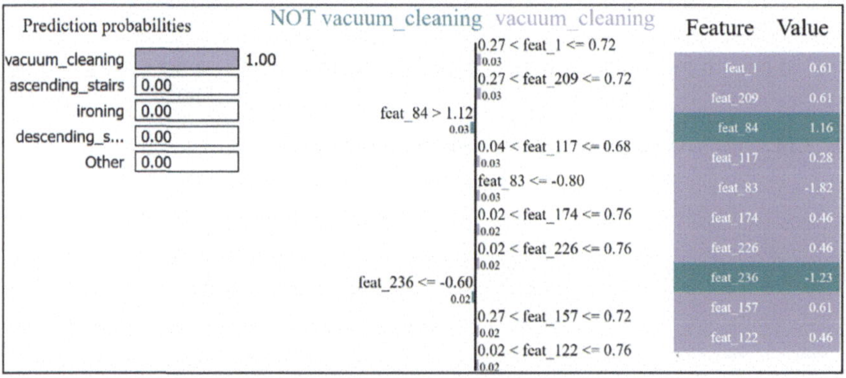

Fig. 5.16 LIME on GRU on the PAMAP2 dataset

```
import numpy as np
import pandas as pd
import seaborn as sns
from matplotlib import pyplot as plt
from IPython.display import display
from sklearn.linear_model import LinearRegression,LogisticRegression
from sklearn.metrics import confusion_matrix,accuracy_score,log_loss
from sklearn.ensemble import RandomForestClassifier
from sklearn.tree import DecisionTreeClassifier
from sklearn.preprocessing import OneHotEncoder
```

Load the activity map as:

```
def load_activity_map():
    map = {}
    map[0] = 'transient'
    map[1] = 'lying'
    map[2] = 'sitting'
    map[3] = 'standing'
    map[4] = 'walking'
    map[5] = 'running'
    map[6] = 'cycling'
    map[7] = 'Nordic_walking'
    map[9] = 'watching_TV'
    map[10] = 'computer_work'
    map[11] = 'car driving'
    map[12] = 'ascending_stairs'
    map[13] = 'descending_stairs'
    map[16] = 'vacuum_cleaning'
    map[17] = 'ironing'
    map[18] = 'folding_laundry'
    map[19] = 'house_cleaning'
    map[20] = 'playing_soccer'
    map[24] = 'rope_jumping'
    return map
```

```
#Load the data of different subjects:
import pandas as pd
def create_3d_sensor_columns(sensor_type):
    """ Returns a list of three sensor columns for x, y, and z axes.  """
    return [f"{sensor_type}_x", f"{sensor_type}_y", f"{sensor_type}_z"]

def create_4d_sensor_columns(sensor_type):
    """Returns a list of four sensor columns for x, y, z, and w.
    """
    return [f"{sensor_type}_x", f"{sensor_type}_y", f"{sensor_type}_z",
f"{sensor_type}_w"]

def build_imu_sensor_list(base_name):
    """ Constructs a list of column names for a given IMU position (e.g., 'hand',
'chest', 'ankle'). Includes temperature, multiple accelerations, gyroscope,
magnetometer, and orientation. """
    columns = []
    # Temperature
    columns.append(f"{base_name}_temperature")

    # 3D acceleration at 16g
    columns +=
create_3d_sensor_columns(f"{base_name}_3D_acceleration_16")

    # 3D acceleration at 6g
    columns += create_3d_sensor_columns(f"{base_name}_3D_acceleration_6")
    # 3D gyroscope
    columns += create_3d_sensor_columns(f"{base_name}_3D_gyroscope")
    # 3D magnetometer
    columns += create_3d_sensor_columns(f"{base_name}_3D_magnetometer")
    # 4D orientation
    columns += create_4d_sensor_columns(f"{base_name}_4D_orientation")
    return columns
```

```
def assemble_all_imu_columns():
    """ Returns a list of all relevant IMU columns:
    1) Basic time, activity, heart rate.
    2) Hand-based sensor columns.
    3) Chest-based sensor columns.
    4) Ankle-based sensor columns.
    """
    # Basic columns
    all_columns = ["time_stamp", "activity_id", "heart_rate"]
    # Hand IMU
    all_columns += build_imu_sensor_list("hand")
    # Chest IMU
    all_columns += build_imu_sensor_list("chest")
    # Ankle IMU
    all_columns += build_imu_sensor_list("ankle")
    return all_columns

def
load_pamap2_subjects(folder_prefix="./PAMAP2_Dataset/Protocol/subject"):
    """
    Reads all subject files from the PAMAP2 dataset (subject101 to subject109),
    assigns column names, adds a 'subject_id' column,
    and appends each subject's data into a single DataFrame.
    """
    full_df = pd.DataFrame()
    column_names = assemble_all_imu_columns()

    for subject_id in range(101, 110):
        filepath = f"{folder_prefix}{subject_id}.dat"
        df_subject = pd.read_table(filepath, header=None, sep=r"\s+")
        df_subject.columns = column_names
        df_subject["subject_id"] = subject_id
        # Concatenate all subjects
        full_df = pd.concat([full_df, df_subject], ignore_index=True)

    full_df.reset_index(drop=True, inplace=True)
    return full_df
```

```
# Example usage:
data = load_pamap2_subjects()
print(data.head())
def process_data(df):
    # Remove rows where 'activity_id' is zero
    df = df[df['activity_id'] != 0]
    # Interpolate missing values
    df = df.interpolate()
    # Fill any remaining NaNs with the column mean
    for column in df.columns:
        df[column].fillna(df[column].mean(), inplace=True)
    # (Optional) Compute the mean for each activity group
    activity_means = df.groupby('activity_id').mean().reset_index()
    return df
data = process_data(data)
```

After processing the data, the data.describe() should show the description of the data. Following figure shows the parital picture with a few columns from 55 total columns in the dataset.

```
import matplotlib.pyplot as plt
import numpy as np

def bar_plot(df, x_col, label_col, title, figsize=(10,6)):
    # Adjust the font size used in the plot
    plt.rcParams.update({'font.size': 16})

    # Create the figure and axes
    fig, ax = plt.subplots(figsize=figsize)

    # Generate a range for positioning the bars along the x-axis
    positions = range(len(df))

    # Draw the bar plot using a custom color
    ax.bar(positions, df[x_col], color='green')

    # Label the x-axis ticks with the values from the label column
    ax.set_xticks(np.arange(len(df)))
    ax.set_xticklabels(df[label_col])
```

```
    # Add a legend and title, then display the plot
    ax.legend([x_col], fontsize=20)
    ax.set_title(title)
    plt.show()

# Example usage: count how many rows each subject_id has, and create a new
DataFrame
samples = data.groupby('subject_id').count().reset_index()

samples_by_subject = pd.DataFrame()
samples_by_subject['subject_id'] = samples['subject_id']
samples_by_subject['samples'] = samples['time_stamp']
samples_by_subject = samples_by_subject.sort_values(by='samples')

bar_plot(
    samples_by_subject,
    'samples',
    'subject_id',
    'Number of Samples by User'
)

# Load activity map
activity_map = load_activity_map()

# Count rows by activity_id and reset the index
activity_counts = data.groupby('activity_id').count().reset_index()

# Create a new DataFrame that maps   each activity_id to its corresponding
activity name
activity_df = pd.DataFrame()
activity_df['activity'] = [activity_map[a_id] for a_id in
activity_counts['activity_id']]
activity_df['samples'] = activity_counts['time_stamp']
# Sort the DataFrame by the number of samples
activity_df = activity_df.sort_values(by='samples')

# Visualize the number of samples for each activity
bar_plot(
```

```
        activity_df,
        'samples',
        'activity',
        'Number of Samples by Activity',
        figsize=(40, 7)
    )
    # Create a new DataFrame for heart rate information
    heart_rate_df = pd.DataFrame()
    heart_rate_df['subject_id'] = ids_mean['subject_id']
    heart_rate_df['heart_rate'] = ids_mean['heart_rate']

    # Sort by the heart_rate column
    heart_rate_df = heart_rate_df.sort_values(by='heart_rate')

    # Visualize the average heart rate by subject
    custom_bar_plot(
        heart_rate_df,
        'heart_rate',
        'subject_id',
        'Average Heart Rate by Subject'
    )
```

#Get subject 102 and 105 as testing and rest as training data.

```
from sklearn.preprocessing import StandardScaler
def create_train_test_sets(dataset):
    # Separate out the test data from subjects 102 and 105
    test_data_102 = dataset[dataset['subject_id'] == 102]
    test_data_105 = dataset[dataset['subject_id'] == 105]
    test_data = test_data_102.append(test_data_105)
```

```
    # Everything else becomes training data
    train_data = dataset[(dataset['subject_id'] != 102) &
(dataset['subject_id'] != 105)]

    # Remove identifiers before splitting
    test_data = test_data.drop(['subject_id'], axis=1)
    train_data = train_data.drop(['subject_id'], axis=1)

    # Separate features (X) from labels (y)
    X_train = train_data.drop(['activity_id', 'time_stamp'], axis=1).values
    y_train = train_data['activity_id'].values
    X_test = test_data.drop(['activity_id', 'time_stamp'], axis=1).values
    y_test = test_data['activity_id'].values

    # Scale the feature data
    scaler = StandardScaler()
    X_train = scaler.fit_transform(X_train)
    X_test = scaler.transform(X_test)

    return X_train, X_test, y_train, y_test


X_train, X_test, y_train, y_test = create_train_test_sets(data)
print("Shape of X_train:", X_train.shape, " y_train:", y_train.shape)
print("Shape of X_test:", X_test.shape, " y_test:", y_test.shape)
```

```
#Apply shallow learning:
import numpy as np
import pandas as pd
import matplotlib.pyplot as plt

from sklearn.metrics import accuracy_score
from sklearn.linear_model import LogisticRegression
from sklearn.svm import SVC
from sklearn.tree import DecisionTreeClassifier
from sklearn.ensemble import (
    RandomForestClassifier,
    GradientBoostingClassifier,
    ExtraTreesClassifier
)
from sklearn.neighbors import KNeighborsClassifier
from sklearn.naive_bayes import GaussianNB

# Example training data (X_train, X_test, y_train, y_test) should already exist
# ...

# Dictionary of models
models = {
    "LogisticRegression": LogisticRegression(max_iter=1000),
    "SVC": SVC(),  # RBF kernel by default (no feature_importances_ or coef_ in
the same sense)
    "DecisionTree": DecisionTreeClassifier(),
    "RandomForest": RandomForestClassifier(),
    "GradientBoosting": GradientBoostingClassifier(),
    "ExtraTrees": ExtraTreesClassifier(),
    "KNN": KNeighborsClassifier(),
    "GaussianNB": GaussianNB(),
}

results = {}
```

```
for name, clf in models.items():
    # Train the model
    clf.fit(X_train, y_train)
    # Predict on test set
    y_pred = clf.predict(X_test)
    # Compute accuracy
    acc = accuracy_score(y_test, y_pred)
    results[name] = acc

    print(f"{name} Accuracy: {acc:.4f}")

    # -------------------------
    # Print and Plot Top 5 Feature Importance (if available)
    # -------------------------
    if hasattr(clf, "feature_importances_"):
        # Tree-based models
        importances = clf.feature_importances_
        indices = np.argsort(importances)[::-1]
        top_indices = indices[:5]

        print("   Feature Importances (Top 5):")
        for rank, idx in enumerate(top_indices, start=1):
            print(f"       #{rank}: Feature {idx}, Importance:
{importances[idx]:.4f}")

        # --- Plot the top 5 features ---
        plt.figure()
        plt.bar(range(len(top_indices)), importances[top_indices])
        plt.title(f"Top 5 Feature Importances for {name}")
        plt.xticks(range(len(top_indices)), top_indices)
        plt.xlabel("Feature Index")
        plt.ylabel("Importance")
        plt.show()
```

```
elif hasattr(clf, "coef_"):
    # Linear models: logistic regression, etc.
    coefs = clf.coef_
    # Handle multiclass case by taking mean absolute value across classes
    if coefs.ndim > 1 and coefs.shape[0] > 1:
        importances = np.mean(np.abs(coefs), axis=0)
    else:
        importances = np.abs(coefs).ravel()

    indices = np.argsort(importances)[::-1]
    top_indices = indices[:5]

    print("  Coefficients (Top 5 by absolute value):")
    for rank, idx in enumerate(top_indices, start=1):
        print(f"    #{rank}: Feature {idx}, Coef: {importances[idx]:.4f}")
            # --- Plot the top 5 features ---
            plt.figure()
            plt.bar(range(len(top_indices)), importances[top_indices])
            plt.title(f"Top 5 Coefficients (Absolute) for {name}")
            plt.xticks(range(len(top_indices)), top_indices)
            plt.xlabel("Feature Index")
            plt.ylabel("Coefficient Magnitude (Absolute)")
            plt.show()

        else:
            # Models like SVC with RBF, KNN, GaussianNB, etc.
            # do not have built-in feature importance
            print("  (No direct feature importance or coefficient attribute.)")

        print("--------------------------------------------------------")

    # Print final accuracies
    print("Summary of model accuracies:")
    for model_name, accuracy in results.items():
        print(f"{model_name}: {accuracy:.4f}")
```

```
#lets create a function to make rnn time-sequential data with 5 step-back
def create_rnn_data(X, y, step_back = 5, step_forword = 1):
    out_X = []
    out_y = []
    size = len(X)
    for i, features in enumerate(X):
        if i >= step_back and i < size - step_forword:
            tmp_X = []
            tmp_y = []
            for j in range(i-step_back,i):
                tmp_X.extend([X[j]])
            out_X.append(tmp_X)
            for j in range(i,i+step_forword):
                tmp_y.extend([y[j]])
            out_y.append(tmp_y)
    return np.array(out_X), np.array(out_y)

X_rnn_train, y_rnn_train = create_rnn_data(X_train, y_train)
X_rnn_test, y_rnn_test = create_rnn_data(X_test, y_test)
print('Train shape X :',X_rnn_train.shape,' y ', y_rnn_train.shape)
print('Test shape X :',X_rnn_test.shape,' y ', y_rnn_test.shape)
```

That makes the shape of the training and testing as:

```
Train shape X : (1407075, 5, 52) y (1407075, 12)
Test shape X : (535785, 5, 52) y (535785, 12)
```

Lets start with LSTM now:

```
from tensorflow.keras import Sequential
from tensorflow.keras.layers import Dense, LSTM, GRU, SimpleRNN, Dropout
lstm_model = Sequential()
lstm_model.add(LSTM(12,input_shape=(X_rnn_train.shape[1],X_rnn_train.shap
e[2])))
```

```
lstm_model.add(Dense(10 ,activation='relu'))
lstm_model.add(Dense(y_rnn_train.shape[1], activation='softmax'))

lstm_model.summary()
lstm_model.compile(loss='categorical_crossentropy',optimizer='adam',metrics=['
accuracy'])

#Now let us train the model.

from tensorflow.keras.callbacks import EarlyStopping
early_stopping_monitor = EarlyStopping(patience=3)
history = lstm_model.fit(X_rnn_train, y_rnn_train, validation_split = 0.2 , epochs
= 5, callbacks=[early_stopping_monitor])
# taken from https://keras.io/visualization/
def plot_history(history):

# Plot training & validation accuracy values
plt.plot(history.history['accuracy'])
plt.plot(history.history['val_accuracy'])
plt.title('Model accuracy')
plt.ylabel('Accuracy')
plt.xlabel('Epoch')
plt.legend(['Train', 'Validation'], loc='upper left')
plt.show()
```

```
        # Plot training & validation loss values
        plt.plot(history.history['loss'])
        plt.plot(history.history['val_loss'])
        plt.title('Model loss')
        plt.ylabel('Loss')
        plt.xlabel('Epoch')
        plt.legend(['Train', 'Validation'], loc='upper left')
        plt.show()
    plot_history(history)


#Test the model
y = y_test[5:-1]
preds = lstm_model.predict(X_rnn_test)
preds_cat = np.argmax(preds,axis=1)
# building a map of result to activity
result = np.unique(preds_cat).tolist()
expected = np.unique(y).tolist()
combined = list(zip(result,expected))
conf_map = dict(combined)
# transfoms the prediction to an activity
results = [conf_map[x] for x in preds_cat]
print('model accuracy on test :',accuracy_score(y,results)*100)
```

The yielded accuracy is 25%. More training should make more accuracies in this case. One just needs to raise the number of epochs. Lets plot the confusion matrix now:

```
#Let's apply LIME to explain a testing result.

# 1) Flatten
X_train_flat = X_rnn_train.reshape((X_rnn_train.shape[0], -1))
X_test_flat  = X_rnn_test.reshape((X_rnn_test.shape[0], -1))
y_train_indices = np.argmax(y_rnn_train, axis=1)
y_test_indices  = np.argmax(y_rnn_test,  axis=1)
# 2) Explainer
from lime import lime_tabular
class_names = labels
feature_names = [f"feat_{i}" for i in range(X_train_flat.shape[1])]
explainer = lime_tabular.LimeTabularExplainer(
    training_data=X_train_flat,
    feature_names=feature_names,
    class_names=class_names,
    mode='classification'
)
# 3) Prediction wrapper
def predict_fn(input_2d):
    num_samples = input_2d.shape[0]
    timesteps   = X_rnn_train.shape[1]
    num_feats   = X_rnn_train.shape[2]
    x_reshaped  = input_2d.reshape(num_samples, timesteps, num_feats)
    return lstm_model.predict(x_reshaped)
# 4) Pick a sample to explain
i = 1
sample_to_explain = X_test_flat[i]
print("True class:", y_test_indices[i])
# 5) Explain
exp = explainer.explain_instance(
    data_row     = sample_to_explain,
    predict_fn   = predict_fn,
    num_features = 10,
    top_labels   = 1
)

# 6) Show result in notebook
exp.show_in_notebook(show_table=True)
```

That makes the explanation as (Fig. 5.8).

Then lets apply SimleRNN model as bellow:

```
# ---------------------------------------------------------------
# Simple RNN Model
# ---------------------------------------------------------------
rnn_model = Sequential()
rnn_model.add(SimpleRNN(32,                 input_shape=(X_rnn_train.shape[1],
X_rnn_train.shape[2])))
rnn_model.add(Dense(16, activation='relu'))
rnn_model.add(Dense(y_rnn_train.shape[1], activation='softmax'))

rnn_model.summary()

rnn_model.compile(loss='categorical_crossentropy',
                  optimizer='adam',
                  metrics=['accuracy'])

print("\nTraining Simple RNN Model...")
history_rnn = rnn_model.fit(X_rnn_train, y_rnn_train,
                            validation_split=0.05,
                            epochs=5)


    plot_history(history_rnn)

    #Prediction
    preds = rnn_model.predict(X_rnn_test)
    preds_cat = np.argmax(preds,axis=1)
    # building a map of result to activity
    result = np.unique(preds_cat).tolist()
    expected = np.unique(y).tolist()
    combined = list(zip(result,expected))
    conf_map = dict(combined)
    # transfoms the prediction to an activity
    results = [conf_map[x] for x in preds_cat]
    print('model accuracy rnn on test :',accuracy_score(y,results)*100)

    labels = [activity_map[conf_map[x]] for x in result]
    plot_con_matrix(y,results, labels)

    #LIME
    # Prediction wrapper
    def predict_fn(input_2d):
        num_samples = input_2d.shape[0]
        timesteps    = X_rnn_train.shape[1]
        num_feats     = X_rnn_train.shape[2]
        x_reshaped   = input_2d.reshape(num_samples, timesteps, num_feats)
        return rnn_model.predict(x_reshaped)
```

```
# Pick a sample to explain
i = 2
sample_to_explain = X_test_flat[i]
print("True class:", y_test_indices[i])
# Explain
exp = explainer.explain_instance(
    data_row      = sample_to_explain,
    predict_fn    = predict_fn,
    num_features = 10,
    top_labels    = 1
)

#Show result in notebook
exp.show_in_notebook(show_table=True)
```

The accuracy here was 41%. The following shows model characteristics, confusion matric and LIME explanation for sample.

Then GRU was applied as follows that yielded the accuracy of 40%.

```
gru_model = Sequential()
gru_model.add(GRU(32,input_shape=(X_rnn_train.shape[1],
X_rnn_train.shape[2])))
gru_model.add(Dense(16, activation='relu'))
gru_model.add(Dense(y_rnn_train.shape[1], activation='softmax'))

gru_model.summary()

gru_model.compile(loss='categorical_crossentropy',
                  optimizer='adam',
                  metrics=['accuracy'])

print("\nTraining GRU Model...")
history_gru = gru_model.fit(X_rnn_train, y_rnn_train,
                            validation_split=0.05,
                            epochs=2)

plot_history(history_gru)

preds = gru_model.predict(X_rnn_test)
```

```
        preds_cat = np.argmax(preds,axis=1)
        # building a map of result to activity
        result = np.unique(preds_cat).tolist()
        expected = np.unique(y).tolist()
        combined = list(zip(result,expected))
        conf_map = dict(combined)
        # transfoms the prediction to an activity
        results = [conf_map[x] for x in preds_cat]
        print('model accuracy gru on test :',accuracy_score(y,results)*100)

        labels = [activity_map[conf_map[x]] for x in result]
        lot_con_matrix(y,results, labels)

# Prediction wrapper
def predict_fn(input_2d):
    num_samples = input_2d.shape[0]
    timesteps   = X_rnn_train.shape[1]
    num_feats   = X_rnn_train.shape[2]
    x_reshaped  = input_2d.reshape(num_samples, timesteps, num_feats)
    return gru_model.predict(x_reshaped)

# Pick a sample to explain
i = 2
sample_to_explain = X_test_flat[i]
print("True class:", y_test_indices[i])

# Explain
exp = explainer.explain_instance(
    data_row      = sample_to_explain,
    predict_fn    = predict_fn,
    num_features = 10,
    top_labels    = 1
)
#  Show result in notebook
exp.show_in_notebook(show_table=True)
```

5.2 Human Activities and Postural Transitions Dataset

The "Smartphone-Based Recognition of Human Activities and Postural Transitions" dataset is a collection of data recorded by smartphone sensors to recognize common human movements. In the study, volunteers carried smartphones while doing everyday actions like walking, sitting, standing, and changing posture. The phones recorded sensor data during each activity, and every segment was labeled to indicate what the person was doing [3, 4]. Because smartphones are widely used, this dataset has become a popular choice for testing machine learning models that try to recognize human activities from sensor data. The data was collected in controlled settings where participants performed specific tasks like walking upstairs and downstairs, lying down, or standing still. The smartphone, placed in a consistent location on each participant, recorded information using two sensors: an accelerometer and a gyroscope. These sensors captured both linear movement and rotation. Each time a participant started or changed an activity, it was marked in the data, which helps researchers teach models to match sensor patterns to real actions.

Many people took part in this project, and their unique styles of walking, sitting, or moving helped create a diverse dataset. This variety makes models trained on this data more flexible and better prepared for real-world use. The different ways participants carried or held the phone also made the data more realistic and useful for practical applications.

The accelerometer measured how fast the phone was moving in straight lines, while the gyroscope measured how it was rotating. These two types of signals provided a full picture of each action. For example, walking often has a repetitive pattern, while climbing stairs might show stronger and more angled movements. Sudden transitions like sitting or standing show up as short bursts in the data. Researchers often process these signals by calculating averages, changes, or even converting them into frequency-based patterns to make the data easier to work with. The dataset supports a wide range of applications. In healthcare, it can be used to monitor patients and detect early signs of risk, such as instability or fatigue. In fitness, it helps track exercises automatically. In smart systems, it can help adjust device settings based on what the user is doing—like muting notifications if they're sleeping or focusing. Since the dataset includes transitions, it offers deeper insights into daily behavior than those that only track static activities. Even though the data was collected using specific phones and sampling settings, its structure allows researchers to apply it in many different contexts. Future research can expand on this by including new devices or environments, but the basic method—using accelerometer and gyroscope data to classify activity—remains the same. The clear labeling and diverse participants make this dataset a strong foundation for studying human activity recognition.

The columns in this dataset capture a comprehensive spectrum of signals derived from accelerometer and gyroscope readings, which were gathered at a fixed sampling rate of 50 Hz. Initially, the raw signals were subjected to both a median filter and a third-order Butterworth filter with a corner frequency of 20 Hz. These steps aim to mitigate noise and ensure that only meaningful motion data remain. The dataset labels the time-domain signals with the prefix "t," indicating temporal information, resulting in vectors such as tBodyAcc-XYZ, tGravityAcc-XYZ, tBodyAccJerk-XYZ, tBodyGyro-XYZ, and tBodyGyroJerk-XYZ. Here, "XYZ" denotes three separate axes—X, Y, and Z—that capture the motion in different directional planes, which is vital for recognizing multidimensional movement patterns in human activity.

A critical element in these measurements involves distinguishing between body acceleration and gravity acceleration. The tGravityAcc-XYZ signal captures primarily the gravitational component through an additional low pass Butterworth filter tuned to a corner frequency of 0.3 Hz. Separating the gravitational influence ensures that tBodyAcc-XYZ can concentrate on the dynamic portion of motion relevant to daily activities, exercises, or transitions in posture. From these time-domain signals, further transformations led to "Jerk" signals, such as tBodyAccJerk-XYZ and tBodyGyroJerk-XYZ. The idea behind Jerk is to quantify abrupt changes in acceleration or angular velocity, thus highlighting transitions or sudden shifts in movement. Beyond the time domain, the dataset includes frequency-domain representations marked with an "f" prefix (for example, fBodyAcc-XYZ and fBodyGyro-XYZ). These arise from applying a Fast Fourier Transform (FFT), enabling the extraction of periodic characteristics. Additional magnitude calculations, indicated by terms like tBodyAccMag or fBodyGyroMag, involve taking the Euclidean norm of the three axes. This procedure condenses the three-dimensional signal into a single measure, simplifying certain analyses and providing insight into overall motion intensity.

For each of these raw or transformed signals, an extensive set of features was computed. These features reveal various statistical properties or shape characteristics of the signals. For instance, mean() and std() capture average trends and overall variability, respectively. The median absolute deviation, mad(), offers a robust statistic less influenced by outliers, while max() and min() highlight the largest and smallest observed values in a given window. Signal magnitude area, or sma(), sums the absolute values to reflect accumulated signal strength. Additionally, iqr() and entropy() measure the spread and unpredictability of the signal distribution, respectively. Other advanced measures, such as the autorregresion coefficients (arCoeff()) and frequency-based metrics like meanFreq() or bandsEnergy(), delve into how the signal behaves across different spectral bins or how it correlates with itself.

The angle() feature captures the orientation between two signal vectors, which can reveal alignment or discrepancies between different motion components, such as body acceleration and gravity acceleration. Altogether, these columns provide a holistic view of human activity, spanning from low-frequency postural shifts to the higher-frequency subtleties of abrupt transitions. By combining time and frequency insights with a diverse suite of statistical features, the dataset becomes a powerful tool for recognizing, quantifying, and analyzing human motion in a variety of real-world or experimental scenarios. So, the dataset consist of 7767 rows and 563 columns where position column is the activity that is extracted and considered for as labels for machine learning.

Figure 5.17 illustrates the distribution of the feature tBodyAcc-Mean-1 across six basic postures and movements using kernel density estimates, box plots, and violin plots. Figure 5.18 provides a similar visualization for the feature tBodyAccJerk-Mean-1, comparing how its values vary across the same set of activities. Figure 5.19 continues the analysis by showing the distribution of tBodyAccMag-Mean-1 with detailed KDE, box, and violin plots for walking, sitting, standing, and laying postures. Figure 5.20 presents the same set of visualizations for tBodyAcc-Mean-1, but focusing on transitional activities such as STAND_TO_SIT and SIT_TO_LIE. To explore high-dimensional feature structure, Fig. 5.21 visualizes the activity clusters generated by t-SNE, showing clear groupings of positions based on reduced features. Figure 5.22 displays the confusion matrix of the K-Nearest Neighbors (KNN) classifier on the HAPT dataset, while Fig. 5.23 presents the corresponding matrix for Support Vector Machines (SVM). Figure 5.24 shows the classification performance of the Extra Trees model using a confusion matrix. In Fig. 5.25, the most important features identified by the Random Forest classifier are ranked, highlighting those with the greatest influence on classification. Finally, Fig. 5.26 presents the confusion matrix of the Random Forest model on the HAPT dataset, summarizing its predictive accuracy across all activity classes. The code segments are as follows.

```
import pandas as pd
import inflection
import math
import numpy as np
import seaborn as sns
import matplotlib.pyplot as plt
import matplotlib.gridspec as gridspec
import datetime
from IPython.display import Image
from IPython.core.display import HTML
```

```
from imblearn import over_sampling as os
from imblearn import combine as c
from sklearn.manifold import TSNE
from sklearn import model_selection as ms
from sklearn import ensemble as en

from boruta import BorutaPy
import random
from sklearn import metrics as m
from scikitplot import metrics as mt
from sklearn import neighbors as nb
from sklearn import linear_model as lm
from sklearn import svm

df_cols_name = pd.read_csv('./data/features.txt', sep=" ", header=None)
cols_name = df_cols_name[0].tolist()
df_X_raw = pd.read_csv('./data/train/X_train.txt', sep=" ", header=None)
df_y_raw = pd.read_csv('./data/train/y_train.txt', sep=" ", header=None)
df_subject_raw = pd.read_csv('./data/train/subject_id_train.txt', sep=" ",
header=None)
df_X_raw.columns = cols_name
# join
df_raw = df_X_raw
```

```
df_raw['subject'] = df_subject_raw
df_raw['position'] = df_y_raw

df_raw['position'] = df_raw['position'].map( {  1 : 'WALKING',
                                                2 : 'WALKING_UPSTAIRS',
                                                3 : 'WALKING_DOWNSTAIRS',
                                                4 : 'SITTING',
                                                5 : 'STANDING',
                                                6 : 'LAYING',
                                                7 : 'STAND_TO_SIT',
                                                8 : 'SIT_TO_STAND',
                                                9 : 'SIT_TO_LIE',
                                                10 : 'LIE_TO_SIT',
                                                11 : 'STAND_TO_LIE',
                                                12 : 'LIE_TO_STAND' } )
sns.kdeplot(  df1[df1['position']  ==  'WALKING']['tBodyAcc-Mean-1'],
label='WALKING', shade=True )
sns.kdeplot( df1[df1['position'] == 'WALKING_UPSTAIRS']['tBodyAcc-Mean-1'],
label='WALKING_UPSTAIRS', shade=True )
sns.kdeplot(  df1[df1['position']  ==  'WALKING_DOWNSTAIRS']['tBodyAcc-
Mean-1'], label='WALKING_DOWNSTAIRS', shade=True )
sns.kdeplot(  df1[df1['position']  ==  'SITTING']['tBodyAcc-Mean-1'],
label='SITTING', shade=True )
sns.kdeplot(  df1[df1['position']  ==  'STANDING']['tBodyAcc-Mean-1'],
label='STANDING', shade=True )
sns.kdeplot(  df1[df1['position']  ==  'LAYING']['tBodyAcc-Mean-1'],
label='LAYING', shade=True )

sns.boxplot(x='position',                              y='tBodyAcc-Mean-
1',data=df1[(df1['position']=='WALKING')                            |
(df1['position']=='WALKING_UPSTAIRS')                               |
(df1['position']=='WALKING_DOWNSTAIRS') | (df1['position']=='SITTING') |
(df1['position']=='STANDING')    |    (df1['position']=='LAYING')    ],
showfliers=False)
sns.violinplot(x='position',y='tBodyAcc-Mean-1',
data=df1[(df1['position']=='WALKING')|(df1['position']=='WALKING_UPSTAI
RS')|(df1['position']=='WALKING_DOWNSTAIRS')|(df1['position']=='SITTING')
| (df1['position']=='STANDING') | (df1['position']=='LAYING') ],
cut=0,          # controls how far the violin extends beyond extreme data
    scale='width',    # can be 'area', 'count', or 'width'
    inner=None,       # remove the default "box" lines inside the violin
    showfliers=False
)
```

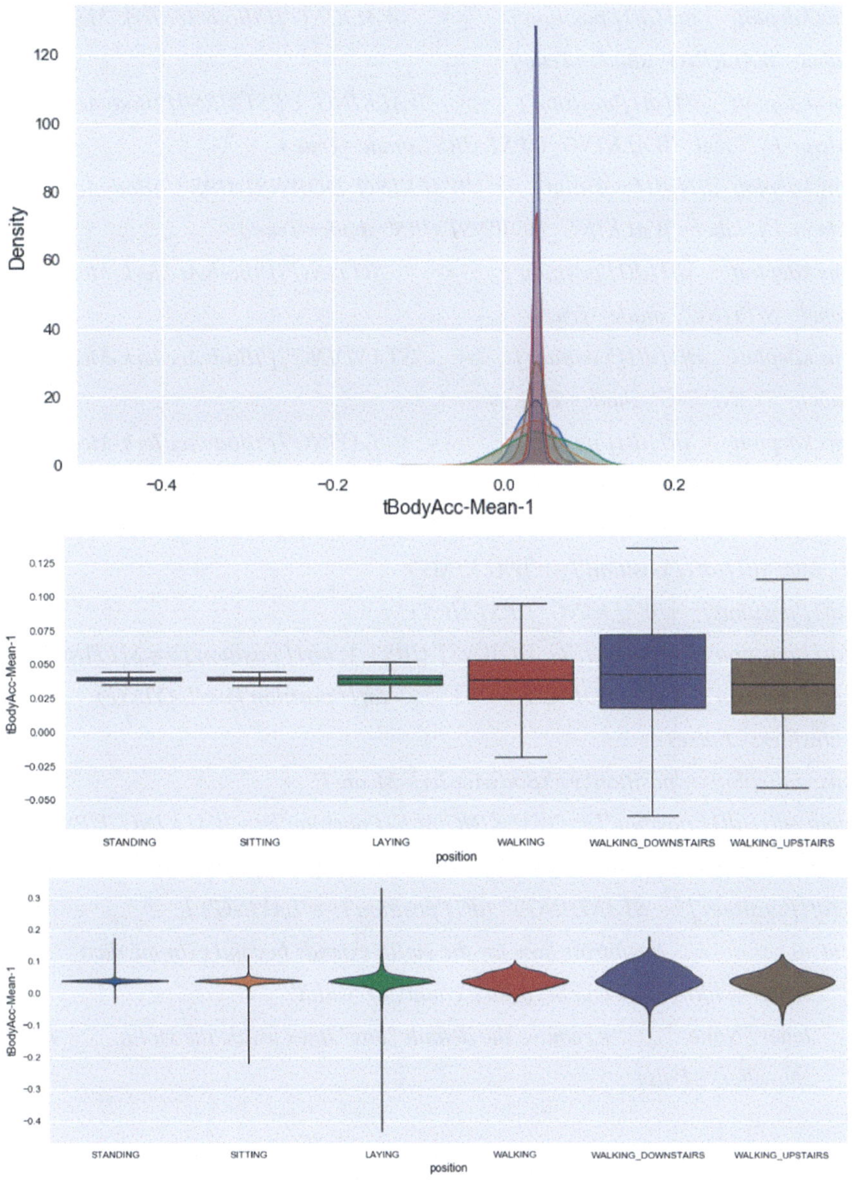

Fig. 5.17 Kernel density estimate, box, and violin plot for tBodyAcc-Mean-1 feature across six basic postures

```
sns.kdeplot( dfl[dfl['position'] == 'WALKING']['tBodyAccJerk-Mean-1'], label='WALKING', shade=True )
sns.kdeplot( dfl[dfl['position'] == 'WALKING_UPSTAIRS']['tBodyAccJerk-Mean-1'], label='WALKING_UPSTAIRS', shade=True )
sns.kdeplot( dfl[dfl['position'] == 'WALKING_DOWNSTAIRS']['tBodyAccJerk-Mean-1'], label='WALKING_DOWNSTAIRS', shade=True )
sns.kdeplot( dfl[dfl['position'] == 'SITTING']['tBodyAccJerk-Mean-1'], label='SITTING', shade=True )
sns.kdeplot( dfl[dfl['position'] == 'STANDING']['tBodyAccJerk-Mean-1'], label='STANDING', shade=True )
sns.kdeplot( dfl[dfl['position'] == 'LAYING']['tBodyAccJerk-Mean-1'], label='LAYING', shade=True )
sns.boxplot(x='position', y='tBodyAccJerk-Mean-1',data=dfl[(dfl['position']=='WALKING') | (dfl['position']=='WALKING_UPSTAIRS') | (dfl['position']=='WALKING_DOWNSTAIRS') | (dfl['position']=='SITTING') | (dfl['position']=='STANDING') | (dfl['position']=='LAYING') ], showfliers=False)
sns.violinplot(x='position',y='tBodyAccJerk-Mean-1',
data=dfl[(dfl['position']=='WALKING')|(dfl['position']=='WALKING_UPSTAIRS')|(dfl['position']=='WALKING_DOWNSTAIRS')|(dfl['position']=='SITTING') | (dfl['position']=='STANDING') | (dfl['position']=='LAYING') ],
cut=0,              # controls how far the violin extends beyond extreme data
    scale='width',      # can be 'area', 'count', or 'width'
    inner=None,         # remove the default "box" lines inside the violin
    showfliers=False
)
```

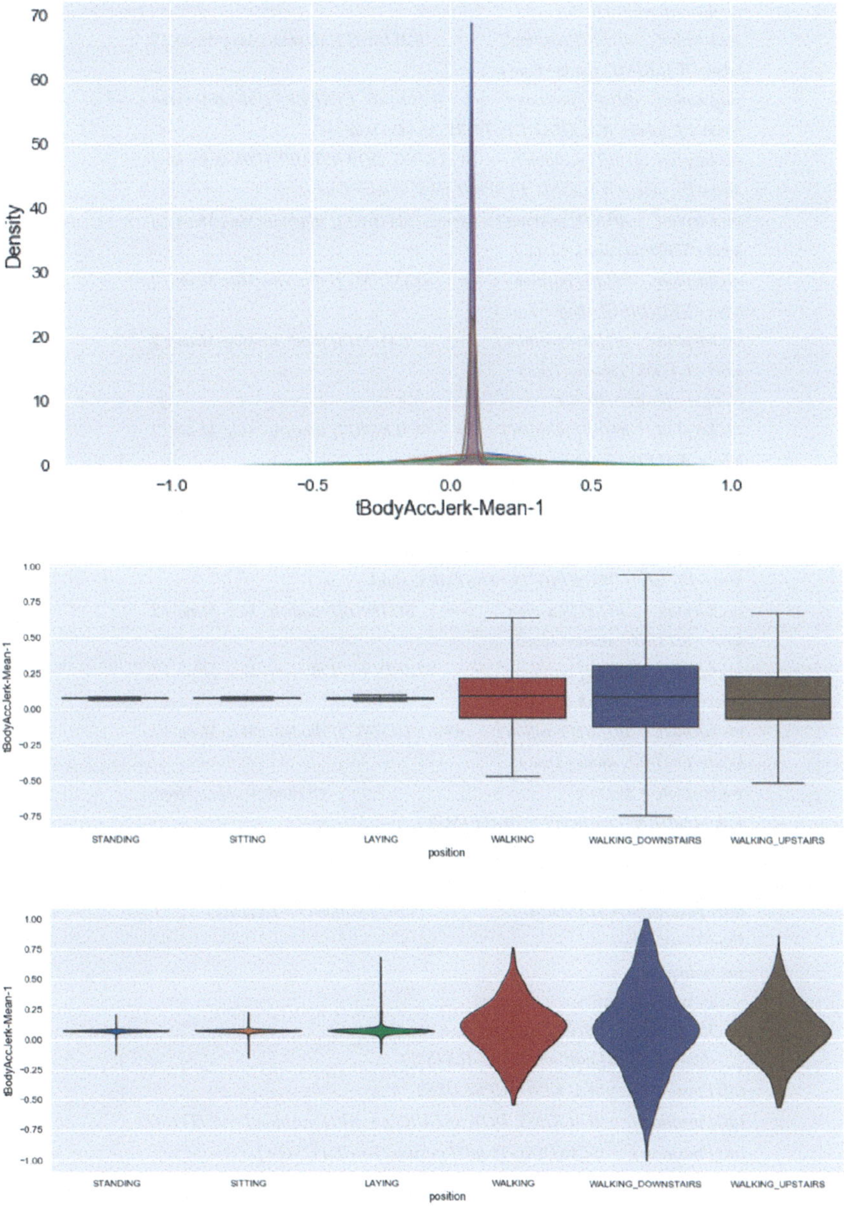

Fig. 5.18 Kernel density estimate, box, and violin plot for tBodyAccJerk-Mean-1 feature

```
plt.figure(figsize=(10, 6))
sns.kdeplot( df1[df1['position'] == 'WALKING']['tBodyAccMag-Mean-1'],
label='WALKING', shade=True )
sns.kdeplot( df1[df1['position'] == 'WALKING_UPSTAIRS']['tBodyAccMag-
Mean-1'], label='WALKING_UPSTAIRS', shade=True )
sns.kdeplot( df1[df1['position'] == 'WALKING_DOWNSTAIRS']['tBodyAccMag-
Mean-1'], label='WALKING_DOWNSTAIRS', shade=True )
sns.kdeplot( df1[df1['position'] == 'SITTING']['tBodyAccMag-Mean-1'],
label='SITTING', shade=True )
sns.kdeplot( df1[df1['position'] == 'STANDING']['tBodyAccMag-Mean-1'],
label='STANDING', shade=True )
sns.kdeplot( df1[df1['position'] == 'LAYING']['tBodyAccMag-Mean-1'],
label='LAYING', shade=True )
plt.figure(figsize=(10, 6))
sns.kdeplot( df1[df1['position'] == 'WALKING']['tBodyAccMag-Mean-1'],
label='WALKING', shade=True )
sns.kdeplot( df1[df1['position'] == 'WALKING_UPSTAIRS']['tBodyAccMag-
Mean-1'], label='WALKING_UPSTAIRS', shade=True )
sns.kdeplot( df1[df1['position'] == 'WALKING_DOWNSTAIRS']['tBodyAccMag-
Mean-1'], label='WALKING_DOWNSTAIRS', shade=True )
sns.kdeplot( df1[df1['position'] == 'SITTING']['tBodyAccMag-Mean-1'],
label='SITTING', shade=True )
sns.kdeplot( df1[df1['position'] == 'STANDING']['tBodyAccMag-Mean-1'],
label='STANDING', shade=True )
sns.kdeplot( df1[df1['position'] == 'LAYING']['tBodyAccMag-Mean-1'],
label='LAYING', shade=True )
sns.boxplot(x='position', y='tBodyAccMag-Mean-
1',data=df1[(df1['position']=='WALKING') |
(df1['position']=='WALKING_UPSTAIRS') |
(df1['position']=='WALKING_DOWNSTAIRS') | (df1['position']=='SITTING') |
(df1['position']=='STANDING') | (df1['position']=='LAYING') ],
showfliers=False)
sns.violinplot(
    x='position',
    y='tBodyAccMag-Mean-1',
    data=df1[(df1['position']=='WALKING') |
(df1['position']=='WALKING_UPSTAIRS') |
(df1['position']=='WALKING_DOWNSTAIRS') | (df1['position']=='SITTING') |
(df1['position']=='STANDING') | (df1['position']=='LAYING') ],
    cut=0,            # controls how far the violin extends beyond extreme data
    scale='width',    # can be 'area', 'count', or 'width'
    inner=None,       # remove the default "box" lines inside the violin
    showfliers=False
)
```

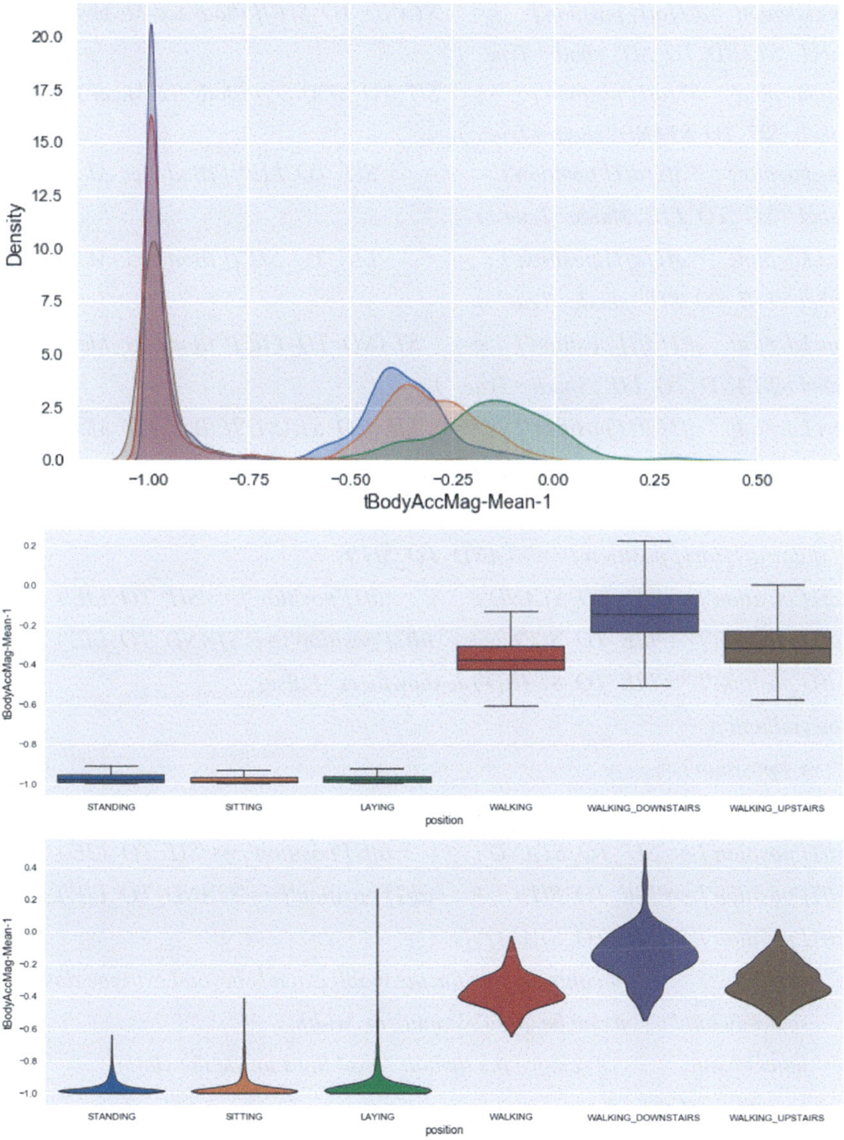

Fig. 5.19 Kernel density estimate, box, and violin plot for tBodyAccMag-Mean-1 feature

```
sns.kdeplot( df1[df1['position'] == 'STAND_TO_SIT']['tBodyAcc-Mean-1'],
label='STAND_TO_SIT', shade=True )
sns.kdeplot( df1[df1['position'] == 'SIT_TO_STAND']['tBodyAcc-Mean-1'],
label='SIT_TO_STAND', shade=True )
sns.kdeplot( df1[df1['position'] == 'SIT_TO_LIE']['tBodyAcc-Mean-1'],
label='SIT_TO_LIE', shade=True )
sns.kdeplot( df1[df1['position'] == 'LIE_TO_SIT']['tBodyAcc-Mean-1'],
label='LIE_TO_SIT', shade=True )
sns.kdeplot( df1[df1['position'] == 'STAND_TO_LIE']['tBodyAcc-Mean-1'],
label='STAND_TO_LIE', shade=True )
sns.kdeplot( df1[df1['position'] == 'LIE_TO_STAND']['tBodyAcc-Mean-1'],
label='LIE_TO_STAND', shade=True )
sns.boxplot(x='position', y='tBodyAcc-Mean-
1',data=df1[(df1['position']=='STAND_TO_SIT') |
(df1['position']=='SIT_TO_STAND') | (df1['position']=='SIT_TO_LIE') |
(df1['position']=='LIE_TO_SIT') | (df1['position']=='STAND_TO_LIE') |
(df1['position']=='LIE_TO_STAND') ], showfliers=False)
sns.violinplot(
    x='position',
    y='tBodyAcc-Mean-1',data=df1[(df1['position']=='STAND_TO_SIT') |
(df1['position']=='SIT_TO_STAND') | (df1['position']=='SIT_TO_LIE') |
(df1['position']=='LIE_TO_SIT') | (df1['position']=='STAND_TO_LIE') |
(df1['position']=='LIE_TO_STAND')],
    cut=0,          # controls how far the violin extends beyond extreme data
    scale='width',  # can be 'area', 'count', or 'width'
    inner=None,     # remove the default "box" lines inside the violin
    showfliers=False
)
```

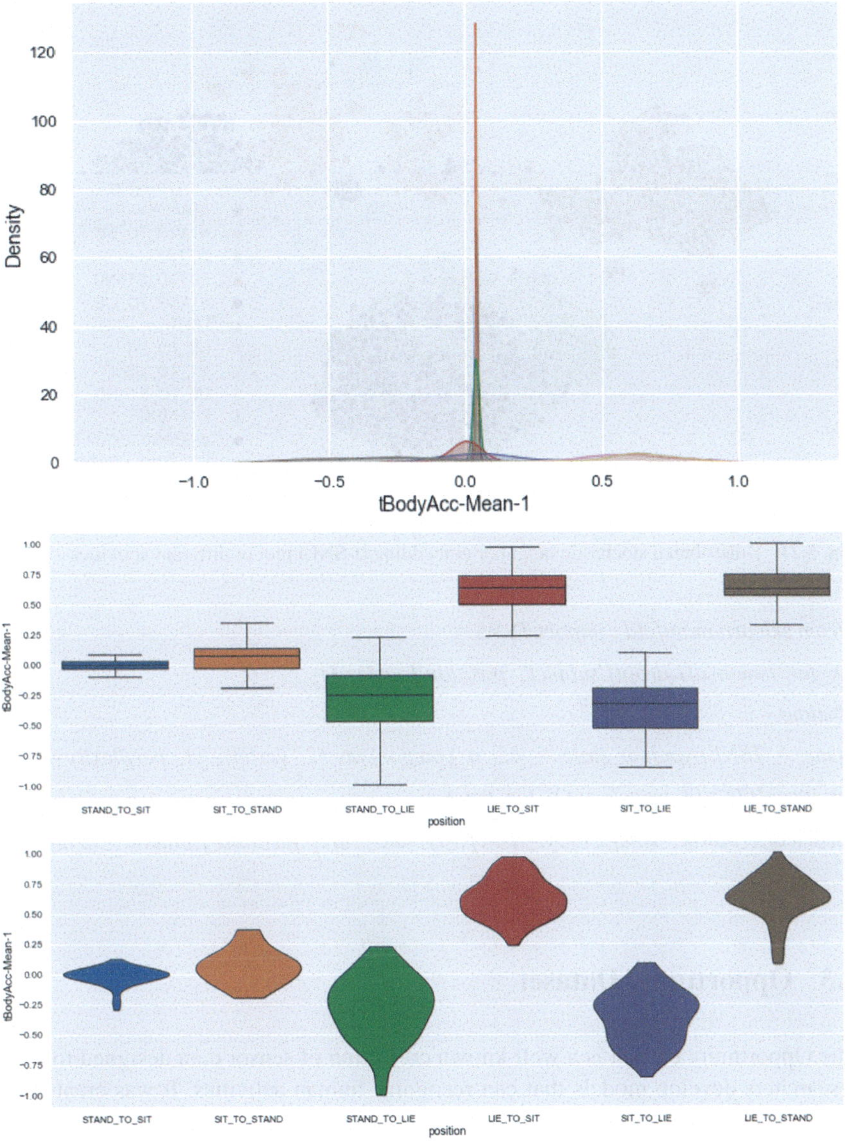

Fig. 5.20 Kernel density estimate, box, and violin plot for BodyAcc-Mean-1 feature focusing on transitional activities such as STAND_TO_SIT and SIT_TO_LIE

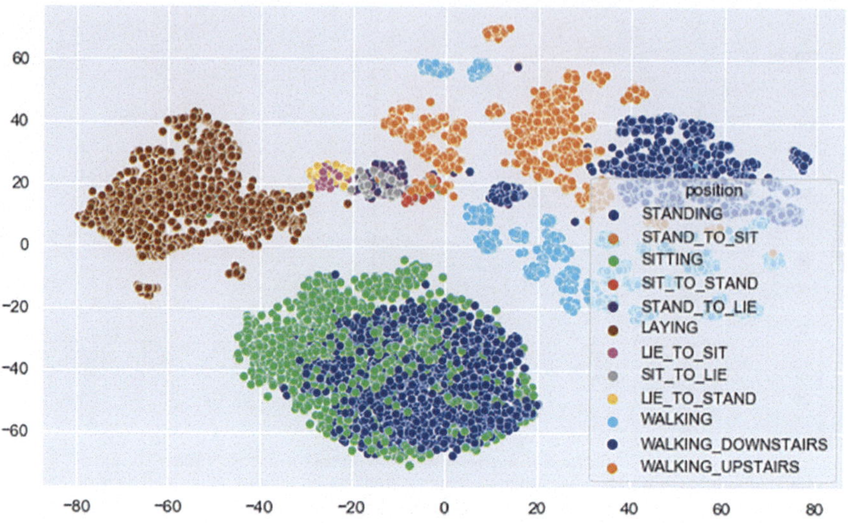

Fig. 5.21 T-distributed stochastic neighbor embedding (t-SNE) plot of different activities

```
from sklearn.manifold  import TSNE
X_for_tsne = df1.drop(['subject', 'position'], axis=1)
%time
tsne = TSNE(random_state = 42, n_components=2, verbose=1, perplexity=50,
n_iter=1000).fit_transform(X_for_tsne)
sns.scatterplot(x =tsne[:, 0], y = tsne[:, 1], hue = df1["position"],palette="bright")
```

5.3 Opportunity Dataset

The Opportunity dataset is a well-known collection of sensor data designed to help researchers develop models that can recognize human activities. It was created as part of a project focused on context-aware computing, where devices or systems can adapt to what a person is doing in real-time. This dataset is especially useful for training machine learning models that aim to understand actions based on data collected from body-worn sensors and objects in the environment.

The data was collected in a controlled environment where participants performed a series of daily activities in a smart home-like setup. These activities included getting up, walking, opening and closing doors, drinking, and cleaning. Some of the actions were scripted, while others were done more naturally [5, 6]. The goal was to mimic real-world behavior as closely as possible while still capturing labeled data. Each participant wore several sensors on their body: on the arms, legs, and back. These

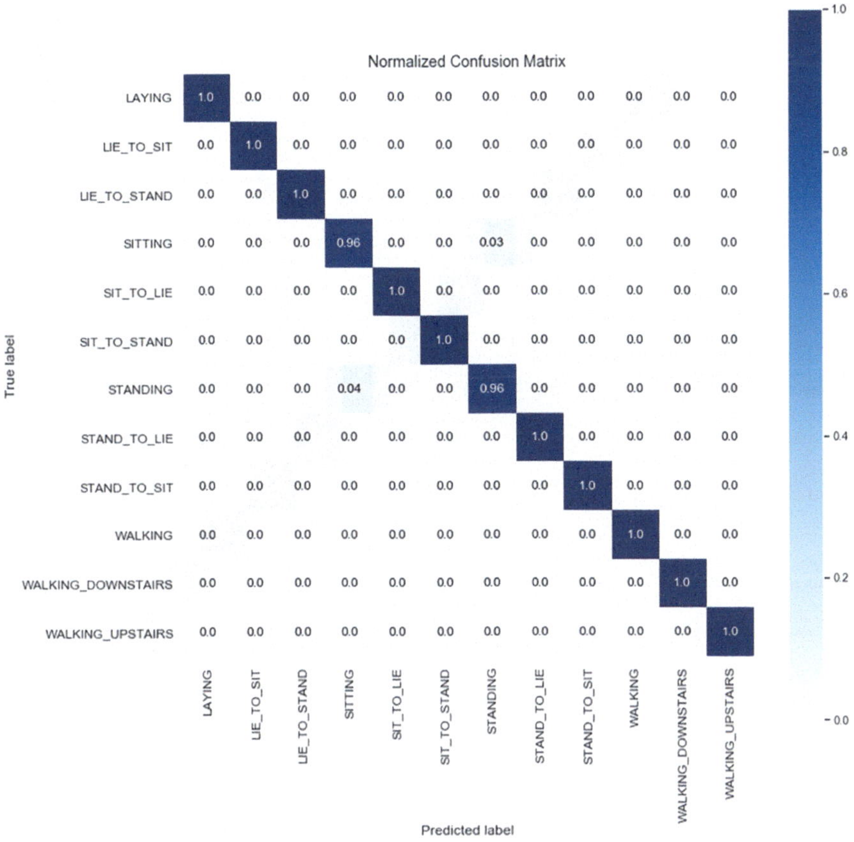

Fig. 5.22 Confusion matrix of KNN on the HAPT dataset

sensors recorded things like acceleration, angular velocity, and magnetic fields. In addition to body-worn sensors, there were also sensors placed in the environment—like on doors, drawers, and kitchen appliances—to capture interactions with objects. This combination of body and ambient sensors made it possible to recognize not only movements but also the use of everyday items.

One of the main features of the Opportunity dataset is that it includes both high-level and low-level activity labels. High-level labels describe general actions, such as "open door" or "drink." Low-level labels provide information about the posture or limb movements of the participant, like "left arm up" or "right foot forward." These labels help researchers develop models that understand complex activities made up of many smaller motions. The dataset is organized into recordings, each representing a full session of activity by a participant. The data is time-stamped and synchronized across all sensors, allowing for easy segmentation into windows or events. There is missing data in some parts due to sensor loss or signal dropout, which is common in real-world sensing and makes the dataset more realistic for testing robust algorithms.

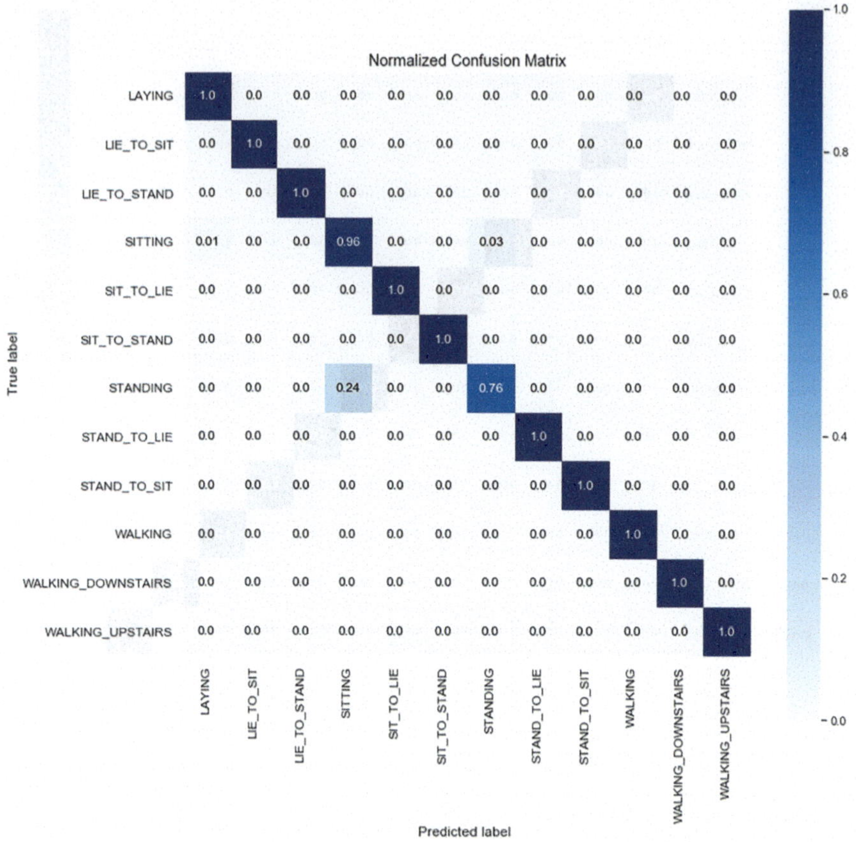

Fig. 5.23 Confusion matrix of SVM on the HAPT dataset

People often use this dataset to explore activity recognition, sensor fusion, feature engineering, and deep learning techniques. Because it contains multiple sensor types and a rich set of labels, it offers many possibilities for experimentation. Models trained on this data can be used in health monitoring, smart homes, rehabilitation, and even robotics. The Opportunity dataset is a valuable resource for anyone interested in human activity recognition. It provides real sensor data from people doing normal tasks, collected using both wearable and environmental sensors. The detailed labeling and structure of the dataset make it a strong benchmark for developing and testing machine learning models. Whether you're building a system to detect when someone falls, automate smart home behavior, or track daily routines, the Opportunity dataset is a great place to start. It offers a realistic and challenging set of data that pushes researchers to build more accurate and flexible activity recognition systems.

Figure 5.27 presents the distribution of activity samples from the Opportunity dataset, providing an overview of class imbalance across different movements. Figure 5.28 summarizes the performance of various classical machine learning

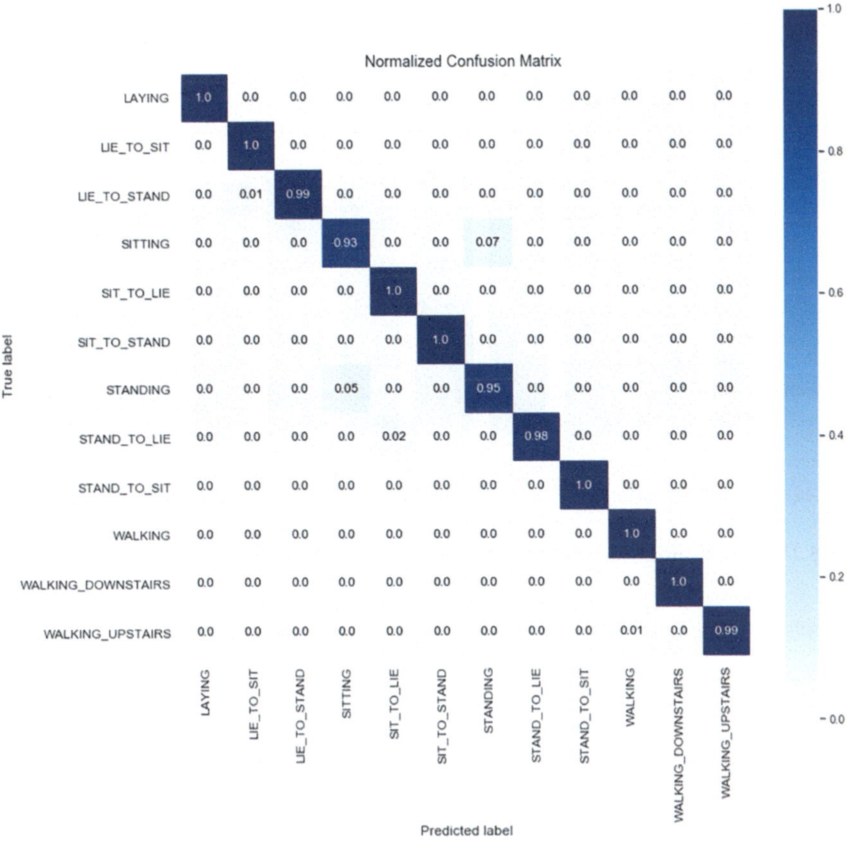

Fig. 5.24 Confusion matrix of extra trees on the HAPT dataset

models on the Opportunitydataset, reporting their accuracy scores and highlighting the top five most important features for models that support feature interpretability. Lastly, Fig. 5.29 illustrates training epochs and testing accuracies for deep learning models (Simple RNN, LSTM, and GRU) applied to segmented time-series data, and includes a LIME explanation visualizing the most influential features for a specific LSTM prediction. The code is as follows:

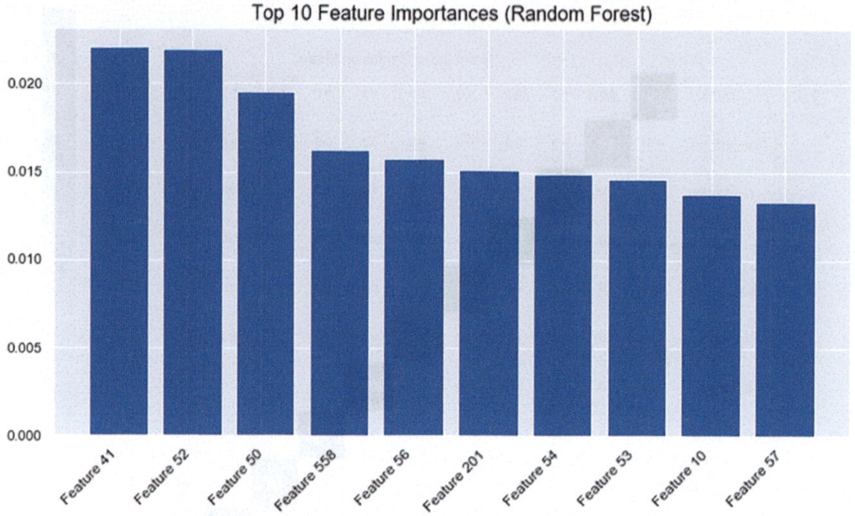

Fig. 5.25 Feature importance of random forests on the HAPT dataset

```
import os
import pandas as pd
import warnings
from sklearn.preprocessing import StandardScaler
warnings.filterwarnings("ignore")
def locate_first_alpha(string_value):
    """
    Finds the position of the first alphabetic character in a string,
    starting the search from the 9th character onward.
    Parameters:
    -----------
    string_value : str
        The string to inspect.
    Returns:
    --------
    int
```

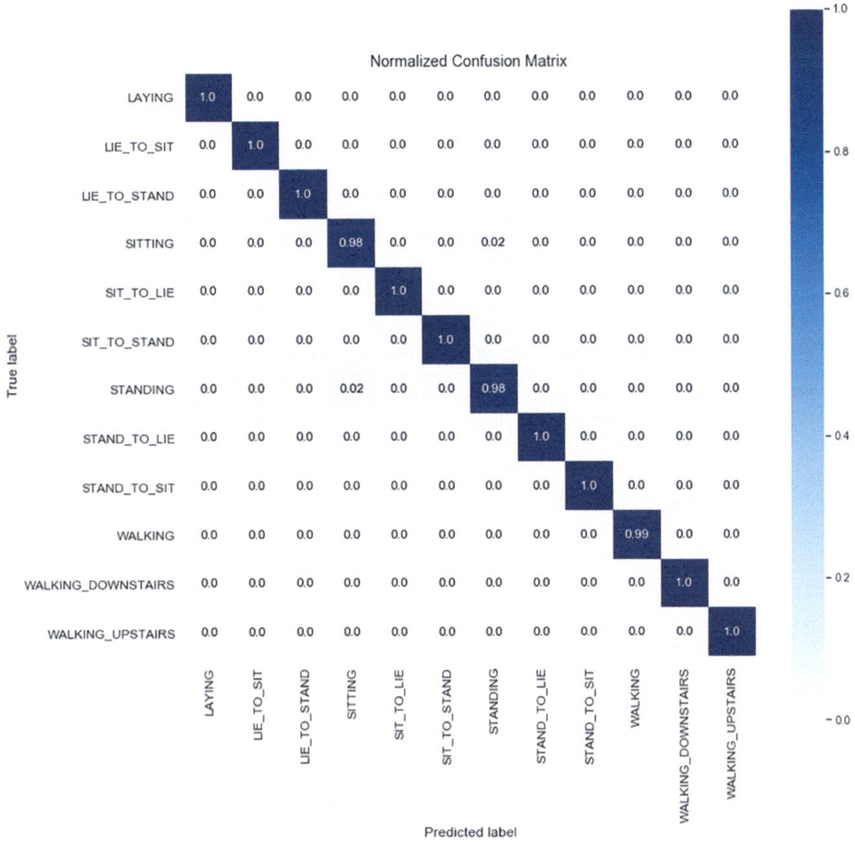

Fig. 5.26 Confusion matrix of random forests on the HAPT dataset

```
        Index of the first alphabetic character found after the 8th character,
        or -1 if none is found.
    """
    for index in range(9, len(string_value)):
        if string_value[index].isalpha():
            return index
    return -1
def collect_data_files():
    """
    Gathers data from .dat files within 'OpportunityUCIDataset/dataset',
excluding
    any files containing 'Drill'. Assigns proper column labels from
'column_names.txt'
    and returns a consolidated pandas DataFrame.

    Returns:
    --------
    pd.DataFrame
        A single DataFrame containing all rows from the relevant .dat files.
    """
    base_path = "OpportunityUCIDataset/dataset"
    all_files = [file for file in os.listdir(base_path) if file.endswith('.dat')]

    # Exclude Drills
    relevant_files = [f for f in all_files if "Drill" not in f]
```

```
    # Prepare column headers using 'column_names.txt'
    column_headers = []
    with open(os.path.join(base_path, "column_names.txt"), "r") as col_file:
        lines = col_file.read().splitlines()
        for line in lines:
            if "Column" in line:
                start_index = locate_first_alpha(line)
                if start_index != -1:
                    col_name = line[start_index:].split(";")[0]
                    column_headers.append(col_name)
    # Initialize a DataFrame with the extracted columns
    combined_data = pd.DataFrame(columns=column_headers)
    # Read all relevant files and append to the DataFrame
    for data_file in relevant_files:
        temp_df = pd.read_table(
            os.path.join(base_path, data_file),
            sep=r"\s+",
            header=None
        )
        temp_df.columns = column_headers
        combined_data = pd.concat([combined_data, temp_df],
ignore_index=True)

    return combined_data

def cleanse_data(data_frame):
    """
    Cleans the provided DataFrame by:
     1) Dropping columns with over 10% missing values.
     2) Converting non-numeric values to NaN.
     3) Performing interpolation to fill NaNs.

    Parameters:
    -----------
    data_frame : pd.DataFrame
        The original DataFrame to be cleaned.

    Returns:
    --------
    pd.DataFrame
        A cleaned and interpolated version of the original DataFrame.
    """
```

```
    # Drop columns that have more than 10% NaNs
    threshold = int(len(data_frame.columns) * 0.9)
    data_frame = data_frame.dropna(thresh=threshold, axis=1)

    # Convert problematic values to NaN
    data_frame = data_frame.apply(pd.to_numeric, errors='coerce')

    # Interpolate to fill NaNs
    data_frame = data_frame.interpolate()

    return data_frame


def remap_labels(data_frame):
    """
    Modifies the label columns in the DataFrame based on the definitions
    found in 'label_legend.txt'. This includes a special handling for
    the 'Locomotion' category.

    Parameters:
    -----------
    data_frame : pd.DataFrame
        The DataFrame whose labels need to be remapped.

    Returns:
    --------
    pd.DataFrame
        The DataFrame with updated label values.
    """
    legend_path = "OpportunityUCIDataset/dataset/label_legend.txt"
    label_legend = pd.read_csv(legend_path, sep=r"\s+-\s+", header=0)
    track_groups = label_legend['Track name'].unique()
```

```
        # Build a dictionary with track name -> ( unique index -> label name )
        mapping_dict = {}
        for track in track_groups:
            subset = label_legend.loc[label_legend['Track name'] == track]
            mapping_dict[track] = dict(subset[["Unique index", "Label
name"]].to_numpy())

        # Adjust 'Locomotion' specifically
        for track in mapping_dict:
            if track == 'Locomotion':
                mapping_dict[track][1] = 1
                mapping_dict[track][2] = 2
                mapping_dict[track][4] = 3
                mapping_dict[track][5] = 0
            else:
                counter = 0
                for key in sorted(mapping_dict[track]):
                    mapping_dict[track][key] = counter
                    counter += 1

        # Apply the dictionary mapping to the DataFrame
        for track in mapping_dict:
            for unique_idx, new_label in mapping_dict[track].items():
                data_frame.loc[data_frame[track] == unique_idx, track] =
new_label

        return data_frame
    def standardize_numeric_columns(data_frame):
        """
        Applies StandardScaler normalization to all numeric columns except the last
7,
        assuming the final 7 columns are not intended for scaling (e.g., label
columns).
```

```
        Parameters:
        -----------
        data_frame : pd.DataFrame
            The DataFrame whose numeric columns will be standardized.

        Returns:
        --------
        pd.DataFrame
            DataFrame with standardized numeric columns.
        """
        scaler = StandardScaler()
        data_frame[data_frame.columns[:-7]]                          =
scaler.fit_transform(data_frame[data_frame.columns[:-7]])
        return data_frame


    # Example Usage:
    raw_data = collect_data_files()
    cleaned_data = cleanse_data(raw_data)
    labeled_data = remap_labels(cleaned_data)
    final_data = standardize_numeric_columns(labeled_data)
df=final_data


import pandas as pd
import numpy as np
import seaborn as sns
import matplotlib.pyplot as plt

# Gather contiguous indices for each class in 'HL_Activity'
contiguous_sequences = []
activity_categories = df["HL_Activity"].unique()
```

```
for activity in activity_categories:
    temp_sequence = []
    matching_indices = df.loc[df["HL_Activity"] == activity].index.tolist()

    for idx in matching_indices:
        # If the next index is still in the same activity, extend the sequence
        if (idx + 1) in matching_indices:
            temp_sequence.append(idx)
        else:
            # Once the sequence is broken, stop and store it
            break
    contiguous_sequences.append(temp_sequence)

# Check the length of each contiguous sequence
for seq in contiguous_sequences:
    print(len(seq))

def plot_activity_segments(
    dataframe,
    sequence_list,
    column_index,
    class_labels,
    subplot_shape=(2, 3),
    figure_size=(15, 7),
    color_of_plot="red",
    y_limits=(-2, 2)
):
    """
    Plots specified data segments from the dataframe based on contiguous indices.

    Parameters
    ----------
    dataframe : pd.DataFrame
```

```
        The dataset containing the columns to be plotted.
    sequence_list : list of lists
        Each element is a list of contiguous indices for a specific class.
    column_index : int
        The column index in `dataframe.columns` that we want to plot.
    class_labels : list of str
        The names of the classes/activities corresponding to each sequence.
    subplot_shape : tuple, default=(2, 3)
        The layout for the subplots (rows, cols).
    figure_size : tuple, default=(15, 7)
        The overall size of the generated figure (width, height).
    color_of_plot : str, default='red'
        The color used for plotting each sequence.
    y_limits : tuple, default=(-2, 2)
        The y-axis range for all subplots.
    """
    fig, axes = plt.subplots(*subplot_shape, figsize=figure_size)
    row_index, col_index = 0, 0
    label_idx = 0

    # Extract the actual data for the chosen column
    data_to_plot = dataframe[dataframe.columns[column_index]].to_numpy()

    # Iterate over each set of contiguous indices
    for seq in sequence_list:
        if len(seq) > 1:  # Need at least a start and an end index
            axes[row_index,            col_index].plot(data_to_plot[seq[0]:seq[-1]],
color=color_of_plot)
            axes[row_index, col_index].set_title(class_labels[label_idx])
            axes[row_index, col_index].set_ylim(y_limits)


        label_idx += 1
        col_index += 1
```

```
            # Move to next row of subplots if we've filled one row
            if col_index == subplot_shape[1]:
                col_index = 0
                row_index += 1

    fig.suptitle(dataframe.columns[column_index], fontsize=14)
    plt.show()

# Define a list of class/segment names
class_names = ["Relaxing", "Coffee time", "Early morning", "Cleanup",
"Sandwich time"]

# Define a dictionary for label replacements
activity_mapping = {
    0: 'Relaxing',
    1: 'Coffee time',
    2: 'Early morning',
    3: 'Cleanup',
    4: 'Sandwich time'
}

# Replace numerical labels with descriptive labels
df['HL_Activity'] = df['HL_Activity'].replace(activity_mapping)

# Choose a fancy Seaborn palette (e.g., Set2, husl, pastel, etc.)
palette = sns.color_palette('Set2', n_colors=df['HL_Activity'].nunique())

# Plot the bar chart using the color palette
df['HL_Activity'].value_counts().plot(
    kind='bar',
    color=palette,
    edgecolor='black'
)

# Add labels and title
plt.xlabel('HL_Activity')
plt.ylabel('Count')
plt.title('Distribution of HL_Activity', fontsize=14)
plt.xticks(rotation=15)
plt.tight_layout()
plt.show()
```

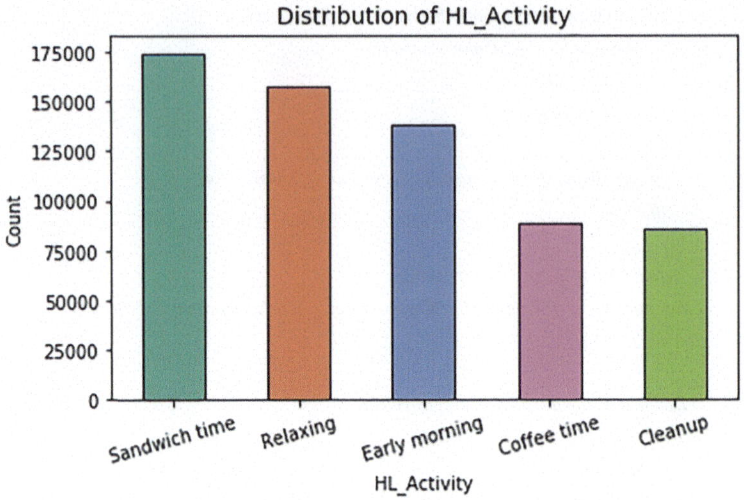

Fig. 5.27 Distribution of samples of different activities from the opportunity dataset

```
from sklearn.model_selection import train_test_split
from sklearn.decomposition import PCA
from sklearn.metrics import confusion_matrix
from sklearn.metrics import classification_report
from sklearn.metrics import accuracy_score, cohen_kappa_score, roc_curve,
auc, roc_auc_score, precision_recall_curve

from bayes_opt import BayesianOptimization

import tensorflow as tf
from tensorflow.keras.utils import to_categorical
from tensorflow.keras.models import Sequential
from tensorflow.keras.layers import Conv1D, MaxPooling1D, Dropout, Flatten
from tensorflow.keras.optimizers import Adam
```

```
import numpy as np
import pandas as pd
from sklearn.preprocessing import StandardScaler
from sklearn.model_selection import train_test_split

def segment_data(data_source, segment_length, target_label):
    """
    Splits the provided DataFrame into overlapping windows of size
`segment_length`,
    ensuring that each segment contains rows with the same activity label and
belongs
    to the same 'file/object' if applicable.

    Parameters
    ----------
    data_source : pd.DataFrame
        The DataFrame holding all data to be segmented.
    segment_length : int
        The fixed size of each segment.
    target_label : str
        Name of the column whose values act as the classification target.

    Returns
    -------
    np.ndarray
        Array of segmented input features of shape (num_segments,
segment_length, num_columns).
    np.ndarray
        Array of corresponding labels of shape (num_segments,).
```

```
"""

# Identify the column index of the target
target_idx = data_source.columns.get_loc(target_label)


# Convert DataFrame to NumPy for speed/efficiency
data_matrix = data_source.to_numpy()
dataset_length = len(data_matrix)


# Prepare containers for the features and labels
feature_segments = []
label_segments = []


left_ptr = 0
while left_ptr + segment_length <= dataset_length:
    right_ptr = left_ptr + segment_length - 1

    # If the segment starts and ends with the same label and same 'file/object'
    if                    (data_matrix[left_ptr][target_idx]                    ==
data_matrix[right_ptr][target_idx] and
            data_matrix[left_ptr][-1] == data_matrix[right_ptr][-1]):

        # Take this window as a valid segment
        feature_segments.append(data_matrix[left_ptr:right_ptr + 1, :])
        label_segments.append(data_matrix[left_ptr][target_idx])

        # Move the left pointer by half the segment length to allow 50%
overlap
        left_ptr += segment_length // 2
    else:
        # If label or file/object is inconsistent across the window,
        # increment `left_ptr` until label changes or we reach the window
end
        while left_ptr + segment_length <= dataset_length:
```

```
                if data_matrix[left_ptr][target_idx] != data_matrix[left_ptr + 1][target_idx]:
                    break
                left_ptr += 1
            left_ptr += 1

    return np.array(feature_segments), np.array(label_segments)

# Example usage
features, targets = segment_data(data_source=df, segment_length=25, target_label="HL_Activity")

num_segments = features.shape[0]
segment_len = features.shape[1]
num_columns = features.shape[2]
print(f"Features shape: {features.shape}")
print(f"Targets shape : {targets.shape}")

# Reshape features into a 2D array for scaler and model input
reshaped_features = features.reshape(num_segments, -1)

# Apply standard scaling
scaler = StandardScaler()
scaled_features = scaler.fit_transform(reshaped_features)

# Replace potential NaNs with zero
scaled_features = np.nan_to_num(scaled_features, nan=0.0)

# Convert targets to integer type (if not already)
targets = targets.astype(int)

# Number of distinct classes
num_classes = len(np.unique(targets))
```

```
# Split data into training and testing sets
X_train, X_test, y_train, y_test = train_test_split(
    scaled_features,
    targets,
    test_size=0.2,
    random_state=42
)

print(f"Training set size: {X_train.shape[0]}")
print(f"Testing set size : {X_test.shape[0]}")


import numpy as np
import pandas as pd

# ------------------------
# 1. Basic ML Imports
# ------------------------
from sklearn.preprocessing import StandardScaler
from sklearn.metrics import accuracy_score

# Classical ML Models
from sklearn.linear_model import LogisticRegression
from sklearn.svm import SVC
from sklearn.tree import DecisionTreeClassifier
from sklearn.ensemble import (
    RandomForestClassifier,
    GradientBoostingClassifier,
    ExtraTreesClassifier
)
from sklearn.neighbors import KNeighborsClassifier
from sklearn.naive_bayes import GaussianNB
```

```
from sklearn.discriminant_analysis import LinearDiscriminantAnalysis
from sklearn.neural_network import MLPClassifier

# -------------------------
# 2. XAI Imports
# -------------------------
from sklearn.inspection import partial_dependence, PartialDependenceDisplay
from lime import lime_tabular
import matplotlib.pyplot as plt

# -------------------------
models = {
    "LogisticRegression": LogisticRegression(max_iter=1000),
    "SVC": SVC(),  # By default, this is an RBF kernel SVC (no coef_ or
feature_importances_)
    "DecisionTree": DecisionTreeClassifier(),
    "RandomForest": RandomForestClassifier(),
    "GradientBoosting": GradientBoostingClassifier(),
    "ExtraTrees": ExtraTreesClassifier(),
    "KNN": KNeighborsClassifier(),
    "GaussianNB": GaussianNB(),
    "LDA": LinearDiscriminantAnalysis(),
    "MLP": MLPClassifier(max_iter=1000)
}

results = {}
num_features = X_train.shape[1]

for name, clf in models.items():
    clf.fit(X_train, y_train)
    y_pred = clf.predict(X_test)
    acc = accuracy_score(y_test, y_pred)
    results[name] = acc
```

```
    print(f"{name} Accuracy: {acc:.4f}")

    # ------------------------
    # Print Top 5 "Feature Importance" (if available)
    # ------------------------
    if hasattr(clf, "feature_importances_"):
        # Tree-based models
        importances = clf.feature_importances_
        indices = np.argsort(importances)[::-1]
        top_indices = indices[:5]
        print("  Feature Importances (Top 5):")
        for rank, idx in enumerate(top_indices, start=1):
            print(f"      #{rank}:   Feature   {idx},   Importance:
{importances[idx]:.4f}")

    elif hasattr(clf, "coef_"):
        # Linear models: logistic regression, linear SVC, LDA (in 1-vs-rest or
multi-class scenario)
        # We'll use the average absolute coefficient across classes if multiclass
        coefs = clf.coef_
        if coefs.ndim > 1 and coefs.shape[0] > 1:
            # e.g., shape (n_classes, n_features)
            importances = np.mean(np.abs(coefs), axis=0)
        else:
            # shape (1, n_features) or (n_features,)
            importances = np.abs(coefs).ravel()

        indices = np.argsort(importances)[::-1]
        top_indices = indices[:5]
        print("  Coefficients (Top 5 by absolute value):")
        for rank, idx in enumerate(top_indices, start=1):
            print(f"    #{rank}: Feature {idx}, Coef: {importances[idx]:.4f}")
        else:
            # Some models (SVC with RBF, KNN, GaussianNB, MLP) don't have
  built-in feature importance
            print("  (No direct feature importance or coefficient attribute.)")

        print("-------------------------------------------------------")
```

```
LogisticRegression Accuracy: 0.9939
  Coefficients (Top 5 by absolute value):
    #1: Feature 1494, Coef: 0.0914
    #2: Feature 2494, Coef: 0.0914
    #3: Feature 3494, Coef: 0.0914
    #4: Feature 2244, Coef: 0.0914
    #5: Feature 5244, Coef: 0.0914
--------------------------------------------------------
SVC Accuracy: 0.9915
  (No direct feature importance or coefficient attribute.)
--------------------------------------------------------
DecisionTree Accuracy: 1.0000
  Feature Importances (Top 5):
    #1: Feature 6244, Importance: 0.5089
    #2: Feature 5744, Importance: 0.2275
    #3: Feature 4244, Importance: 0.1830
    #4: Feature 2994, Importance: 0.0806
    #5: Feature 2076, Importance: 0.0000
--------------------------------------------------------
RandomForest Accuracy: 1.0000
  Feature Importances (Top 5):
    #1: Feature 3994, Importance: 0.0335
    #2: Feature 4244, Importance: 0.0334
    #3: Feature 2994, Importance: 0.0312
    #4: Feature 3494, Importance: 0.0301
    #5: Feature 1744, Importance: 0.0294
--------------------------------------------------------
GradientBoosting Accuracy: 0.9988
  Feature Importances (Top 5):
    #1: Feature 3744, Importance: 0.1509
    #2: Feature 4763, Importance: 0.1012
    #3: Feature 494, Importance: 0.0971
    #4: Feature 3494, Importance: 0.0846
    #5: Feature 5494, Importance: 0.0823
--------------------------------------------------------
ExtraTrees Accuracy: 1.0000
  Feature Importances (Top 5):
    #1: Feature 3494, Importance: 0.0299
    #2: Feature 5744, Importance: 0.0255
    #3: Feature 5494, Importance: 0.0254
    #4: Feature 4244, Importance: 0.0252
    #5: Feature 4994, Importance: 0.0246
--------------------------------------------------------
```

Fig. 5.28 Accuracies and top feature importances of different approaches on the opportunity dataset

```
import numpy as np
import tensorflow as tf
from tensorflow.keras.utils import to_categorical
from tensorflow import keras
from tensorflow.keras import layers

# For LIME
from lime import lime_tabular

# ------------------------------------------------------------------
# 1. Suppose you've loaded or defined X_train, y_train, X_test, y_test
#     - X_train.shape -> (3297, 2000),   X_test.shape -> (825, 2000)
#     - y_train.shape -> (3297,),          y_test.shape -> (825,)
#     - Each label in [0..4] if you have 5 classes
# ------------------------------------------------------------------

# Example:
# X_train, y_train, X_test, y_test = ...
# L, M = 25, 250   # timesteps=25, features=250
# num_classes = 5

# Reshape X to (samples, timesteps=25, features=250)
X_train = X_train.reshape(X_train.shape[0], L, M)
X_test  = X_test.reshape(X_test.shape[0],  L, M)

print("X_train shape:", X_train.shape)    # (3297, 25, 250)
print("X_test shape: ", X_test.shape)     # (825, 25, 250)

# Convert integer labels to one-hot, shape becomes (samples, 5)
y_train = to_categorical(y_train)
y_test  = to_categorical(y_test)

print("y_train shape:", y_train.shape)    # (3297, 5)
print("y_test shape: ", y_test.shape)     # (825, 5)
```

```
# ---------------------------------------------------------------
# 2. Build RNN, LSTM, GRU Models
# ---------------------------------------------------------------
def build_rnn_model(input_shape, num_classes):
    """SimpleRNN model."""
    model = keras.Sequential([
        layers.SimpleRNN(64, input_shape=input_shape),
        layers.Dense(num_classes, activation='softmax')
    ])
    return model

def build_lstm_model(input_shape, num_classes):
    """LSTM model."""
    model = keras.Sequential([
        layers.LSTM(64, input_shape=input_shape),
        layers.Dense(num_classes, activation='softmax')
    ])
    return model

def build_gru_model(input_shape, num_classes):
    """GRU model."""
    model = keras.Sequential([
        layers.GRU(64, input_shape=input_shape),
        layers.Dense(num_classes, activation='softmax')
    ])
    return model

# ---------------------------------------------------------------
# 3. Compile & Train Function (for one-hot labels)
# ---------------------------------------------------------------
def train_tf_model(model, X_tr, y_tr, epochs=5, batch_size=32):
    model.compile(
```

```
        optimizer='adam',
        loss='categorical_crossentropy',    # <--- For one-hot labels
        metrics=['accuracy']
    )
    history = model.fit(
        X_tr, y_tr,
        epochs=epochs,
        batch_size=batch_size,
        verbose=1
    )
    return model, history

# Decide input shape & number of classes
timesteps   = L          # 25
n_features = M           # 250
num_classes = y_train.shape[1]     # 5
input_shape = (timesteps, n_features)

# ----------------------------------------------------------------
# 4. Train SimpleRNN, LSTM, GRU
# ----------------------------------------------------------------
print("\n--- Training Simple RNN ---")
rnn_model = build_rnn_model(input_shape, num_classes)
rnn_model, rnn_hist = train_tf_model(rnn_model, X_train, y_train)

print("\n--- Training LSTM ---")
lstm_model = build_lstm_model(input_shape, num_classes)
lstm_model, lstm_hist = train_tf_model(lstm_model, X_train, y_train)

print("\n--- Training GRU ---")
gru_model = build_gru_model(input_shape, num_classes)
gru_model, gru_hist = train_tf_model(gru_model, X_train, y_train)
```

```
# ---------------------------------------------------------------
# 5. Evaluate on the Test Set
# ---------------------------------------------------------------
def evaluate_tf_model(model, X_te, y_te):
    loss, acc = model.evaluate(X_te, y_te, verbose=0)
    return loss, acc


rnn_loss,  rnn_acc  = evaluate_tf_model(rnn_model,  X_test, y_test)
lstm_loss, lstm_acc = evaluate_tf_model(lstm_model, X_test, y_test)
gru_loss,  gru_acc  = evaluate_tf_model(gru_model,  X_test, y_test)


print(f"\nTest Accuracies:")
print(f"Simple RNN: {rnn_acc:.4f}")
print(f"LSTM:       {lstm_acc:.4f}")
print(f"GRU:        {gru_acc:.4f}")


# ---------------------------------------------------------------
# 6. LIME Explanation on the LSTM model
#    Flatten each sample (25, 250) -> (25*250=6250) for LIME
# ---------------------------------------------------------------
X_test_flat = X_test.reshape(X_test.shape[0], -1)  # shape = (825, 6250)

def lstm_predict_proba(x_flat):
    """
    x_flat: shape (batch, timesteps * n_features)
    We'll reshape to (batch, 25, 250), then predict using the LSTM,
    which returns a (batch, 5) softmax output.
    """
    x_reshaped = x_flat.reshape(x_flat.shape[0], timesteps, n_features)
    preds = lstm_model.predict(x_reshaped)  # shape (batch, 5)
    return preds  # Probability distribution already

explainer = lime_tabular.LimeTabularExplainer(
```

```
    training_data = X_train.reshape(X_train.shape[0], -1),
    feature_names = [f"feature_{i}" for i in range(timesteps * n_features)],
    class_names   = [f"class_{c}" for c in range(num_classes)],
    discretize_continuous=True
)

# Explain 1 test instance (index=0)
instance_idx = 1
instance_flat = X_test_flat[instance_idx]

lime_exp = explainer.explain_instance(
    data_row    = instance_flat,
    predict_fn = lstm_predict_proba,
    num_features = 5   # Show top-5 features
)

print(f"\nLIME Explanation for test instance {instance_idx} (LSTM):")
for feature, importance in lime_exp.as_list():
    print(f"{feature}: {importance:.4f}")
```

5.4 USC-HAD Dataset

The University of Southern California Human Activity Dataset (USC-HAD) is a highly regarded benchmark in the human activity recognition (HAR) field, designed particularly for analyzing signals from inertial sensors worn on the body. Developed by researchers at USC, this dataset aims to support the creation, assessment, and refinement of algorithms capable of detecting and categorizing regular activities performed in everyday life. As wearable sensor technology has grown more sophisticated and user-friendly, the curators of USC-HAD focused on obtaining genuine, day-to-day behaviors from individuals carrying out a variety of tasks, thereby enabling

```
--- Training Simple RNN ---
Epoch 1/5
104/104 [==============================] - 1s 4ms/step - loss: 0.6063 - accuracy: 0.7889
Epoch 2/5
104/104 [==============================] - 0s 4ms/step - loss: 0.1597 - accuracy: 0.9612
Epoch 3/5
104/104 [==============================] - 0s 4ms/step - loss: 0.0610 - accuracy: 0.9897
Epoch 4/5
104/104 [==============================] - 0s 4ms/step - loss: 0.0275 - accuracy: 0.9964
Epoch 5/5
104/104 [==============================] - 0s 4ms/step - loss: 0.0227 - accuracy: 0.9964

--- Training LSTM ---
Epoch 1/5
104/104 [==============================] - 2s 10ms/step - loss: 0.5141 - accuracy: 0.8353
Epoch 2/5
104/104 [==============================] - 1s 10ms/step - loss: 0.0773 - accuracy: 0.9860
Epoch 3/5
104/104 [==============================] - 1s 9ms/step - loss: 0.0220 - accuracy: 0.9970
Epoch 4/5
104/104 [==============================] - 1s 9ms/step - loss: 0.0079 - accuracy: 1.0000
Epoch 5/5
104/104 [==============================] - 1s 10ms/step - loss: 0.0039 - accuracy: 1.0000

--- Training GRU ---
Epoch 1/5
104/104 [==============================] - 3s 9ms/step - loss: 0.5332 - accuracy: 0.8192
Epoch 2/5
104/104 [==============================] - 1s 10ms/step - loss: 0.1110 - accuracy: 0.9727
Epoch 3/5
104/104 [==============================] - 1s 9ms/step - loss: 0.0295 - accuracy: 0.9961
Epoch 4/5
104/104 [==============================] - 1s 9ms/step - loss: 0.0144 - accuracy: 0.9985
Epoch 5/5
104/104 [==============================] - 1s 9ms/step - loss: 0.0103 - accuracy: 0.9982

Test Accuracies:
Simple RNN: 0.9697
LSTM:       0.9939
GRU:        0.9915

LIME Explanation for test instance 0 (LSTM):
feature_5992 > 0.32: 0.0285
feature_6236 > 0.66: 0.0249
feature_6242 > 0.33: 0.0227
feature_6084 <= -0.99: 0.0226
feature_4064 > 0.70: 0.0218
```

Fig. 5.29 Training epochs, testing accuracies of different approaches, and Lime on LSTM on the opportunity dataset

algorithms to be tested in conditions that closely resemble real-world environments [7, 8].

Within USC-HAD, you will find motion-tracking data primarily recorded by accelerometers and gyroscopes affixed to participants' bodies. Each participant carried out numerous daily tasks, such as walking, jogging, ascending and descending stairs, standing, and other routine actions that depict the broad range of activities people undertake. These sensors gather signals along multiple axes, producing distinct motion signatures for each activity type. Equipped with this comprehensive sensor data, researchers can harness both classic and modern machine learning approaches—ranging from feature-based methods to sophisticated deep neural networks—to accurately classify and forecast human movements. Furthermore, the variability in personal biomechanics, including posture and walking style, is captured by USC-HAD's diverse group of subjects, helping models to generalize better across different populations. Beyond its initial role in activity recognition research, USC-HAD extends into other meaningful applications. For instance, it has proven valuable in medical monitoring scenarios, such as tracking subtle changes in patients with Parkinson's disease or identifying early indicators of mobility difficulties. Care providers can detect warning signs—for example, a shift in gait or posture—and intervene before serious injuries occur. In fitness and sports, meanwhile, coaches and athletes can analyze motion data to spot inefficiencies or heightened fatigue, streamlining training sessions and reducing the risk of injury. The dataset's methodical labeling of each recorded activity, along with the standardized manner of data collection, makes it simpler to construct reliable pipelines for real-time monitoring or offline research, ensuring adaptability to different real-world settings.

One of the dataset's major advantages is its accessibility for users at all levels of expertise. Students and novices can learn the fundamentals of feature extraction, classification, and performance evaluation using USC-HAD, thanks to its balanced assortment of simple and complex movements. In parallel, advanced investigators can build upon the dataset to refine cutting-edge techniques, experiment with transfer learning, or investigate specialized areas such as anomaly detection in motion patterns. This flexibility highlights why USC-HAD remains a cornerstone in inertial sensor research and why it continues to be embraced by scholars seeking to expand the frontiers of human activity recognition. Figure 5.30 shows confusion matrix and LIME output from LSTM on the USC-HAD dataset.

```python
# Imports and setup
import os
import gc
import numpy as np
import pandas as pd
import seaborn as sns
import matplotlib.pyplot as plt
from sklearn.model_selection import train_test_split
from sklearn.preprocessing import LabelEncoder, StandardScaler
from sklearn.metrics import classification_report, confusion_matrix,
accuracy_score
from sklearn.utils.class_weight import compute_class_weight

import tensorflow as tf
from tensorflow.keras.models import Model
from tensorflow.keras.layers import Input, Dense, Dropout, BatchNormalization,
LSTM
from tensorflow.keras.optimizers import Adam
from tensorflow.keras.utils import to_categorical
from tensorflow.keras.callbacks import EarlyStopping, ReduceLROnPlateau,
ModelCheckpoint
```

```
from tensorflow.keras.regularizers import l2

# : Load Data from Directory
def load_chunks(directory, chunk_size=1000):
    data_frames = []
    for folder in sorted(os.listdir(directory)):
        if 'Subject' in folder and 'converted' in folder.lower():
            path = os.path.join(directory, folder)
            if not os.path.isdir(path):
                continue

            csv_files = sorted([f for f in os.listdir(path) if f.endswith('.csv')])
            meta_files = sorted([f for f in os.listdir(path) if f.endswith('.txt')])

            for csv_file, meta_file in zip(csv_files, meta_files):
                with open(os.path.join(path, meta_file), 'r') as f:
                    lines = f.readlines()
                    activity = next((line.split(":")[1].strip().strip(']') for line in
lines if line.startswith('activity')), None)

                for chunk in pd.read_csv(os.path.join(path, csv_file),
chunksize=chunk_size):
                    if all(col in chunk.columns for col in ['accelerometer_x',
'accelerometer_y', 'accelerometer_z',
                                                              'gyroscope_x',
'gyroscope_y', 'gyroscope_z']):
                        chunk['activity'] = activity
                        data_frames.append(chunk)
    return pd.concat(data_frames, ignore_index=True)

base_dir = "./USC-HAD/"
df = load_chunks(base_dir)
```

```
# : Preprocess Data
le = LabelEncoder()
df['activity'] = le.fit_transform(df['activity'])

features = df[['accelerometer_x', 'accelerometer_y', 'accelerometer_z',
               'gyroscope_x', 'gyroscope_y', 'gyroscope_z']].values
labels = df['activity'].values

acc_mag = np.linalg.norm(features[:, :3], axis=1)
gyro_mag = np.linalg.norm(features[:, 3:], axis=1)
features = np.column_stack((features, acc_mag, gyro_mag))
features = StandardScaler().fit_transform(features)

# : Create Windows
window_size = 20
X, y = [], []
for i in range(len(features) - window_size):
    X.append(features[i:i+window_size])
    y.append(labels[i + window_size - 1])
X, y = np.array(X), to_categorical(y)

# : Train-Test Split
train_idx, test_idx = train_test_split(np.arange(len(X)), test_size=0.15,
stratify=np.argmax(y, axis=1), random_state=42)
train_idx, val_idx = train_test_split(train_idx, test_size=0.15,
stratify=np.argmax(y[train_idx], axis=1), random_state=42)
X_train, X_val, X_test = X[train_idx], X[val_idx], X[test_idx]
y_train, y_val, y_test = y[train_idx], y[val_idx], y[test_idx]

# : Class Weights
class_weights = compute_class_weight('balanced',
classes=np.unique(np.argmax(y, axis=1)), y=np.argmax(y, axis=1))
class_weights = {i: w*4.0 if i in [0, 1] else w for i, w in enumerate(class_weights)}
```

```
# : Define LSTM Model
def build_lstm_model(input_shape, num_classes, l2_reg=1e-4):
    inputs = Input(shape=input_shape)
    x = LSTM(64, return_sequences=True, kernel_regularizer=l2(l2_reg))(inputs)
    x = BatchNormalization()(x)
    x = LSTM(64, return_sequences=False, kernel_regularizer=l2(l2_reg))(x)
    x = BatchNormalization()(x)
    x = Dropout(0.5)(x)
    x = Dense(128, activation='relu', kernel_regularizer=l2(l2_reg))(x)
    x = BatchNormalization()(x)
    x = Dropout(0.5)(x)
    outputs = Dense(num_classes, activation='softmax')(x)
    return Model(inputs, outputs)

model = build_lstm_model(input_shape=X_train.shape[1:],
num_classes=y_train.shape[1])
model.compile(optimizer=Adam(1e-4), loss='categorical_crossentropy',
metrics=['accuracy'])
model.summary()

# : Train Model
callbacks = [
    ModelCheckpoint("best_lstm_model.keras", save_best_only=True,
monitor="val_loss"),
    EarlyStopping(monitor="val_loss", patience=10,
restore_best_weights=True),
    ReduceLROnPlateau(monitor="val_loss", factor=0.2, patience=3, min_lr=1e-
6, verbose=1)
]

history = model.fit(
    X_train, y_train,
```

```
    validation_data=(X_val, y_val),
    epochs=50,
    batch_size=64,
    callbacks=callbacks,
    class_weight=class_weights,
    verbose=1
)

# : Evaluate
loss, acc = model.evaluate(X_test, y_test)
print(f"Test Accuracy: {acc * 100:.2f}%")

# Confusion Matrix
preds = model.predict(X_test)
y_true = np.argmax(y_test, axis=1)
y_pred = np.argmax(preds, axis=1)

plt.figure(figsize = (16,12))
conf_matrix = confusion_matrix(y_true, y_pred)
sns.heatmap(conf_matrix, annot=True, fmt='d', cmap='viridis')
plt.title("Confusion Matrix")
plt.xlabel("Predicted")
plt.ylabel("True")

print(classification_report(y_true, y_pred))

# : LIME Example
from lime.lime_tabular import LimeTabularExplainer

explainer = LimeTabularExplainer(
    training_data=X_train.reshape((X_train.shape[0], -1)),
    feature_names=[f"f{i}" for i in range(X_train.shape[1] * X_train.shape[2])],
    class_names=[str(cls) for cls in le.classes_],
    discretize_continuous=True
)

sample_idx = 5
sample_input = X_test[sample_idx].reshape(1, X_test.shape[1], X_test.shape[2])
pred_func = lambda x: model.predict(x.reshape(-1, X_test.shape[1],
X_test.shape[2]))

explanation = explainer.explain_instance(
    X_test[sample_idx].reshape(-1),
    pred_func,
    num_features=10,
    top_labels=1
)

explanation.show_in_notebook(show_table=True)
```

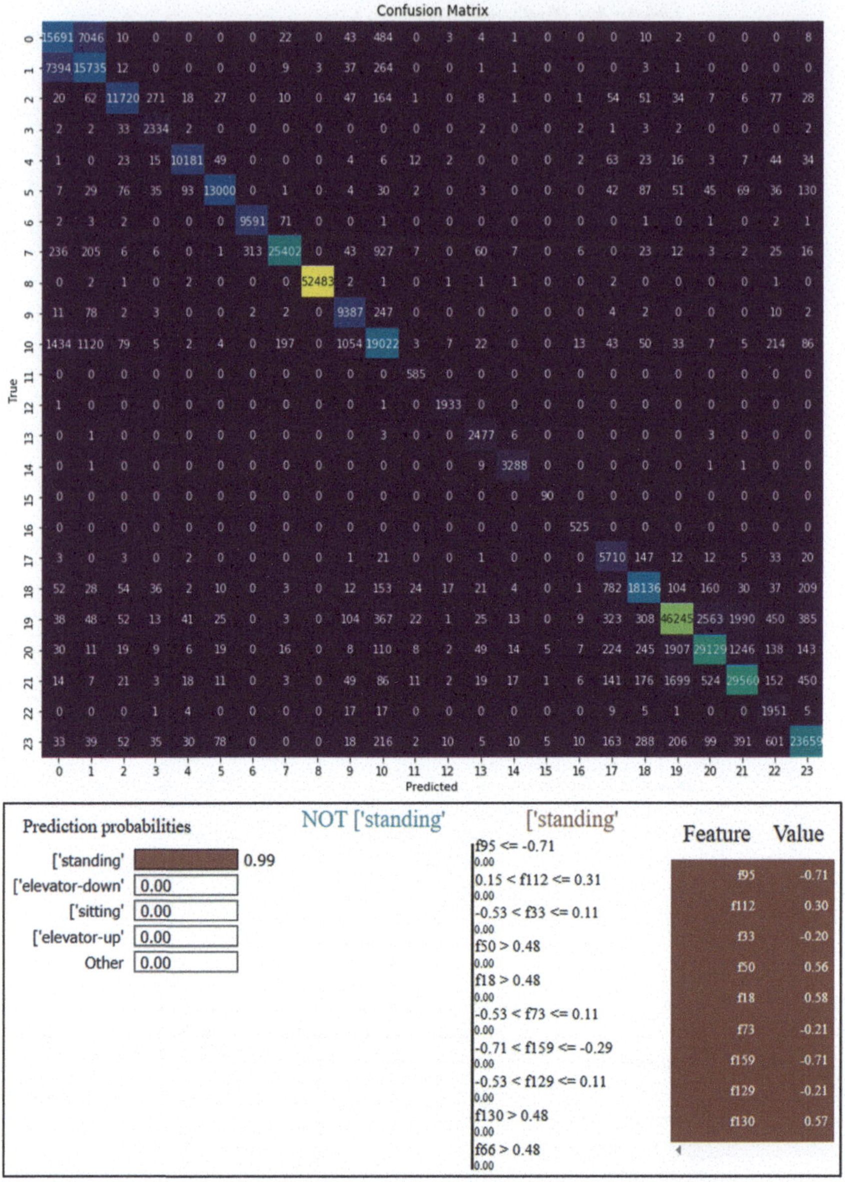

Fig. 5.30 Confusion matrix and LIME output from LSTM on the USC-HAD dataset

5.5 Center for Advanced Studies in Adaptive Systems

Center for Advanced Studies in Adaptive Systems (CASAS) dataset is widely used in research areas such as activity recognition, elder care, health monitoring, and home automation. The CASAS dataset is a large and useful collection of smart home sensor data developed by researchers at Washington State University. It's part of a broader effort to create intelligent environments that can understand and respond to people's daily lives [9, 10].

At its core, the CASAS dataset captures how people move through and interact with their living space using non-intrusive sensors. These sensors are installed throughout smart homes or apartments and collect data such as motion, door openings, and temperature readings. This data is stored over time to build a picture of a person's behavior and daily habits. What makes this data valuable is that it allows researchers to build systems that can recognize activities like cooking, sleeping, or leaving the house without using cameras or microphones. One of the key strengths of the CASAS dataset is its real-world application. Rather than collecting information in a lab, the researchers installed sensors in actual homes and allowed people to go about their regular routines. This makes the data more natural and realistic, which is important when building systems that are meant to work in real environments. Since the sensors are silent and do not capture images or sound, they also help protect the privacy of the people living in these smart homes.

Each smart home in the dataset is equipped with a number of basic environmental sensors. These usually include motion sensors to detect presence or movement in rooms, magnetic sensors on doors and cupboards, light switches, and sometimes temperature or water flow sensors. For example, if someone opens a refrigerator and then moves into the kitchen area, those two events might be recorded and used to infer that the person is cooking or getting a snack. The data format is generally simple but highly detailed. Each event includes a timestamp, a sensor ID, a sensor value (like "ON" or "OFF"), and sometimes an activity label. A sample entry might say that motion sensor M001 was triggered at 3:42 PM, and the activity at that moment was "Cook." With thousands of such entries collected each day, researchers can trace full routines, understand habits, and even spot unusual behavior patterns.

Another important feature of CASAS is the variety of datasets it offers. There are datasets from different types of homes and different countries. Some datasets involve a single person living in the home, while others have multiple residents, which makes activity recognition more complex. Examples include the Kyoto dataset and Milan dataset, which contains two-resident activity data. Each of these has its own unique layout and collection period, adding to the richness of the overall dataset. The CASAS datasets are often used to train machine learning models. These models learn patterns from the sensor data and use those patterns to predict or recognize what a person is doing. For example, after analyzing many "sleep" activities in the data, the model may learn that a person sleeping usually triggers bedroom motion sensors only once or twice in several hours. Once trained, these models can be used in real-time systems that alert caregivers if something unusual happens—like no movement in the kitchen during breakfast time.

Figure 5.31 highlights the top-ranked feature importances identified by various classical machine learning approaches on the CASAS dataset, offering insight into which variables most influence activity classification. Figure 5.32 presents the training loss and accuracy curves for three deep learning models—SimpleRNN, LSTM, and GRU—demonstrating their learning progress over epochs and comparative performance. Finally, Fig. 5.33 illustrates a LIME explanation applied to the LSTM model on a specific test instance, showing the top contributing features responsible for the model's prediction and offering a window into its interpretability. The code is as follows:

```
import argparse
import csv
from datetime import datetime
import tensorflow.keras
import numpy as np
from tensorflow.keras.callbacks import ModelCheckpoint, CSVLogger
from sklearn.metrics import confusion_matrix, classification_report
from sklearn.model_selection import StratifiedKFold
from sklearn.utils import compute_class_weight
from sklearn.preprocessing import LabelEncoder
from sklearn.model_selection import KFold
from tensorflow.keras.models import Sequential, load_model
X, Y, dictActivities =  data.getData("milan")
import numpy as np
import pandas as pd
import matplotlib.pyplot as plt
```

```
# ------------------------
# 1. Basic ML Imports
# ------------------------
from sklearn.model_selection import train_test_split
from sklearn.preprocessing import StandardScaler
from sklearn.metrics import accuracy_score

# Classical ML Models
from sklearn.linear_model import LogisticRegression
from sklearn.svm import SVC
from sklearn.tree import DecisionTreeClassifier
from sklearn.ensemble import (
    RandomForestClassifier,
    GradientBoostingClassifier,
    ExtraTreesClassifier
)
from sklearn.neighbors import KNeighborsClassifier
from sklearn.naive_bayes import GaussianNB
from sklearn.discriminant_analysis import LinearDiscriminantAnalysis
from sklearn.neural_network import MLPClassifier

# ------------------------
# 2. XAI Imports
# ------------------------
from sklearn.inspection import PartialDependenceDisplay
```

```
from lime import lime_tabular

# For demonstration, assume you have X, Y loaded
# X.shape -> (n_samples, n_features)
# Y.shape -> (n_samples, )

# ------------------------
# 3. Train/Test Split
# ------------------------
X_train, X_test, y_train, y_test = train_test_split(
    X, Y, test_size=0.2, random_state=42
)

# ------------------------
# 4. Feature Scaling
# ------------------------
scaler = StandardScaler()
X_train_scaled = scaler.fit_transform(X_train)
X_test_scaled = scaler.transform(X_test)

# ------------------------
# 5. Train Multiple Models
# ------------------------
models = {
    "LogisticRegression": LogisticRegression(max_iter=1000),
    "SVC": SVC(),   # No built-in feature_importances_ or coef_ in RBF SVC
    "DecisionTree": DecisionTreeClassifier(),
    "RandomForest": RandomForestClassifier(),
    "GradientBoosting": GradientBoostingClassifier(),
    "ExtraTrees": ExtraTreesClassifier(),
    "KNN": KNeighborsClassifier(),   # No feature_importances_ or coef_
    "GaussianNB": GaussianNB(),      # No feature_importances_ or coef_
    "LDA": LinearDiscriminantAnalysis(),
```

```
    "MLP": MLPClassifier(max_iter=1000)  # No feature_importances_ or direct
coef_
}

results = {}
num_features = X_train.shape[1]

for name, clf in models.items():
    clf.fit(X_train_scaled, y_train)
    y_pred = clf.predict(X_test_scaled)
    acc = accuracy_score(y_test, y_pred)
    results[name] = acc

    print(f"{name} Accuracy: {acc:.4f}")

    # -------------------------
    # Plot Top 5 Feature Importance or Coefficients
    # -------------------------
    if hasattr(clf, "feature_importances_"):
        # Tree-based models
        importances = clf.feature_importances_
        indices = np.argsort(importances)[::-1]  # descending sort
        top_indices = indices[:5]

        print("   Feature Importances (Top 5):")
        for rank, idx in enumerate(top_indices, start=1):
            print(f"          #{rank}:    Feature    {idx},    Importance:
{importances[idx]:.4f}")

        # ----- Show bar chart -----
        plt.figure()
        plt.bar(range(5), importances[top_indices])
        plt.xticks(range(5), [f"Feature {idx}" for idx in top_indices], rotation=45)
```

```
        plt.ylabel("Importance")
        plt.title(f"{name}: Top 5 Feature Importances")
        plt.tight_layout()
        plt.show()

    elif hasattr(clf, "coef_"):
        # Linear models: logistic regression, linear SVC, LDA
        coefs = clf.coef_
        if coefs.ndim > 1 and coefs.shape[0] > 1:
            # If it's multiclass (shape = [n_classes, n_features])
            importances = np.mean(np.abs(coefs), axis=0)
        else:
            # shape (1, n_features) or (n_features,)
            importances = np.abs(coefs).ravel()

        indices = np.argsort(importances)[::-1]
        top_indices = indices[:5]

        print("   Coefficients (Top 5 by absolute value):")
        for rank, idx in enumerate(top_indices, start=1):
            print(f"     #{rank}: Feature {idx}, Coef: {importances[idx]:.4f}")

        # ----- Show bar chart -----
        plt.figure()
        plt.bar(range(5), importances[top_indices])
        plt.xticks(range(5), [f"Feature {idx}" for idx in top_indices], rotation=45)
        plt.ylabel("Coefficient (abs)")
        plt.title(f"{name}: Top 5 Coefficients (abs)")
        plt.tight_layout()
        plt.show()

    else:
        # For SVC with RBF kernel, KNN, GaussianNB, MLP, etc.
            print("   (No direct feature importance or coefficient attribute.)")

        print("-------------------------------------------------------")


    #  Final Accuracy Results
    # ------------------------
    print("\nFinal Accuracy Results of All Models:")
    for name, acc in results.items():
        print(f"{name}: {acc:.4f}")
```

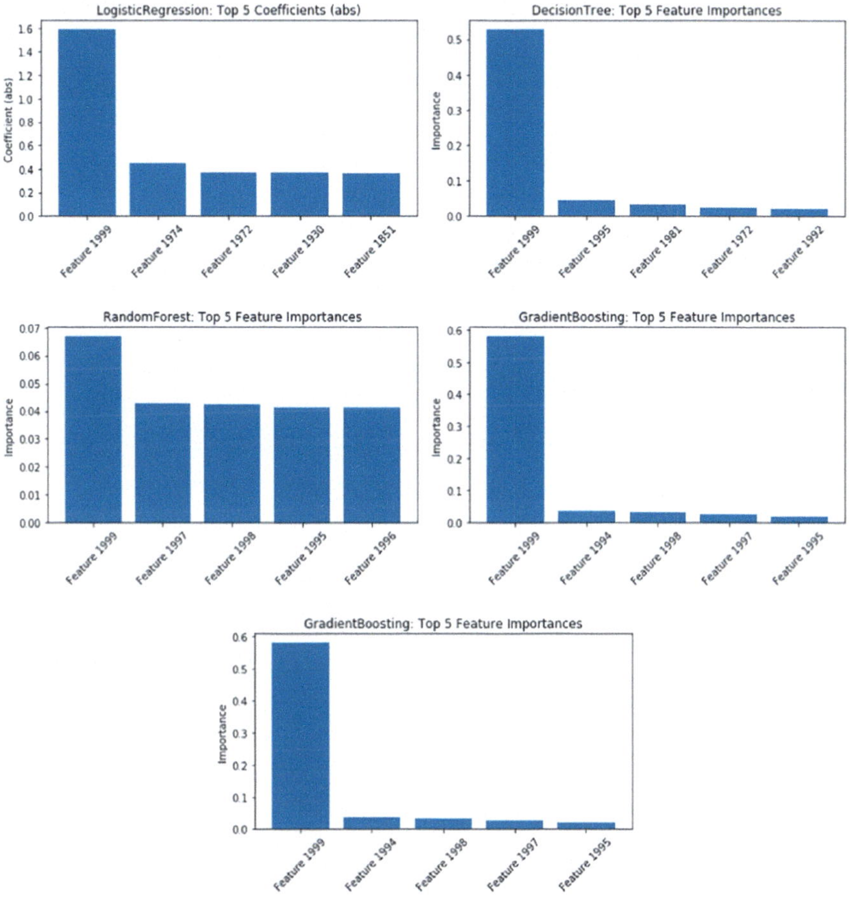

Fig. 5.31 Feature importances of different approaches on CASAS

The final accuracy results are Logistic Regression (0.4383), SVC (0.4759), Decision Tree (0.7521), Random Forest (0.7650), Gradient Boosting (0.8402), Extra Trees (0.7286), KNN (0.5194), GaussianNB (0.0306), LDA (0.4113), and MLP (0.5358).

```
import numpy as np
import torch
import torch.nn as nn
import torch.optim as optim
from sklearn.model_selection import train_test_split
from sklearn.preprocessing import StandardScaler
from sklearn.metrics import accuracy_score
import matplotlib.pyplot as plt

# For LIME
from lime import lime_tabular

# --------------------------------------------------------------------------
# Assume X_train_scaled, X_test_scaled, y_train, y_test are already defined.
# Example shapes:
#   - X_train_scaled: (train_size, 2000)
#   - X_test_scaled : (test_size, 2000)
#   - y_train        : (train_size,)
#   - y_test         : (test_size,)
# --------------------------------------------------------------------------
# Reshape X to (N, 20, 100) as in your example
train_size = X_train_scaled.shape[0]
X_train = X_train_scaled.reshape((train_size, 20, 100))

test_size = X_test_scaled.shape[0]
X_test = X_test_scaled.reshape((test_size, 20, 100))

# Convert to Torch tensors
X_train_tensor = torch.FloatTensor(X_train)
y_train_tensor = torch.LongTensor(y_train)

X_test_tensor = torch.FloatTensor(X_test)
y_test_tensor = torch.LongTensor(y_test)

print("\nFinal Tensor Shapes:")
print("X_train_tensor:", X_train_tensor.shape)  # (train_size, 20, 100)
print("y_train_tensor:", y_train_tensor.shape)  # (train_size,)
```

```
print("X_test_tensor: ", X_test_tensor.shape)    # (test_size, 20, 100)
print("y_test_tensor: ", y_test_tensor.shape)    # (test_size,)

num_classes = 10

# ---------------------------------------------------------------------------
# Define three simple RNN-based classifiers (SimpleRNN, LSTM, GRU)
# ---------------------------------------------------------------------------
class SimpleRNNClassifier(nn.Module):
    def __init__(self, input_size=100, hidden_size=64, num_layers=2,
num_classes=10):
        super(SimpleRNNClassifier, self).__init__()
        self.rnn = nn.RNN(input_size, hidden_size, num_layers, batch_first=True)
        self.fc = nn.Linear(hidden_size, num_classes)

    def forward(self, x):
        out, _ = self.rnn(x)
        out = out[:, -1, :]
        logits = self.fc(out)
        return logits

class LSTMClassifier(nn.Module):
    def __init__(self, input_size=100, hidden_size=64, num_layers=2,
num_classes=10):
        super(LSTMClassifier, self).__init__()
        self.lstm = nn.LSTM(input_size, hidden_size, num_layers,
batch_first=True)
        self.fc = nn.Linear(hidden_size, num_classes)

    def forward(self, x):
        out, _ = self.lstm(x)
        out = out[:, -1, :]
        logits = self.fc(out)
```

```
        return logits


class GRUClassifier(nn.Module):
    def __init__(self, input_size=100, hidden_size=64, num_layers=2, num_classes=10):
        super(GRUClassifier, self).__init__()
        self.gru = nn.GRU(input_size, hidden_size, num_layers, batch_first=True)
        self.fc = nn.Linear(hidden_size, num_classes)

    def forward(self, x):
        out, _ = self.gru(x)
        out = out[:, -1, :]
        logits = self.fc(out)
        return logits

# ---------------------------------------------------------------------------
# Training function: returns the model, plus arrays for loss & accuracy each epoch
# ---------------------------------------------------------------------------
def train_model(model, X_tr, y_tr, epochs=5, lr=1e-3, batch_size=32):
    criterion = nn.CrossEntropyLoss()
    optimizer = optim.Adam(model.parameters(), lr=lr)

    n_samples = X_tr.shape[0]

    # Lists to store the metrics after each epoch
    all_train_losses = []
    all_train_accuracies = []

    for epoch in range(epochs):
        permutation = torch.randperm(n_samples)
        total_loss = 0.0
        correct = 0
```

```
        model.train()
        for i in range(0, n_samples, batch_size):
            idx = permutation[i : i + batch_size]
            batch_x = X_tr[idx]
            batch_y = y_tr[idx]

            optimizer.zero_grad()
            logits = model(batch_x)
            loss = criterion(logits, batch_y)
            loss.backward()
            optimizer.step()

            total_loss += loss.item() * batch_x.size(0)
            preds = torch.argmax(logits, dim=1)
            correct += (preds == batch_y).sum().item()

        train_loss = total_loss / n_samples
        train_acc = correct / n_samples

        all_train_losses.append(train_loss)
        all_train_accuracies.append(train_acc)

        print(f"Epoch [{epoch+1}/{epochs}], "
              f"Train Loss: {train_loss:.4f}, "
              f"Train Acc: {train_acc:.4f}")

    return model, all_train_losses, all_train_accuracies

# ------------------------------------------------------------------------------
# Instantiate and train each model (SimpleRNN, LSTM, GRU), collecting metrics
# ------------------------------------------------------------------------------
print("\n--- Training SimpleRNN ---")
```

```
rnn_model = SimpleRNNClassifier(input_size=100, hidden_size=64,
num_layers=2, num_classes=num_classes)
rnn_model, rnn_losses, rnn_accs = train_model(rnn_model, X_train_tensor,
y_train_tensor, epochs=30, lr=1e-3, batch_size=32)

print("\n--- Training LSTM ---")
lstm_model = LSTMClassifier(input_size=100, hidden_size=64, num_layers=2,
num_classes=num_classes)
lstm_model, lstm_losses, lstm_accs = train_model(lstm_model, X_train_tensor,
y_train_tensor, epochs=30, lr=1e-3, batch_size=32)

print("\n--- Training GRU ---")
gru_model = GRUClassifier(input_size=100, hidden_size=64, num_layers=2,
num_classes=num_classes)
gru_model, gru_losses, gru_accs = train_model(gru_model, X_train_tensor,
y_train_tensor, epochs=30, lr=1e-3, batch_size=32)

# ---------------------------------------------------------------------------
# Plotting the training loss and accuracy for each model
# (One figure for loss, one figure for accuracy)
# ---------------------------------------------------------------------------

# -- SimpleRNN Loss --
plt.figure()
plt.plot(rnn_losses)
plt.title("SimpleRNN Training Loss over Epochs")
plt.xlabel("Epoch")
plt.ylabel("Loss")
plt.show()

# -- SimpleRNN Accuracy --
plt.figure()
plt.plot(rnn_accs)
```

```
plt.title("SimpleRNN Training Accuracy over Epochs")
plt.xlabel("Epoch")
plt.ylabel("Accuracy")
plt.show()

# -- LSTM Loss --
plt.figure()
plt.plot(lstm_losses)
plt.title("LSTM Training Loss over Epochs")
plt.xlabel("Epoch")
plt.ylabel("Loss")
plt.show()

# -- LSTM Accuracy --
plt.figure()
plt.plot(lstm_accs)
plt.title("LSTM Training Accuracy over Epochs")
plt.xlabel("Epoch")
plt.ylabel("Accuracy")
plt.show()

# -- GRU Loss --
plt.figure()
plt.plot(gru_losses)
plt.title("GRU Training Loss over Epochs")
plt.xlabel("Epoch")
plt.ylabel("Loss")
plt.show()

# -- GRU Accuracy --
plt.figure()
plt.plot(gru_accs)
plt.title("GRU Training Accuracy over Epochs")
```

```
plt.xlabel("Epoch")
plt.ylabel("Accuracy")
plt.show()

# ---------------------------------------------------------------------------
# Final evaluation on the test set
# ---------------------------------------------------------------------------
def evaluate_model(model, X_te, y_te):
    model.eval()
    with torch.no_grad():
        logits = model(X_te)
        preds = torch.argmax(logits, dim=1)
    return accuracy_score(y_te.numpy(), preds.numpy())

acc_rnn  = evaluate_model(rnn_model, X_test_tensor, y_test_tensor)
acc_lstm = evaluate_model(lstm_model, X_test_tensor, y_test_tensor)
acc_gru  = evaluate_model(gru_model, X_test_tensor, y_test_tensor)

print("\nFinal Test Accuracies:")
print(f"SimpleRNN: {acc_rnn:.4f}")
print(f"LSTM:      {acc_lstm:.4f}")
print(f"GRU:       {acc_gru:.4f}")
```

The final test accuracies are SimpleRNN (0.6134), LSTM (0.6263), and GRU (0.6228). Now, lets see a LIME example.

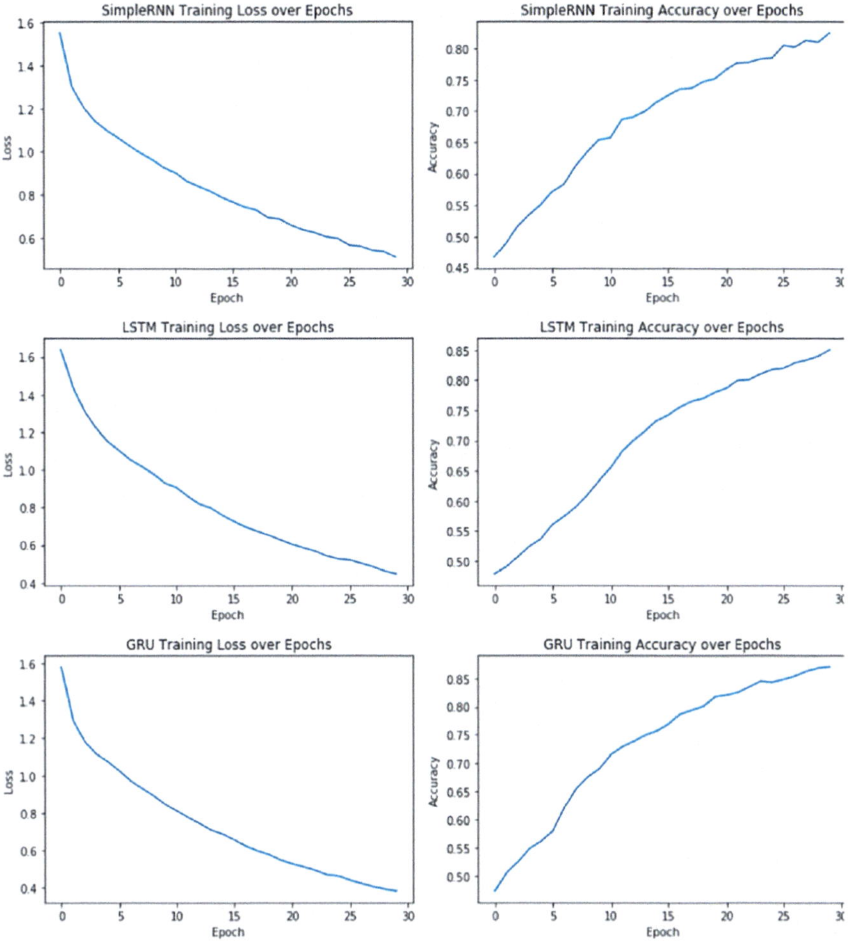

Fig. 5.32 Loss and accuracy plot of different deep learning approaches on CASAS

```
# Prepare the training data for LIME's reference:
# Typically, LIME expects training or reference data in flattened form.
X_train_flat_for_lime = X_train_tensor.reshape(L, -1).numpy()
lime_explainer = lime_tabular.LimeTabularExplainer(
    training_data=X_train_flat_for_lime,
    feature_names=[f"feature_{i}" for i in range(2000)],
    class_names=[f"Class{i}" for i in range(num_classes)],
    discretize_continuous=True
)

# Pick a test instance for local explanation, e.g. the first one
test_instance_idx = 0
X_test_flat_for_lime = X_test_tensor.reshape(M, -1).numpy()
instance_flat = X_test_flat_for_lime[test_instance_idx]  # shape (2000,)

# Explain with LIME
lime_exp = lime_explainer.explain_instance(
    data_row=instance_flat,
    predict_fn=lstm_predict_proba,
    num_features=5  # show top 5 features
)

print(f"\nLIME Explanation for test instance {test_instance_idx} (LSTM):")
for feature_desc, contribution in lime_exp.as_list():
    print(f"{feature_desc}: {contribution:.4f}")

# (Optional) In Jupyter, display or save:
lime_exp.show_in_notebook()
# lime_exp.save_to_file("lime_lstm_explanation.html")
```

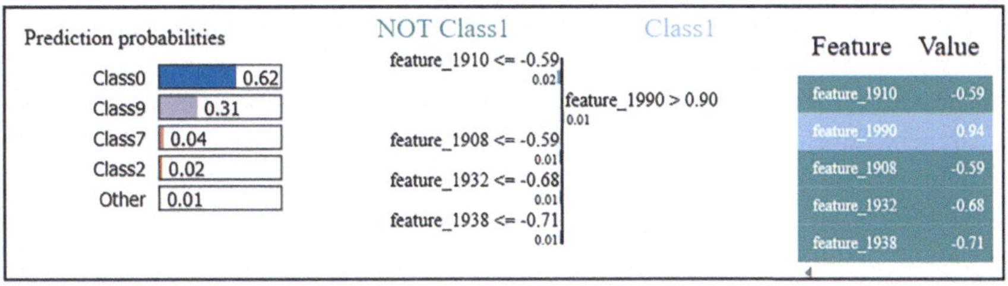

Fig. 5.33 LIME with LSTM on CASAS

5.6 Other Distinguished Datasets

The Silhouettes for Human Posture Recognition dataset, available through IEEE DataPort, offers a comprehensive and structured set of silhouette-based images specifically developed to facilitate research in the field of automated human posture recognition. This dataset addresses a critical need within computer vision and machine learning communities by providing standardized images that clearly depict human forms in various postural states. Silhouettes are particularly valuable because they emphasize shape and contours without background noise, making them ideal for training algorithms focused solely on human posture identification.

This dataset comprises a total of 4,800 silhouette images, categorized evenly into four distinct human posture groups: sitting, standing, bending, and lying. Each category contains precisely 1200 images, maintaining consistency across the dataset [11]. All images within this collection share uniform dimensions of 512 × 512 pixels, ensuring standardization. Such consistency allows researchers to directly compare their methods and algorithms without needing additional preprocessing or size normalization. Moreover, standardized image resolution simplifies the integration of this dataset into existing machine learning frameworks and allows for straightforward benchmarking and comparative analysis across different research initiatives.

The images in this dataset were carefully prepared to eliminate extraneous visual elements, leaving only the essential outlines of the human figures. Silhouette-based datasets are particularly useful for posture recognition tasks because the absence of texture, color, and background simplifies the computational complexity associated with image processing tasks. This allows algorithms to focus exclusively on the geometric shape of the human body, promoting higher accuracy in posture recognition. As a result, the Silhouettes for Human Posture Recognition dataset serves as an excellent foundation for developing and evaluating both classical machine learning approaches and deep learning models, including convolutional neural networks (CNNs) and recurrent neural networks (RNNs), that specifically target posture detection.

The human–computer interaction (HCI) community can employ posture recognition technologies developed from silhouette images to enhance interaction models. Such interfaces might allow users to interact with computers or other digital devices through natural movements and postures, facilitating a more intuitive and engaging user experience. Access to the dataset is open and straightforward. IEEE Data-Port provides this dataset under a Creative Commons Attribution license, enabling researchers, developers, and industry professionals to freely share, adapt, and reuse the data, provided appropriate acknowledgment is given. This open-access model encourages broad usage, collaborative research, and innovation across academic institutions and industries worldwide.

Looking toward the future, the dataset also offers considerable potential for expansion. While currently encompassing four primary postures, incorporating additional complex or intermediate poses can enhance the dataset's versatility. Expanding the dataset to include dynamic sequences rather than isolated static images would help researchers investigate transitions between postures. Including a broader demographic range—covering diverse body types, ages, and clothing styles—and introducing variability in lighting and background settings would also improve the real-world robustness of posture recognition models developed from this resource. Figure 5.34 shows GradCAM results on a testing posture.

```
import tensorflow as tf
from tensorflow.keras.preprocessing import image_dataset_from_directory

# Load training and test sets
train_dir = './train/'
test_dir = './test/'

img_size = (224, 224)
batch_size = 32

train_ds = image_dataset_from_directory(
    train_dir,
    image_size=img_size,
    batch_size=batch_size,
    label_mode='categorical'  #for softmax output
)
```

```
test_ds = image_dataset_from_directory(
    test_dir,
    image_size=img_size,
    batch_size=batch_size,
    label_mode='categorical'
)

class_names = train_ds.class_names
print("Class names:", class_names)
```

So, there were A total of 2000 files belonging to 2 classes were found for training, and 400 files belonging to the same 2 classes were found for testing. The class names were: lying and standing. Let us initialize a CNN model and train for 50 epochs.

```
from tensorflow.keras import layers, models
model = models.Sequential([
    layers.Rescaling(1./255, input_shape=(224, 224, 3)),
    layers.Conv2D(32, (3, 3), activation='relu'),
    layers.MaxPooling2D(),
    layers.Conv2D(64, (3, 3), activation='relu'),
    layers.MaxPooling2D(),
    layers.Conv2D(128, (3, 3), activation='relu'),
    layers.MaxPooling2D(),
    layers.Flatten(),
    layers.Dense(64, activation='relu'),
    layers.Dense(len(class_names), activation='softmax')
])

model.compile(optimizer='adam',
              loss='categorical_crossentropy',
              metrics=['accuracy'])

model.summary()
history = model.fit(train_ds,  epochs=50)
```

Lets apply GradCAM on a testing image to see the result.

```
import numpy as np
import matplotlib.pyplot as plt
import tensorflow.keras.backend as K
from tensorflow.keras.preprocessing import image
import cv2
import os

def get_img_array(img_path, size):
    img = image.load_img(img_path, target_size=size)
    array = image.img_to_array(img)
    array = np.expand_dims(array, axis=0)
    return array / 255.0

def make_gradcam_heatmap(img_array, model, last_conv_layer_name,
pred_index=None):
    grad_model = tf.keras.models.Model(
        [model.inputs], [model.get_layer(last_conv_layer_name).output,
model.output]
    )
    with tf.GradientTape() as tape:
        conv_outputs, predictions = grad_model(img_array)
        if pred_index is None:
            pred_index = tf.argmax(predictions[0])
        class_channel = predictions[:, pred_index]

    grads = tape.gradient(class_channel, conv_outputs)
    pooled_grads = tf.reduce_mean(grads, axis=(0, 1, 2))
    conv_outputs = conv_outputs[0]

    heatmap = conv_outputs @ pooled_grads[..., tf.newaxis]
    heatmap = tf.squeeze(heatmap)
    heatmap = tf.maximum(heatmap, 0) / tf.math.reduce_max(heatmap)
    return heatmap.numpy()
```

```
# Example image path
img_path = './test/standing/117.jpg'  # <-- replace with your image

# Preprocess
img_array = get_img_array(img_path, size=(224, 224))

# Choose the last conv layer name
last_conv_layer_name = 'conv2d_1'  # <-- adjust based on model.summary()

# Generate heatmap
heatmap = make_gradcam_heatmap(img_array, model, last_conv_layer_name)

# Superimpose heatmap on original image
img = cv2.imread(img_path)
img = cv2.resize(img, (224, 224))
heatmap = cv2.resize(heatmap, (img.shape[1], img.shape[0]))
heatmap = np.uint8(255 * heatmap)
heatmap = cv2.applyColorMap(heatmap, cv2.COLORMAP_JET)
superimposed_img = heatmap * 0.4 + img

# Show
plt.imshow(cv2.cvtColor(superimposed_img.astype(np.uint8),
cv2.COLOR_BGR2RGB))
plt.axis('off')
plt.title("Grad-CAM")
plt.show()
```

There is another UCI dataset for activity analysis which is known as Occupancy. The Occupancy Detection dataset from the UCI Machine Learning Repository includes sensor data collected to determine whether a room is occupied or not. It is commonly used for developing and testing machine learning models that predict room occupancy based on indoor environmental factors. The dataset was gathered in an office setting using sensors that recorded data such as temperature, humidity, light, and carbon dioxide (CO_2) levels [12]. It also includes the humidity ratio, which combines temperature and humidity into a single measure. The goal of collecting this data was to identify whether someone was present in the room. Occupancy is shown as a binary value (0 for unoccupied, 1 for occupied), making the dataset

Fig. 5.34 GradCAM results on a testing posture

well-suited for supervised learning methods. The dataset is split into three parts: one for training and two for testing. Each part was collected at different times and includes timestamps along with sensor readings. These features—especially CO_2 levels, temperature, humidity, and light—are strongly linked to human presence. For example, high CO_2 levels often suggest that people are in the room, and changes in light or temperature may indicate movement or activity. This type of data is useful in real-world applications such as smart buildings. Knowing whether a room is occupied can help control heating, cooling, and lighting systems more efficiently, saving energy and improving comfort. Researchers typically start by cleaning and preparing the data, then apply machine learning models like decision trees, logistic regression, or neural networks to make predictions [13].

Overall, the UCI Occupancy dataset is a valuable tool for anyone working on smart environments, as it helps build intelligent systems that can respond to human presence and improve energy management. Similar code structure is follows as discussed in other sections above. Figure 5.35 presents violin plots for selected features in the Occupancy dataset, visually comparing their distributions under occupied and unoccupied conditions. Figure 5.36 displays a cluster plot separating occupancy from non-occupancy instances, offering a visual assessment of feature separability and class structure. Lastly, Fig. 5.37 summarizes the feature importances derived from various classical machine learning models, highlighting the most influential variables in predicting occupancy status. However, the final accuracy results show that Random Forest achieve highest accuracy in this regard (97%).

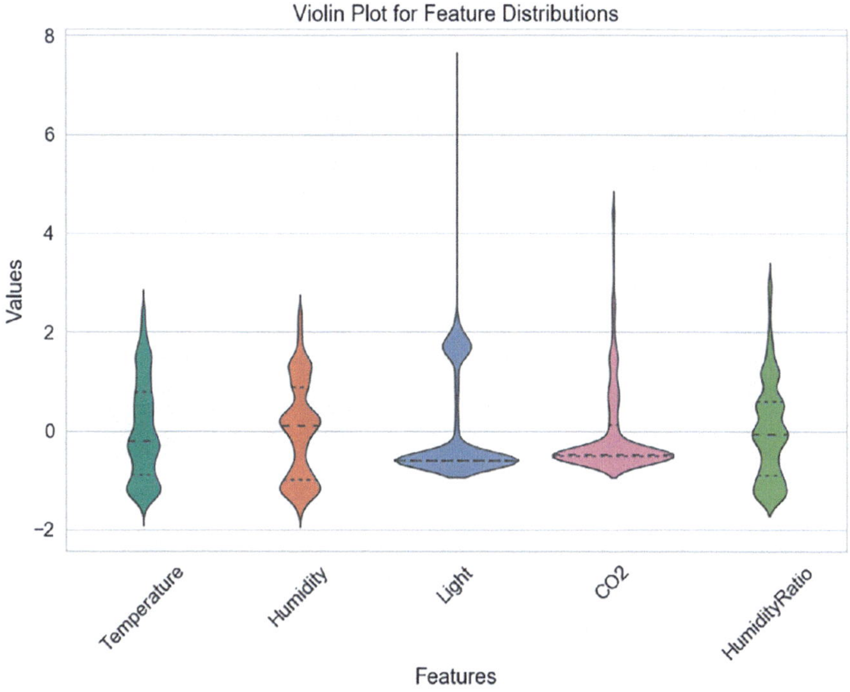

Fig. 5.35 Violin plot of different features on occupancy dataset

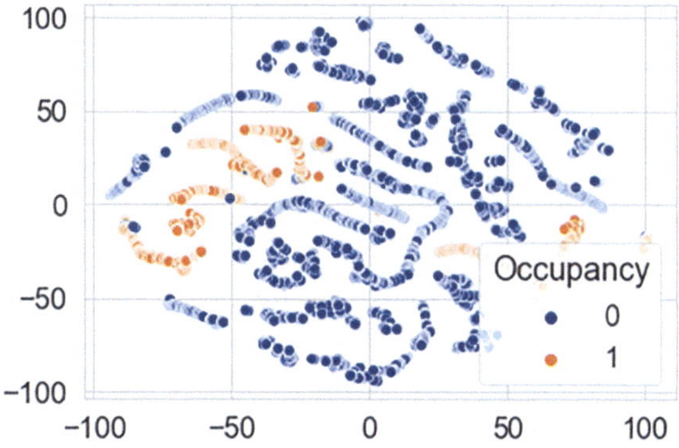

Fig. 5.36 Cluster plot of occupancy versus non-occupancy

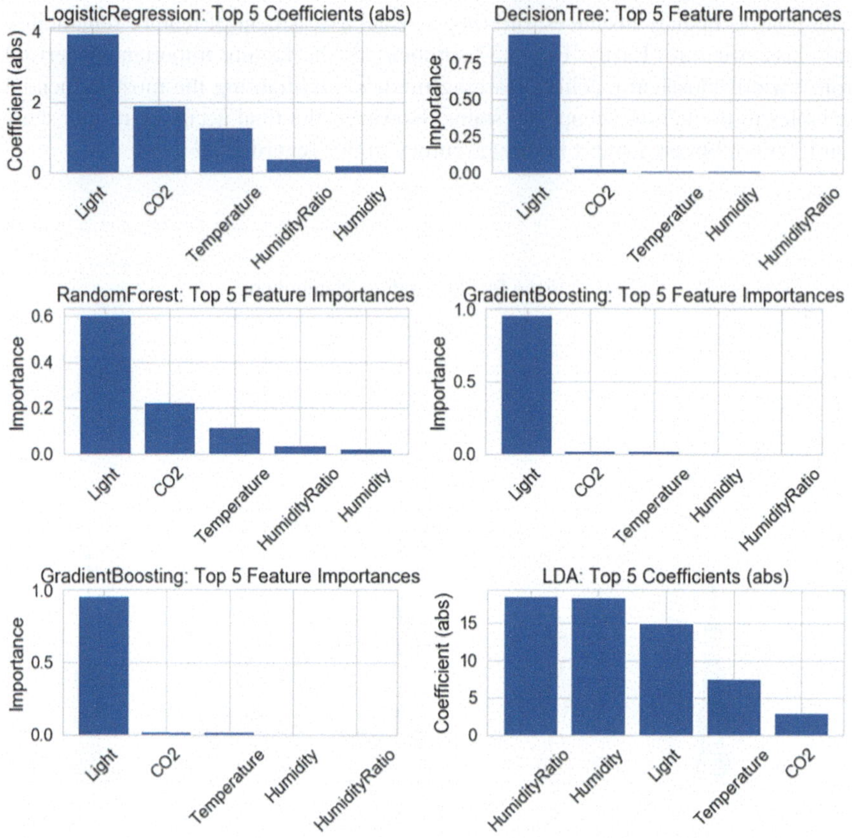

Fig. 5.37 Feature importance using different classical machine learning approaches on occupancy dataset

5.7 Conclusion

This chapter highlights key strategies for analyzing wearable and ambient sensor data using deep learning and explainable artificial intelligence within a Python-centric framework. The overarching aim has been to illustrate how modern sensor setups—ranging from wrist-worn devices and chest straps to unobtrusive ambient solutions—can capture rich streams of behavioral information, which in turn support Deciding whether wearable, ambient, or hybrid configurations are best for a given application involves considering trade-offs such as user acceptance, ease of deployment, and system reliability. A wide array of publicly available datasets collectively demonstrate the breadth of potential learning tasks, from simple activity recognition (e.g., running vs. walking) to more granular transitions (e.g., sitting-to-stand, lying-to-sit) and object-interaction events (e.g., opening a door, making coffee). These datasets are benchmark tools for exploring supervised learning pipelines, from data wrangling and feature extraction to model training and performance evaluation. At each stage, Python-based implementations highlight both well-established machine learning approaches (e.g., Random Forest, Logistic Regression, SVM) and more advanced methods (e.g., LSTM, GRU, convolutional neural networks). The examples confirm that deep architectures can automatically uncover hidden temporal patterns, but they also require careful parameter tuning and often face issues such as data imbalance or sensor placement variability. Explainable AI serves as a unifying theme for evaluating model interpretability. Methods like LIME offer a lens into black-box classifiers, providing individualized feature importance measures that clarify why certain decisions are made. Such insights can be especially valuable for stakeholders like clinicians, caregivers, or the monitored individuals themselves, who may rely on these systems for day-to-day wellbeing or medical oversight. By blending theoretical foundations with hands-on coding examples, this chapter offers a foundation from which readers can design, experiment with, and refine their own sensor-based AI projects. Whether the goal is to develop fall detection systems for the elderly, optimize athletic training regimens, or create multifaceted smart homes, the presented methodologies and case studies provide a robust springboard for employing deep learning and explainable AI in real-world health and behavior monitoring.

References

1. N.Y. Hammerla, S. Halloran, and T. Plötz, "Deep, convolutional, and recurrent models for human activity recognition using wearables," arXiv preprint arXiv:1604.08880, 2016.
2. A. Reiss and D. Stricker, "Creating and benchmarking a new dataset for physical activity monitoring," Proceedings of the 5th International Conference on Pervasive Technologies Related to Assistive Environments, 2012, p. 40.
3. D. Anguita, A. Ghio, L. Oneto, X. Parra, and J.L. Reyes-Ortiz, "A public domain dataset for human activity recognition using smartphones," Proceedings of the 21st European Symposium on Artificial Neural Networks, Computational Intelligence and Machine Learning, 2013, pp. 437–442.
4. J.L. Reyes-Ortiz, L. Oneto, A. Samà, X. Parra, and D. Anguita, "Transition-aware human activity recognition using smartphones," Neurocomputing, vol. 171, pp. 754–767, 2016.
5. D. Roggen, A. Calatroni, M. Rossi, T. Holleczek, K. Förster, G. Tröster, P. Lukowicz, D. Bannach, G. Pirkl, A. Ferscha, J. Doppler, C. Holzmann, M. Kurz, G. Holl, R. Chavarriaga, M. Creatura, and J.D.R. Millán, "Collecting complex activity datasets in highly rich networked sensor environments," INSS 2010 Conference Proceedings, pp. 233–240.
6. D. Roggen, A. Calatroni, K. Förster, G. Tröster, A. Ferscha, M. Kurz, G. Hoelzl, P. Lukowicz, D. Bannach, H. Sagha, H. Bayati, J.D.R. Millán, and R. Chavarriaga, "Activity recognition in opportunistic sensor environments," European Future Technologies Conference and Exhibition (FET11), 2011, pp. 2–5.
7. M. Zhang and A.A. Sawchuk, "USC-HAD: A daily activity dataset for ubiquitous activity recognition using wearable sensors," Proceedings of the ACM International Conference on Ubiquitous Computing, 2012, pp. 1036–1043.
8. M. Zhang and A.A. Sawchuk, "Human daily activity recognition with sparse representation using wearable sensors," IEEE Journal of Biomedical and Health Informatics, vol. 17, no. 3, pp. 553–560, 2013.

9. D.J. Cook, M. Schmitter-Edgecombe, A. Crandall, C. Sanders, and B. Thomas, "Collecting and disseminating smart home sensor data in the CASAS project," CHI Workshop on Developing Shared Home Behavior Datasets, 2009.
10. D.J. Cook and M. Schmitter-Edgecombe, "Assessing the quality of activities in a smart environment," Methods of Information in Medicine, vol. 48, no. 5, pp. 480–485, 2009.
11. A. Kumar and E. D. Raj, "Silhouettes for human posture recognition," IEEE Dataport, August 6, 2020, https://doi.org/10.21227/9c9b-3j44.
12. L.M. Candanedo and V. Feldheim, "Accurate occupancy detection of an office room from light, temperature, humidity and CO_2 measurements using statistical learning models," Energy and Buildings, vol. 112, pp. 28–39, 2016.
13. Z. Yang, N. Li, B. Becerik-Gerber, and M. Orosz, "A systematic approach to occupancy modeling in ambient sensor-rich buildings," Simulation, vol. 90, no. 8, pp. 960–977, 2014.

Chapter 6
Case Studies: Health Monitoring and Analysis

Abstract The healthcare landscape has seen a transformative shift towards personalized and continual monitoring, with wearable sensors playing a pivotal role. These devices, ranging from smartwatches to specialized medical wearables, have the potential to revolutionize patient care by providing real-time data and insights into various physiological parameters. Oxygen saturation, a critical parameter for respiratory health, can be accurately predicted from wearable sensor data using advanced machine learning techniques. Respiration, a fundamental physiological process, serves as a vital indicator of an individual's overall health. Monitoring respiratory rate, depth, and patterns is crucial for the early detection of respiratory conditions, assessing cardiorespiratory fitness, and optimizing medical interventions. Traditional methods of respiratory monitoring often involve intrusive devices or cumbersome equipment, limiting their application in continuous and real-time monitoring scenarios. Ultra-Wideband (UWB) technology, initially developed for communication and radar applications, has found new horizons in healthcare. UWB sensors operate across a broad frequency spectrum, enabling high precision in the localization and tracking of objects. The ability of UWB sensors to capture detailed temporal and spatial information makes them well-suited for monitoring dynamic physiological processes such as respiration. UWB sensors utilize short-duration, low-power pulses transmitted across a wide frequency range. When these pulses encounter surfaces or objects, they generate echoes that are captured by the sensor. By analyzing the time delay and amplitude of these echoes, UWB sensors can precisely determine the distance and movement of objects in their vicinity. Applied to respiratory monitoring, UWB sensors detect subtle chest movements associated with inhalation and exhalation. UWB sensors offer a contactless solution for respiratory monitoring, eliminating the need for physical attachments or uncomfortable devices. Placed in the environment or integrated into everyday objects, UWB sensors can capture respiratory data without direct contact with the individual, ensuring a non-intrusive and user-friendly experience. In home healthcare settings, UWB sensors

© The Author(s), under exclusive license to Springer Nature Switzerland AG 2025

M. Z. Uddin, *Trustworthy Multimodal Intelligent Systems for Independent Living*, Cognitive Technologies, https://doi.org/10.1007/978-3-031-97359-8_6

contribute to Ambient Assisted Living (AAL) by continuously monitoring respiratory patterns. This is particularly valuable for aging populations or individuals with chronic respiratory conditions. UWB-enabled systems can detect deviations from normal respiratory patterns, triggering timely interventions or alerts to caregivers. In clinical settings, UWB sensors offer an innovative alternative to traditional respiratory monitoring devices. Patients can be monitored remotely, reducing the burden on healthcare infrastructure and providing healthcare professionals with real-time data. UWB sensors can be integrated into hospital beds, rooms, or wearable devices to enable seamless monitoring during hospital stays.

6.1 Time-Series Respiration Data

Ultra-Wideband (UWB) sensors use short, low-power pulses across a wide frequency range to precisely detect movement and position. In healthcare, they enable contactless, accurate monitoring of breathing by tracking subtle chest movements, making respiratory monitoring more comfortable and unobtrusive [1, 2]. For the case studies of respiration prediction using machine learning, the time-series data is recorded by author himself to show the examples. However, any other floating number data sequences can be used for prediction. Figure 6.1 shows the actual data versus prediction with different models i.e.,, LSTM, GRU, and Dense models. Figure 6.2 shows the loss versus epoch for the different models. Figure 6.3 an XAI example of using SHAP on the data.

```
import numpy as np
import matplotlib.pyplot as plt
from pandas import read_csv
import math
import shap
import tensorflow as tf
from tensorflow.keras.models import Sequential
from tensorflow.keras.layers import Dense, LSTM, GRU
from sklearn.preprocessing import MinMaxScaler
from sklearn.metrics import mean_squared_error
```

```
# Fix random seed for reproducibility
tf.random.set_seed(7)
np.random.seed(7)

# Function to create X, Y pairs for time series
def create_dataset(dataset, look_back=1):
    dataX, dataY = [], []
    for i in range(len(dataset)-look_back-1):
        a = dataset[i:(i+look_back), 0]
        dataX.append(a)
        dataY.append(dataset[i + look_back, 0])
    return np.array(dataX), np.array(dataY)

# Load and normalize the dataset
dataframe = read_csv('Respiration.csv', usecols=[1], engine='python')
dataset = dataframe.values.astype('float32')
scaler = MinMaxScaler(feature_range=(0, 1))
dataset = scaler.fit_transform(dataset)

# Train/test split
train_size = int(len(dataset) * 0.30)
test_size = train_size + 1000
train, test = dataset[0:train_size, :], dataset[train_size:test_size, :]
```

```
# Create supervised datasets
look_back = 1
trainX, trainY = create_dataset(train, look_back)
testX, testY = create_dataset(test, look_back)

# Reshape for recurrent models
trainX_seq = np.reshape(trainX, (trainX.shape[0], 1, trainX.shape[1]))
testX_seq = np.reshape(testX, (testX.shape[0], 1, testX.shape[1]))

# Dense model input stays 2D
trainX_dense = trainX
testX_dense = testX

### LSTM Model
model_lstm = Sequential()
model_lstm.add(LSTM(10, input_shape=(1, look_back)))
model_lstm.add(Dense(1))
model_lstm.compile(loss='mean_squared_error', optimizer='adam')
history_lstm = model_lstm.fit(trainX_seq, trainY, epochs=10, batch_size=1,
verbose=2)

### GRU Model
model_gru = Sequential()
model_gru.add(GRU(10, input_shape=(1, look_back)))
model_gru.add(Dense(1))
model_gru.compile(loss='mean_squared_error', optimizer='adam')
```

```
history_gru = model_gru.fit(trainX_seq, trainY, epochs=10, batch_size=1,
verbose=2)

### Dense Model
model_dense = Sequential()
model_dense.add(Dense(10, input_dim=look_back, activation='relu'))
model_dense.add(Dense(1))
model_dense.compile(loss='mean_squared_error', optimizer='adam')
history_dense = model_dense.fit(trainX_dense, trainY, epochs=10, batch_size=1,
verbose=2)

### Predict and Inverse
def predict_and_inverse(model, X, Y):
    pred = model.predict(X)
    pred = scaler.inverse_transform(pred)
    true = scaler.inverse_transform(Y.reshape(-1, 1))
    return pred, true

pred_lstm, true_lstm = predict_and_inverse(model_lstm, testX_seq, testY)
pred_gru, true_gru = predict_and_inverse(model_gru, testX_seq, testY)
pred_dense, true_dense = predict_and_inverse(model_dense, testX_dense, testY)

### Evaluation
def evaluate(pred, true):
    return math.sqrt(mean_squared_error(true, pred))

print("RMSE LSTM:", evaluate(pred_lstm, true_lstm))
print("RMSE GRU:", evaluate(pred_gru, true_gru))
print("RMSE Dense:", evaluate(pred_dense, true_dense))
```

```
### Plot Predictions
plt.figure(figsize=(15, 5))
plt.plot(true_lstm, label='Actual', linewidth=2)
plt.plot(pred_lstm, label='LSTM')
plt.plot(pred_gru, label='GRU')
plt.plot(pred_dense, label='Dense')
plt.title('Time Series Prediction Comparison')
plt.xlabel('Time Steps')
plt.ylabel('Respiration Value')
plt.legend()
plt.show()

### Plot Loss per Epoch for All Models
plt.figure(figsize=(10, 5))
plt.plot(history_lstm.history['loss'], label='LSTM Loss')
plt.plot(history_gru.history['loss'], label='GRU Loss')
plt.plot(history_dense.history['loss'], label='Dense Loss')
plt.title('Model Loss per Epoch')
plt.xlabel('Epoch')
plt.ylabel('Loss (MSE)')
plt.legend()
plt.grid(True)
plt.show()
explainer = shap.Explainer(model_dense, trainX_dense[:100])
shap_values = explainer(testX_dense[:100])
shap.summary_plot(shap_values, testX_dense[:100], feature_names=['Previous
Value'])
```

6.2 Sleep Analysis

Sleep plays a vital role in human health and is necessary for our physical and mental well-being. Getting enough high-quality sleep supports clear thinking, emotional balance, a strong immune system, and healthy metabolism [3]. To predict whether a person has sleep apnea, a small dataset was used, called the Sleep Health and Lifestyle Dataset, available on Kaggle: https://www.kaggle.com/datasets/uom190346a/sleep-health-and-lifestyle-dataset. This dataset includes 400 entries and 13 features related to sleep patterns and daily habits. It contains details such as gender, age, job type, sleep duration and quality, activity levels, stress, BMI category, blood pressure, heart rate, daily step count, and whether the individual has a sleep disorder. For this project, we worked with the "Sleep_health_and_lifestyle_dataset.csv" file. The following sections describe the

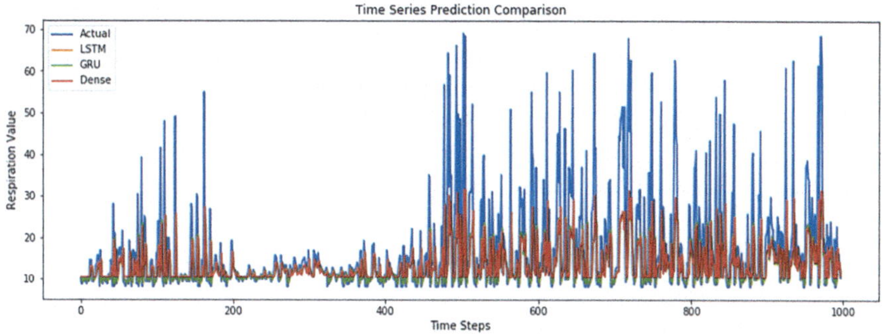

Fig. 6.1 Actual data versus prediction with different models

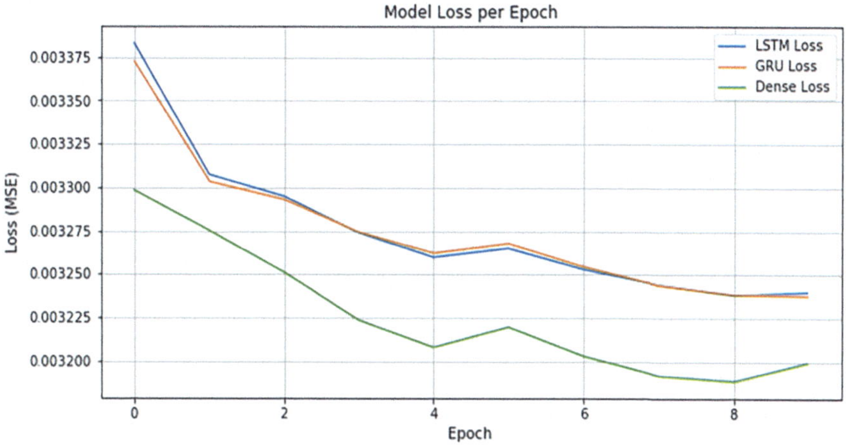

Fig. 6.2 Different model loss versus epochs

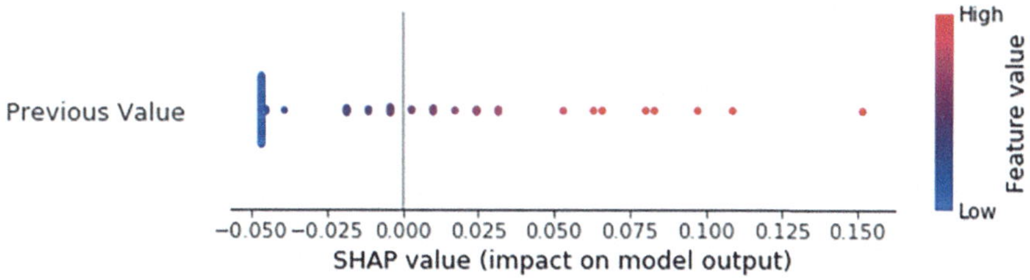

Fig. 6.3 XAI using SHAP on the data

data, preprocessing steps, and the machine learning classification models used in our analysis. Figure 6.4 displays violin plots for various features, capturing the underlying distributions and spread across categories. Figure 6.5 illustrates the distribution of samples across different sleep categories, highlighting class imbalance or prevalence patterns. Figure 6.6 through Fig. 6.11 present feature importance rankings as identified by a range of classical machine learning models: Decision Trees (Fig. 6.6), Random Forests (Fig. 6.7), Gradient Boosting (Fig. 6.8), Extra Trees (Fig. 6.9), Logistic Regression (Fig. 6.10), and Support Vector Machines (Fig. 6.11), allowing for comparative analysis of the most influential predictors in sleep classification.

```
import pandas as pd
import numpy as np
import matplotlib.pyplot as plt
import seaborn as sns
import seaborn as sns
import matplotlib.pyplot as plt

# Set consistent style and font
sns.set(style="whitegrid", font_scale=1.2)
df = pd.read_csv('./Sleep_health_and_lifestyle_dataset.csv', sep = ',')

# List of numeric variables to plot
variables = [
    "Age",
    "Sleep Duration",
    "Quality of Sleep",
    "Physical Activity Level",
    "Stress Level",
    "Heart Rate",
    "Daily Steps"
]

# Generate a violin plot for each variable
for var in variables:
    plt.figure(figsize=(8, 6))
    sns.violinplot(x="Sleep Disorder", y=var, data=df, inner="quartile",
palette="muted")
    plt.title(f"{var} Distribution by Sleep Disorder")
    plt.tight_layout()
    plt.show()
```

```
# ---- Barplot: Sleep Disorder Frequency ----
plt.figure(figsize=(8, 6))
sns.countplot(x="Sleep Disorder", data=df)
plt.title("Sleep Disorder Frequency")
plt.tight_layout()
plt.show()

df = df.drop('Person ID', axis = 1)
hot = pd.get_dummies(df[['Gender', 'Occupation', 'BMI Category', 'Blood Pressure']])
df = pd.concat([df, hot], axis = 1)
df = df.drop(['Gender', 'Occupation', 'BMI Category', 'Blood Pressure'], axis = 1)

X = df.drop('Sleep Disorder', axis = 1)
X = X.values

import pandas as pd
import numpy as np
import seaborn as sns
import matplotlib.pyplot as plt

from sklearn.model_selection import train_test_split
from sklearn.preprocessing import StandardScaler
from sklearn.metrics import accuracy_score
from sklearn.linear_model import LogisticRegression
from sklearn.ensemble import RandomForestClassifier, GradientBoostingClassifier, ExtraTreesClassifier
from sklearn.tree import DecisionTreeClassifier
from sklearn.naive_bayes import GaussianNB
from sklearn.svm import SVC
from sklearn.neighbors import KNeighborsClassifier
from sklearn.discriminant_analysis import LinearDiscriminantAnalysis

# ------------------------
```

```
# 1. Prepare Data
# ------------------------
X = df.drop("Sleep Disorder", axis=1)
y = df["Sleep Disorder"]

feature_names = X.columns

# Standardize features
scaler = StandardScaler()
X_standard = scaler.fit_transform(X)

# Train-test split
X_train, X_test, y_train, y_test = train_test_split(X_standard, y, test_size=0.3,
random_state=0)

# ------------------------
# 2. Define Models
# ------------------------
models = {
    "Decision Tree": DecisionTreeClassifier(criterion='entropy',
min_samples_split=6, max_depth=6, random_state=0),
    "Random Forest": RandomForestClassifier(random_state=0),
    "Gradient Boosting": GradientBoostingClassifier(random_state=0),
    "Extra Trees": ExtraTreesClassifier(random_state=0),
    "Logistic Regression": LogisticRegression(max_iter=1000),
    "LDA": LinearDiscriminantAnalysis(),
    "Gaussian NB": GaussianNB(),
    "KNN": KNeighborsClassifier(),
    "SVC": SVC(kernel='linear')  # Linear kernel for coef_
}
```

```
# -------------------------
# 3. Train Models and Show Feature Importances
# -------------------------
accuracies = {}

for name, model in models.items():
    model.fit(X_train, y_train)
    y_pred = model.predict(X_test)
    acc = accuracy_score(y_test, y_pred)
    accuracies[name] = acc

    print(f"\n{name} Accuracy: {acc:.4f}")

    # Feature importances (tree-based) or coefficients (linear models)
    if hasattr(model, "feature_importances_"):
        importances = model.feature_importances_
        top_idx = np.argsort(importances)[-10:][::-1]
        top_features = feature_names[top_idx]
        top_values = importances[top_idx]

        plt.figure(figsize=(8, 6))
        sns.barplot(x=top_values, y=top_features)
        plt.title(f"{name} - Top 10 Feature Importances")
        plt.tight_layout()
        plt.show()

    elif hasattr(model, "coef_"):
        coefs = model.coef_
        if coefs.ndim > 1:
            importances = np.mean(np.abs(coefs), axis=0)
        else:
            importances = np.abs(coefs)
```

```
        top_idx = np.argsort(importances)[-10:][::-1]
        top_features = feature_names[top_idx]
        top_values = importances[top_idx]

        plt.figure(figsize=(8, 6))
        sns.barplot(x=top_values, y=top_features)
        plt.title(f"{name} - Top 10 Coefficients (abs)")
        plt.tight_layout()
        plt.show()

    else:
        print(f"{name} does not provide feature importances or coefficients.")

# -------------------------
# 4. Final Accuracy Summary
# -------------------------
print("\nFinal Accuracy Results of All Models:")
for name, acc in accuracies.items():
    print(f"{name}: {acc:.4f}")
```

The classification accuracy scores for the evaluated models are: Decision Tree (89.38%), Random Forest (87.61%), Gradient Boosting (89.38%), Extra Trees (89.38%), Logistic Regression (91.15%), Linear Discriminant Analysis (87.61%), Gaussian Naive Bayes (53.10%), K-Nearest Neighbors (88.50%), and Support Vector Classifier (88.50%).

6.3 Synthetic Data

Health data, especially related to vital signs, is sensitive and often comes with privacy concerns. Synthetic data offers a safer alternative by creating artificial datasets that reflect the patterns of real data without exposing personal information. This is important for following healthcare rules and using data responsibly in research and development.

Training models for vital sign monitoring requires varied and realistic data to handle different situations. Synthetic data helps by adding variety to small real-world datasets, offering a wider range of patient types and conditions [4]. This helps machine learning models perform better and more accurately in real scenarios.

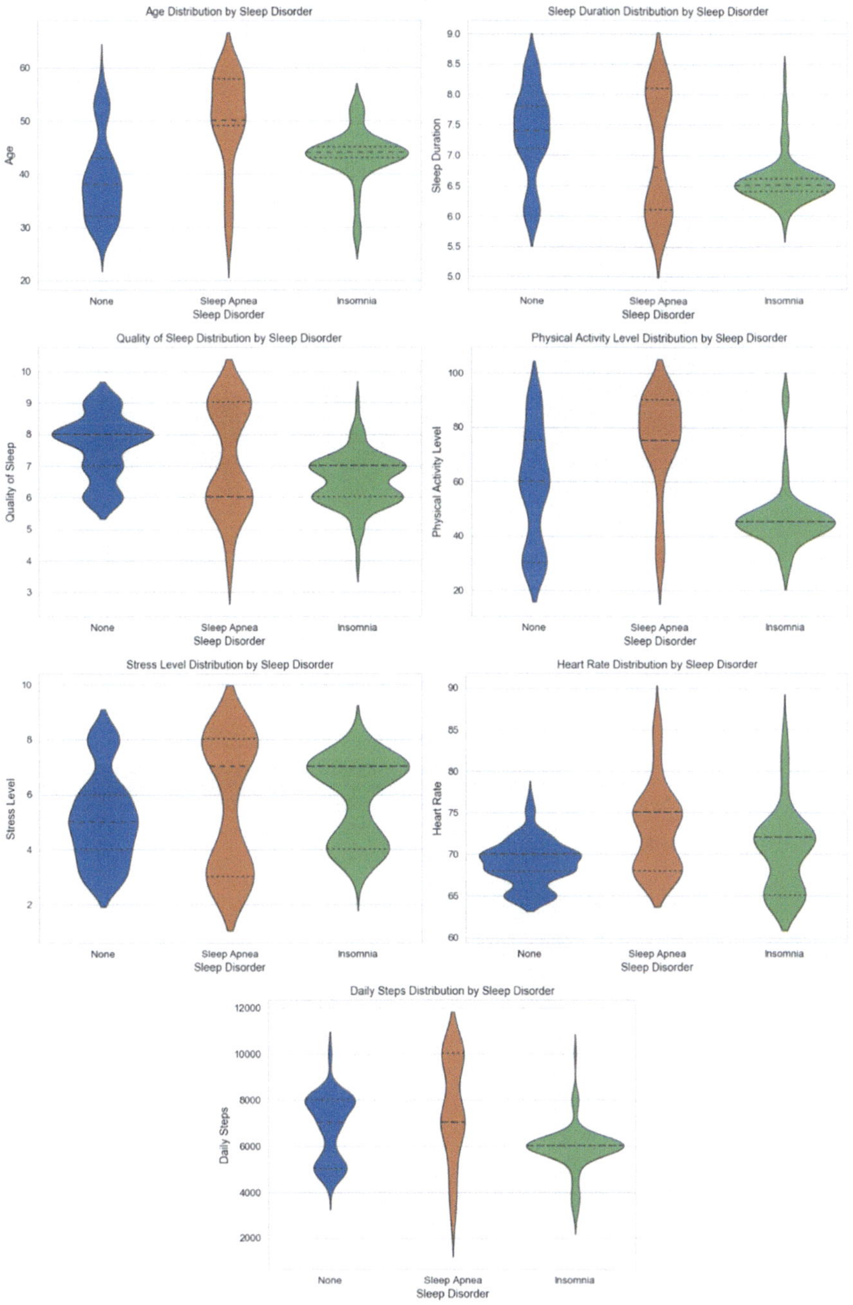

Fig. 6.4 Violin plots for different distributions

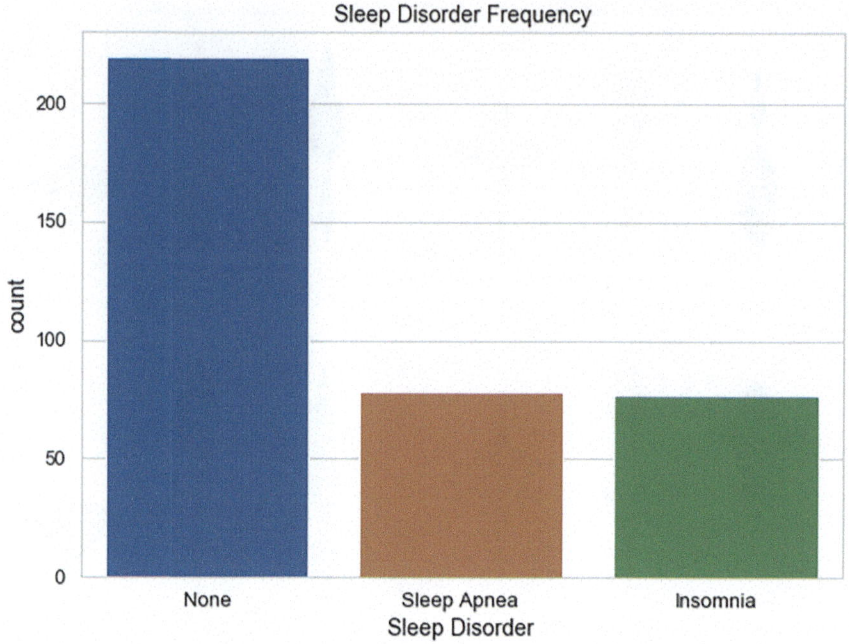

Fig. 6.5 Distribution of samples for different categories of sleep

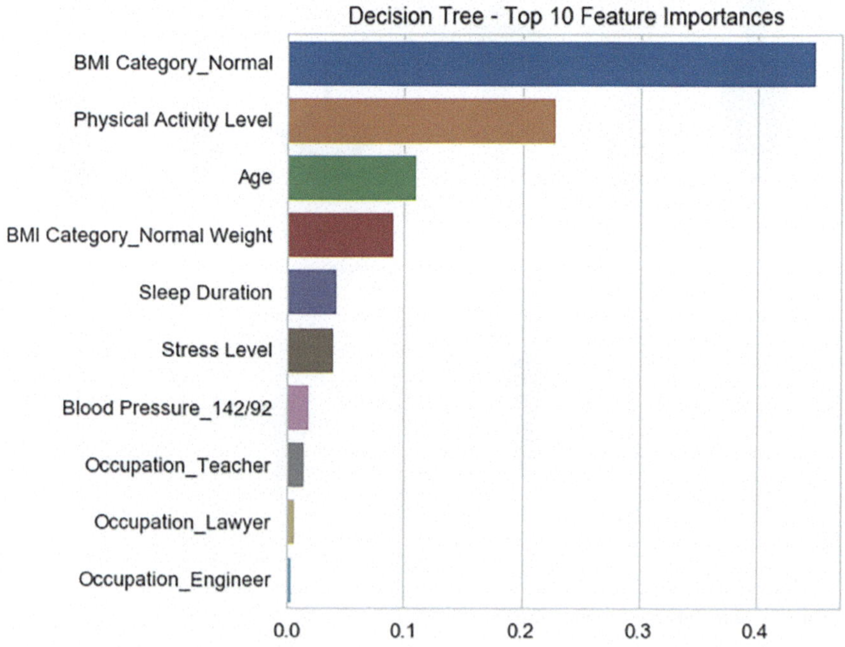

Fig. 6.6 Feature importance using decision trees

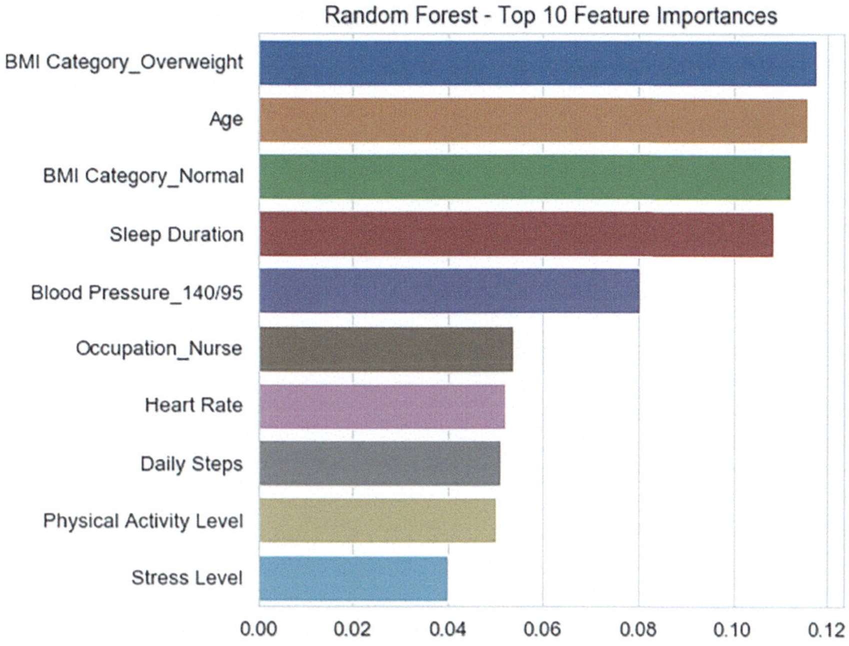

Fig. 6.7 Feature importance using random forests

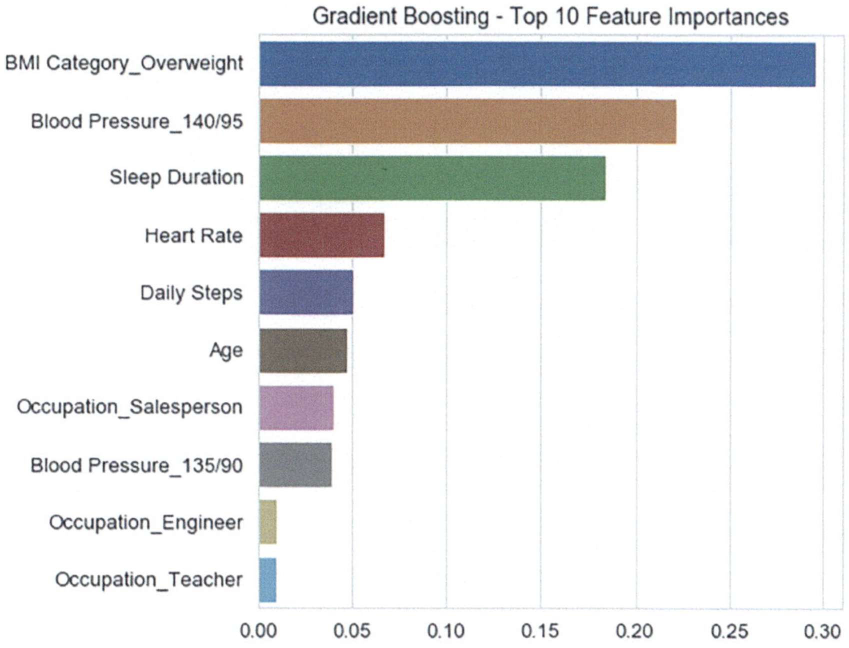

Fig. 6.8 Feature importance using gradient boosting

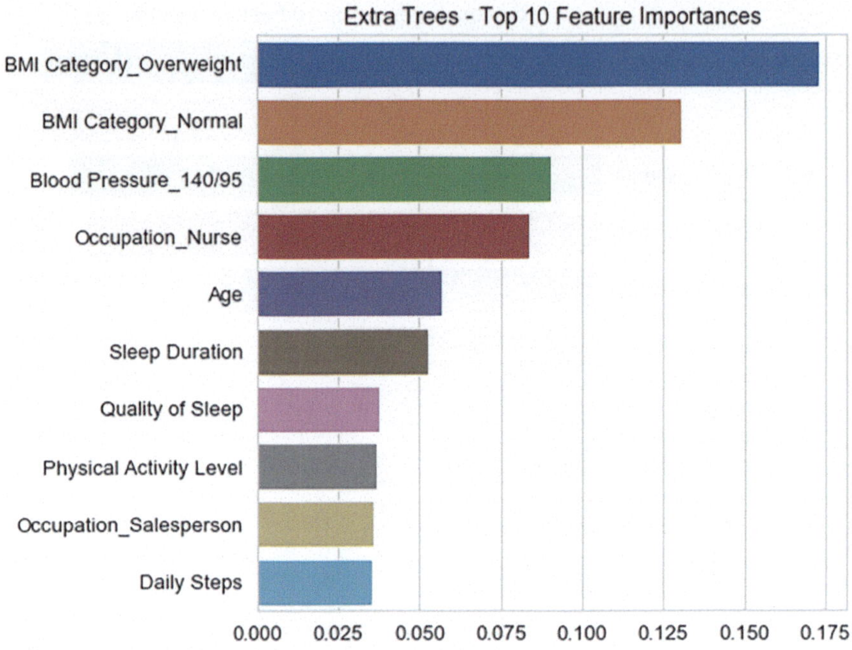

Fig. 6.9 Feature importance using extra trees

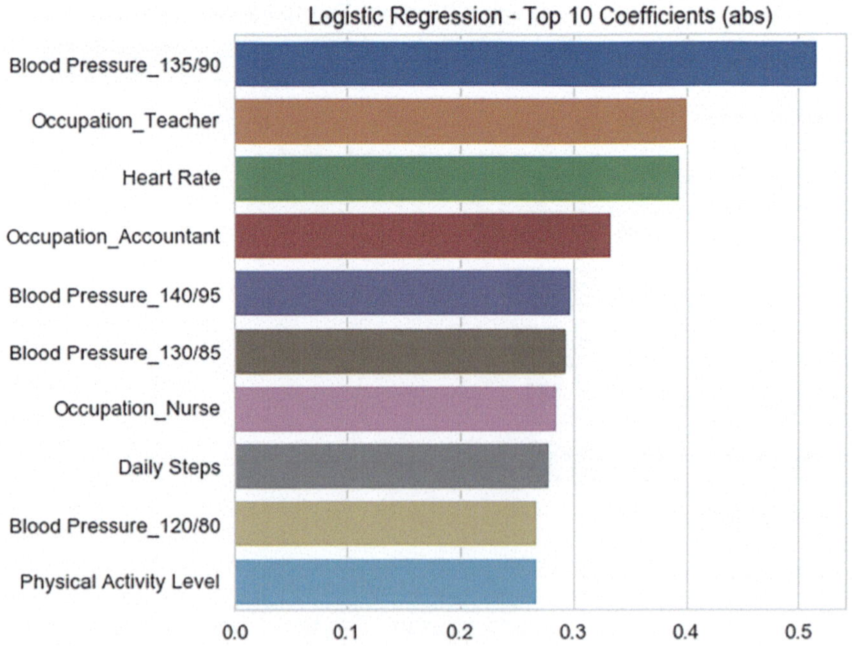

Fig. 6.10 Feature importance using logistic regressions

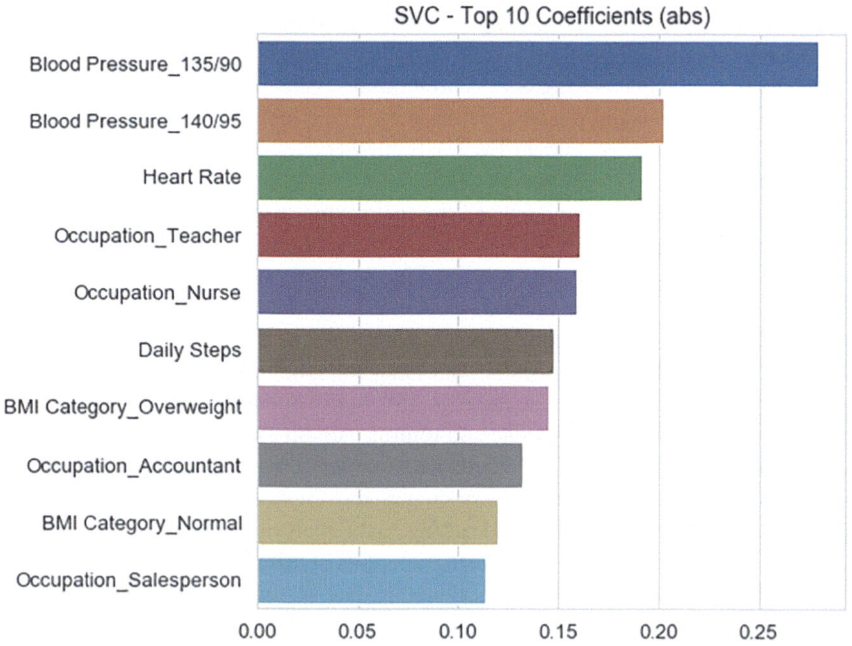

Fig. 6.11 Feature importance using SVM

In medical diagnostics, synthetic data is useful for improving how vital signs like heart rate, pulse, oxygen levels, and breathing are analyzed. By simulating different patterns in these signals, researchers can train models to detect unusual changes early. This can lead to faster diagnosis and better care for patients.

Following is a sample code to generate respiration data discussed in previous subsection. Synthetic Data Vault (SDV) library, which is designed to generate high-quality synthetic data that preserves the statistical properties of real-world datasets. SDV provides a variety of models that can be applied to different data types and use cases, especially for tabular data. One of the key models is the Gaussian Copula Synthesizer, which models the relationships between variables using copulas, allowing it to capture statistical correlations in a straightforward and efficient way. This method is particularly suitable for structured data with continuous and numerical values. Another powerful model is the CTGAN Synthesizer, which uses Conditional Generative Adversarial Networks (GANs) to learn complex data distributions. It is especially effective in handling both continuous and categorical data, making it suitable for more diverse and mixed-type datasets. The TVAE Synthesizer, based on a Tabular Variational Autoencoder (TVAE), is another deep learning-based model that learns a probabilistic representation of the data. This approach is useful for generating realistic synthetic samples when the underlying distribution of the dataset is complex or non-linear.

In addition to these synthesizers, SDV includes supporting tools such as *SingleTableMetadata*, which is used to automatically detect and define the schema of the dataset before generation. This metadata informs the synthesizers about the structure, types, and constraints of the data. Once the synthetic data is generated, SDV also provides evaluation tools like the *evaluate_quality* function, which compares the synthetic dataset to the original one and returns a quality score. This score helps in understanding how closely the synthetic data matches the original in terms of statistical properties. Overall, these tools work together to create synthetic data that is safe, realistic, and suitable for machine learning, data analysis, and privacy-preserving applications. Figure 6.12 shows the histogram plots of different synthetic data generation methods. Figure 6.13 represents synthetic data versus real data using Gaussian Copula and CTGAN. Figure 6.14 depicts synthetic data versus real data using TVAE and NumPy.

```
import pandas as pd
import numpy as np
import matplotlib.pyplot as plt
from sdv.metadata import SingleTableMetadata
from sdv.single_table import GaussianCopulaSynthesizer, CTGANSynthesizer,
TVAESynthesizer
from sdv.evaluation.single_table import evaluate_quality
```

```
# === Load Data ===
sample = pd.read_csv('./Respiration.csv', index_col=0)
column_name = 'Respirations'

# === Metadata Detection ===
metadata = SingleTableMetadata()
metadata.detect_from_dataframe(data=sample)

# === GaussianCopula ===
gc = GaussianCopulaSynthesizer(metadata)
gc.fit(sample)
synthetic_gc = gc.sample(num_rows=2000)

# === CTGAN ===
ctgan = CTGANSynthesizer(metadata)
ctgan.fit(sample)
synthetic_ctgan = ctgan.sample(num_rows=2000)

# === TVAE ===
tvae = TVAESynthesizer(metadata)
tvae.fit(sample)
synthetic_tvae = tvae.sample(num_rows=2000)

# === NumPy Normal Generator (for benchmark only) ===
```

```
synthetic_np = pd.DataFrame({
    'Respirations': np.random.normal(loc=sample['Respirations'].mean(),
                                     scale=sample['Respirations'].std(),
                                     size=2000)
})
synthetic_np.index.name = 'id'

# === Evaluation Scores ===
report_gc = evaluate_quality(sample, synthetic_gc, metadata)
score_gc = report_gc.get_score()

report_ctgan = evaluate_quality(sample, synthetic_ctgan, metadata)
score_ctgan = report_ctgan.get_score()

report_tvae = evaluate_quality(sample, synthetic_tvae, metadata)
score_tvae = report_tvae.get_score()

print("\n=== Quality Scores ===")
print(f"GaussianCopula: {score_gc:.4f}")
print(f"CTGAN:          {score_ctgan:.4f}")
print(f"TVAE:           {score_tvae:.4f}")
print("NumPy Normal:   N/A (no metadata for eval)")

# === Matplotlib Histograms ===
def plot_hist(real, synth, title):
    plt.figure(figsize=(10, 4))
    plt.hist(real, bins=50, alpha=0.5, density=True, label='Real', color='red')
    plt.hist(synth, bins=50, alpha=0.5, density=True, label='Synthetic',
color='blue')
    plt.title(title)
    plt.xlabel('Respirations')
    plt.ylabel('Density')
    plt.legend()
```

```
    # Removed the grid for a cleaner look
    plt.tight_layout()
    plt.show()

# Plot histogram comparisons
plot_hist(sample[column_name], synthetic_gc[column_name], 'GaussianCopula vs Real')
plot_hist(sample[column_name], synthetic_ctgan[column_name], 'CTGAN vs Real')

# === Plot 500 Samples (Real vs Synthetic) ===
def plot_samples(real, synth, title):
    """Plot the first 500 samples of real vs. synthetic data as a line plot."""
    plt.figure(figsize=(10, 4))
    plt.plot(real.head(500).values, label='Real', color='red')
    plt.plot(synth.head(500).values, label='Synthetic', color='blue')
    plt.title(title)
    plt.xlabel('Index')
    plt.ylabel('Respirations')
    plt.legend()
    plt.tight_layout()
    plt.show()

# Show real vs. synthetic for 500 samples in separate plots
plot_samples(sample[column_name], synthetic_gc[column_name], 'GaussianCopula (First 500 Samples)')
plot_samples(sample[column_name], synthetic_ctgan[column_name], 'CTGAN (First 500 Samples)')
plot_samples(sample[column_name], synthetic_tvae[column_name], 'TVAE (First 500 Samples)')
plot_samples(sample[column_name], synthetic_np[column_name], 'NumPy Normal (First 500 Samples)')
```

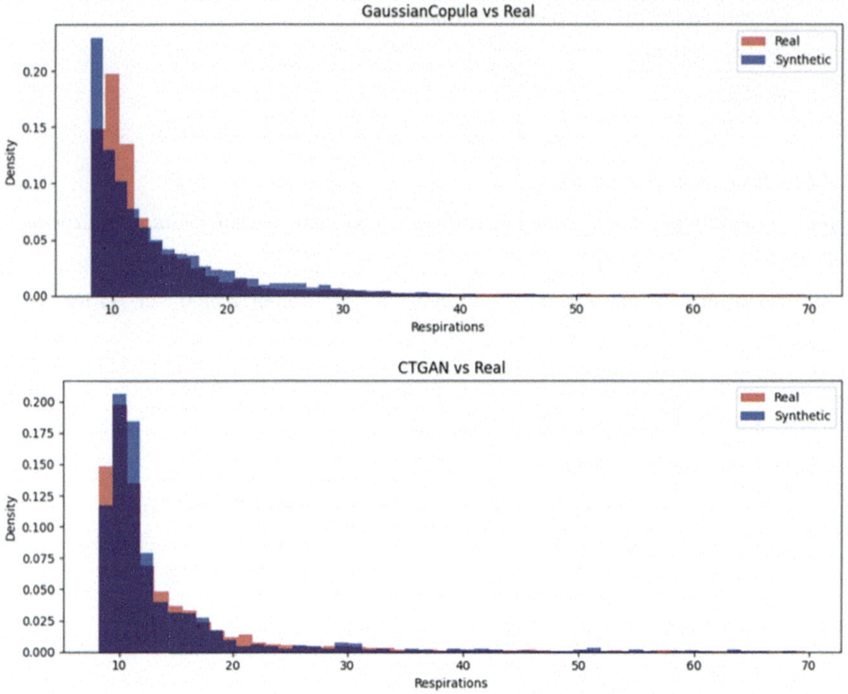

Fig. 6.12 Histogram plots of different synthetic data generation methods

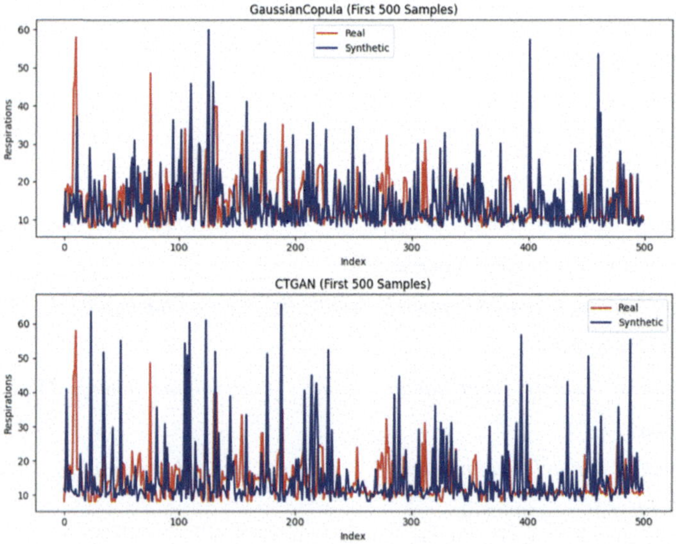

Fig. 6.13 Synthetic data versus real data using GaussianCopula and CTGAN

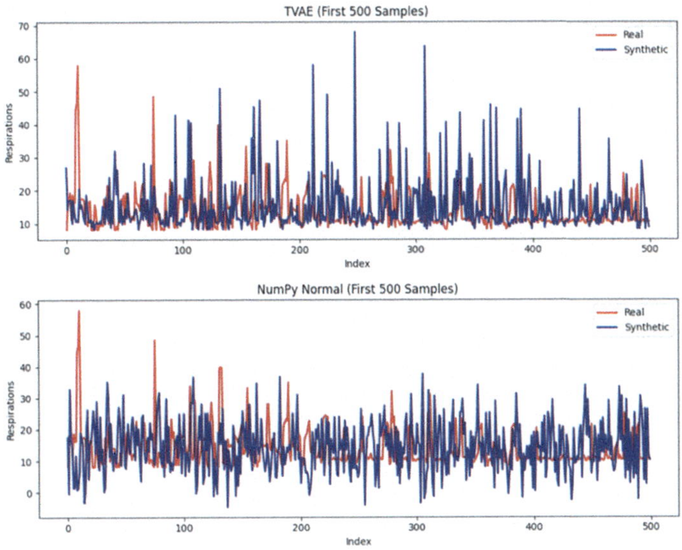

Fig. 6.14 Synthetic data versus real data using TVAE and NumPy

6.4 Conclusion

In this chapter, the application of wearable sensors, Ultra-Wideband (UWB) technology, and machine learning techniques for healthcare monitoring was presented. The prediction of oxygen saturation, respiration rates, and sleep disorders was achieved using real-world and synthetic datasets. Contactless respiratory monitoring was enabled through UWB sensors, allowing detailed chest movements to be detected without physical attachments. Machine learning models, including LSTM, GRU, and dense networks, were trained and evaluated, demonstrating strong predictive performance. Additionally, synthetic data was generated using SDV tools such as GaussianCopula, CTGAN, and TVAE synthesizers, ensuring that data privacy was preserved while enhancing model training with diverse examples. Feature importance was analyzed across multiple classification algorithms to better understand sleep health factors. By leveraging these technologies, a pathway toward continuous, non-invasive, and intelligent healthcare monitoring was established. Future healthcare solutions can be greatly enhanced when real-time physiological monitoring and machine learning are effectively integrated and responsibly deployed.

References

1. F. M. Noori, M. Z. Uddin, and J. Torresen, "Ultra-Wideband radar-based activity recognition using deep learning," IEEE Access, vol. 9, pp. 138132–138143, 2021..
2. M. Z. Uddin, F. M. Noori, and J. Torresen, "In-home emergency detection using an ambient ultra-wideband radar sensor and deep learning," in Proc. 2020 IEEE Ukrainian Microwave Week (UkrMW), Kharkiv, Ukraine, pp. 1089–1093, 2020.
3. M. Ogasawara, M. Takeshima, S. Kosaka, A. Imanishi, Y. Itoh, D. Fujiwara, K. Yoshizawa, N. Ozaki, K. Nakagome, and K. Mishima, "Exploratory validation of sleep-tracking devices in patients with psychiatric disorders," Nature and Science of Sleep, pp. 301–312, 2023.
4. A. Kiran and S. S. Kumar, "A methodology and an empirical analysis to determine the most suitable synthetic data generator," IEEE Access, vol. 12, pp. 12209–12228, 2024.

Chapter 7
Case Studies: Understanding Emotions

Abstract Emotion prediction from images is achieved by enabling computers to recognize human emotions based solely on facial appearances. Images or audio recordings of individuals are used to infer whether emotions such as happiness, sadness, anger, surprise, fear, or others are being displayed. In the case of images, facial features including the eyes, mouth, and eyebrows are analyzed, and patterns of change associated with different emotional expressions are learned. These features are carefully examined to identify subtle differences that correspond to specific emotions. Regarding audio, essential characteristics such as pitch, tone, loudness, and speech rate are extracted to assist in the emotion prediction process. Various machine learning and deep learning models are then trained on labeled datasets to enable accurate predictions. Through these approaches, emotion recognition systems are developed to support applications in areas such as healthcare, education, entertainment, and human–computer interaction.

7.1 Emotion Prediction in Images and XAI

To teach the computer, we use a large group of images where each face is already labeled with the correct emotion. This helps the computer learn what each emotion looks like. A popular method for this is using a deep learning model called a convolutional neural network (CNN), which is very good at finding patterns in images.

Before training the model, the images are prepared through a process called preprocessing. This includes changing the size of the images, turning them into grayscale, and making sure the faces are centered and clear. Sometimes we also change the images a bit, like flipping or rotating them, so the model can learn from different examples. Then, XAI techniques such as Grad-CAM can be applied. Figure 7.1 shows an example of Grad-CAM output of a happy facial expression testing image.

© The Author(s), under exclusive license to Springer Nature Switzerland AG 2025

M. Z. Uddin, *Trustworthy Multimodal Intelligent Systems for Independent Living*, Cognitive Technologies, https://doi.org/10.1007/978-3-031-97359-8_7

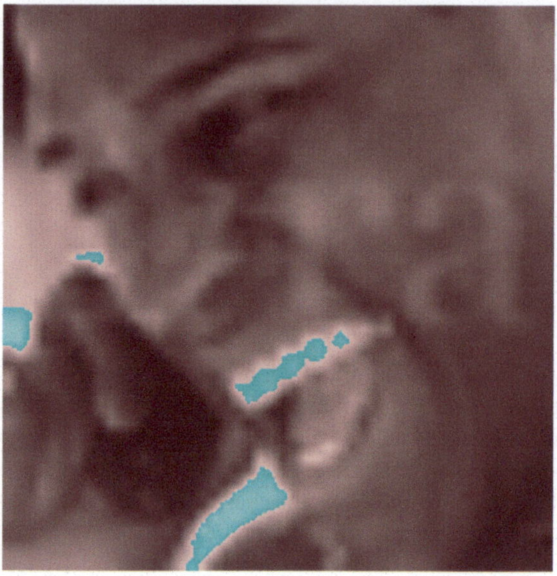

Fig. 7.1 A Grad-CAM output of a facial expression testing image

After the training is done, the model can look at a new image and predict the emotion. This is useful in apps and systems that need to understand how users feel, like in online learning, video games, customer support, or health monitoring. Even though emotion prediction from images works well, it still has challenges. People express emotions differently based on their culture, personality, or situation. Because of this, the model might not always be right. But as the technology improves and more training data is used, these systems are getting better and more accurate in recognizing emotions from faces. For typical CNN, we can follow the same pattern of posture predictions part where there are two classes in this regard: Sad and Happy. Figure 7.2 shows a LIME output of a facial expression testing image using the code shown bellow.

```python
from lime import lime_image
from skimage.segmentation import mark_boundaries
from tensorflow.keras.preprocessing import image as keras_image
from tensorflow.keras.applications.imagenet_utils import preprocess_input

# Load and preprocess image
def load_image_tf(img_path, size=(224, 224)):
    img = keras_image.load_img(img_path, target_size=size)
    img_array = keras_image.img_to_array(img)
    return img, img_array.astype(np.uint8), img_array / 255.0

# Prediction function for LIME (expects list of [H, W, 3] images)
def predict_fn(images):
    images = np.array(images) / 255.0   # normalize
    preds = model.predict(images)
    return preds

# Path to test image
img_path = './fer_dataset/test/happy/PrivateTest_11807115.jpg'   # <-- your image
path

# Load image
pil_img, raw_img, norm_img = load_image_tf(img_path)
raw_img = raw_img.astype(np.uint8)

# Create LIME explainer
explainer = lime_image.LimeImageExplainer()

# Explain prediction
explanation = explainer.explain_instance(
    image=raw_img,
    classifier_fn=predict_fn,
    top_labels=1,
    num_samples=1000,
    hide_color=0
)
```

```
# Get top prediction
pred_class = explanation.top_labels[0]

# Get image and mask from explanation
temp, mask = explanation.get_image_and_mask(
    label=pred_class,
    positive_only=True,
    num_features=10,
    hide_rest=False
)

# Overlay with boundaries
lime_result = mark_boundaries(temp / 255.0, mask, color=(1, 1, 0),
mode='subpixel')

# Display
plt.figure(figsize=(6, 6))
plt.imshow(lime_result)
plt.axis("off")
plt.title(f"LIME - Class {pred_class}")
plt.show()
```

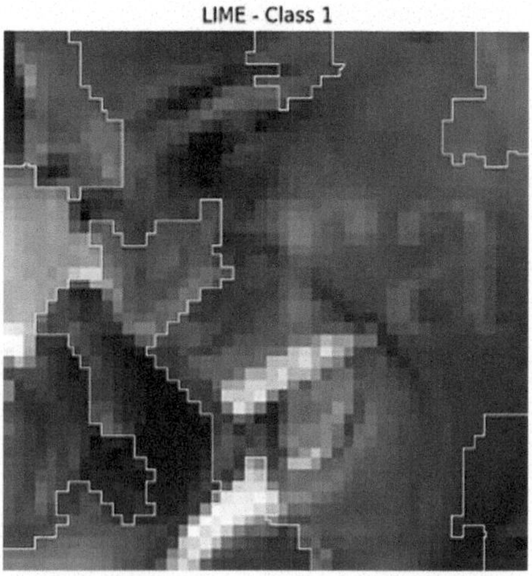

Fig. 7.2 A LIME output of a facial expression testing image

7.2 Emotion Prediction in Images, Pretrained Model, and XAI

One of the most widely used deep learning models for this task has been ResNet (Residual Network). ResNet is a type of Convolutional Neural Network (CNN) that introduced the concept of skip connections, allowing the model to be deeper without running into problems like vanishing gradients [1]. In emotion recognition, ResNet is used to extract detailed features from facial images, such as the shape of the mouth, eyes, and eyebrows. These features help the model learn patterns linked to different emotions. ResNet has been highly effective for tasks involving image classification and has served as a strong backbone model in many emotion prediction systems [2]. Figure 7.3 shows a Grad-CAM output of a facial expression testing image on ResNET18. Figure 7.4 shows a LIME output of a happy facial expression testing the same image on ResNET18.

Transformers were first used in natural language processing but have been adapted for image tasks. Two well-known transformer models for images are the Vision Transformer (ViT) and the Swin Transformer. These models work differently from CNNs. Instead of using filters to scan parts of an image, transformers break the image into smaller patches and process them all at once using attention mechanisms. This allows the model to focus on important areas of the image and understand the relationships between different parts of the face more effectively. The Vision Transformer (ViT) divides an input image into fixed-size patches, flattens each patch into a vector, and feeds them into a transformer encoder. This encoder learns the spatial relationships and patterns across the image, treating the visual data similarly to how it would treat a sequence of words in a sentence. This method gives the model a global view of the image from the beginning, which can be very useful for capturing overall facial structure and expression. Figure 7.5 shows an example of GradCAM++

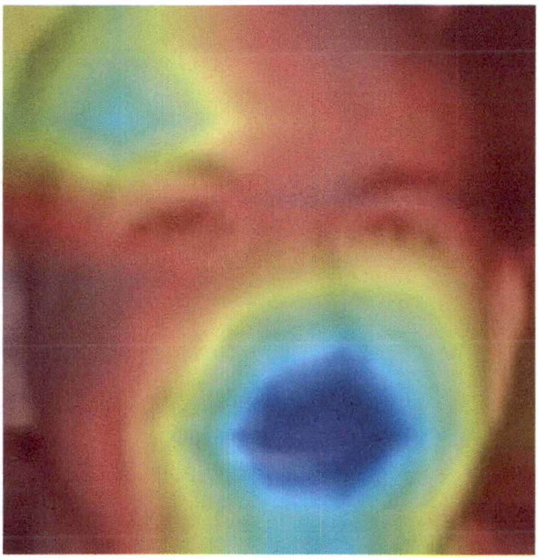

Fig. 7.3 A Grad-CAM output of a facial expression testing image on ResNET18

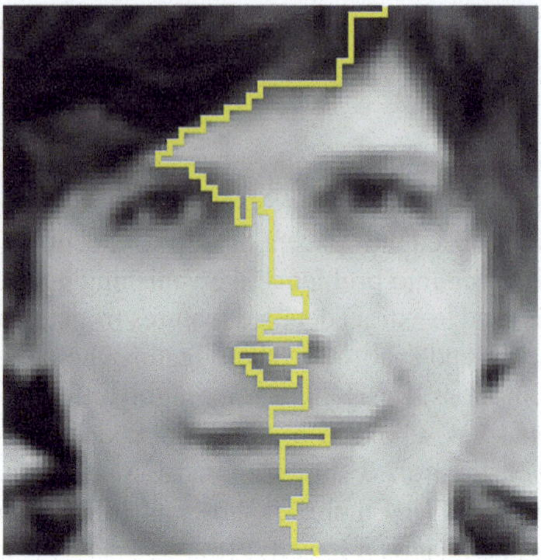

Fig. 7.4 A LIME output of a happy facial expression testing image on ResNET18

output of a happy facial expression testing image on ViT. Figure 7.6 shows a LIME example on a happy facial expression testing image on top of ViT.

On the other hand, the Swin Transformer uses a more structured approach by processing the image in a hierarchical way. It uses shifted windows, meaning it looks at overlapping areas of the image at different stages. This helps the model capture both small details, like the curve of a smile, and larger patterns, like the shape of the whole face. Because of this, Swin is often better at dealing with high-resolution images and recognizing emotions in more complex scenes. Figure 7.7 shows a LIME output of a happy facial expression testing image on SWIN transformers.

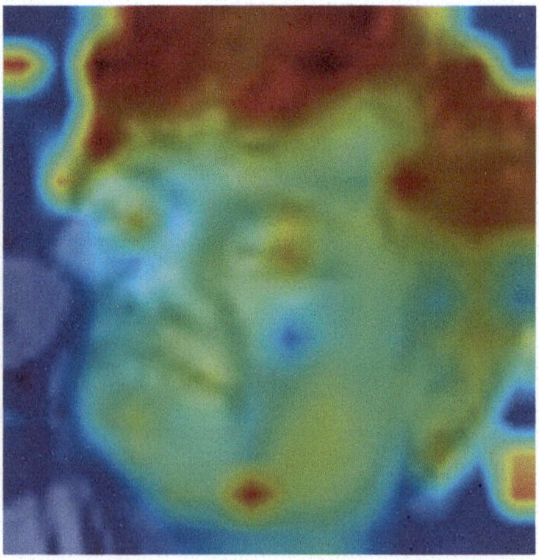

Fig. 7.5 A GradCAM++ output of a happy facial expression testing image on ViT

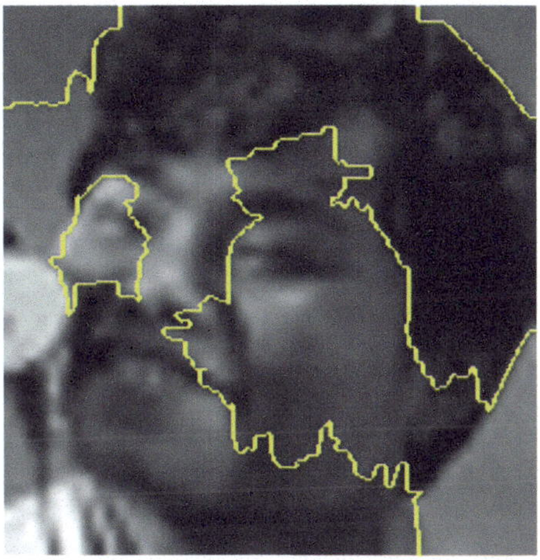

Fig. 7.6 A LIME output of a happy facial expression testing image on ViT

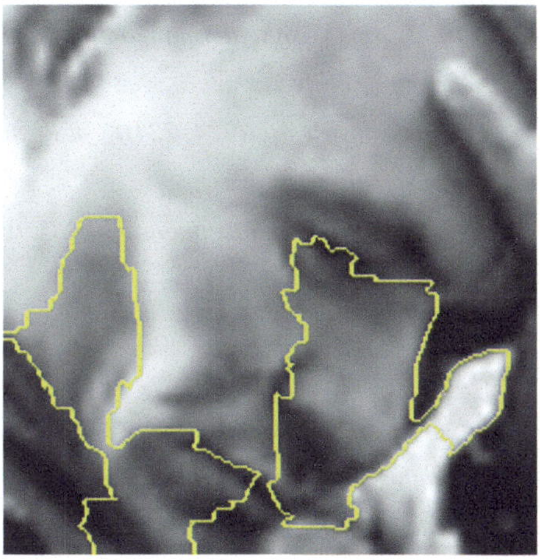

Fig. 7.7 A LIME output of a happy facial expression testing image on SWIN

Using transformer models like ViT and Swin for emotion prediction offers many benefits [3]. They are more flexible in learning different types of features and are often more accurate, especially when dealing with large and diverse datasets. These models also scale well, meaning their performance improves as they are trained on more data. As a result, they are becoming increasingly popular in emotion recognition systems used in fields like healthcare, education, and human–computer interaction.

```
import torch
import torchvision
import torchvision.transforms as transforms
from torch.utils.data import DataLoader
from torchvision.datasets import ImageFolder
# Define image transformations
transform = transforms.Compose([
    transforms.Grayscale(num_output_channels=3),   # Convert to 3 channels for
CNN compatibility
    transforms.Resize((224, 224)),   # Resize for ResNet
    transforms.ToTensor(),
    transforms.Normalize(mean=[0.485, 0.456, 0.406], std=[0.229, 0.224, 0.225])
])

# Load dataset
data_dir = "fer_dataset/"
train_dataset = ImageFolder(root=data_dir + "train", transform=transform)
test_dataset = ImageFolder(root=data_dir + "test", transform=transform)
train_loader = DataLoader(train_dataset, batch_size=32, shuffle=True)
test_loader = DataLoader(test_dataset, batch_size=32, shuffle=False)

# Class names (emotions)
class_names = train_dataset.classes
```

```
import torch.nn as nn
import torchvision.models as models

# Load pre-trained ResNet model
model = models.resnet18(pretrained=True)

# Modify the last layer for 2 emotion classes
num_features = model.fc.in_features
model.fc = nn.Linear(num_features, len(class_names))

# Move model to GPU (if available)
device = torch.device("cuda" if torch.cuda.is_available() else "cpu")
model = model.to(device)

# Define loss and optimizer
criterion = nn.CrossEntropyLoss()
optimizer = torch.optim.Adam(model.parameters(), lr=0.001)

# Training loop
for epoch in range(20):  # Train for 5 epochs
    model.train()
    for images, labels in train_loader:
        images, labels = images.to(device), labels.to(device)
        optimizer.zero_grad()
        outputs = model(images)
        loss = criterion(outputs, labels)
        loss.backward()
        optimizer.step()

print("Training complete.")
import cv2
import numpy as np
import torch
```

```
import matplotlib.pyplot as plt
from pytorch_grad_cam import GradCAM
from pytorch_grad_cam.utils.image import preprocess_image,
show_cam_on_image
from pytorch_grad_cam import GradCAMPlusPlus


# Define Grad-CAM explainer
target_layers = [model.layer4[-1]]  # Ensure model is defined
cam = GradCAM(model=model, target_layers=target_layers)

#cam = GradCAMPlusPlus( model=model,target_layers=target_layers)

# Load a test image
image_path = "./fer_dataset/test/happy/PrivateTest_14548043.jpg"
image = cv2.imread(image_path, cv2.IMREAD_COLOR)
image = cv2.resize(image, (224, 224)).astype(np.float32) / 255.0  # Normalize

# Convert to PyTorch tensor with float32
input_tensor = preprocess_image(image, mean=[0.485, 0.456, 0.406], std=[0.229,
0.224, 0.225]).to(torch.float32)

# Generate Grad-CAM heatmap
grayscale_cam = cam(input_tensor=input_tensor)[0, :]  # Remove batch
dimension

# Overlay heatmap on the original image
visualization = show_cam_on_image(image, grayscale_cam)

# Display result
plt.imshow(visualization)
plt.axis("off")
plt.show()
```

```
import torch
import numpy as np
import matplotlib.pyplot as plt
from lime import lime_image
from skimage.segmentation import mark_boundaries
from torchvision import transforms
from PIL import Image

# Ensure model is in evaluation mode
model.eval()

# Define Image Transformations (same as training)
transform = transforms.Compose([
    transforms.Resize((224, 224)),
    transforms.ToTensor(),
    transforms.Normalize(mean=[0.485, 0.456, 0.406], std=[0.229, 0.224, 0.225])
])

# Load and preprocess image
image_path = "./fer_dataset/test/happy/PrivateTest_13068573.jpg"

image = Image.open(image_path).convert("RGB")
image_np = np.array(image)   # Convert to NumPy array
```

```
input_tensor = transform(image).unsqueeze(0)  # Convert to PyTorch tensor with
batch dimension

# Define LIME Explainer
explainer = lime_image.LimeImageExplainer()

# Define prediction function for LIME
def predict_fn(images):
    batch = torch.stack([transform(Image.fromarray(img)) for img in images])  #
Convert list of images to tensors
    batch = batch.to(torch.float32)  # Ensure correct dtype
    with torch.no_grad():
        outputs = model(batch)  # Get model predictions
        return  torch.nn.functional.softmax(outputs,  dim=1).cpu().numpy()    #
Convert to NumPy

        # Generate LIME Explanation with sufficient perturbations
        explanation = explainer.explain_instance(
            image_np,
            predict_fn,
            top_labels=1,
            hide_color=0,
            num_samples=1000  # More samples for better segmentation
        )
```

```
# Extract the mask and overlay
temp, mask = explanation.get_image_and_mask(
    explanation.top_labels[0],
    positive_only=True,        # Show only contributing regions
    num_features=1000,             # Top N superpixels
    hide_rest=False              # Set to True to only show important parts
)
lime_result = mark_boundaries(
    temp / 255.0,
    mask,
    color=(1, 1, 0),         # red (RGB values in range 0-1)
    mode='subpixel'          # thinner, smoother lines
)

with torch.no_grad():
    pred = model(input_tensor.to(torch.float32))
    pred_class_idx = pred.argmax(dim=1).item()
    pred_class_name = class_names[pred_class_idx]


plt.figure(figsize=(6, 6))
plt.imshow(lime_result)
plt.axis("off")
plt.title(f"LIME Explanation- Predicted: {pred_class_name} ({pred_class_idx})")
plt.show()
```

Let us try ViT now.

```
Let us try ViT now.
import torch
import torch.nn as nn
import torch.optim as optim
from transformers import ViTForImageClassification

device = torch.device("cuda" if torch.cuda.is_available() else "cpu")
# Create the ViT model (pretrained on ImageNet-21k)
model = ViTForImageClassification.from_pretrained(
    "google/vit-base-patch16-224-in21k"
)
model.to(device)

# Example: CrossEntropyLoss
criterion = nn.CrossEntropyLoss()
optimizer = optim.Adam(model.parameters(), lr=1e-4)

NUM_EPOCHS = 2  # example
for epoch in range(NUM_EPOCHS):
    model.train()
    for images, labels in train_loader:
        images = images.to(device)
        labels = labels.to(device)

        # The Hugging Face ViT expects the argument pixel_values=...
        outputs = model(pixel_values=images)
        logits = outputs.logits  # shape [B, num_classes]

        loss = criterion(logits, labels)
        loss.backward()
        optimizer.step()
        optimizer.zero_grad()

    print(f"Epoch {epoch+1} complete.")

# ----------------------------------------
# SAVE THE TRAINED MODEL (Hugging Face style)
# ----------------------------------------
save_directory = "my_vit_model"
```

```
model.save_pretrained(save_directory)
print(f"Model saved to: {save_directory}")
import torch
import torch.nn as nn
import torchvision.transforms as transforms
import numpy as np
import matplotlib.pyplot as plt
from PIL import Image

# Hugging Face ViT
from transformers import ViTForImageClassification

# Grad-CAM++
from pytorch_grad_cam import GradCAMPlusPlus
from pytorch_grad_cam.utils.model_targets import ClassifierOutputTarget
from pytorch_grad_cam.utils.image import show_cam_on_image

##########################################################################
###############
# 1) Simple wrapper to return logits for Grad-CAM
##########################################################################
###############
class ViTModelWrapper(nn.Module):
    def __init__(self, hf_vit):
        super().__init__()
        self.hf_vit = hf_vit

    def forward(self, pixel_values):
        outputs = self.hf_vit(pixel_values=pixel_values)
        return outputs.logits    # Grad-CAM requires raw logits
```

```
###############################################################################
# 2) Setup model, device, and load pretrained or custom checkpoint
###############################################################################
device = torch.device("cpu")

# Load pretrained model or your custom model
hf_vit_model = ViTForImageClassification.from_pretrained("my_vit_model")
hf_vit_model.eval()
model = ViTModelWrapper(hf_vit_model).to(device)

###############################################################################
# 3) Image preprocessing pipeline (adapt to your training setup)
###############################################################################
transform = transforms.Compose([
    transforms.Grayscale(num_output_channels=3),
    transforms.Resize((224, 224)),
    transforms.ToTensor(),
    transforms.Normalize(mean=[0.5, 0.5, 0.5],
                         std=[0.5, 0.5, 0.5])
])

###############################################################################
# 4) Reshape for Grad-CAM from [B, tokens, D] to [B, D, H, W]
###############################################################################
def vit_reshape_transform(tensor, height=14, width=14):
    tensor = tensor[:, 1:, :]  # Remove CLS token
    tensor = tensor.reshape(tensor.size(0), height, width, tensor.size(2))
```

```
    tensor = tensor.permute(0, 3, 1, 2)   # [B, D, H, W]
    return tensor

#########################################################################
###############
# 5) Load and prepare an input image
#########################################################################
###############
image_path = "./fer_dataset/test/happy/PrivateTest_10470092.jpg"
pil_img = Image.open(image_path).convert("RGB")
input_tensor = transform(pil_img).unsqueeze(0).to(device)

resized = pil_img.resize((224, 224))
img_for_cam = np.array(resized, dtype=np.float32) / 255.0

#########################################################################
###############
# 6) Pick a target transformer layer for Grad-CAM++
#########################################################################
###############
target_layer = hf_vit_model.vit.encoder.layer[10].output   # last encoder block
output

#########################################################################
###############
# 7) Initialize Grad-CAM++ object
#########################################################################
###############
cam = GradCAMPlusPlus(
    model=model,
    target_layers=[target_layer],
    reshape_transform=vit_reshape_transform
)
```

```
################################################################################
###############
# 8) Forward pass & get prediction
################################################################################
###############
with torch.no_grad():
    logits = model(input_tensor)
    pred_class = logits.argmax(dim=1).item()
    print("Predicted class index:", pred_class)

targets = [ClassifierOutputTarget(pred_class)]

################################################################################
###############
# 9) Generate and overlay Grad-CAM++
################################################################################
###############
grayscale_cam = cam(input_tensor=input_tensor, targets=targets)[0] # [224,
224]
visualization = show_cam_on_image(img_for_cam, grayscale_cam,
use_rgb=True)

plt.imshow(visualization)
plt.axis("off")
plt.title("Grad-CAM++ on Hugging Face ViT")
plt.show()
```

```
import torch
import torch.nn as nn
import torchvision.transforms as transforms
import numpy as np
import matplotlib.pyplot as plt
from PIL import Image

# Hugging Face ViT
from transformers import ViTForImageClassification

# LIME
from lime import lime_image
from skimage.segmentation import mark_boundaries

######################################################################
###############
# 1) Simple wrapper to return logits
######################################################################
###############
class ViTModelWrapper(nn.Module):
    def __init__(self, hf_vit):
        super().__init__()
        self.hf_vit = hf_vit


            def forward(self, pixel_values):
                outputs = self.hf_vit(pixel_values=pixel_values)
                return outputs.logits   # for prediction probabilities
```

```
##########################################################################
###############
# 2) Setup model, device, and load pretrained or custom checkpoint
##########################################################################
###############
device = torch.device("cpu")

# Load pretrained model (or your own if available)
hf_vit_model = ViTForImageClassification.from_pretrained("my_vit_model")
hf_vit_model.eval()
model = ViTModelWrapper(hf_vit_model).to(device)

##########################################################################
###############
# 3) Image preprocessing pipeline (adapt to your training setup)
##########################################################################
###############
transform = transforms.Compose([
    transforms.Grayscale(num_output_channels=3),
    transforms.Resize((224, 224)),
    transforms.ToTensor(),
    transforms.Normalize(mean=[0.5, 0.5, 0.5],
                         std=[0.5, 0.5, 0.5])
])

##########################################################################
###############
# 4) Load and prepare an input image
```

```
###########################################################################
###############
image_path = "./fer_dataset/test/happy/PrivateTest_10470092.jpg"
pil_img = Image.open(image_path).convert("RGB")
resized = pil_img.resize((224, 224))
input_tensor = transform(resized).unsqueeze(0).to(device)

###########################################################################
###############
# 5) Predict class
###########################################################################
###############
with torch.no_grad():
    logits = model(input_tensor)
    pred_class = logits.argmax(dim=1).item()
    print("Predicted class index:", pred_class)

###########################################################################
###############
# 6) Define LIME prediction function
###########################################################################
###############
def predict_fn(images_np):
    images_tensor = []
    for img in images_np:
        img_pil = Image.fromarray(img.astype('uint8')).convert("RGB")
        tensor = transform(img_pil)
        images_tensor.append(tensor)

    batch = torch.stack(images_tensor).to(device)
    with torch.no_grad():
        outputs = model(batch)
        probs = torch.nn.functional.softmax(outputs, dim=1)
```

```
    return probs.cpu().numpy()

##########################################################################
###############
# 7) Run LIME explainer
##########################################################################
###############
explainer = lime_image.LimeImageExplainer()

explanation = explainer.explain_instance(
    np.array(resized),           # Original image as numpy array
    classifier_fn=predict_fn,    # Prediction function
    top_labels=5,                 # Number of top labels to explain
    hide_color=0,
    num_samples=1000                # Number of perturbed samples
)

# Get explanation for the predicted class
temp, mask = explanation.get_image_and_mask(
    label=pred_class,
    positive_only=True,
    num_features=10,
    hide_rest=False
)

##########################################################################
###############
# 8) Visualize LIME result
##########################################################################
###############
plt.imshow(mark_boundaries(temp, mask))
plt.title("LIME on Hugging Face ViT")
plt.axis("off")
plt.show()
```

```
#Lets use SWIN now.

################################################################################
###############
# 5. Load Swin Transformer + Processor
################################################################################
###############
model = SwinForImageClassification.from_pretrained("microsoft/swin-base-
patch4-window7-224")
model.to(device)

image_processor = AutoImageProcessor.from_pretrained("microsoft/swin-base-
patch4-window7-224")

################################################################################
###############
# 6. Loss & Optimizer
################################################################################
###############
criterion = nn.CrossEntropyLoss()
optimizer = optim.Adam(model.parameters(), lr=1e-4)

################################################################################
###############
# 7. Training Loop
################################################################################
###############
```

```
for epoch in range(NUM_EPOCHS):
    model.train()
    total_loss = 0.0

    for images, labels in train_loader:
        # Preprocess with Hugging Face processor
        inputs = image_processor(images=images,
return_tensors="pt").to(device)
        labels = labels.to(device)

        outputs = model(**inputs)
        logits = outputs.logits

        loss = criterion(logits, labels)
        loss.backward()
        optimizer.step()
        optimizer.zero_grad()

        total_loss += loss.item()

    print(f"Epoch [{epoch+1}/{NUM_EPOCHS}], Loss: {total_loss:.4f}")

#######################################################################
##############
# 8. Save Trained Model
#######################################################################
##############
save_dir = "my_swin_model"
```

```
model.save_pretrained(save_dir)
image_processor.save_pretrained(save_dir)
print(f"Model saved to: {save_dir}")import torch
import torch.nn as nn
import numpy as np
import matplotlib.pyplot as plt
from PIL import Image

from transformers import SwinForImageClassification, AutoImageProcessor

# Grad-CAM++
from pytorch_grad_cam import GradCAMPlusPlus
from pytorch_grad_cam.utils.model_targets import ClassifierOutputTarget
from pytorch_grad_cam.utils.image import show_cam_on_image

##########################################################################
###############
# 1) Wrapper to return logits for Grad-CAM++
##########################################################################
###############
class SwinModelWrapper(nn.Module):
    def __init__(self, hf_model):
        super().__init__()
        self.hf_model = hf_model

    def forward(self, pixel_values):
        outputs = self.hf_model(pixel_values=pixel_values)
        return outputs.logits

##########################################################################
###############
# 2) Load your fine-tuned Swin model
```

```
###########################################################################
###############
device = torch.device("cuda" if torch.cuda.is_available() else "cpu")

save_dir = "my_swin_model"
hf_swin_model = SwinForImageClassification.from_pretrained(save_dir)
hf_swin_model.eval()
model = SwinModelWrapper(hf_swin_model).to(device)
import torch
import torch.nn.functional as F
import numpy as np
from PIL import Image
from lime import lime_image
from skimage.segmentation import mark_boundaries
import matplotlib.pyplot as plt
from transformers import AutoImageProcessor, SwinForImageClassification
import torch.nn as nn

###########################################################################
###############
# 1. SwinModelWrapper
###########################################################################
###############
class SwinModelWrapper(nn.Module):
    def __init__(self, model_path):
        super().__init__()
        self.hf_model                                                      =
SwinForImageClassification.from_pretrained(model_path)

    def forward(self, **kwargs):
        return self.hf_model(**kwargs).logits
```

```
##########################################################################
###############
# 2. Setup model and processor
##########################################################################
###############
device = torch.device("cuda" if torch.cuda.is_available() else "cpu")

model_path = "./my_swin_model/"
model = SwinModelWrapper(model_path).to(device).eval()
image_processor = AutoImageProcessor.from_pretrained(model_path)

##########################################################################
###############
# 3. LIME prediction wrapper
##########################################################################
###############
def predict_fn(images_np):
    # Convert each [H, W, 3] float image back to PIL and process
    images = [Image.fromarray((img * 255).astype(np.uint8)) for img in
images_np]
    inputs = image_processor(images=images, return_tensors="pt").to(device)
    with torch.no_grad():
        logits = model(**inputs)
        probs = F.softmax(logits, dim=1).cpu().numpy()
    return probs   # shape: [batch_size, num_classes]

##########################################################################
###############
# 4. Run LIME on one image
##########################################################################
###############
image_path = "./fer_dataset/test/sad/PrivateTest_11574818.jpg"
pil_img = Image.open(image_path).convert("RGB").resize((224, 224))
```

```
img_np = np.array(pil_img).astype(np.float32) / 255.0   # shape: [224, 224, 3]

explainer = lime_image.LimeImageExplainer()

explanation = explainer.explain_instance(
    image=img_np,
    classifier_fn=predict_fn,
    top_labels=5,
    hide_color=0,
    num_samples=1000
)

##########################################################################
###############
# 5. Visualize result
##########################################################################
###############
pred_class = explanation.top_labels[0]
temp, mask = explanation.get_image_and_mask(
    label=pred_class,
    positive_only=True,
    num_features=5,
    hide_rest=False
)

lime_result = mark_boundaries(temp, mask)

plt.imshow(lime_result)
plt.axis("off")
plt.title(f"LIME Explanation - Class {pred_class}")
plt.show()
```

7.3 Emotion Prediction in Audio

Emotion prediction in audio is the process of teaching a computer to understand how a person is feeling just by listening to their voice. When we talk, we express emotions not only through the words we use but also through the way we say them. For example, if someone is angry, they might speak louder and faster [4]. If they are sad, their voice may sound soft and slow. These changes in how we speak can give clues about our emotions, and computers can be trained to recognize these clues.

To predict emotions from audio, the process usually starts with collecting voice recordings. These recordings can come from phone calls, interviews, videos, or any other situation where people speak. Once the audio is collected, it needs to be cleaned. This means removing background noise and focusing on the parts of the recording that matter most. After cleaning, the next step is to study the voice and pull out important patterns [5]. These patterns are called features. Some examples of features include how high or low the voice sounds, how loud it is, and how fast the person is speaking. One of the most important features is something called MFCCs, which stands for Mel-Frequency Cepstral Coefficients [6]. These are mathematical patterns that help describe the shape of the sound and are very useful in recognizing emotions. Once all these features are taken from the voice recording, they are given to a machine learning model. This model is like a smart program that can learn from examples. The model is trained using many examples of voice recordings where the emotion is already known. For instance, a recording might be labeled as "happy" or "sad," and the model uses these labels to learn how different emotions sound.

After training, the model is ready to listen to new recordings. When you give it a new piece of audio, it will try to guess the emotion based on what it learned. These kinds of systems can be used in many ways. For example, in customer service, they can help detect if a caller is upset so the company can respond better. In mental health, emotion prediction can help detect early signs of depression or anxiety. It can also be used in smart home devices that react differently depending on how you sound. Even though this technology is powerful, it is not perfect. People express emotions in different ways depending on their culture, language, and personality. Some people might sound sad even when they are not. Also, noisy environments or poor-quality recordings can make it harder for the system to understand emotions correctly. To improve accuracy, some systems combine voice with other types of information, like facial expressions or text messages.

In short, emotion prediction in audio is a way for computers to understand how we feel by listening to how we talk. It has many useful applications and is becoming more common in everyday technology. As the systems improve, they can become more helpful, more accurate, and more sensitive to human emotions. Figures 7.8 and 7.9 show the prediction scores of a happy and neutral sample audio on Hubert model, respectively.

```
import os

# If TensorFlow is installed but we only want PyTorch, disable TF in Transformers:
os.environ["TRANSFORMERS_NO_TF"] = "1"

from transformers import pipeline

# List of 10 model IDs (examples)
model_ids = [

        "superb/wav2vec2-base-superb-er",
        "superb/hubert-base-superb-er",
        "superb/wavlm-base-superb-er",
        "superb/wavlm-base-plus-superb-er",
        "superb/wav2vec2-large-superb-er",
        "superb/xls_r-300m-superb-er",
        "superb/wav2vec2-large-xlsr-53-superb-er",
        "superb/wav2vec2-base-plus-librispeech-250h-superb-er",
        "superb/wav2vec2-large-robust-ft-libri-960-superb-er",
        "superb/hubert-large-superb-er"
    ]

    # Input audio file
    audio_file = "./dataset/Happy/03a01Fa.wav"
    import matplotlib.pyplot as plt

    for model_id in model_ids:
        print(f"\n=== Using model: {model_id} ===")
        try:
```

```
        # 1) Create an audio-classification pipeline for the current model
        classifier = pipeline(task="audio-classification", model=model_id)

        # 2) Classify the audio
        results = classifier(audio_file)

        # 3) Print the predictions (label + score)
        print("Emotion recognition results:")
        for entry in results:
            print(f"  Label: {entry['label']}, Score: {entry['score']:.3f}")

        # 4) Plot the scores
        #    results is typically sorted by descending score,
        #    but we'll just map them in the order they're returned.

        labels = [entry['label'] for entry in results]
        scores = [entry['score'] for entry in results]

        plt.figure()  # Make a new figure for each model
        plt.bar(labels, scores)
        plt.title(f"Scores for model: {model_id}")
        plt.xlabel("Predicted Label")
        plt.ylabel("Score")
        plt.tight_layout()
        plt.show()

    except Exception as e:
            print(f"ERROR loading or using model '{model_id}': {e}")
```

For *audio_file = "./dataset/Neutral/03b09Nc.wav"*, we obtain following scores.

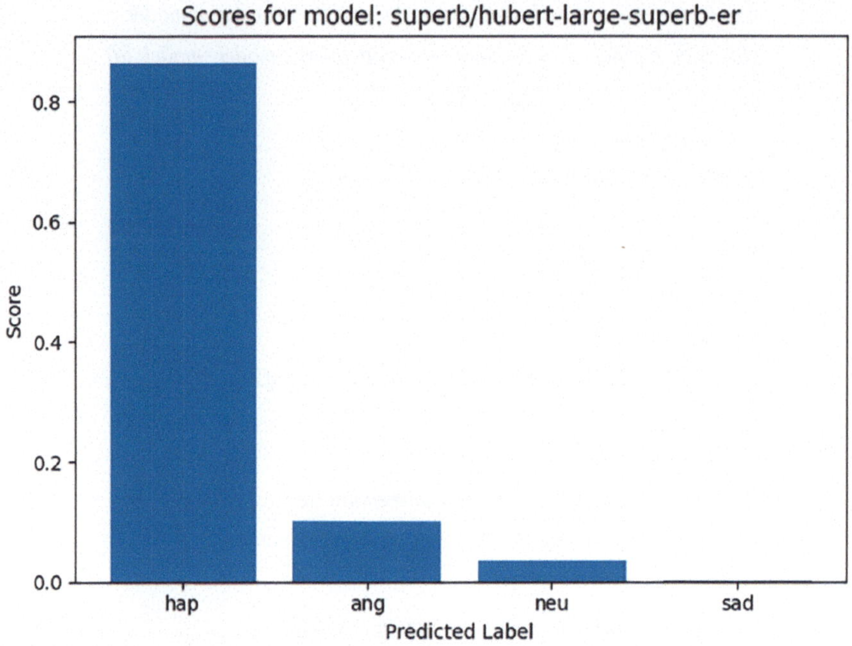

Fig. 7.8 Prediction scores of a happy sample audio on Hubert model

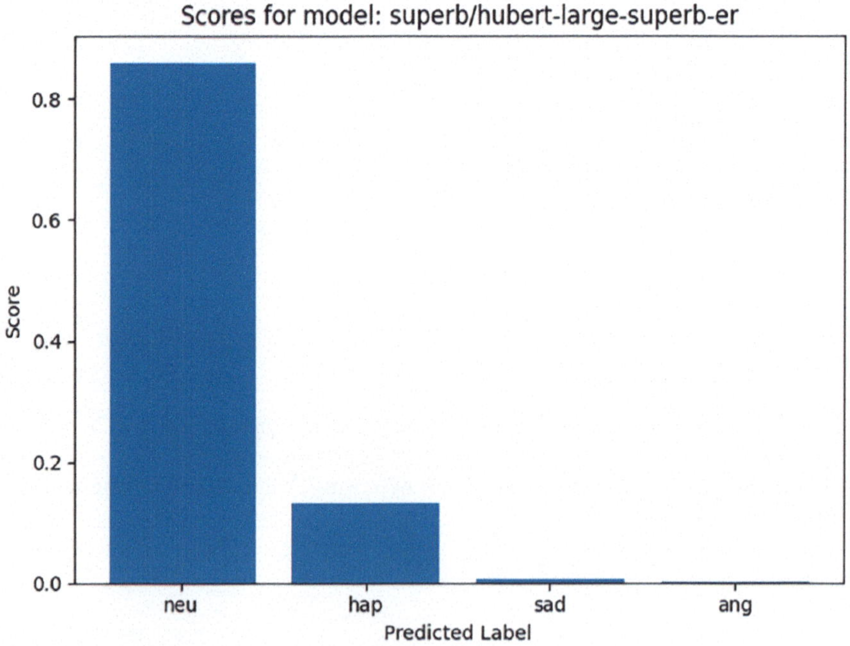

Fig. 7.9 Prediction scores of a neutral sample audio on Hubert model

7.4 Conclusion

In this chapter, the prediction of emotions from images and audio was explored through deep learning techniques. CNNs, ResNet, Vision Transformer (ViT), and Swin Transformer models were utilized to classify emotions such as happy and sad, with preprocessing steps carefully applied to enhance performance. XAI methods like LIME and Grad-CAM were implemented to visualize and interpret model decisions. For audio-based emotion prediction, features such as MFCCs were extracted, and transformer-based models pretrained on large datasets were employed. Emotions from voice signals were successfully classified by several fine-tuned models. Challenges such as cultural variability, recording noise, and expression diversity were recognized as factors affecting prediction accuracy. Nevertheless, improvements were demonstrated through the use of advanced architectures and explainability techniques. It was shown that by combining robust models with interpretability tools, more trustworthy and accurate emotion recognition systems can be developed, offering significant potential for applications in healthcare, education, and user experience.

References

1. M. K. Chowdary, T. N. Nguyen, and D. J. Hemanth, "Deep learning-based facial emotion recognition for human–computer interaction applications," *Neural Computing and Applications*, vol. 35, no. 32, 2023, pp. 23311–23328.
2. F. X. Gaya-Morey, S. Ramis-Guarinos, C. Manresa-Yee, and J. M. Buades-Rubio, "Unveiling the human-like similarities of automatic facial expression recognition: An empirical exploration through explainable AI," *Multimedia Tools and Applications*, vol. 83, 2024, pp. 85725–85753.
3. S. Khan, M. Naseer, M. Hayat, S. W. Zamir, F. S. Khan, and M. Shah, "Transformers in vision: A survey," *ACM Computing Surveys*, vol. 54, no. 10, Art. 200, 2022, pp. 1–41.
4. A. Dosovitskiy, L. Beyer, A. Kolesnikov, D. Weissenborn, X. Zhai, T. Unterthiner, M. Dehghani, M. Minderer, G. Heigold, S. Gelly, J. Uszkoreit, and N. Houlsby, "An image is worth 16×16 words: Transformers for image recognition at scale," *International Journal of Computer Vision*, vol. 131, no. 3, 2023, pp. 620–644.
5. S. M. George and P. M. Ilyas, "A review on speech emotion recognition: A survey, recent advances, challenges, and the influence of noise," *Neurocomputing*, vol. 568, 2024, Art. 127015.
6. D. S. Johnson, O. Hakobyan, and H. Drimalla, "Towards interpretability in audio and visual affective machine learning: A review," arXiv:2306.08933, 2023.

Chapter 8
Real-Time Applications

Abstract Imagine you ask an intelligent system to play your favorite music, audiobooks, or TV shows. It learns your preferences and suggests content you might enjoy based on your past choices. Imagine the system detects an unusual change in your vital signs through wearable sensors, it automatically alerts caregivers or emergency services and provides them with relevant health data. From assisting in healthcare to enhancing daily living, these technologies are hot topics for research. In this regard, machine learning is being explored quite profoundly to make the systems more intelligent and more intuitive. In a real-world smart assisted living facility, where numerous sensors are deployed to monitor behavior, environmental conditions, and health status, it is preferred that the collected data be stored in controlled, private storage systems rather than commercial devices or cloud services. This approach can better safeguard user privacy and enhance data security.

8.1 Real-Time Activity Recognition from Wearable Sensors

For recognizing human activities in real time, a small device called MetaMotionR is used. This sensor is made by a company called MbientLab [1]. MetaMotionR is popular because of its small size and powerful features. Even though it is tiny, it contains several important sensors inside it. These include an accelerometer, a gyroscope, and a magnetometer. Each of these sensors collects different types of data that help track motion, direction, and the surrounding environment.

The accelerometer measures how fast something is moving or changing direction. For example, it can detect if a person is walking, running, or standing still. The gyroscope helps measure how something is rotating. This is useful for detecting if someone is turning, spinning, or tilting in different directions. The magnetometer senses the Earth's magnetic field and helps with figuring out orientation, like which way a person or object is facing. When all three sensors work together, they give a clear picture of how something is moving in three dimensions.

© The Author(s), under exclusive license to Springer Nature Switzerland AG 2025
M. Z. Uddin, *Trustworthy Multimodal Intelligent Systems for Independent Living*, Cognitive Technologies, https://doi.org/10.1007/978-3-031-97359-8_8

One of the best things about the MetaMotionR is that it can send data in real time using Bluetooth Low Energy, also known as BLE [2]. This means it can connect wirelessly to phones, tablets, or computers without needing any cables. Real-time communication is especially useful for situations where immediate feedback is important. For example, in sports training, therapy sessions, or activity tracking, the data can be seen and analyzed right away. To help developers and researchers work with the MetaMotionR sensor, MbientLab offers software tools, guides, and coding examples. These are available on their official website and on GitHub. One of the main tools used in this project is the Python SDK from their GitHub page, which allows developers to communicate with the sensor, collect data, and build their own activity recognition systems. The tools provided are simple to use and allow for custom code to be written to process the data collected from the device.

For instance, data from the accelerometer can be used to detect when someone starts walking, jumps, or falls. The gyroscope can help track when someone rotates their body, like turning their head or twisting their waist. The magnetometer adds more detail by helping determine the direction of movement or heading. All this combined information makes MetaMotionR a powerful tool for understanding human movement in real time. In healthcare, this sensor can play an important role in monitoring how patients move during physical therapy. If a patient is recovering from an injury, the sensor can be used to make sure they are doing exercises the right way. Doctors or therapists can check the quality of each movement and give better feedback. This helps create more effective and personal treatment plans.

Overall, MetaMotionR stands out because of its mix of useful sensors, wireless connection, and easy-to-use tools for developers. Its small size, built-in battery, and detailed documentation make it a good choice for many different fields. Whether you're an experienced developer or just starting out, the MetaMotionR offers everything needed to start working with real-time motion tracking and activity recognition. Figure 8.1 shows a real-time activity recognition output where the sensors is worn on the belt and the image is shows just for ground truth, using the following code.

```
#!/usr/bin/env python3
import os, sys, re, csv, time, math, pytz
import numpy as np, pandas as pd, tensorflow as tf
from time import sleep
from datetime import datetime
from scipy.signal import find_peaks
from mbientlab.metawear import MetaWear, libmetawear, parse_value
from mbientlab.metawear.cbindings import *
```

Fig. 8.1 A real-time activity recognition output where the sensors is worn on the belt and the image is shows just for ground truth

```
# Clear terminal and set timezone
os.system("clear")
os.environ['TZ'] = 'Norway/Oslo'
time.tzset()

# Global lists to hold sensor values
acc_x, acc_y, acc_z = [], [], []
gyr_x, gyr_y, gyr_z = [], [], []

# Class for handling sensor data callbacks
class SensorState:
    def __init__(self, device):
        self.dev = device
        self.samples = 0
        self.acc_cb = FnVoid_VoidP_DataP(self.on_acc)
```

```
        self.gyr_cb = FnVoid_VoidP_DataP(self.on_gyr)

    def on_acc(self, ctx, data):
        self.samples += 1
        vals = list(map(float, re.findall(r"\d+\.\d+", str(parse_value(data)))))
        acc_x.append(vals[0])
        acc_y.append(vals[1])
        acc_z.append(vals[2])

    def on_gyr(self, ctx, data):
        self.samples += 1
        vals = list(map(float, re.findall(r"\d+\.\d+", str(parse_value(data)))))
        gyr_x.append(vals[0])
        gyr_y.append(vals[1])
        gyr_z.append(vals[2])

# Write initial HTML content indicating sensor not connected
now = datetime.now(pytz.timezone('Europe/Oslo')).strftime('%Y-%m-%dT%H:%M:%SZ')
init_msg = f'<meta http-equiv="refresh" content="2"/> <br><font size=16>Time: {now} Activity: SORRY! SENSOR NOT CONNECTED</font>'
with open('/var/www/html/index.html', 'w') as f:
    f.write(init_msg)

# Connect to devices provided as arguments
states = []
for mac in sys.argv[1:]:
    dev = MetaWear(mac)
    dev.connect()
    conn_type = "USB" if dev.usb.is_connected else "BLE"
    print(f"Connected to {dev.address} over {conn_type}")
    states.append(SensorState(dev))
```

```
# Configure each device
for state in states:
    board = state.dev.board
    libmetawear.mbl_mw_settings_set_connection_parameters(board, 7.5, 7.5, 0,
6000)
    sleep(1.5)
    # Accelerometer configuration
    libmetawear.mbl_mw_acc_bmi270_set_odr(board, AccBmi270Odr._50Hz)
    libmetawear.mbl_mw_acc_bosch_set_range(board, AccBoschRange._4G)
    libmetawear.mbl_mw_acc_write_acceleration_config(board)
    # Gyroscope configuration
    libmetawear.mbl_mw_gyro_bmi270_set_range(board,
GyroBoschRange._1000dps)
    libmetawear.mbl_mw_gyro_bmi270_set_odr(board, GyroBoschOdr._50Hz)
    libmetawear.mbl_mw_gyro_bmi270_write_config(board)
    # Subscribe to signals
    acc_sig = libmetawear.mbl_mw_acc_get_acceleration_data_signal(board)
    gyr_sig                                                              =
libmetawear.mbl_mw_gyro_bmi270_get_rotation_data_signal(board)
    libmetawear.mbl_mw_datasignal_subscribe(acc_sig, None, state.acc_cb)
    libmetawear.mbl_mw_datasignal_subscribe(gyr_sig, None, state.gyr_cb)
    # Start sensor sampling
    libmetawear.mbl_mw_acc_enable_acceleration_sampling(board)
    libmetawear.mbl_mw_acc_start(board)
    libmetawear.mbl_mw_gyro_bmi270_enable_rotation_sampling(board)
    libmetawear.mbl_mw_gyro_bmi270_start(board)

# Load the TensorFlow model weights once (inside loop only if you need to
reinitialize each time)
model = tf.keras.Sequential([
    tf.keras.Input((300, 6)),
    tf.keras.layers.LSTM(20),
    tf.keras.layers.Dense(4, activation='softmax')
```

```
])
model.compile(loss='categorical_crossentropy', optimizer='rmsprop',
metrics=['accuracy'], run_eagerly=True)
model.load_weights("./HARV1.h5")
activity_names = ['Standing', 'Sitting', 'Lying', 'Walking']
action_chars   = ['S', 's', 'L', 'W']

# Main loop: process and predict every 10 seconds
while True:
    sleep(10)
    n_samples = min(len(acc_x), len(gyr_x))
    print(n_samples)
    if n_samples < 1:
        now = datetime.now(pytz.timezone('Europe/Oslo')).strftime('%Y-%m-
%dT%H:%M:%SZ')
        msg = f'Time: {now} Activity: SORRY! SENSOR NOT CONNECTED'
        with open('/var/www/html/index.html', 'w') as f:
            f.write(f'<meta http-equiv="refresh" content="2"/> <br><font
size=16>{msg}</font>')
        sys.exit()

    # Process sensor data into segments
    df = pd.DataFrame({
        'AX': acc_x[:n_samples],
        'AY': acc_y[:n_samples],
        'AZ': acc_z[:n_samples],
        'GX': gyr_x[:n_samples],
        'GY': gyr_y[:n_samples],
        'GZ': gyr_z[:n_samples]
    })
    data_arr = df.to_numpy()
    seg_count = data_arr.shape[0] // 300
    data_arr = data_arr[:seg_count * 300].reshape(seg_count, 300, 6)
```

```
    # Run prediction
    prediction = model.predict(data_arr)
    act_idx = int(np.argmax(prediction[0]))
    act_text = activity_names[act_idx]
    act_char = action_chars[act_idx]

    cur_time =
datetime.now(pytz.timezone('Europe/Oslo')).strftime('%H:%M:%SZ')
    result_txt = f"Time: {cur_time} : {act_text}"

    # Step counting from accelerometer magnitude
    power = np.power(np.array(acc_x[:n_samples]), 2) +
np.power(np.array(acc_y[:n_samples]), 2) +
np.power(np.array(acc_z[:n_samples]), 2)
    mag = np.sqrt(power) - np.mean(np.sqrt(power))
    threshold = np.std(mag)
    peak_idxs = find_peaks(mag, height=threshold)[0]
    steps = int(len(peak_idxs) / 3.0) if threshold > 0.01 else 0

    if (np.array(acc_x[:n_samples]).sum() + np.array(acc_y[:n_samples]).sum()
+ np.array(acc_z[:n_samples]).sum()) < 101:
        result_txt = f"Time: {cur_time} Others"
        act_char = 'O'

    # Write updated HTML output
    with open('/var/www/html/index.html', 'w') as f:
        f.write(f'<meta http-equiv="refresh" content="2"/> <br><font
size=16>{result_txt}</font>')
    print(result_txt)
    print(f"Time: {cur_time} steps: {steps}")

    # Log steps and activity
```

```
        with open('/home/sintef/MetaWear-SDK-Python/examples/steps.csv', 'a') as f:
            csv.writer(f).writerow([cur_time, steps, act_char])

        # Clear sensor lists for next batch
        acc_x.clear(); acc_y.clear(); acc_z.clear()
        gyr_x.clear(); gyr_y.clear(); gyr_z.clear()

# Stop and clean up devices when done
for state in states:
    board = state.dev.board
    libmetawear.mbl_mw_acc_stop(board)
    libmetawear.mbl_mw_acc_disable_acceleration_sampling(board)
    libmetawear.mbl_mw_gyro_bmi270_stop(board)
    libmetawear.mbl_mw_gyro_bmi270_disable_rotation_sampling(board)

libmetawear.mbl_mw_datasignal_unsubscribe(libmetawear.mbl_mw_acc_get_acc
eleration_data_signal(board))

libmetawear.mbl_mw_datasignal_unsubscribe(libmetawear.mbl_mw_gyro_bmi27
0_get_rotation_data_signal(board))
    libmetawear.mbl_mw_debug_disconnect(board)
```

8.2 Real-Time Fall Detection from Camera Images

Real-time fall detection using camera images plays a vital role in enhancing safety, especially for elderly individuals or people with mobility issues. This technology relies on computer vision and deep learning methods to monitor human movements and recognize when a fall occurs [3]. By continuously analyzing video frames captured from a camera, the system can detect unusual posture changes or rapid downward movements, which may indicate a fall. Once detected, the system can immediately send alerts to caregivers or emergency services. One popular approach for fall detection involves the use of YOLO (You Only Look Once), a deep learning-based object detection model known for its speed and accuracy. YOLO can quickly identify and locate people within each video frame, making it well-suited for real-time applications. To improve fall detection accuracy, YOLO can be combined with pose estimation or human activity recognition techniques to distinguish between normal actions (like sitting or lying down) and actual falls. These models can be deployed on low-power devices such as the Raspberry Pi or NVIDIA Jetson, allowing for edge-based processing and reducing the need for cloud computation. Overall, this method offers an efficient, real-time solution to monitor and respond to potential fall incidents in various environments [4]. Figure 8.2 shows a real-time fall detection output from camera images using YOLO model.

Fig. 8.2 A real-time fall detection from camera images

```
import cv2
import cvzone
import math
from ultralytics import YOLO

# Load video file
video = cv2.VideoCapture('fall.mp4')

# Initialize YOLO model
detector = YOLO('yolov8s.pt')

# Read class names from file
with open('classes.txt', 'r') as file:
    labels = file.read().splitlines()

while True:
    success, img = video.read()
    if not success:
        break

    # Resize for consistent display
    img = cv2.resize(img, (980, 740))

    # Run detection
    detections = detector(img)

    for detection in detections:
        all_boxes = detection.boxes
```

```
    for b in all_boxes:
        x_start, y_start, x_end, y_end = map(int, b.xyxy[0])
        label_idx = int(b.cls[0])
        confidence = float(b.conf[0])
        label = labels[label_idx]

        # Calculate width, height, and threshold for fall detection
        w = x_end - x_start
        h = y_end - y_start
        fall_risk = h - w

        # Draw bounding box and label if person is detected confidently
        if confidence > 0.8 and label == 'person':
            cvzone.cornerRect(img, [x_start, y_start, w, h], l=30, rt=6)
            cvzone.putTextRect(img, f'{label}', [x_start + 10, y_start - 10],
scale=2, thickness=2)

            if fall_risk < 0:
                cvzone.putTextRect(img, 'Fall Detected', [h, w], scale=2,
thickness=2)

    # Display result
    cv2.imshow('Fall Detection', img)
    if cv2.waitKey(1) & 0xFF == ord('t'):
        break

video.release()
cv2.destroyAllWindows()
```

8.3 Real-Time Home Monitoring Using Ambient Sensors

In modern smart homes, ambient sensors play a key role in enhancing safety, efficiency, and overall living quality. These sensors, which detect environmental changes, are essential components in the development of intelligent and responsive home systems. For example, motion sensors help detect movement within or around the home, triggering actions such as alarms or notifications to enhance security. When integrated with smart surveillance systems, they allow homeowners to receive live updates and monitor their property remotely. Ambient sensors also contribute to better health and comfort. Air quality sensors monitor indoor environments and detect harmful substances or allergens, helping residents take timely action by adjusting ventilation or using air purifiers.

In water management, leak detection sensors identify leaks early, reducing the risk of water damage. Sound sensors can recognize abnormal noises and activate responses like turning on lights or sending alerts. These devices also support automated control of temperature, lighting, and other systems, making homes more adaptive and user-friendly. As technology advances, ambient sensors are expected to become even more sophisticated, delivering smarter, more sustainable solutions. Figure 8.3 illustrates how these sensors communicate with a central storage system using MQTT (Message Queuing Telemetry Transport) and a gateway device, a lightweight messaging protocol ideal for IoT environments. The below code is for that.

```
import subprocess
import yaml
import time
import datetime
import os
import pytz
```

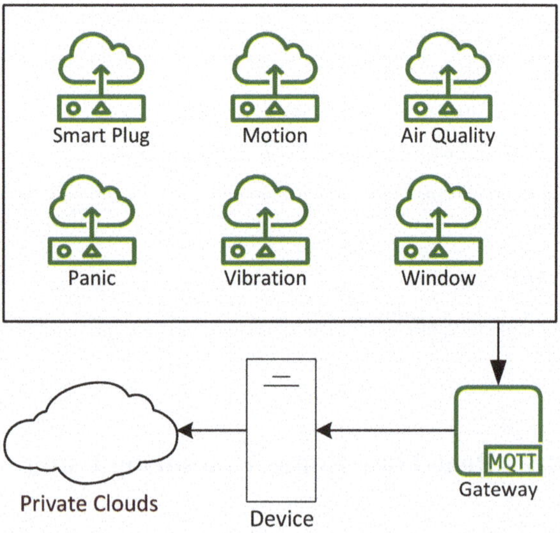

Fig. 8.3 Ambient sensors, data communication and storage

```
import csv

##########################################################################
##############
# Configuration
##########################################################################
##############
BROKER_HOST = "192.168.2.11"
SUBSCRIBE_TOPIC = "#"
OUTPUT_FOLDER = "/home/sintef/Dataset"

LOCAL_TIMEZONE = "Europe/Oslo"
ENV_TIMEZONE = "Norway/Oslo"   # For OS environment

os.environ["TZ"] = ENV_TIMEZONE
time.tzset()

##########################################################################
##############
# Global State
##########################################################################
##############
last_power_state = 0   # Track on/off transitions for device 5 (SmartPlug)

##########################################################################
##############
# Utility Functions
##########################################################################
##############
def is_float(value):
    """Return True if value can be cast to float, otherwise False."""
    try:
        float(value)
```

```
        return True
    except ValueError:
        return False

def parse_mqtt_message(mqtt_line):
    """
    Extract device ID, sensor name, and sensor value from an MQTT line.
    Returns (None, None, None) if minimal checks fail.
    """
    mqtt_line = mqtt_line.strip()
    if not mqtt_line:
        return None, None, None

    if '{' not in mqtt_line or '/dev/' not in mqtt_line or '/ldev/' not in mqtt_line:
        return None, None, None

    # Device ID
    dev_part = mqtt_line.split('/dev/')[1]
    if '/ldev/' not in dev_part:
        return None, None, None
    device_id = dev_part.split('/ldev/')[0]

    # YAML parse
    payload_str = mqtt_line[mqtt_line.find('{'):]
    loaded_data = yaml.safe_load(payload_str)

    sensor_name = loaded_data.get("name")
    sensor_value = loaded_data.get("value")

    if sensor_name is None or sensor_value is None:
        return None, None, None

    return device_id, sensor_name, str(sensor_value)
```

```
def determine_event(device_id, sensor_name, sensor_value):
    """
    Based on the device ID, sensor name, and sensor value, return
    (code_label, sensor_type, final_value) or (None, None, None) if no match.
    """
    global last_power_state

    # Boolean-based sensors
    boolean_map = {
        ("1", "Alarm"):             ("AMB-NOR-001", "Door Opening"),
        ("2", "Vibration Alarm"):   ("AMB-NOR-002", "Vibration"),
        ("3", "Occupancy"):          ("AMB-NOR-005", "Motion")
    }

    # Check simple True/False sensors
    if (device_id, sensor_name) in boolean_map and sensor_value in ["True",
"False"]:
        code_label, sensor_desc = boolean_map[(device_id, sensor_name)]
        return code_label, sensor_desc, sensor_value

    # Device 5 -> SmartPlug logic
    if device_id == "5" and sensor_name == "Instantaneous Energy Use":
        if not is_float(sensor_value):
            return None, None, None
        measured_power = float(sensor_value)

        # Only log transitions from 0->>0 or >0->0
        if last_power_state == 1 and measured_power > 0:
            return None, None, None
        if last_power_state == 0 and measured_power == 0:
            return None, None, None
```

```
        last_power_state = 1 if measured_power > 0 else 0
        return "AMB-NOR-003", "SmartPlug", str(last_power_state)

    # Device 4 -> Air Quality sensors
    if device_id == "4" and sensor_name in [
        "Relative Humidity",
        "Air quality - Level",
        "Air quality - Recommendation",
        "Measured Temperature",
    ]:
        return "AMB-NOR-004", "Air Quality", sensor_value

    # No match
    return None, None, None

def append_to_csv(folder_path, date_str, row_data):
    """
    Append the row_data to <date_str>.csv in folder_path.
    """
    csv_file = os.path.join(folder_path, f"{date_str}.csv")
    with open(csv_file, "a", encoding="UTF8", newline="") as outfile:
        writer = csv.writer(outfile)
        writer.writerow(row_data)

##########################################################################
##############
# Set Up MQTT Subscriber
##########################################################################
##############
mqtt_command = f"mosquitto_sub -h {BROKER_HOST} -t
\"{SUBSCRIBE_TOPIC}\" -v"
mqtt_process = subprocess.Popen(mqtt_command, shell=True,
stdout=subprocess.PIPE, universal_newlines=True)
```

```
###########################################################################
##############
# Main Loop: No try/except
###########################################################################
##############
while True:
    line = mqtt_process.stdout.readline(
    dev_id, s_name, s_value = parse_mqtt_message(line)
    if not dev_id or not s_name:
        continue

    now = datetime.datetime.now(pytz.timezone(LOCAL_TIMEZONE))
    iso_time = now.strftime("%Y-%m-%dT%H:%M:%SZ")
    date_str = now.strftime("%Y-%m-%d")

    code_label, sensor_desc, final_val = determine_event(dev_id, s_name,
s_value)
    if code_label:
        print(f"Time: {iso_time}, Device: {dev_id}, Sensor: {code_label}
{sensor_desc}, Event: {s_name}, Value: {final_val}")
        row = [iso_time, f"{code_label} {sensor_desc}", s_name, final_val]
        append_to_csv(OUTPUT_FOLDER, date_str, row)
```

A real-time event log provides continuous updates from both ambient and wearable sensors within a smart home environment. This log displays key status indicators such as door state (open: true/false), humidity levels, air quality index, step count from wearable devices, and respiration rates monitored over time. By presenting this data in a clear, timestamped format, the system allows users to track activity and environmental conditions as they occur. Such real-time monitoring improves safety, comfort, and health awareness in the home. Figure 8.4 illustrates a real time log showing live sensor data collected from various sources across the smart home setup. The data is completely anonymous.

Date	Sensor	Status	Event
2024-12-01T13:17:37Z	Wearable-001	6	Wearable Steps:6
2024-12-01T13:17:37Z	Wearable-001	6	Wearable Steps:6
2024-12-01T13:18:40Z	AMB-001	TRUE	Door Opening
2024-12-01T13:20:58Z	9279-1	26.53542698	Respiration:26.53Movement Type:1.0
2024-12-01T13:22:04Z	AMB-001	FALSE	Door Opening
2024-12-01T13:23:11Z	AMB-002	TRUE	Vibration
2024-12-01T13:23:15Z	AMB-003	1	SmartPlug
2024-12-01T13:23:33Z	AMB-002	TRUE	Vibration
2024-12-01T13:27:07Z	AMB-004	36	Relative Humidity
2024-12-01T13:27:07Z	AMB-004	27.2	Measured Temperature
2024-12-01T13:28:40Z	AMB-004	32.1	Relative Humidity
2024-12-01T13:28:41Z	AMB-001	TRUE	Door Opening
2024-12-01T13:29:57Z	AMB-002	TRUE	Vibration
2024-12-01T13:30:07Z	AMB-004	35.4	Relative Humidity
2024-12-01T13:30:10Z	AMB-004	24	Measured Temperature
2024-12-01T13:30:30Z	AMB-001	TRUE	Door Opening
2024-12-01T13:30:53Z	9279-1	OK	Respiration:23MovementT ype:1
2024-12-01T13:31:11Z	AMB-004	23.5	Measured Temperature
2024-12-01T13:31:31Z	AMB-001	FALSE	Door Opening
2024-12-01T13:32:12Z	AMB-004	23	Measured Temperature
2024-12-01T13:32:20Z	AMB-002	TRUE	Vibration
2024-12-01T13:32:24Z	AMB-001	TRUE	Door Opening
2024-12-01T13:32:39Z	AMB-002	FALSE	Vibration
2024-12-01T13:32:39Z	AMB-001	FALSE	Door Opening
2024-12-01T13:32:41Z	AMB-002	TRUE	Vibration
2024-12-01T13:33:00Z	Wearable-001	24	Wearable Steps:24
2024-12-01T13:33:02Z	AMB-002	TRUE	Vibration
2024-12-01T13:33:13Z	AMB-004	22.6	Measured Temperature
2024-12-01T13:33:18Z	AMB-001	TRUE	Door Opening
2024-12-01T13:34:11Z	AMB-004	40.9	Relative Humidity
2024-12-01T13:34:14Z	AMB-004	22.4	Measured Temperature
2024-12-01T13:35:59Z	AMB-002	TRUE	Vibration
2024-12-01T13:36:05Z	9279-1	OK	Respiration:16Movement Type:1
2024-12-01T13:36:06Z	AMB-002	TRUE	Vibration
2024-12-01T13:36:09Z	AMB-004	42.3	Relative Humidity
2024-12-01T13:36:12Z	AMB-002	TRUE	Vibration
2024-12-01T13:36:16Z	AMB-004	23.3	Measured Temperature
2024-12-01T13:36:17Z	AMB-002	TRUE	Vibration
2024-12-01T13:36:44Z	AMB-004	Good	Air quality - Level

Fig. 8.4 Real-time event status using ambient and wearable sensors

8.4 Real-Time Emotion Recognition from Camera

Real-time emotion recognition from camera input is a powerful technique that analyzes facial expressions captured through a live video feed to identify emotional states such as happiness, sadness, anger, surprise, or neutrality. This technology is used in applications like smart assistants, healthcare monitoring, interactive learning, and customer service systems to make interactions more responsive and emotionally aware [5, 6]. The process begins with detecting faces in each video frame, followed by analyzing facial features to classify emotions. Pretrained deep learning models like DeepFace are widely used for this task, as they have been trained on large-scale facial datasets and can accurately extract and interpret expression patterns without the need for training from scratch. These models are efficient and capable of providing instant feedback, making them suitable for real-time environments. For example, a virtual assistant can adapt its tone or suggestions based on the user's detected mood. This approach enhances the emotional intelligence of systems, allowing for more natural and personalized user experiences. Figure 8.5 illustrates how real-time emotion recognition is implemented using a camera and a pretrained model, showing live emotion predictions based on facial input.

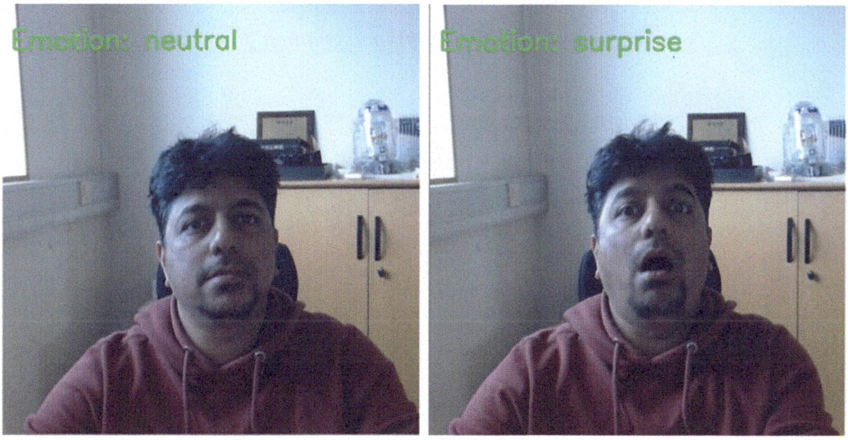

Fig. 8.5 Real-time emotion recognition using camera

```
import cv2
from deepface import DeepFace

# Initialize webcam
cap = cv2.VideoCapture(0)

while True:
    ret, frame = cap.read()
    if not ret:
        break

    try:
        # Perform emotion analysis

        result = DeepFace.analyze(frame, actions=["emotion"],
enforce_detection=False)
        emotion = result[0]["dominant_emotion"]

        # Display emotion on the frame
        cv2.putText(frame, f"Emotion: {emotion}", (10,
50),cv2.FONT_HERSHEY_SIMPLEX, 1, (0, 255, 0), 2)
    except Exception as e:
    print("e")

    # Show the frame
    cv2.imshow("Emotion Recognition", frame)

    # Exit condition
    if cv2.waitKey(1) & 0xFF == ord("q"):
        break

# Release resources
cap.release()
cv2.destroyAllWindows()
```

8.5 Real-Time Emotion Recognition from Audio

Real-time emotion recognition from audio is a technique used to detect a speaker's emotional state by analyzing their voice. It focuses on vocal features such as tone, pitch, volume, and speech rate to identify emotions like happiness, anger, sadness, or neutral. This technology is useful in applications like virtual assistants, mental health monitoring, customer service, and interactive systems. The process begins with capturing live audio through a microphone. From this input, important acoustic features such as Mel-Frequency Cepstral Coefficients (MFCCs), pitch, and energy are extracted [7]. These features are then fed into pre-trained models that have been trained on large emotion-labeled audio datasets. Models such as Wav2Vec 2.0, HuBERT, or OpenSMILE-based classifiers can recognize emotional cues from speech effectively without needing to be trained from scratch. Since these models are optimized for speech understanding, they can process audio in real time, making them ideal for applications that require quick responses. For example, a smart assistant could adjust its tone if it detects irritation, or a wellness app could track emotional trends over time [8]. Using pre-trained models allows developers to build reliable emotion-aware systems with less computational effort and more accurate results. Following code is for real time emotion recognition from audio.

```
import os
import time
import pyaudio
import numpy as np
import torch
from transformers import pipeline

##########################################################################
##############
# 1) Disable TensorFlow if you only want PyTorch in Transformers (optional).
##########################################################################
##############
os.environ["TRANSFORMERS_NO_TF"] = "1"
```

```
##########################################################################
##############
# 2) Choose One Pretrained Emotion Model
#
#       Uncomment exactly ONE line below to pick your model.
##########################################################################
##############
MODEL_ID = "superb/wav2vec2-base-superb-er"
# MODEL_ID = "superb/hubert-base-superb-er"
# MODEL_ID = "superb/wavlm-base-superb-er"
# MODEL_ID = "superb/wavlm-base-plus-superb-er"
# MODEL_ID = "superb/wav2vec2-large-superb-er"
# MODEL_ID = "superb/xls_r-300m-superb-er"
# MODEL_ID = "superb/wav2vec2-large-xlsr-53-superb-er"
# MODEL_ID = "superb/wav2vec2-base-plus-librispeech-250h-superb-er"
# MODEL_ID = "superb/wav2vec2-large-robust-ft-libri-960-superb-er"
# MODEL_ID = "superb/hubert-large-superb-er"

##########################################################################
##############
# 3) Create the Audio-Classification Pipeline
#       GPU if available, else CPU (device=-1).
##########################################################################
##############
classifier = pipeline(
    task="audio-classification",
    model=MODEL_ID,
    device=0 if torch.cuda.is_available() else -1
)

##########################################################################
##############
```

```
# 4) Setup PyAudio for Real-Time Mic Capture
###########################################################################
#############
CHUNK = 16000       # frames per buffer (1 second * 16kHz)
FORMAT = pyaudio.paInt16
CHANNELS = 1
RATE = 16000

p = pyaudio.PyAudio()
stream = p.open(
    format=FORMAT,
    channels=CHANNELS,
    rate=RATE,
    input=True,
    frames_per_buffer=CHUNK
)

print(f"Using model: {MODEL_ID}")
print("Listening... press Ctrl+C to stop.")

###########################################################################
#############
# 5) Real-Time Loop
#    Capture 1-second chunks, run emotion inference, print top label.
###########################################################################
#############
try:
    while True:
        # Read a 1-second chunk from the mic
        audio_data = stream.read(CHUNK, exception_on_overflow=False)

        # Convert raw bytes to float32 array
```

```
            audio_np = np.frombuffer(audio_data,
    dtype=np.int16).astype(np.float32)
            # Optional scaling to [-1.0, 1.0]
            audio_np = audio_np / 32768.0

            # Classify (some pipeline versions require sampling_rate=RATE)
            results = classifier(audio_np, sampling_rate=RATE)

            if results:
                top_emotion = results[0]    # highest confidence
                label = top_emotion["label"]
                score = top_emotion["score"]
                print(f"Predicted: {label} (score={score:.3f})")

            # Tiny sleep to avoid overloading console
            time.sleep(0.1)

    except KeyboardInterrupt:
        print("Stopping...")

    finally:
        stream.stop_stream()
        stream.close()
        p.terminate()
```

8.6 Real-Time Emotion Recognition from Text

Real-time emotion recognition from text is a technique that identifies a person's emotional state based on the content of their written or spoken words [9]. This approach is useful in areas such as virtual assistants, mental health applications, chatbots, and customer service platforms, where understanding user emotions can improve communication and response quality. The system begins by receiving text input, either typed directly or generated from speech using speech-to-text tools.

This text is then processed using natural language processing (NLP) methods [10]. Pretrained models like GPT-2, which have been trained on large-scale text data, are capable of understanding language patterns, context, and subtle emotional cues. When adapted with emotion-labeled datasets, these models can recognize and classify different emotional expressions in text. Thanks to their ability to generate quick and accurate predictions, models like GPT-2 are well-suited for real-time applications. They can analyze and respond to user input almost instantly, enabling emotionally responsive interactions. For example, a chatbot could respond more supportively if it detects frustration or sadness in a user's message. By using pretrained models, developers can build emotion-aware systems without needing extensive training from scratch, saving both time and resources. Following code is for real time emotion recognition from audio.

```
import torch
from transformers import AutoTokenizer, AutoModelForSequenceClassification
import torch.nn.functional as F

# Load model
model_name = "bhadresh-savani/distilbert-base-uncased-emotion"
tokenizer = AutoTokenizer.from_pretrained(model_name)
model = AutoModelForSequenceClassification.from_pretrained(model_name)

#  Other Pretrained Emotion Models :
# ----------------------------------------------------------------
# "bhadresh-savani/distilbert-base-uncased-emotion"
#        → 6 emotions: anger, joy, sadness, fear, love, surprise
#
# "j-hartmann/emotion-english-distilroberta-base"
#        → 7 emotions: anger, disgust, fear, joy, neutral, sadness, surprise
#
# "SamLowe/roberta-base-go_emotions"
#        → 28 emotions + neutral (GoEmotions dataset)
```

```
#
# "monologg/bert-base-cased-goemotions-original"
#       → Multi-label classification (can detect multiple emotions)
# ---------------------------------------------------------------

# Put model in evaluation mode
model.eval()

# Label mapping
id2label = model.config.id2label

def detect_emotion(text):
    inputs = tokenizer(text, return_tensors="pt", truncation=True, padding=True)
    with torch.no_grad():
        outputs = model(**inputs)
        probs = F.softmax(outputs.logits, dim=1)
        prediction = torch.argmax(probs, dim=1).item()
        confidence = probs[0][prediction].item()

    emotion = id2label[prediction]
    return emotion.capitalize(), confidence

# Real-time input loop
if __name__ == "__main__":
    print("Real-Time Emotion Detector (type 'exit' to quit)\n")
    while True:
        user_input = input("User: ")
        if user_input.lower() in ['exit', 'quit']:
            print("Goodbye!")
            break
        emotion, conf = detect_emotion(user_input)
        print(f"→ Emotion: {emotion} (Confidence: {conf:.2f})\n")
```

8.7 Real-Time Sleep Quality Prediction from Ambient Sensor

Real-time sleep quality prediction using machine learning can be effectively realized by analyzing respiratory data captured through privacy-preserving ultrawideband (UWB) sensors. These sensors offer a non-intrusive solution by recording detailed respiration patterns without requiring physical contact. In the proposed methodology, a UWB sensor is positioned near the subject's bed, ideally close to the chest area, to monitor breathing signals continuously throughout the night. The use of UWB sensors ensures privacy and minimal disruption to the sleep environment, which is especially important in healthcare and home-monitoring applications. However, one of the primary challenges in developing machine learning models for sleep quality prediction is the limited availability of real-world data. To address this, synthetic data generation techniques are incorporated into the system. Using the Synthetic Data Vault (SDV), a tool designed to create synthetic data that statistically mirrors real datasets, additional respiration data samples are generated. These synthetic samples preserve the underlying structure, distribution, and temporal characteristics of the actual respiration signals. This augmentation helps overcome the data scarcity issue, making the model more robust and generalizable.

To enable supervised machine learning, both the real and synthetic respiration data need to be categorized into meaningful sleep quality labels. Subjective feedback from users is used to define these labels, which are typically divided into different classes: Bad, Okay, and Good. The K-Nearest Neighbors (K-NN) algorithm, a simple yet effective classification technique, is applied to assign sleep quality labels to synthetic data instances. K-NN uses Euclidean distance to determine the similarity between data points and classifies new samples based on the majority class among their nearest neighbors, ensuring consistency between synthetic and real data labels. Once the dataset is labeled, a bidirectional Long Short-Term Memory (Bi-LSTM) model is trained to predict sleep quality from respiration patterns. The Bi-LSTM model takes sequences of respiration data as input and is trained using optimization techniques such as stochastic gradient descent or Adam optimizer. The model's objective is to minimize a loss function, commonly categorical cross-entropy, which quantifies the difference between predicted and actual sleep quality labels. Through iterative training and parameter updates, the Bi-LSTM model learns to accurately map respiration patterns to the appropriate sleep quality category.

The illustrated diagram in Fig. 8.6 outlines a two-phase system for sleep quality prediction using respiration data collected via an ultrawideband (UWB) radar sensor on a Raspberry Pi. In the upper part of the diagram, representing the training phase, the system begins by capturing overnight respiratory signals through the UWB sensor positioned near the user's bed. Simultaneously, the user provides subjective sleep quality feedback—**categorized** as Bad, Okay, or Good—through a conversational agent (CA). This feedback is linked to the corresponding respiration data and securely transmitted to a private cloud infrastructure. Here, machine learning models—particularly bidirectional Long Short-Term Memory (Bi-LSTM) networks—are trained to learn the relationship between respiratory patterns and sleep quality labels. This personalized training phase is crucial for building a robust and privacy-preserving model tailored to individual sleep characteristics.

The lower part of the diagram illustrates the real-time prediction and feedback loop. On subsequent nights, the UWB radar again records respiration data from the same user. This new data is fed into the previously trained ML model, which generates a sleep quality prediction. The result is communicated back to the user through the

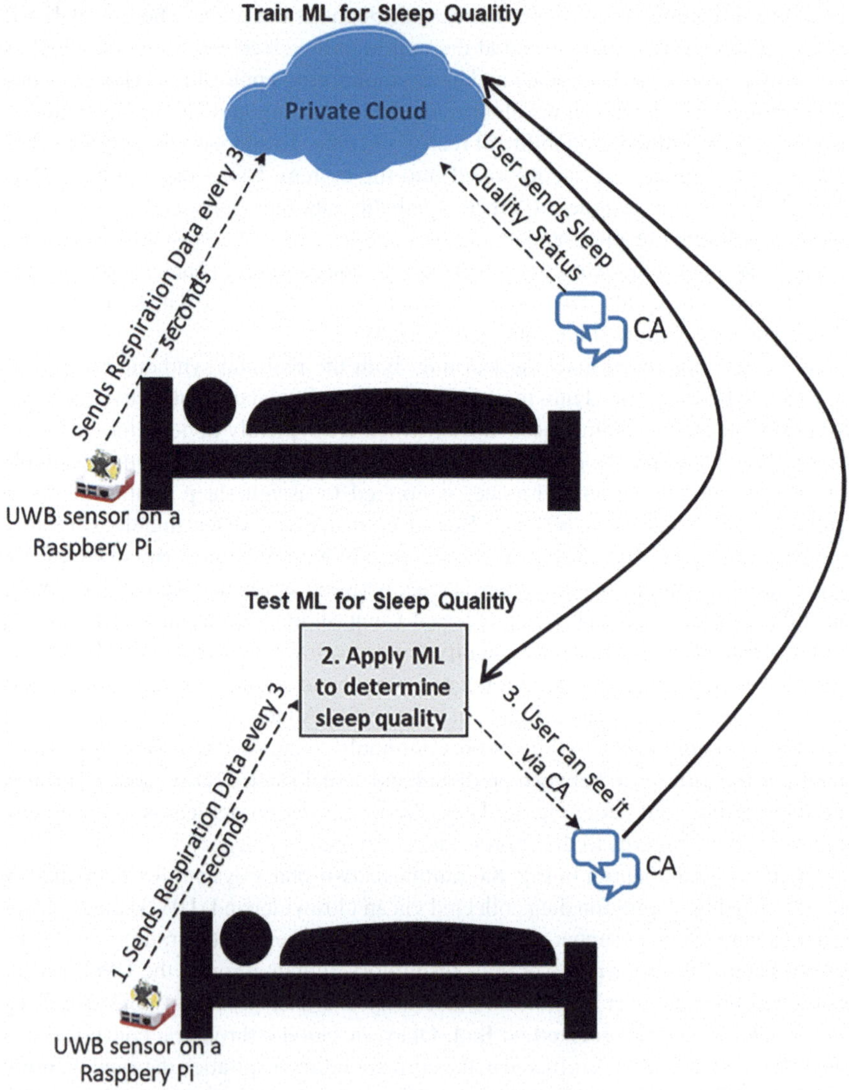

Fig. 8.6 Real-time sleep quality prediction using respiration data

CA. If the user disagrees with the prediction, they can correct it by providing updated feedback via the CA. This corrected label is then used to refine the model, ensuring it adapts to the user's sleep patterns over time. This continuous learning loop not only improves accuracy but also maintains user engagement and model relevance, enabling a dynamic and privacy-aware approach to sleep quality monitoring in home environments.

Figure 8.7 presents a structured log of daily sleep quality predictions generated by a machine learning model using real-time anonymous respiration data for November 2024. The entries reflect system-generated sleep quality feedback." Most days are labeled as "Bad," indicating consistently poor respiratory patterns during sleep across the month. Only a few days, such as November 18 and 21, are marked as "Good," showing improved sleep quality on those nights. The table highlights the model's consistency in daily monitoring and offers valuable insights into individual sleep trends over time, essential for identifying long-term health or behavioral interventions.

Date and Time	Type	Value
15 November 2024	Sleep Quality-Machine Feedback	Bad
15 November 2024	Sleep Quality-User Feedback	Bad
16 November 2024	Sleep Quality-Machine Feedback	Bad
17 November 2024	Sleep Quality-Machine Feedback	Bad
18 November 2024	Sleep Quality-Machine Feedback	Good
19 November 2024	Sleep Quality-Machine Feedback	Bad
19 November 2024	Sleep Quality-User Feedback	Bad
20 November 2024	Sleep Quality-Machine Feedback	Bad
21 November 2024	Sleep Quality-Machine Feedback	Good
22 November 2024	Sleep Quality-Machine Feedback	Bad
24 November 2024	Sleep Quality-User Feedback	Good
23 November 2024	Sleep Quality-Machine Feedback	Bad
25 November 2024	Sleep Quality-Machine Feedback	Bad
25 November 2024	Sleep Quality-User Feedback	Okay
26 November 2024	Sleep Quality-Machine Feedback	Bad
27 November 2024	Sleep Quality-Machine Feedback	Bad
28 November 2024	Sleep Quality-Machine Feedback	Bad
29 November 2024	Sleep Quality-Machine Feedback	Bad
30 November 2024	Sleep Quality-Machine Feedback	Bad
30 November 2024	Sleep Quality-User Feedback	Bad

Fig. 8.7 Sleep quality feedback from machine and user

8.8 Conclusion

This chapter presented the use of real-time smart sensing technologies for activity, fall, health, and emotion recognition. Various sensors, including wearable devices, cameras, and ambient sensors, were deployed to monitor daily activities and detect critical events such as falls or emotional changes. Machine learning models were utilized to process sensor data, enabling activities and emotions to be recognized accurately and efficiently. Privacy considerations were addressed by ensuring that sensitive data were stored locally rather than transmitted to commercial platforms. Wearable devices like MetaMotionR were used for physical activity monitoring, while deep learning models such as YOLO, DeepFace, and Transformer-based networks were applied for visual and audio emotion analysis. Ambient sensors were integrated to capture environmental data and enhance home monitoring systems. Through these approaches, real-time and reliable feedback systems were developed, offering significant benefits for healthcare, assisted living, and smart home environments. Future improvements are anticipated through continued research.

References

1. S. Zhang, Y. Li, S. Zhang, F. Shahabi, S. Xia, Y. Deng, and N. Alshurafa, "Deep learning in human activity recognition with wearable sensors," Sensors, vol. 22, no. 4, Art. 1476, 2022.
2. N. Zhang, Y. Song, D. Fang, and Y. Yan, "An improved deep convolutional LSTM for human activity recognition using wearable sensors," IEEE Sensors Journal, vol. 24, p. 1717, 2024.
3. X. Kan, S. Zhu, Y. Zhang, and C. Qian, "A lightweight human fall detection network," Sensors, vol. 23, no. 22, Art. 9069, 2023.
4. X. Huang, X. Li, L. Yuan, Z. Jiang, H. Jin, W. Wu, W. Cai, R. Zheng, M. Bai, and H. Bai, "SDES-YOLO: A high-precision and lightweight model for fall detection in complex environments," Scientific Reports, vol. 15, Art. 2026, 2025.
5. P. Albert, F. Haider, and S. Luz, "CUSCO: An unobtrusive custom secure audio-visual recording system for ambient assisted living," Sensors, vol. 24, no. 5, Art. 1506, 2024.
6. N. S. Dasappa, K. G. Kumar, and N. Somu, "Multi-sensor data fusion framework for energy optimization in smart homes," Renewable and Sustainable Energy Reviews, vol. 193, Art. 114235, 2024.
7. B. Nasersharif and M. Namvarpour, "Exploring the potential of Wav2vec 2.0 for speech emotion recognition using classifier combination and attention-based feature fusion," Journal of Supercomputing, vol. 80, pp. 23667–23688, 2024.
8. W.-C. Lin, K. Sridhar, and C. Busso, "An interpretable deep mutual information curriculum metric for a robust and generalized speech emotion recognition system," IEEE/ACM Transactions on Audio, Speech and Language Processing, vol. 32, pp. 5117–5130, 2024.
9. F. A. Acheampong, H. Nunoo-Mensah, and W. Chen, "Comparative analyses of BERT, RoBERTa, DistilBERT and XLNet for text-based emotion recognition," Proceedings of the 17th International Computer Conference on Wavelet Active Media Technology and Information Processing, pp. 117–121, 2020.
10. Y. Zhou, X. Kang, and F. Ren, "Prompt consistency for multi-label textual emotion detection," IEEE Transactions on Affective Computing, vol. 15, no. 1, pp. 121–129, 2024.

The manufacturer's authorised representative in the EU is Springer Nature Customer Service Centre GmbH, Europaplatz 3, 69115 Heidelberg, Germany. If you have any concerns regarding our products, please contact ProductSafety@springernature.com

Printed and bound by CPI Group (UK) Ltd, Croydon, CR0 4YY
01/10/2026
02225971-0011